ROUTLEDGE LIBRARY EDITIONS: PERCY SHELLEY

Volume 1

SHELLEY'S TEXTUAL SEDUCTIONS

SHELLEY'S TEXTUAL SEDUCTIONS
Plotting Utopia in the Erotic and Political Works

SAMUEL LYNDON GLADDEN

LONDON AND NEW YORK

First published in 2002 by Routledge

This edition first published in 2016
by Routledge
4 Park Square, Milton Park, Abingdon, Oxon OX14 4RN
605 Third Avenue, New York, NY 10017

Routledge is an imprint of the Taylor & Francis Group, an informa business

© 2002 Taylor & Francis

All rights reserved. No part of this book may be reprinted or reproduced or utilised in any form or by any electronic, mechanical, or other means, now known or hereafter invented, including photocopying and recording, or in any information storage or retrieval system, without permission in writing from the publishers.

Trademark notice: Product or corporate names may be trademarks or registered trademarks, and are used only for identification and explanation without intent to infringe.

British Library Cataloguing in Publication Data
A catalogue record for this book is available from the British Library

ISBN: 978-1-138-65476-1 (Set)
ISBN: 978-1-315-62261-3 (Set) (ebk)
ISBN: 978-1-138-64054-2 (Volume 1) (hbk)
ISBN: 978-1-138-64057-3 (Volume 1) (pbk)
ISBN: 978-1-315-62822-6 (Volume 1) (ebk)

Publisher's Note
The publisher has gone to great lengths to ensure the quality of this reprint but points out that some imperfections in the original copies may be apparent.

Disclaimer
The publisher has made every effort to trace copyright holders and would welcome correspondence from those they have been unable to trace.

Shelley's Textual Seductions
Plotting Utopia in the Erotic and Political Works

Samuel Lyndon Gladden

ROUTLEDGE
NEW YORK & LONDON

Published in 2002 by
Routledge
29 West 35th Street
New York, NY 10001
www.Routledgeny.com

Published in Great Britain by
Routledge
11 New Fetter Lane
London EC4P 4EE

Routledge is a member of the Taylor & Francis Group.

Copyright © 2002 by Routledge.

All rights reserved. No part of this book may be reprinted or reproduced or utilized in any form or by any electronic, mechanical, or other means, now known or hereafter invented, including photocopying and recording, or in any information storage or retrieval system, without written permission from the publishers.

10 9 8 7 6 5 4 3 2 1

Library of Congress Cataloging-in-Publication Data

Gladden, Samuel L.
  Shelley's textual seductions : plotting Utopia in the erotic and political works / by Samuel L. Gladden.
    p. cm. — (Studies in major literary authors)
  Includes bibliographical references (p.) and index.
  ISBN 0-415-93702-7
  1. Shelley, Percy Bysshe, 1792–1822—Views on sex. 2. Shelley, Percy Bysshe, 1792–1822—Political and social views. 3. Politics and literature—Great Britain—History—19th century. 4. Political poetry, English—History and criticism. 5. Erotic poetry, English—History and criticism. 6. Seductions in literature. 7. Utopias in literature. 8. Sex in literature. I. Title. II. Series.

PR5442.S47 G58 2002
821'.7—dc21

2001045725

Printed on acid-free, 250 year-life paper
Manufactured in the United States of America

For my parents

Contents

LIST OF ABBREVIATIONS   xi

ACKNOWLEDGMENTS   xiii

PREFACE   xv

Chapter I
   INTRODUCTION
   SITUATING THE EROTIC: THE PLACES AND
   SPACES OF EXCESS   1

PART ONE: THE PROBLEM

Chapter II
   SHELLEY'S AGENDA WRIT LARGE:
   RECONSIDERING *ŒDIPUS TYRANNUS; OR,*
   SWELLFOOT THE TYRANT   49
      Tyranny   79
      Liberty   92
      Language   94
      Sexual Transgression   102

Chapter III
   TYRANNY AND LIBERATION, OR RIGIDITY AND
   OOZINESS: PHYSICAL AND PSYCHOLOGICAL
   LANDSCAPES IN *THE CENCI* AND *JULIAN AND*
   MADDALO   121
      Love, Landscape, and Revolution   121
      The Vanishing Points of Patriarchy   129
      Private and Public, Family and Society   132

Torture, Retaliation, and Eroticism	140
The Feminine Community	143
Landscape, Psychology, and Unconnectedness	147
Somatic Inscription (Body, Text, Madness)	154
Vanishings	157

PART TWO: THE SOLUTION

Chapter IV
REVOLUTIONARY LANDSCAPES AND THE POLITICS
OF LOVE: *EPIPSYCHIDION* AS EROTIC CARTOGRAPHY 173
Love	190
The Other	194
The Female and the Feminine	197
Androgyny	201
Rejection of the Imaginary	207
" . . . honeyed words betray"	210
Reconfiguration	212

Chapter V
MAPPING THE IDEAL: PLEASURE AND DISPLACEMENT
IN *LAON AND CYTHNA* AND *PROMETHEUS
UNBOUND* 225
Pedagogy	231
Eroticism	235
Landscape and Liminality	242
Prometheus as Redeemer	253
Language, Love, and Revolution	257
Landscape and Utopia	263

Chapter VI
CONCLUSION
RE-TRACING SEDUCTION: THE INFLUENCE OF
SHELLEY ON NINETEENTH-CENTURY
BRITISH CULTURE 285
Shelley's Contemporaries	290
The Pre-Raphaelites	294
The Aesthetes	301

REFERENCES	319
INDEX	339

List of Abbreviations

In citing Shelley's works in the notes, I have generally used short titles. Works frequently cited are indicated by the following abbreviations:

Letters   Shelley, Percy Bysshe. *The Letters of Percy Bysshe Shelley.* Edited by Frederick L. Jones. 2 vols. Oxford, England: Clarendon Press, 1964.

SPP   Shelley, Percy Bysshe. *Shelley's Poetry and Prose.* Edited by Donald H. Reiman and Sharon B. Powers. New York: W. W. Norton, 1977.

WPS   Shelley, Percy Bysshe. *The Complete Works of Percy Bysshe Shelley.* Edited by Roger Ingpen and Walter E. Peck. 10 vols. New York: Charles Scribner's Sons, 1928.

Acknowledgments

Writing is primarily a social act, as countless literary theorists and literary historians have demonstrated; certainly, this book arises from personal and intellectual engagements of my own, from debts I can only hope to repay by saying "thank you." Chief among these are those I owe to the members of my dissertation committee—Melanie C. Hawthorne, Margaret J. M. Ezell, and Robert D. Newman—who nurtured this project and its author from rather humble beginnings. Most especially, I owe a debt of gratitude to the chair of that committee, Jeffrey N. Cox, whose continued advice, support, and encouragement have buoyed me through the early years of my professional life, and whose enviable career continues to serve as a model for my own. Robert Boenig and Terence Allan Hoagwood, two of my early mentors, guided me through some tricky intellectual waters and never failed to convey enthusiasm about my pursuits, this book chief among them. Dennis Berthold, James L. Harner, and Mary Ann O'Farrell offered valuable advice on the marketing of this book to publishers, and Larry J. Reynolds worked with me closely to ensure that the final version of my prospectus proved seductive. To all of these, I express my sincere gratitude.

A great number of friends and colleagues have listened to me talk through my ideas and have reviewed my work, some at conference presentations and some in less formal settings; to these also I express gratitude for the gentle guidance and moral support they have provided over the years of this project's gestation. These include Harriette Andreadis, Susan Bolet Egenolf, Joanna Gibson, Patricia Timmons, and Staci Lynn von Boeckmann; Cole Daugherty, Ann Dizdar-Nelson, Amy Earhart, Jeannie Griffith, Rebecca Jackson, Molly Johnson, Trent Masiki, Krista May, Amy McWilliams, Charles Snodgrass, and J. P. Song; Samantha Cantrell, Alan Cox, Renee Dechert, Dianna J. LeFevre, Virginia Miller, Suzanne Bowers Richardson, Darrian Lea Williams, and Susan Williams. James M.

Rosenheim continues to invigorate me from afar, as does Magnolia Helen, the four-pawed wonder here at home. To those new but dear friends who saw me through the final difficult months of revision—Janet R. Hurley, without whom I might have lost my mind, and Adam R. Clark, because of whom I very nearly did—I say thank you, and now let us return to our lives of scandal, decadence, and everyday elegance.

I am deeply grateful for the financial support of Dean James B. Lubker and Associate Dean Reinhold Bubser of the College of Humanities and Fine Arts at the University of Northern Iowa, whose generous project grant enabled me to hire as manuscript proofreaders two quite promising graduate students, Kevin H. Gaffney and Marcea K. Seible; and to the generosity of the Department of English Language and Literature, especially to Jeffrey S. Copeland and Richard Utz, who as Department Head and English Graduate Coordinator, respectively, assigned Susan Santha Kerns to assist me during the Fall of 2001 with the editing of page proofs; and to Gail Moehlis, one of our department's secretaries, who tirelessly photocopied ream after ream of corrected material for me, often "on demand" and with a very short turn-around time. Without the assistance of these administrators, faculty, and staff, my work would have progressed far less smoothly. And without the diligent efforts in editing and proofreading—not to mention the astonishing precision—of three extraordinarily talented graduate students, Kevin, Marcea, and Susan, the final revision of the book would have proven much more burdensome; truly, they are responsible for much of what appears on these pages, and I thank them for making my work easier and my writing cleaner. Finally, I am grateful for the guidance offered by my editors at Routledge, Erin Herlihy, Damian Treffs, and Damon Zucca, and for the diligent work on the index provided by my colleague Vince Gotera.

An excerpt from Chapter II, under the same title as the chapter in this book, was originally published electronically on the University of Maryland's *Romantic Circles* website as part of a volume in the *Praxis* series entitled "Reading Shelley's Interventionist Poetry, 1819-1820," edited by Michael Henry Scrivener. I am grateful to *Romantic Circles* for permission to reprint that excerpt in this book.

Preface

In the four years since I completed the basis for this book in the form of a Ph.D. dissertation entitled *Cartographizing Seduction: Mapping the Political in Percy Shelley's Erotic Narratives,* I have continued to investigate the strategies of textual seduction Shelley develops throughout his œuvre by contextualizing his work in more extensive and, in many cases, more recent scholarship about politics, the erotic, landscape, and representationality, all in an effort to articulate more fully and complexly the model of erotic cartography so crucial to the poet's vision of a world liberated, to his plottings of utopia. In its present form, this book represents what I believe is a more highly refined discussion of those matters. Recently, my thought has been greatly influenced by work in Romanticism by Tedi Chichester Bonca and Deborah Elise White; by work in the erotic by Pierre Saint-Amand, Lucienne Frappier-Mazur, and Vernon A. Rosario; by work in landscape and cartography by Geoff King; and by work in phenomenology and representationality by Kaja Silverman. My book, I hope, offers appropriate homage to those whose writing has influenced me; from their ideas as well as from their sometimes startlingly beautiful prose, I have benefited greatly.

∞ ∞ ∞ ∞ ∞

Shelley's Textual Seductions charts new territory in Romantic scholarship by drawing on a range of interpretive methodologies to investigate two models key to understanding all of Shelley's work, as well as the maneuvers of nineteenth-century revolutionary writing in general and Romanticism in particular. Where traditional models for reading nineteenth-century British literature have located revolution in the space of an imaginative apocalypse or an artist's thoroughgoing communion with the natural world, *Shelley's Textual Seductions* unveils political engagements within the seemingly apolitical reaches of the erotic narrative. Reversing traditional models of the body as a text upon which power continues to be written, the Shelleyan body emerges as a generative site that inscribes its own emancipatory narrative, a productive device according to which freedom may be cartographized, or mapped. Throughout his *œuvre*, Shelley privileges mapping as a hermeneutic strategy that allows for the exploration of the intersections of the sexual, the textual, and the political, for mapping enables Shelley to navigate the gulphs and chasms between the real world and the imagination, between politics and poetry, between the reader and the text. According to Shelley's model, physical space (the public or exterior world) and psychological space (the private or interior experience of the individual, lived both within and apart from the exterior world) ultimately dissolve into a radical contingency, so that the boundaries, the limits, of the public and private become increasingly difficult—and increasingly rewarding—to plot, to map, to cartographize. Turning from the corporeal to the textual body to eroticize the text itself, Shelley poses the erotic as a textual rupture, or split, between traditional British culture and what we might think of as its "other," yet he resists defining the erotic as a specific pleasure or even as a catalogue of pleasures. As such, the erotic activates a blurring of the parameters of existing social codes, including the various institutionalizations of tyranny through which individuals or groups are empowered at the very real and often very physical expense of others: through the processes of textual seduction, the division between text and reader dissolves, as two bodies—one physical, the other textual—mix and melt into each other, modeling the erotic engagement and the psychospatial configuration so crucial to Shelley's conception of liberty-through-love.

Through close readings of six works central to Shelley's aesthetic and political agenda, I uncover the political engagements embedded in Shelley's erotic narratives to consider the public implications of private relationships. I begin the first half of my study with *Œdipus Tyrannus; or, Swellfoot the Tyrant*, a satire that demonstrates Shelley's understanding of the intrinsic connections between political and sexual machinations; next, I consider *The Cenci*, a tragedy that exemplifies the links between political and domestic oppression and gestures toward the family as the locus from which an alternative political model might be developed, and *Julian and Maddalo*, a conversation poem that poses friendship and fellow-feeling as antidotes to erotic disappointment and its very public manifestation in exile and containment. In the second half of my study, I examine *Epipsychidion*, an erotic fantasy that provides not only a rich analysis of Shelley's model of love but also a vivid description of the utopia from which the poem's lover and beloved remain forever barred. Finally, I consider *Laon and Cythna* and *Prometheus Unbound* to discover Shelley's alternative to the fallen utopia of *Epipsychidion*, his return to natural wonderlands not merely as correctives to the tyrannical orders that beset each poem's heroes, but as viable alternatives—tangible utopias—to the never-never land of

Epipsychidion's "far Eden of the purple East." Throughout, I demonstrate that the processes of textual seduction model political strategies for displacing larger, oppressive social structures: time and again, Shelley stages the erotic as a device for renegotiating power and privilege, so that every context in which the erotic figures must be understood as a resolutely political one.

I divide my discussion into two sections, "Part I: The Problem" and "Part II: The Solution." While these categories may strike one, at first glance, as absurdly reductive, they exemplify the significance of Shelley's work to broader, ongoing discussions of the intersections of the political and the erotic at the site of the textual, for Shelley resists the naïve belief that every textual representation of transgressive eroticism promotes political subversion. Instead, Shelley investigates the full range of potential embedded within representations of such relationships, acknowledging that the presence or absence of equality within any relationship determines whether that relationship tends toward liberation or oppression, as well as whether the relationship plots the liberation of the world or simply anatomizes the systems of oppression that mark Shelley's own historical moment. In short, Shelley maps utopia and reality upon the bodies of his lovers: focusing in extreme close-up—shifting to synecdoche—Shelley traces upon the bodies of disproportionately empowered lovers the structures of power and injustice that maintain oppression in the real world, while upon the bodies of equal lovers, true partners, Shelley charts the contours of a new vision of the world in which selfless erotic embrace models a politics and psychology that activate the liberation of humankind. In Part I, I consider three works in which Shelley examines erotic relationships that exemplify inequities in power, where one partner is privileged—and pleasured—at the psychic and, sometimes, the physical expense of others, and I establish the correlation between each of these relationships and the mechanisms of political injustice against which Shelley rails.

While I begin my project by interrogating Shelley's investigation of "the problem" of the erotic—its potential to oppress—in "Part II: The Solution," I consider the alternative Shelley offers to systemic injustice by examining the place and function of love as it is mapped throughout some of the poet's best-known works. In these poems, three erotic relationships emerge as paradigms for a new social order, and by considering those relationships in terms of feminist theory, Lacanian psychoanalysis, spatial theory, and ecocriticism, I develop an understanding of the links Shelley charts between politics and love, the public and the private, and the "civilized" and natural worlds. I argue that in these poems Shelley envisions what I describe as the erotic cartography of a liberated world, a figurative map that charts personal relationships and political orders according to the contours of individual love-unions, which the poet sharply contrasts to the inflexibility of oppressive relationships and social structures. Throughout Part II, I demonstrate the textual processes that allow Shelley to subvert the unbending order of tyrannical regimes to peer beyond what I call the "vanishing points" of patriarchy and to imagine a space over the horizon where rigidity dissolves into permeability as oppression succumbs to ecstatic union.

Shelley's Textual Seductions

CHAPTER I

Introduction
Situating the Erotic:
The Spaces and Places of Excess

According to legend, the fall of the Bastille on 14 July 1789 was instigated when Donatien Alphonse, the Marquis de Sade, a notorious French aristocrat and pornographer, leaned out of his prison-cell window and shouted to the crowd below, describing the deplorable conditions under which he was held captive. Outraged by this fresh proof of the government's tyrannical excesses, the crowd stormed the fortress and ignited the political time bomb of the French Revolution. In this cultural fantasy, political engagement and subversive eroticism coalesce in a libertine's gesture and utterance, which "makes" public policy by goading the disgruntled, downtrodden French masses into action; thus, the impetus for Revolution takes its cue from the mere display of a privileged outcast, an aristocrat whose private life and public performances so outraged the keepers of law and order that they reacted by containing and confining the renegade scrivener under lock and key. This legend of the Marquis de Sade remains significant to our understanding of the French Revolution because it provides a specific incident around which subversive sexuality and political revolution are imagined to coalesce, and it insinuates what we might call the erotic alphabet in which the history of the French Revolution has always been written. The legend, however fantastic, is also quite untrue. What, then, is the usefulness of this anecdote, and how does one explain its origin and continued transmission some two hundred years after the "fact"?[1]

The story of Sade reminds us of the overcodings of eroticism and politics, particularly in turbulent times and across highly contested political terrain. In his study of the place of sexual power in the Romantic imagination, Daniel P. Watkins observes that "[t]he three admittedly nonparallel categories of society, philosophy, and sexuality seem . . . to be crucial in the attempt to locate and explain, in historical terms, the [R]omantic imagination and [R]omantic textuality."[2] (xvi). Pierre Saint-Amand finds such a link in the corpus—both the physical and textual bodies—of Sade, who, "[p]oised at the twilight of the Enlightenment" functions as "a clamorous harbinger of the nineteenth century" (114), and Watkins insists that "*any* social reading of [R]omanticism must contend with the ideas and logic of Sade" (132 n 8). Surely, the literary and ideological indebtedness of nineteenth-century British radical writers to the Marquis de Sade cannot be overlooked. A member of the privileged class, Sade was frequently held prisoner for erotic transgressions against the laws and social codes of his day, thrown in jail for real-life sex crimes such as rape. In fact, Sade completed the manuscript of one of his most notorious works, *Cent Vingt Journées de Sodome* [The 120 Days of Sodom], in the Bastille, and the scroll on which he composed that text was stolen from his cell by the mob that stormed the fortress (Lever 352). Years later, Sade's work would continue to function politically and would contribute to revolutionary action, as during the Revolution of 1848, when copies of *La Philosophe dans le Boudoir* [Philosophy in the Bedroom] were distributed along the Paris barricades.[3] So while the myth of Sade leaning out of his window to provoke the mob to riot is nothing more than post-Revolutionary fiction—Maurice Lever provides evidence that the writer had been transferred to Charenton ten days before the storming of the Bastille (352)—Sade nevertheless comes to occupy a space in the nineteenth-century cultural imagination that always co-aligns the sexually transgressive and the politically revolutionary; moreover, his physical absence from the Bastille is balanced by his textual presence in that fortress, both in the manuscript that was recovered from his cell and in his mythic role as instigator of that firestorm, a legend reproduced throughout a variety of narratives about the "origin" of the French Revolution,[4] just as representations of the primary instrument of Revolutionary democracy, the guillotine, percolated throughout popular commercial culture, appearing in the least seemingly political spaces—drawing rooms—as trinkets and *objets d'art*. On a more tangible and resolutely political level, portions of the Bastille itself were appropriated as reminders of the shock of Revolution: Ronald Paulson writes that "[s]mall images of the prison were made from the dismantled stones [of the razed structure] and disseminated to every department in France" as a reminder of the horrors of the despotism of the overthrown order.[5] While cultural legend inaccurately portrays Sade—pornographer, libertine, prisoner of an oppressive, pre-Revolutionary French regime—as the literal instigator of the French Revolution, I believe we should regard him nonetheless as a symbolic figurehead for that astounding transfer of political power; for as Lucienne Frappier-Mazur has argued, the Sadean text draws a connection between the erotic body and the social body, collapsing distinctions between private acts/experiences of pleasure or unpleasure and public policies/conditions of empowerment or oppression (7). The body of Sade occupies a particularly important place in the contests for authority, for visibility amidst clogged and contested political and ideological terrains, his "nonnormative practices [exposing] the weak links in normative regimes, [exposing] the regimes' arbitrariness."⁶ The imprisoning of the Marquis de Sade, a moment in which an oppressive order inscribes its authority on the body of an erotic transgressor, marks a crucial moment in the ideological development of the textual strategies I will show Percy Bysshe Shelley to extend: erotic transgression, stigmatized by excoriation, approbation, and censure, activates the opening of an experiential space out of which the call for revolution may arise as new models for a liberated world are generated. To borrow from the language of Sade, as translated by Robert Darnton, "[v]oluptuousness and philosophy produce the happiness of the sensible man."⁷ Much of the power of "voluptuousness" to produce happiness derives from the role of the erotic in regulating pleasure and, with such an end in mind, behavior—action and reaction. Jean Grimshaw observes that the erotic teaches us strategies of negotiation, of mediating a self/other split, which necessitates "some sense of 'loss' of the boundaries of self; the temporary erosion of the bodily boundaries between one person and another, and the temporary obliteration of one's normal or everyday sense of oneself."⁸ Such erosions will take form in Shelley's commitment to ideological interpenetration and psychic commingling, to his mappings of "ooziness," a trope I consider below, as well as in the negotiations of power and pleasure—and, indeed, of power *as* pleasure—that underwrite many of his works.

The nuances of the term "transgression" and its derivatives inform my descriptions of Shelley, his work, and the intellectual milieu to which he belongs. In her review of feminist readings of pornography, Constance Penley describes transgression as " . . . no simple thing. . . . It means knowing the culture inside and out, discerning the secret shames and grubby secrets, and knowing best how to humiliate it."⁹ In general, I follow the *OED*'s definition of "transgression" as "a violation," but I also keep in play the spatial relationships that term invokes, the notion of stepping over into a marked-off space, the bodily violation of a spatialized and restricted order.¹⁰ As we see in both Sade and Shelley, "transgressive" acts are those that complicate or rupture some sort of code by stepping over—violating—the boundaries between the spheres of public and private engagement. Political pornography invokes transgression through its imbrication of the public and private spheres—or discourses—of power and pleasure, of politics and the erotic. In geology, "transgression" denotes "[t]he spread of the sea over the land along a subsiding shore-line, producing an overlap . . ."; and in musicology, transgression describes sounds that come in an irregular sequence, sounds that "overlap" (*OED*). In my discussions of the transgressive qualities of political pornography—a category in which I include not only the corpus of Sade but also the works by Shelley I discuss throughout this book—I explore the potential of the transgressive to violate, or break, social norms and laws, as well as to dissolve or, at the very least, *to erode* the distinctions between binary elements, such as public/private, masculine/feminine, and politics/pleasure, and thus to introduce the condition of liminality we see in geological transgression—the overlapping of one space by another and the erasure of any clear line of demarcation between, for example, sea and land. Such a condition of liminality might be explained in terms of the artistic concept of sfumato, which Tedi Chichester Bonca offers as a model for understanding the ceaseless commminglings Shelley imagines with so many lovers; sfumato describes "a painting or drawing technique in which contours, colours, and tonal gradations are softened or blurred into one another without abrupt transitions."[11] One example of the place of such spaces or registers of indeterminacy in Shelley's work may be found in *Rosalind and Helen: A Modern Eclogue* (1818), in which Helen speaks of " . . . Gray Power . . . seated / Safely on her ancestral throne."[12] Helen's description of power as "gray" acknowledges its indeterminacy, its between-ness and, thus, its potential to shift one way or another, toward either of the strong poles (black and white) its ambiguity mixes. "Grayness" serves as an apt metaphor for Shelley's thinking about power and its movements, for, as we shall see, power may be directed in the service of good or ill, of liberation or oppression, depending, as I shall demonstrate, upon the motivations for its shift, as well as upon the mechanisms of engagement through which such shifts occur. In *The Triumph of Life* (1822), the fragment left at his death, Shelley describes the mechanics of engagement that lead to individual enlightenment and social improvement, to liberation at the psychological and political levels; such shifts follow from a reversal of gendered positionalities, a giving-up of masculinity for femininity, of dominance for submission, so that the potential for both extremes circulates throughout the individual body, finding resolution in an intercourse, a coupling, with an equally balanced beloved, whose love lifts us to " . . . a new Vision never seen before."[13] Transgressions—border-crossings, negotiations of positionality—and the conditions of liminality they invoke allow for the generation of alternative social models that are, to varying degrees, liberated from the restrictive, binary classifications that encourage the construction of hierarchies of empowerment and disempowerment, or cultures of oppression.

Sade's groundbreaking texts function not only as "palimpsests" of his personal history (Saint-Amand 115), but they also gesture toward and contribute to a post-Revolutionary canon whose narratives model the transformation of political and social realities through representations of sexually transgressive engagements. Frappier-Mazur argues that the process of writing provided Sade an avenue for mastering both personal and social realities through the textualization of erotic rituals, which establish "a rather sustained parallel between the erotic body . . . and the social body."[14] Though certainly not the first political pornographer, Sade caps a seventeenth- and eighteenth-century French tradition that interpellates pornography within the discursive realms of politics and religion, as Darnton explains: ". . . Frenchmen in the eighteenth century . . . [did not] distinguish a genre of 'pure' pornography from erotic fiction, anti-clerical tracts, and other varieties of 'philosophical books.' The notion of pornography, like the word itself, was developed in the nineteenth century, when librarians sorted out books that they considered dirty and put them under lock and key . . . . Strictly speaking, pornography . . . did not exist in the eighteenth century" (8). By including descriptions of erotic acts within what would have been recognized as "philosophical" texts, seventeenth- and eighteenth-century French pornographers secured the "place" of such representations by protecting them from censure; in this way, one of the most important precursors to the works of Sade, *Thérèse Philosophe* (1748), announces its "place" among philosophical literature in its very title, a gimmick Sade would repeat in *La Philosophe dans le Boudoir* almost 50 years later.

Roland Barthes reads what he describes as the Sadian scene—any of the orgiastic vignettes the writer's books describe—as microcosms of the social order, in which existing hierarchies of gender and class remain clearly and firmly demarcated.[15] Barthes points to the Sadian scene—"Sadian theater," he calls it—to demonstrate the place of language in pornographic fantasy: enthroned as a God at the center of the scene, Speech finds incarnation at the edges of the stage—or, to use a metaphor to which I will return in my reading of *The Cenci*, at the vanishing points of power, which demarcate the horizon (148): that is, occupying both the center and the margins, Speech is everywhere, making its God-like claims over the entire scene indisputable. For Sade, eroticism and language prove inseparable; indeed, Sade locates eroticism within language to reveal texts themselves as erotic sites (26), as Barthes observes: "[f]or Sade, there is no eroticism unless the crime is 'reasoned'; *to reason* means to philosophize, to dissertate, to harangue, in short, to subject crime (a generic term designating all the Sadian passions) to a system of articulated language . . . ." (27); Sade's writing "'seduces,' 'animates,' 'misleads,' 'electrifies,' 'inflames'; in the series of orgies, it indubitably functions as a rest period, but this rest is not merely for ordinary recuperation: during the dissertation, erotic energy is renewed" (146). Throughout the works of Sade, pleasure proceeds from language and returns to language for its renewal,[16] so that in Sade's system, language and pleasure remain inextricably related, as the dissemination of one *is* the dissemination of the other: throughout the orgiastic exchange, pleasure and text multiply in their transmission from one locutor to another, and so on. As Deborah Elise White has observed of Shelley's work, "[w]riting, like reading . . . unites action with suffering—political aspiration with reflective consciousness."[17] As pleasure and pain register upon the bodies of victims and victimizers, Sadian theater demonstrates the profound social effects of language—the imbrications of human and textual bodies as mediated by the erotic encounter.

Eva Lajer-Burcharth recognizes that "Sade does not simply speak . . . for the random pursuit of pleasure; what he proposes is a kind of libidinal imperative for the new republican self."[18] That central theater of Sadean activity, the bedroom, therefore takes on a resolutely public "space," far exceeding the confines of private space to which we might otherwise assign it: "[a]nd it is as a space of desire that the Sadean boudoir . . . represents the symbolic interior of the Republic itself," the uncharted insides of power (290). Following Carole Pateman, Lynn Hunt extends Barthes' understanding of the social effects of language by arguing that in Sade's works, "the sexual contract is the foundation of the social contract,"[19] so that in Sade's fantasy worlds, order—whether traditional or anarchic—develops synecdochally from individual erotic relationships. Sade's masterpiece, *La Philosophie dans le Boudoir*, details the education of the innocent Eugénie by Dolmancé and Saint-Ange, two figures who respond to their pupil's questions through words and deeds "which . . . carry perversion to its utmost extreme" (Lever, *Sade* 476). Sade intersperses his accounts of characters' sexual activities with didactic passages that consider aspects of nature, crime, religion, morality, politics, and revolution; and in the middle of *La Philosophie*, Sade inserts the pamphlet-length "Français, encore un effort, si vous voulez être républican [Frenchmen, yet another effort if you would become republican]," a political tract that calls on the downtrodden masses to rise in collective revolt against the regime that oppresses them by overthrowing Christianity in order to inaugurate a republican age in which theft, murder, incest, and sodomy are not merely sanctioned but, shockingly, encouraged. The novel thus overlaps political discourse and descriptions of sex acts to create what Barthes might call a "hyphology," a narrative in which "*text* means *tissue*," a space composed by the interweavings of webs of meaning.[20] In the end, *La Philosophie dans le boudoir* describes a world in which the sexual and the political always intersect,[21] and the novel may thus be cited as an important precedent for the politicization of the erotic I will show Shelley to explore.

Like his Romantic inheritors, the Marquis de Sade speaks from an oddly privileged social position: born into the aristocracy, he looms in the cultural imagination as an erotic criminal, a scandal-plagued writer whose life proves so central to his age and those to follow that an entire experience or identity assumes his name. From Sade, we inherit the notion of the "sadist," a term that marks the outsider, who finds pleasure in the infliction of pain—in the register of his own power—and his transgressively eroticized, criminalized body is always positioned in opposition to hegemonic values, institutions, and experiences. Sade contributes to a libertine tradition that centers around an erotic figure whose intimate engagements

Introduction

embed political significance by and through the condition of their transgressiveness.[22] From Sade to the Romantics, we may chart the movement of this libertine tradition from France to England, a tradition that, at least in theory, arrives in England on the back of the French Revolution.[23]

The migration from France to England of what we might call a "politicized erotic" follows two real-life, historical precedents. First, in 1660, Charles II returned to England accompanied by an aristocratic French court, and rumors of the deviant sexual practices of his circle spread rapidly.[24] The political reversals of the Restoration, the movement of the "proper" or "Divine Right" order out of exile back to the seat of power, must also be understood in the context of the cultural fantasy of those who opposed the restoration of Charles II and regarded his accession as symbolic of the "infection" of England by the vices and excesses of France, all of which were hypostasized in the person of the restored monarch.[25] Second, looming large in the Romantic imagination was the notorious "Queen Caroline Affair" of 1820, an incident in which King George IV's wife, long rumored to have been involved in scandalous extramarital relationships, found praise and adoration as a revolutionary hero in a variety of cheap English publications. Certainly motivated by a collective resistance to the rule and order of the day, tales of the transgressively erotic behavior of the Queen found material form in countless stories, sketches, cartoons, and songs, all of which celebrated the Queen's participation in a variety of deviant sexual activities.[26] In these salacious rumors and drawings, we find manifestations of the erotic employed as tools for political resistance and appropriated as a vocabulary for the articulation of revolutionary fervor. In the resistance to the accession of Charles II and in the media frenzy over the Queen Caroline Affair, we see played out on the stage of history the same ideological strategy that structures the post-Revolutionary legends that place the Marquis de Sade at the Bastille on 14 July 1789: specifically, we observe the conjoining of the political and the erotic in a symbolic system that articulates the threat—or, from a different perspective, the promise—of revolution.

∞ ∞ ∞ ∞ ∞

Throughout *Shelley's Textual Seductions*, I examine how and to what effects Shelley conflates representations of political and erotic engagements to generate new models for re-making the world in the aftermath of the French Revolution or, more generally, in the wake of the ceaseless turbulence that characterized the Romantic age.[27] I argue that Shelley masks political rhetoric by way of erotic narratives in order to seduce readers with a wide variety of sexual milieux in which pleasure and love are posed as symbols for liberation from oppressive regimes and selfishly invested individuals. Saint-Amand recognizes the pedagogical potential of seduction (117), yet he notes too the propensity for seduction to function as hypnosis, as possession, as poisoning (13): "seduction ... is above all fascination, mesmerism, sorcery," and it operates through "the magic of magnetic gestures, in the intimidation of the gaze that transfixes" (3). In so saying, Saint-Amand acknowledges the dynamics of power that lurk in seduction and its deployments, using even the language of military maneuvers to describe their goals: "[s]eduction is a military *occupation*" (9). But for Shelley, I will argue, the appropriation of so power-laden a strategy is offset by its intended effects: if first he must lure a reader into his web, Shelley then liberates the reader through that seductive engagement, encouraging a shift in perspective and an alteration in engagement that perpetuates the individual's liberation by encouraging its extension to others around him or her, ultimately to the whole social structure—the world, even—in which he or she lives.

"[T]he only authentic act available to human beings in the society that had emerged after the French Revolution was coming to be that of questioning," John Beer argues,[28] and the act of questioning suggests a desire for some form of engagement, a reciprocal activity, an intellectual give-and-take, which the writings of the Romantics seem to offer, given their avant-garde aesthetic and ideological programs. Saint-Amand locates seductive power in the gaze of irresistibility; similarly, the Romantics embed seduction in texts that lure through the controversial or otherwise provocative nature of their engagements—political, sexual, spiritual, and so on. A work by Shelley appropriates the seductive power of the gaze within its own pages, so that any reader who chooses to glance through it will, ideally, stand transfixed, hypnotized, mesmerized by the images there construed.

Perhaps the most important study of seduction to date is Jean Baudrillard's, although his ultimate assessment of the motivations for and the effects of seduction (always selfish, and always an inequity in power) run counter to the means and ends to which Shelley applies those strategies. Baudrillard argues that seduction is always a conspiracy of signification,[29] a manipulation of language, one version of Paulson's claim that "revolution makes words mean something else" (15), that the language emerging from chaos (revolution generally, the French Revolution in the specific case of the Romantics) must be read differently, that is, for different effect. Baudrillard poses seduction as an alternative to sex and power, and he relates seduction to "the strength of the feminine" (7), situating seduction in exactly the position of "other" that Romanticism in general (as a charge against the status quo, as a form of ideological questioning, of skepticism) comes to occupy and which Shelley in particular celebrates throughout his work. And while I depart from Baudrillard's assertion that seduction ultimately has nothing to do with sexual or political power (8)—for I will show how Shelley links those powers by and through the mechanisms of seduction—I follow Baudrillard in imagining the seductive universe as one no longer divisible into diacritical oppositions (7), for surely this kind of oozy world that dissolves the rigid rules of "propriety," themselves structural links between and among systems of oppression, is exactly the world Shelley heralds in works such as *Epipsychidion*, *Laon and Cythna*, and *Prometheus Unbound*, which offer a vision of a world liberated by love.

Shelley's visionary works, as we shall see, postulate utopias on the comminglings of lovers and on the establishment of free-love communities. In moderating a discussion between Theodor Adorno and Ernst Bloch about the concept of utopia, Horst Krüger observes that "utopia refers to what is missing," for that which is absent, and Bloch points to the French Revolution as germinating from a utopic ideal.[30] Perhaps, then, the key tactical mistake that doomed the French Revolution to failure was the absence of an original plot for a changed culture, a map of freedom. Shelley's works provide such a map: they plot utopia, only to discover that the utopic is, at present, absent, that at best it can merely be gestured toward, imagined, and thus activated only on an intellectual level. But the inability to arrive at the utopic never slows Shelley in his quest for the betterment of his society, for he believes that repeated imaginings and the dissemination of those imaginings through textual forms—consciousness-raising writing, we might say—gradually lead us to utopia's shores, finally to deliver us there once and for all, if not in his time, and if not in ours, then in some time in the not-too-distant future. This hope, this dream, forms a significant component of the lure of Shelley's writing, a chief aspect of his strategy of textual seduction. Representations of the distant world prompt erotic longing, Bloch argues (281), and thus such representations enact seduction, as my examination of Shelley's work will suggest.[31]

Ross Chambers points to seduction as one strategy that underwrites what he describes as oppositional narrative, a text that enables readers to see through structures of oppression in order to devise strategies for re-mediating power and authority in the world. Chambers argues that the politics of oppositionality are concerned with "the possibilities for social change in a world where the violence of revolutionary reversals is less and less felt to be justified while modern apparatuses of social control are increasingly experienced as alienating and intolerable."[32] Such a condition characterizes the first third of the nineteenth century, as Shelley and his contemporaries come to regard the French Revolution as a political failure given its "fall" into tactics of domination alarmingly reminiscent of those it initially opposed; more broadly, such a condition characterizes the entire nineteenth century as a complex of economic, political, technological, and cultural forces profoundly transforms the lived experience of public and private life in Britain. The politics of oppositionality are thus crucial to making sense of the seductive political engagements I find embedded in works by Shelley as well as in works throughout the nineteenth century that derive from the Shelleyan model of "textual seduction," or the political coercion of the reader through the lure of the sexy text. In his "Essay on Christianity" (ca. 1813-1819), Shelley argues that moral revolution must precede any real and sustained political change, and he recognizes the success of Christ as largely a function of effective rhetoric, of Christ's ability to deploy speech as a means of seduction.[33] Frappier-Mazur equates speech with desire, and she argues that speech "triggers sexual pleasure and nurtures the imaginary" (77). Shelley's writing—his speech—articulates a desire for liberation and, by means of that articulation, manifests his vision of freedom, if only on an imaginary level, but one made to seem real through the elaborate plots Shelley designs—the maps he makes—which render the utopic tantalizingly tangible. We crave maps, Geoff King argues, in part because we know that in making maps we are making our experience of the world, shaping the world to reflect our desires, for maps do more than represent space; they *assert* it.[34] In exactly this way, Shelley deploys the strategies of textual seduction to lure his readers into plotting utopia with him, to imagining the idealized worlds he predicts. Thus, Shelley inaugurates a counter-tradition in nineteenth-century British literature in which radical political narratives are displaced into the seemingly apolitical realms of erotic utopia, which he maps according to the parameters of idealized erotic relationships. By locating the political in Shelley's erotic-utopic narratives, I plot the strategies through which Shelley seduces his readers into radical political engagements, and I demonstrate how Shelley's narratives map liberation according to the contours of erotic union, ultimately in an attempt to articulate a sociopolitical ideal, to plot utopia.[35]

Like Sade, Shelley turns to the erotic body and, more generally, to the theater of the erotic-as-spectacle for the central device that activates the strategies of textual seduction. As I demonstrate in the chapters to follow, Shelley's vision of a liberated world proceeds from his idealized model of erotic engagement, in which the bodies of lover and beloved "mix and melt" into one, erasing all markers of difference and division.[36] Romanticism in general encourages and attempts to provide modes for social change that proceed from the level of the individual and his or her relationships with others. For this reason, Romanticism offers what we must recognize as a profoundly psychological model, and its methods depend upon interpersonal relationships, as reflected in and mediated through textual engagements. In seeking to call forth a radically democratized view of the world, Romanticism aims to legislate lived experience in order to activate a profoundly liberating vision, one that results from the raising of intellectual processes to the level of social interaction—a move from the self to the larger world, from the one to the other, which may be mapped exactly alongside William Wordsworth's model for the processes of writing and reading poetry, a pattern that depends on perpetual negotiations of inside and outside, self and world, perception and imagination—constant crossings and re-crossings of binary divisions, finally to the point of blurring the edges that separate each from the other. And while Wordsworth may have introduced the psychopolitics of reading that

Introduction

inform the whole of the Romantic project, such a model is most consistently deployed and most fully explored in the works of Shelley, whose writings proceed from the notion that social revolution emerges from psychological insights manifested in writing and realized through both textual and extra-textual interpersonal engagements. Shelley's notorious system of free love follows his model of erotic cartography, which charts the physical universe and one's experience of it according to aspects of personal engagement—of lovers, of loving, and finally of all modes of interpersonal exchange—indeed, of eroticism in its most elastic sense. For Shelley, the text serves as a hinge between writer and reader, and the fruit of that union proves contingent upon the writer's ability to work through the instrument of the text to move the reader, to seduce the reader and, thus, to interpenetrate the reader, infusing him or her with the writer's own ideas and ideals. Shelley regards reading as a liminal experience, one in which, ideally, all distinctions between writer and reader dissolve as the two melt into union, a blurry, oozy state we will see to be key to many of the relationships Shelley describes in the works I examine. For Shelley, the text operates as a hinge of contingency; when that hinge achieves the goal of uniting Shelley and his reader, the resulting intercourse replicates at the level of the textual/psychological the rhythms, pulses, and pleasures of lovemaking, the tender gestures of reciprocity and the melting into one that prefigures the transformation and resuscitation of a fractured and fractious world. Shelley's textual seductions, then, model strategies for repairing the damage done to the world by institutionalized forms of hierarchy and separation, of stratification and (d)evaluation. In this way, Shelley's model of reading operates transgressively, for it anticipates and encourages a breaking down of all divisions between writer and reader, so that the text becomes the magic-space in which the two merge, overcoming all manners and modes of difference and division in their embrace.

Shelley's breakings-down may be mapped according to the geological sense of transgression, for his lover and beloved overlap in a seamless combination that complicates traditional order by introducing the condition of indeterminacy, or ooziness, just as states of matter—physical or geographical entities—dissolve into each other and combine in complete and indivisible unions.[37] Generating liberation from the erotic union, Shelley emphasizes the political potential of his lovers' comminglings to articulate a conception of the social order that indeed offers a re-vision of the age-old notion of the body-politic;[38] but in the age-to-come of Shelleyan liberation, the traditional "head" of the body-politic, the individual ruler, the patriarch, the King—always a tyrannical figure, according to Shelley—disappears as the map of the social order is re-drawn in the image of idealized erotic unions. By opposing tyranny with pleasure, Shelley calls forth a liberated world in which (political) division succumbs to (erotic) overlap to generate a radically democratized order that finds its structural and ideological bases in Shelley's own model of love.

∞ ∞ ∞ ∞ ∞

Shelley's strategies of textual seduction derive from the premise that the text is pedagogical, that writing teaches the reader something about the larger world. Shelley considers the pedagogical function of the text at some length in his essay *A Defence of Poetry* (1821): "[Poetry] awakens and enlarges the mind by rendering it the receptacle of a thousand unapprehended combinations of thought. Poetry lifts the veil from the hidden beauty of the world, and makes familiar objects as if they were not familiar; it reproduces all that it represents, and the impersonations clothed in its Elysian light stand thenceforward in the minds of those who have once contemplated them, as memorials of that gentle and exalted content which extends itself over all thoughts and actions with which it coexists."[39] Elsewhere in the *Defence,* Shelley delineates the functions of poetry in terms of the creation of knowledge, power, and pleasure (503), a constellation whose terminological codes overlap education, politics, and eroticism. Shelley's agenda draws on the function of pornography, which, as Darnton indicates, was frequently employed in the service of sexual stimulation: so-called "'Wicked' books celebrated reading as a stimulus of sexual pleasure . . ." (89). Shelley draws on the seductive power of language (or, to borrow a description from Darnton, "the evocative power of reading itself" [103]), the potential for a narrative to draw a reader in, to tease a reader with the guarantee of some sort of erotic pleasure. This erotic draw is the hallmark of textual seduction, for it promises the reader the reward of pleasure in one form or another; and in Shelley's vision of liberation, erotic pleasure (love) and political pleasure (freedom) prove inseparable—indeed, they become interdependent, as we shall see. Such a drawing-in of the reader marks the political effects of Shelley's erotic works: as Gary Kelly observes, "[w]riting the revolutionized subject not only transcends the merely historical revolution, it is one of the few authentic forms of revolutionary action. Writing the revolutionized subject constitutes a claim to be the revolutionary avant-garde and *incorporates* the reader in [the text]" (82, emphasis added). Seducing his readers, Shelley's writing activates the intellectual revolution he so often hails. Seduction may be, as Baudrillard argues, pure artifice, all sign and ritual (2), but for Shelley, its effects are profoundly political, resolutely tangible, both in the psychic world of his individual reader and in that reader's larger society.[40]

Darnton points to a seventeenth-century French text on the art of printing, Louis-Sébastien Mercier's *De la Littérature et des littéraries* (1778), to historicize the social and political effects of the reading process: "[printing] is the most beautiful gift of heaven. . . . It soon will change the countenance of the universe. . . . A despot, surrounded by guards, by fortresses, defended by two thousand naked swords, may be deaf to the call of conscience; but he cannot resist a stroke of the pen: this stroke will fell

Introduction   13

him in the heart of his grandeur" (trans. and qtd. in Darnton 229). The effects of the written word on the body politic—here, on the body of the individual reader—take tangible form: Darnton describes the effects of reading as parallel to the processes of printing, so that just as a page is stamped with characters and designs, the message transmitted through that page is similarly "imprinted in the soul of the reader" (229). This description of the reading process locates textual effects on the body of the individual reader and reminds us of the decidedly physical uses to which "wicked" books were put; in addition, Darnton's description acknowledges the erotic condition that codes the entire act of reading throughout the eighteenth century. Vernon A. Rosario notes that Rousseau feared the effects of reading, since among them lay the introduction of the reader to sexuality, to desire (24); for Rousseau—and certainly for Shelley, though he regards the effect as positive and potentially liberating— literature may well function as a tool of and for the erotic: "[Rousseau blamed l]ascivious talk, romantic novels, and sensual images . . . for igniting the imagination and, by sympathy, inciting the genitals" (26). An "erotics of reading," Bruce Smith explains, "asks the reader to take words, not as symbols . . . but as indexes, signs with a natural or metonymic connection with somatic experience,"[41] and erotic literature clearly fulfills this expectation by transferring the pleasure from its representational form (the text) to its manifestation in the mind and body of the reader of the text. When Darnton describes "the sensation of cutting the first pages [of a book] with a pocket knife . . . and the [reader's] final immersion in the texts late at night, as the wick of the lantern sputtered and burned down to a stub" (230), his account positions the text as one erotic body and the reader as another, so that the process of reading *is* the process of lovemaking, complete with anticipation, arousal, penetration, ejaculation, and detumescence, all of which occur "late at night," perhaps after a hard day's work, or perhaps because of the reader's desire to conceal such "wicked" pleasures from public view.

Shelley inherits more from seventeenth- and eighteenth-century France than this sexy model of reading, however; he also inherits an understanding of the specifically political function of the writer. At the close of *A Defence of Poetry,* Shelley offers what has become one of his most well-known claims, that "Poets are the unacknowledged legislators of the World" (508). Elsewhere, Shelley writes of the poet's creative powers, his or her ability to alter reality through the mere deployment of language, so that the poet emerges as a kind of God who incarnates the very ideals about which s/he writes: " . . . the office and character of a poet participates in the divine nature as regards providence, no less than as regards creation" (492). Poetry " . . . is ever accompanied by pleasure" (486), and, indeed, the poet who, like the philosopher, remains dedicated to preserving such pleasure, activates "[t]he production and assurance of pleasure in [the] highest sense" (502, 501). While in the *Defence* Shelley's definition of "pleasure" seems rather innocuous—"Pleasure . . . is that which the consciousness of a sensitive and intelligent being seeks, and in which when found acquiesces" (500)—my readings of Shelley's works will demonstrate such pleasures to incorporate components that are decidedly erotic, as well.

Describing erotic acts in an effort to elicit corporeal response—readerly stimulation—Shelley's works uncover the textual body as an erotic site—a *sexual* textual body whose investments in pleasure are deployed in an express effort to stimulate the reader's libido, to excite us into some sort of action, real or imagined, tangible or fantasized. Such a rubbing up against the imagination of the reader is the first and foremost effect of Shelley's works, and such are the processes of textual seduction: embracing the text that interpenetrates his or her imagination, Shelley's reader engages in a commingling with the work in exactly the manner of union Shelley will describe in "On Love," an act of commingling—the consummation of the process of textual seduction—through which text and reader become one, as each depends upon the other for fulfillment, and as the two establish a relationship of contingency in which the reader, standing in for the text, stands poised to reproduce in the larger world the message Shelley's words engender.

Just as Shelley composes texts that operate separately and collectively as an erotic body, so too does the twentieth-century poststructuralist critic Roland Barthes regard the text as symbolically erotic (*The Pleasure of the Text* 17). But for Barthes, as for Shelley, the erotic is not clearly definable as a specific pleasure or even as a catalogue of pleasures; instead, the erotic emerges as something of a rupture, or split, between culture and what we might think of as its "other": "Neither culture nor its destruction is erotic; it is the seam between them, the fault, the flaw, which becomes so" (7). Barthes reminds us that "the most erotic portion of a body" is the area in which "*the garment gapes*," (9) and he locates textual eroticism at similar spaces, in similar openings: like the flash of skin we see in the gape of the garment, the erotic appears within the text itself "between two edges," a flash that seduces the reader with the promise of some sort of reward (10).[42] Barthes, again like Shelley, believes that the text solicits the reader into an erotic engagement; to use Barthes' own language, the text *cruises* the reader and invites the reader into the erotic exchange of reading (4), within which text and reader dissolve into one: "[o]n the stage of the text, no footlights: there is not, behind the text, someone active (the writer) and out front someone passive (the reader); there is not a subject and an object. The text supersedes grammatical attitudes: it is the undifferentiated eye which an excessive author (Angelus Silesius) describes: 'The eye by which I see God is the same eye by which he sees me'" (16). As we shall see in my readings of Shelley's texts, the erotic activates an odd blurring of the parameters of existing social codes, including the institutionalization of tyranny through which individuals or groups are empowered at the very real and often very physical expense of others. In the exchange of reading, the division between text and reader breaks down as the two bodies—one physical, the other textual—mix and melt into each other, modeling the erotic connection so crucial to Shelley's concept of love. For Shelley, power is always written on the body, always somatically inscribed, as my readings of *The Cenci* and *Julian and Maddalo* will demonstrate; conversely, Shelley turns to the body as the space from which a new social order may proceed, so that the body emerges as a text from which the model for liberation has already been generated, a model according to which freedom may be cartographized.

Barthes writes that "[t]he text is (should be) that uninhibited person who shows his behind to the *Political Father*" (53). Shelley's texts certainly fulfill Barthes' fantasy, for not only do they expose the artificial, arbitrary nature of power, but they place themselves in a self-consciously oppositional relationship to authority. Showing their behinds to so many political fathers, Shelley's texts challenge tyranny with a renunciation of its claims to power, and they situate themselves as the feminine "others" in opposition to the heteropatriarchal power-structures they reject. In bending over, Shelley's texts invite "Political Fathers"—all who are empowered by exclusive, patriarchal models, as we shall see—to fuck them, and in so doing the texts remark on their status as erotic bodies by unleashing their power to arouse and to unsettle the very powers they confront. In the *Defence*, Shelley writes that "[p]oetry turns all things to loveliness; it exalts the beauty of that which is most beautiful, and it adds beauty to that which is most deformed: it marries exultation and horror, grief and pleasure, eternity and change; it subdues to union under its light yoke all irreconcilable things. It transmutes all that it touches, and every form moving within the radiance of its presence is changed by wondrous sympathy to an incarnation of the spirit which it breathes; its secret alchemy turns to potable gold the poisonous waters which flow from death through life; it strips the veil of familiarity from the world, and lays bare the naked and sleeping beauty which is the spirit of its forms" (*SPP* 505). Self-consciously positioned as feminized/receptive sites of and for erotic pleasure, Shelley's texts—these spaces-to-be-penetrated—lure the powers-that-be into erotic engagements that re-mediate power as pleasure; and in the processes of textual seduction, Shelley's texts trump tyranny with a vision of a new social order in which power is re-distributed as equality, so that the disenfranchised are empowered as the Political Fathers are castrated of their own claims to supremacy, reduced finally—but only—to a status *equal* to that of those whom they have dominated.

∞ ∞ ∞ ∞ ∞

Four terms inform my project, each of which gives rise to a wide variety of sometimes inconsistent interpretations: the public, the private, the erotic and the political. As this list suggests, throughout the book

I interrogate ideological engagements in terms of physical space; that is, I examine with particular interest where the political and the erotic may be located in the texts under consideration, and I demonstrate how Shelley's decision to map ideology onto physical space spectacularizes a shift in the place of revolution from more recognizably public spaces, such as government and organs of the mainstream press, to private ones, such as the home and special-interest publications.[43]

Because my study surveys an array of texts that explore the diverse connections between sex and power as well as the dual ends (oppression and liberation) to which those connections may lead, I want to begin by defining each of those terms in a broad, theoretical sense. Throughout the book, I particularize those definitions according to the specific texts under investigation. At this early moment in my study, I do not presume to offer an absolute definition for each term I employ; instead, I define each term in only the most broad sense, so that in subsequent chapters I may delineate the parameters of these apparently elastic definitions more clearly and distinctly.

In his survey of eighteenth-century France and Germany, Jürgen Habermas describes the "public" sphere as the primary locale for reasoned, non-coercive communication and exchange.[44] The "public sphere," then, is a term we may apply collectively to spaces designated for "proper" interaction and exchange, and in such spaces, we witness what we might characterize as rational, "proper," and non-erotic activity. I consider "the public" any space that labors under the monitorizing gazes of the institutions of power, regulation, and control; specifically, the "public" labors under the gazes of religion and law. The "private" sphere, by contrast, is located quite literally in the physical space of the home, the domestic realm in which the technologies of "public" personæ—affectations, manners, and codes of behavior—begin to be dropped, the space in which erotic exchanges are imagined more "properly" to occur. Thus we see that it is in the very condition of transgression—the overlapping of one space and another, the pushing to erosion of the bounds that demarcate "proper" behavior, or the boundaries that demarcate specific spaces—that the potential for social change begins to emerge; in this give-and-take, transgression takes variously erotic and political forms, but, like the seams between these "public" and "private" spaces, the seams between the erotic and the political, too, begin to cede into a kind of blur, to erode into ooziness, a trope I examine in much greater depth throughout this book, particularly in my discussion of *The Cenci* and *Julian and Maddalo*.

Throughout my study, I consider how the erotic functions as a tool that may be used either as a means for liberation or as a mechanism for oppression. To this end, I use the term "erotic" primarily to denote representations of sexual activity; but in some cases, I consider texts that depict other sorts of emotional engagements, such as familial relationships, to be "erotic" as well. More generally, I refer to particular emotional exchanges, both positive (or fulfilling) and negative (or disappointing) as "erotic," and I shall demonstrate how these relationships either duplicate existing social structures (in the case of oppression) or offer alternative social models (in the case of liberation).[45]

The fourth term that informs my work, the "political," signifies interactions meant to affect change in the public sphere—change, of course, that sometimes arises out of and sometimes intrudes upon "private" life. To put it more simply, my use of the term "political" always refers to the effects of power on people since, for me, "politics" signifies access to power and its negotiations between and among individuals and groups. Throughout my argument, I demonstrate how the works under consideration rely on the titillating potential of the erotic to deploy power in the service of coercion, so that seduction-by-reading functions as a powerful lure into the political agenda each work advances. In contrast to Habermas' model of a public sphere in which coercion is replaced by reason and force by discourse, Shelley's works deploy the erotic as *a discourse of force*; descriptions of love and pleasure are posed to sway readers by mediating the subjective experience of desire rather than by appealing objectively to reason and utility. Such, we shall see, is the work of Shelley's textual seduction.

∞ ∞ ∞ ∞ ∞

Shelley's model of textual seduction clearly derives from the so-called "philosophical" tradition of French Revolution-era pornography. A variety of critics have pointed to the Revolution as a crucial political factor in what we might think of as the evolution of the Romantic attitude. In *Romantics, Rebels, and Reactionaries,* Marilyn Butler observes that the Romantic response to the French Revolution is crucial to making sense of the radical intellectual context of nineteenth-century Britain. While she argues that the storming of the Bastille on 14 July 1789 marked not the origin but the culmination of a revolutionary spirit in Europe that began around 1760, she notes that we should consider the Romantic period of 1798-1830 an age of historical unity in which "England's *ancien régime* faced radical social change and the threat of revolution."[46] Likewise, Raymond Williams argues that industrialization holds the same significance for England as the Revolution does for France, and he suggests that in the Romantic period "political, social, and economic change" are accompanied by "a radical change ... in ideas of art, of the artist, and of their place in society": in Williams' view, "[Romantic] artists ... came to see themselves as agents of the 'revolution for life.'"[47] In a similar vein, Anne K. Mellor demonstrates how a number of Romantic texts by men—Byron and Shelley in particular—were grounded in what she characterizes as "revolutionary Promethean" models that "advocated social change and utopian transformations of the social and political order."[48] Like Butler and Williams,

Mellor recognizes the truth in Shelley's dictum that "Poets are the unacknowledged legislators of the world."

As is true of many of the younger Romantic writers, Shelley's sense of legislation—his self-designated duty as a poet—derives largely from the radical engagements of French Revolution-era discourse. In *The Making of English Reading Audiences, 1790-1832,* Jon P. Klancher provides evidence for the development of a radical readership in England "from the exhilarating first days of the French Revolution to the final prison doors that swung shut on radical leaders persecuted for treason."[49] While Butler's study points to the French Revolution as the moment that marks the conclusion—rather than the origin—of English radicalism, Klancher's work locates the beginning of that movement at the onset of the Revolution to suggest implicit connections between English radicalism and French republicanism. But while Klancher insists that a series of prosecutions of radical writers for treason foreclosed upon the flourishing of English radicalism, one goal of my book is to demonstrate how that radical, anti-hegemonic political impulse found a new voice through the strategies of textual seduction, by way of which Shelley and his inheritors shifted the language of radical politics into a discourse of eroticism. For Shelley, as I hope to demonstrate, radical engagements never disappear but simply get disguised in more highly coded forms so that they may be spoken in what we might think of as a "safe"—yet ultimately transparent—language. Throughout my study, I suggest that Shelley may have innovated the strategies of textual seduction as a shield from prosecution for treason; certainly, his careful transposition—one might even say his deliberate *translation*—of subject matter from politics to the erotic armed Shelley with a parallel language for the production of anti-hegemonic texts and enabled him to speak about political engagements even amidst seemingly apolitical retreats to pleasure, love, and aesthetics.

My understanding of the contingencies of sexual and political discourses follows a lengthy critical tradition. In *The Historicity of Romantic Discourse,* Clifford Siskin recognizes the intrinsic links between Romantic poetry and sexuality and argues that "sex became the code of all pleasure" in the period as "Romanticism wrote and was written by the apparatus of sexuality."[50] Siskin thus establishes a precedent for "reading" Romanticism in terms of erotic pleasure, which he characterizes in only the most general of terms. Stephen Frosh, following psychoanalyst Wilhelm Reich, underscores the polyvalence of the trope of sexuality and locates within that experiential and discursive space a nexus of desires and anxieties—class, economics, and ideology—all of which represent extrinsic realities and may be broadly categorized under the general rubric of "the political" as I shall define it below.[51] While Siskin points to sexuality as the master trope for all ideological figurations in the Romantic period, Judith R. Walkowitz argues more broadly that throughout the nineteenth century, writing about sexual issues functioned as a political act.[52] Like Siskin, she agrees that sexuality stood as a metaphor for other kinds of social issues, "a contested site for other struggles and social divisions, particularly those of class, gender, and race" (8). Concentrating on the dissemination of pornography in the Romantic period, Iain McCalman considers media coverage of the Queen Caroline Affair and argues that such documents exemplify the links between radical political discourse and representations of sexual transgression; further, McCalman gestures toward arguing for the omnipotence of pornographic representation-as-politics by noting that press portrayals of the Queen Caroline Affair became so widespread in England that authorities were rendered powerless in their attempts to suppress them (176, 205). McCalman's discussion of the coverage and reaction to this notorious incident reminds us of the power of prurience-in-print to overcome the regulatory and disciplinary structures entrusted to state apparatuses such as the police: written and pictorial speculations about the erotic intrigues of the Queen completely captivated public interest, seducing countless readers who fell into a sort of textual feeding frenzy, gorging themselves on unlimited narratives whose chief ingredients were always and simultaneously sexual and political.

Textual representations of sexual acts—not to mention readers' gorgings on them—proliferate during periods of political instability and revolutionary upheaval.[53] Lynn Hunt traces the etymology of the word "pornography" throughout the turbulent years of the French Revolution and concludes that by 1806 the term had come to stand for "writing that disturbed the social order and contravened good morals."[54] Following Jeffrey Merrick, Hunt argues that during the French Revolution, the manifestation of sexual disorder in the proliferation of pornography functioned as "a sign of a breakdown in public order" (306), or, as she puts it elsewhere, representations of "sexual degeneration . . . [were imagined to go] hand in hand with political corruption."[55] Hunt's examination of the pornography of revolutionary France provides visual evidence for the political significance of sexual narratives, for even their power to affect political realities: "politically motivated pornography helped to bring about the Revolution by undermining the legitimacy of the ancien régime as a social and political system" ("Pornography and the French Revolution" 301). In the French Revolutionary period, we witness the overlapping of sex and politics in representations at once sexually and socially engaged, in seductive texts whose readerly pleasures derive from the collision-course of the erotic and the political. Hunt observes that republicans valued transparency—a seeing through, a harmony between private selves and public lives.[56] In artistic representations that emphasized the contingent natures of private and public lives, we see such transparencies in images of transgression, of overlap, between inside and outside, self and world, suggesting the less-than-solid nature of those spaces, the permeable borders that delimit their edges, and that allow them to overlap, to overflow, each into the other.

Hunt demonstrates that "in the early years of the Revolution, politically motivated pornography accounted for about half of the obscene literature produced" in France (307), a rather impressive output of approximately 200 "licentious pamphlets and books . . . between 1789 and 1792 alone" (310). Hunt comments on the shifting demographics of the audience for pornography throughout the revolutionary period and notes that while before 1789 the "typography, length, and content" of most pornography deemed it "destined for a very upper-class audience" (316), sometime during 1789, the year of the Revolution, a number of pornographic pamphlets—now mass-produced and less expensive to purchase than books—made pornography "accessible to a large audience" (317). After 1789, a new genre of cheap pornographic pamphlets, usually eight pages in length, became available to a wide range of consumers at the relatively low price of five *sols*, and sometimes for even less than that (317). Hunt concludes that "just as the revolutionary leadership hoped to mobilize all classes of French people, so too did political pornographers hope to tap all classes of readers and viewers" (321), and in the end, the wide accessibility of pornography served in the interest of democratization, for it made the same material available to all potential buyers and participated in an ongoing critique of the monarchial forces that oppressed those buyers by precluding any sort of social movement, by paralyzing them in the space of the lower-class (329). In the newly inexpensive genre of the pornographic pamphlet, licentious narratives, political discourse, and the democratization of France overlap and speak to one and all. Such a democratizing hyphology informs the 1790 pamphlet *La Confédération de la nature, ou L'Art de se reproduire, avec figures* [The Confederation of Nature, or The Reproductive Art, With Pictures], in which a prostitute broadcasts her lower rates for patriots: "'Eighteen sous, instead of twenty-four; It's to that that my national cunt has been reduced'" (qtd. and trans. in Hunt 327). In this narrative—as well as in the democratization of pornographic materials themselves—pornography, manifested here in the actual body of the prostitute, makes pleasure more accessible for the politically engaged.

Hunt argues that from about 1796 French pornography "developed into a medium for the exploration of new sexual pleasures . . . but left behind its political past" (339), and the only exception she makes to this rule is the work of Sade, who "explicitly tied the . . . [revolutionary by-words of] equality and fraternity to the virtues of incest and the community of all women" that his scandalous narratives celebrate (330). But Hunt insists that the very excesses of Sade's texts, his endless catalogs of positions and activities, his countless narratives of erotic torture and murder, "undermined the use of pornography for political ends in the future . . . [because in Sade's works] pornography was now identified with a general assault on morality itself, rather than a specific criticism of the irrationalities of the ancien régime moral system" (330). Hunt thus dismisses Sade's work as ultimately de-politicized, but as I have suggested, I read the same tendencies in those texts—excess and the fetish for cataloguing—as instruments of hyper-politicization, so that Sade's texts are always moving beyond the narrow confines of his own historical moment to critique all structures of reason and law as they exist before, during, and after his lived experience in late eighteenth-century France.

Hunt maintains that from the moment of the revolution of 1789, pornography "came to the surface of the new popular politics in the form of . . . vicious attacks on leading courtiers and, in particular, on the queen, Marie Antoinette" (302).[57] But, as Hunt observes, pornography was deployed in the political interests of an array of individuals and groups: "before the Revolution, anti-Marie Antoinette pamphlets . . . were no doubt sponsored by factions of the court itself" (315); "[t]he 'popular' images of the queen, then, had their origin in the court, not in the streets" ("The Many Bodies of Marie Antoinette" 116).[58] Hunt's findings about the pornographic representations of the French queen bear quoting at length, for they suggest not only the widespread availability of such materials, but also the political importance of those documents:

> Marie Antoinette was, without question, the favorite individual target of pornographic attacks, both before and after 1789. There were not only more pamphlets about her than about any other single figure, but the pamphlets were the most sustained in their attacks; they were also, apparently, best-sellers. Heading the list of pamphlets confiscated by the Paris police in 1790-1791, for example, were *Vie privée, et scandaleuse de Marie Antoinette*, with eighty-eight copies confiscated, and *La Messaline française*, with eighty-one copies confiscated. . . . . [T]he antiqueen pamphlets were sold at the gate to Tuileries palace, in its gardens and right under the king's window. This kind of pornography had a much wider audience than ancien régime libertine literature. (324)

Hunt's study makes clear the political significance of representations of Marie Antoinette's private life: " . . . the trial of the queen, especially in its strange refractions of the pornographic literature, . . . makes manifest, more perhaps than any other single event of the Revolution, the underlying connections between pornography and politics" ("The Many Bodies of Marie Antoinette" 108). Paulson adds that the queen's erotic body functioned symbolically for a society out of control, a phenomenon manifested in Edmund Burke's *Reflections on the Revolution in France*, in which, according to Paulson, "the metaphorical stripping of society has become the literal stripping of the queen."[59] And in the final days before her execution, Marie Antoinette turned to writing—the text—as a locus for taking control of her increasingly unstable world. Following her trial for four counts of conspiracy and treason, "[t]he Queen heard the ruling against her without word or gesture. . . . . As soon as she arrived in her cell, the Queen asked for a pen, paper, and ink and sat down to write a long farewell letter to Madame Elisabeth."[60] Near the end of her life, Marie Antoinette regained at least one of the liberties earlier stripped from her—the ability to write, to communicate her thoughts, which on 29 September 1793 had been denied her, after Louis XV and his family had been taken prisoner, negotiations ceased, and "paper, pens and pencils were taken from them" (285). A site of real-life control, the text figures throughout Marie Antoinette's life as a register for the negotiation of power and reputation, and it is to the text that she turns in an attempt to make sense of her fate, just as it is to the text others turn to undermine her public position. And in the moments before her execution, Marie Antoinette's body continues to operate as a site of erotic interest overcoded with political control: Evelyne Lever recounts the Queen's final moments in her cell, when "she crouched . . . and took off her dress to change her undergarments for the last time. But the officer of the Gendarmerie came closer, stood by the bolster and watched [her] change. Her Majesty quickly put her fichu back on her shoulders and with great gentleness said to the young man: 'In the name of decency, monsieur, allow me to change my undergarments without witnesses.' 'I cannot give my consent,' the gendarme answered" (304), and so the queen stood, exposed to an embodiment of the law that oppressed her, her body now functioning as an erotic spectacle for his consumption, and soon to offer a spectacle of another kind for the masses assembled to observe her beheading—the spectacle of the new law written upon the embodiment of the old, the spectacle of the somatic inscription of Revolution on a former oppressor.

Hunt considers pornographic attacks on Marie Antoinette at length and concludes that "the queen represented not only the ultimate in counterrevolutionary conspiracy but also the menace that the feminine and the feminizing presented to republican notions of manhood and virility" ("The Bad Mother" 94). Because her political position as Queen allowed her to participate in the kind of public life traditionally restricted to men, Marie Antoinette became "emblematic of the much larger problem of the relation between women and the public sphere in the eighteenth century," a problem that "concerned not only the specific status of women but also the grounds of sexual differentiation itself" (90). In the midst of misogynistic panic, the presence of women threatened to feminize the entire public sphere so that, as "Rousseau warned ominously[,]. . . [women] in public might turn men into women" (90); and the effects of Marie Antoinette's private life did in fact spill over into public policy, in, for example, the firing of Louis XV's ministers, whom Marie Antoinette suspected of forming friendships with her husband's mistress, Madame du Barry, and in Marie Antoinette's decision to close to the public the Petit Trianon, a palace at Versailles, and to post the rules of the palace in her name rather than in her husband's.[61] Retrospectively, we may locate in the political presence of Marie Antoinette the literal and symbolic manifestations of cultural anxieties about gender roles and the emerging place of women in late eighteenth-century France. Telescoping cultural anxieties about her public presence to the site of her most private self, her erotic body—a misogynistic tactic as prevalent today as it was over two hundred years ago—revolutionary pornographers exposed not only the "problems" with the ancien régime, but also the Pandora's box that that régime threatened to loose upon the world, the disquieting phenomenon of one woman's invasion of a resolutely masculine public sphere.[62] Hunt writes that "according to pamphlets such as *Les Festes de Louis XV* (1782), the rising influence of women on public life feminized both the king's ministers and the king himself, who was depicted as withdrawing into a 'private, slothful and voluptuous life'" (90). In the panic over "the feared disintegration of gender boundaries that accompanied the Revolution[,] . . . the queen . . . was the emblem (and sacrificial victim)" of the gender wars of late eighteenth-century France (114). Fittingly, then, Marie Antoinette was often portrayed and attacked "as a whore, that is, as a public woman whose sexuality destroyed any possibility of tracing paternity," the line of ancestry central to the maintenance of monarchial order vis-à-vis the legitimization of a king's divine right to rule his country (115). With the execution of Marie Antoinette—the culmination of a trial that focused obsessively on, that fetishized, her sexual proclivities, finally even to accuse her of engaging in an incestuous affair with her son—"republican men were not simply concerned [with punishing] a leading counterrevolutionary. They wanted to separate mothers from any public activity" (121) in order to keep so-called whores such as the Queen out of the crucial processes of policy-making and nation-rebuilding.

Such an anxious response to the Revolution as the feminization of France, as that country's "fall" into pleasure, lawlessness, and social disorder, finds material form in a contemporary engraving by the pro-revolutionary artist A. Clément entitled "La France Républicaine. Ouvrant son Sein à tous les Français" ["Republican France. Offering Her Breasts to all the French"]. Clément's engraving depicts a female figure sporting a cap topped with a rooster and, across her exposed breasts, a medallion made from a carpenter's level. Simon Schama comments on the symbols that appear in this engraving and notes that "the exhibition is an emblem of egalitarian inclusiveness. The equality of 'all Frenchmen' regenerated by the nurturing breasts of the Republic is symbolized by the strategically hung carpenter's level, while the dawn of freedom is represented by another traditional Gallic emblem, the rooster" (768). At once the emblem of salvation and productivity—half-Christ, the halo and bared chest reminding us of so many iconographic representations of the "Sacred Heart," and half-mother, the exposed breasts promising the flow of endless nourishment for the revolutionaries who take shelter at her bosom—Clément's figure is overcoded with the image of the whore, the woman-in-public whose body takes political form in its self-commodification, its easy availability to any and all of the revolutionaries who would "take" it. We see in this particular icon the same images that appeared in the pornographic representations of Marie Antoinette which were deployed as attacks upon the French monarchy: the sexualized female body, firmly situated in the public sphere, hypostasizes the contentious sites of politics and sexuality, so that that body functions as a coded image for all revolutionary activity. At the same time, Clément's engraving anticipates the image Shelley unveils throughout his erotic narratives—the revolutionary icon as the conflation of God and mother, of masculine and feminine, of public and private, of politics and the erotic.

The image of the bare-breasted woman occupies a central position in my argument about the "place" of political engagement within erotic narratives, for where the erotic narrative conflates private engagements and public concerns, the image of the bare-breasted woman similarly conflates public and private iconography: as a mother, the bare-breasted woman symbolizes home, family, and lineage; as a whore, she represents a variety of transgressions that complicate the "place" of pleasure by lifting the private transaction of its purchase to a public matter, both in the location of the whore (that is, on the street) and in the codification of proscriptions against such activity in the language of the law. Both mother and whore, both private woman and public, both nurturer and criminal, the bare-breasted woman defies the public/private split by advertising the pleasures she promises, themselves at once erotic and political. In baring her breasts, the mother-whore confronts the powers-that-be and promises her followers not only freedom, but pleasure and love, as well.

Linda Dowling considers the image of the bare-breasted woman and its place in nineteenth-century narratives about the French Revolution, and she argues that "whenever they appear in the nineteenth century, such images will retain their power of evoking the possibility of [what Catherine Gallagher has called] 'completely chaotic reproduction'—of bodies, of goods, of money, of value."[63] In Dowling's reading, "the image of the half-clothed female would eventually come to symbolize . . . an emergent realm of irrational and unknowable forces" (21). Dowling locates the origin of the English iconography of the bare-breasted woman in what she describes as "the notorious representation of the goddess of Liberty during the Feast of Reason on 10 November 1793" (20). In this dramatization of the French Revolution, the actress Mademoiselle Aubrey "bared her breasts before the onlooking crowd, [encouraging] English writers [to perceive] symbolic sanction for the revolutionary decrees permitting sexual promiscuity and equalizing bastard children which would follow a few months later" (20). According to Dowling, such a costume of déshabillé "taken up by Mlle Aubrey and so many others as *la mode révolutionnaire* signaled, in the view of such commentators as John Robinson, nothing less than the Jacobins' determination to inflame sexual desire and incite profligacy in order to propagate more citizens for the Revolution" (20).

In her account of Victorian responses to the French Revolution, Linda M. Shires argues that by the middle of the nineteenth century a variety of threats to hegemonic values inspired the resurrection of French Revolution-era iconography derivative of that which we have seen in Clément's image of "Republican France"—the mænad or "female fury," the mother and "its other half . . . including feminized males."[64] Shires links such representations of mother-as-maenad to the shifts in power between the genders throughout the age, unmasking this "image of woman as Unnatural" as a direct "transplantation from France to England" of the image of revolution; in fact, according to Shires, the image of the "maenadic fury" was employed in England to describe not only female French revolutionaries, but their male counterparts as well (148). Returning to early Romantic-era anxieties about revolution and the shifting place of gender in English society, Shires traces the links between men and femininity in anti-revolutionary discourse and points to Burke's *Reflections on the Revolution in France* (1790), a text Shelley knew well, to demonstrate how Burke "follows French anti-Jacobins in his association of women with the revolutionary mob, with incoherence or madness, and with explosions of nature, calling insurrectionists 'the furies of hell in the abused shape of the vilest of women'" (151). For Shires, Burke's harangue against "the effeminacy of the Jacobins is particularly important. The point is not merely that women in the Revolution were likened to the fierce furies. Rather, the men were 'reduced' to the state of female furies. Burke condemns all revolutionaries, mixing the sexes together, in his terms of utter condemnation and anxiety. He links them to chaos, to the breeding of utter foulness, to excrement, and to mothers and daughters . . ." (151).[65]

Such a feminization of all parties engaged in anti-hegemonic politics forms the core language of the attacks by "Z" (later revealed to be John Gibson Lockhart and John Wilson) against Leigh Hunt, John Keats, and other members of the so-called "Cockney School" of poetry, which were published in *Blackwood's Edinburgh Magazine* in 1817 and 1818.[66] Like Burke's repudiation of revolutionaries, and like the later Victorian characterization of all revolutionaries as mænads, these attacks cast the members of Hunt's intellectual milieu—which clearly included Shelley, although the poet remained unnamed in the *Blackwood's* attacks—as political transgressors, and the attacks expose the Cockney School members' various embodiments of femininity vis-à-vis their positions in the highly contested arenas of class, education, and morality. Ultimately, the *Blackwood's* attacks attempt to dismantle the public presence of members of the Cockney School by sabotaging them on personal grounds, by dismissing them from the stage of public affairs to confine or contain them in what the attacks carefully construct as the harmless realm of the private; interestingly, this approach anticipates the model of Shelleyan seduction, for it exposes private engagements in the interest of public life in order to dismiss the Cockneys from the public space of fame, reputation, and influence, back into the private space of the coterie or "school." In so doing, the *Blackwood's* attacks wage a very public—and publicized—war against the Cockneys by eroding the writers' reputations on personal grounds in order to expel them from the space of influence—the public stage of reputation and prestige.

Dowling considers the etymology of "Cockney" and argues that it "[derives] from Middle English *cocken-ei* or 'cock's egg,' the ostensible impossible female product of a male fowl" (16). In this reading, "Cockney" "registers at an archaic level of etymological association precisely the sense of brutish and unnatural powers, of uncontrollable appetites—and the monstrous outcomes released by those appetites—which *Blackwood's* invokes by calling Leigh Hunt, for instance, "'the most contemptible little capon of the bantam breed, that ever vainly dropped a wing, or sidled up to a partlet'" (16; *Blackwood's* qtd. in Dowling). Ultimately, Dowling argues that "the significance of the term 'Cockney' is not that it identifies some inferior social class but that it is an attempt to name something perceived to exist unnervingly outside all known categories of order, rank, or status, something the dark threat of which arises out of its very unfathomability" (20). The *OED* proves particularly instructive in making sense of *Blackwood's* attacks on Hunt's "Cockney" school. An obsolete use of "cockney," last seen in print in 1611, described "a squeamish, over-nice, wanton, or affected woman." A century and a half later, the term's gender connotations had switched, so that as late as 1783 "cockney" had come to name "a mother's darling," "a squeamish or effeminate fellow," or "a milksop," and by 1826, the term was employed as "a derisive appellation for a townsman . . . [with regard to his] effeminacy." Significantly, the *OED* offers "a parallel [for 'cockney'] in the French word *coco*, a child's word for an egg, also a term of endearment applied to children and of derision applied to men." We thus may trace in its etymological evolution throughout the eighteenth and nineteenth centuries how the term "cockney" functioned to describe a male whose behavior challenged traditional gender roles, a man who, one might say, "acts like a woman," his attitude and behavior forcing a rupture—opening a gap—in the strict social distinctions his society tried (and failed) to force upon him.

Blackwood's unrelenting feminizing of the Romantics—"The Cockneys" in particular—has much to do, I believe, with the social coding of passion as feminine. Jeffrey C. Robinson notes that "passion and its representation . . . has historically caused in society at large denial and displacement and rationalizations . . . because of its inherent excessiveness, its threat to established boundaries, and probably because the boundarilessness inevitably means the passions of *women*"; "the poetics and thematics of passion contains a strong feminist element, in that passion, always excessive, implies the other, the presence of passion in the other who is often in Romanticism figured as the woman."[67] Whether the "passion" of the Cockneys is specifically sexually expressed, their status as culture's other—given their class standing and their aesthetic and ideological programs—situates them as sites of excess, as embodiments of the feminine in a culture resolved to quash such threats to established (read, traditional, masculine) order.[68]

A close look at two representative reviews, the initial "Cockney School" attack on Hunt in October of 1817 and the attack on Keats in August of 1818, will demonstrate how Z's coding of all anti-hegemonic figures as feminine returns to the particular milieu to which Shelley and Byron are constantly connected, albeit tangentially. Although the attacks never target Shelley and Byron directly, the reputations of both writers remain at stake throughout the attacks, if for no reason other than each writer's numerous intertextual connections to works by members of the Cockney School, each writer's quite literal (guilt by) associations.[69]

The initial Cockney School attack, written by John Gibson Lockhart, appeared in *Blackwood's* in October of 1817 and began by positioning Leigh Hunt, the principle object of the article's fury, in opposition to "what is commonly called THE LAKE SCHOOL" of Wordsworth and Coleridge (*The Romantics Reviewed* 49). Lockhart names Hunt as the "chief Doctor and Professor" of the Cockney School and describes him as a man "of extravagant pretensions both in wit, poetry, and politics, and withal of exquisitely bad taste, and extremely vulgar ... in all respects" (49). This passage sets the tone for the feminization of the writers Z would go on to attack under the general heading of the Cockney School, for it draws on a vocabulary of affectation and naïveté that casts the members of Hunt's "school" as others, that is, as figures who stand in opposition to traditional values—as feminine (and, thus, revolutionary) influences poised to dismantle traditional (and, thus, masculine) order.[70] The phrase "extravagant pretensions" conjures Hunt as one who desires nothing more or less than to wallow in luxury, a charge similar to many leveled at Louis XV in the pornographic pamphlets exposing the putatively dangerous influence of Marie Antoinette. Lockhart's use of the word "vulgar," a term that recurs throughout the attack on Hunt, contributes significantly to the positioning of Hunt as an embodiment of otherness. According to the *OED*, a panoply of meanings for the term "vulgar" held currency in 1817: a person not reckoned as belonging to good society; of language or speech, ordinary, vernacular; having a common and offensively mean character, lacking in refinement or good taste, uncultured and ill-bred; and, perhaps most significantly, "of errors, prejudices, etc." To attack Hunt as "vulgar" is to indict him on charges of reputation, education, personal appearance, class, philosophy, and politics; to suggest his extraordinary deficiencies in each of these arenas is to reduce him to the collective category of lack, to "the feminine."[71]

Finally, the apostrophizing of Hunt as one who displays "extravagant pretensions both in wit, poetry, and politics" reminds us that Lockhart recognizes the intrinsic connections among those engagements, so that just as one's wit finds form in one's poetry, poetry exposes one's politics, and so on. Lockhart's feminization of Hunt continues as he describes his feelings of "disgust" upon reading *The Story of Rimini*: "One feels the same disgust at the idea of opening Rimini, that impresses itself on the mind of a man of fashion, when he is invited to enter, for a second time, the gilded drawing-room of a little mincing boarding-school mistress. . . . Every thing is pretense, affectation, finery, and gaudiness" (50). In the very next paragraph, Lockhart offers "the great poets of our country" as antitypes to Hunt and emphasizes their relative masculinity, that is, their veneration of traditional, civilized values and ideals: "All of the great poets of our country have been men of some rank in society, and there is no vulgarity in any of their writings; but Mr. Hunt cannot utter a dedication, or even a note, without betraying the *Shibboleth* of low birth and low habits. He is the ideal of a Cockney Poet" (50). In Lockhart's view, Hunt's social status, manifested at the level of language, betrays the vulgar origins above which he has never risen—perhaps even has refused to rise—and functions as one more lens by means of which he may be exposed as an embodiment of otherness.

Next, Lockhart turns to a religious vocabulary in yet another attempt to set Hunt against "dignified poetry": "[Hunt] labors under the burden of a sin more deadly than either of these [*viz.*, vulgarity and the foundation of the Cockney School]. The two great elements of all dignified poetry, religious feeling, and patriotic feeling, have no place in his writings. His religion is . . . [blasphemy] . . . his patriotism a crude, vague, ineffectual, and sour Jacobinism" (50). And finally, as if what Lockhart regards as Hunt's failures in religious and patriotic duty were not enough to damn him, Z returns to sexual imagery in his attack on Hunt, warning readers of *Blackwood's* that "the extreme of moral depravity of the Cockney School is another thing which is for ever thrusting itself upon the public attention," so that Hunt's poetry "resembles that of a man who has kept company with kept-mistresses. His muse talks indelicately like a tea-sipping milliner girl" (51). Nicholas Roe indicates that "tea-sipping" functioned as early nineteenth-century code for sedition;[72] coupled with the cross-gendered identification of Hunt, by way of the mediating figure of his muse, as a "milliner girl," we see how Z's feminization of Hunt is motivated in direct response to Hunt's anti-hegemonic political engagements, to his textual inscriptions of sedition.

As his "review" of *The Story of Rimini* closes,[73] Lockhart explodes in rage over Hunt's decision to dedicate that work to Lord Byron, but rather than implicating Byron as Hunt's fellow vulgarian, Lockhart instead props Byron up as Hunt's opposite in terms of class, concluding that the "insult which [Hunt] offered to Lord Byron in the dedication of Rimini" arises from the class-pretensions of the "Doctor and professor" of Cockneyism in assuming that a titled gentry would be flattered by such an invocation "in which [Hunt], a paltry cockney newspaper scribbler, had the assurance to address one of the most nobly-born of English Patricians, and one of the first geniuses whom the world has ever produced, as 'My dear Byron,' . . . [a gesture which has] excited a feeling of utter loathing and disgust in the public mind, which will always be remembered whenever the name of Leigh Hunt is mentioned" (52). Although Lockhart wants to distinguish Byron from Hunt both in terms of class and literary importance, the name "Byron" becomes a kind of simulacrum that weaves in and out of the *Blackwood's* attacks, ultimately to such an extent that in his association with the Cockney School in this context—not to mention by way of Hunt's well-known dedication to him in *The Story of Rimini*—Byron's name constantly overlaps with "the Cockney School of poetry" in the public imagination, if for no other reason than that Byron is always held up in a complicated relationship to the many embodiments of otherness that find form in Hunt. Byron, however tangentially, remains a crucial figure throughout the *Blackwood's* attacks on Hunt and his circle, and Lockhart's repeated invocation of Byron's name in those reviews (as an anti-type to the Cockneys) as well as the nods to Byron in the works of Hunt and, more broadly, of other "Cockneys," subsumes Byron within the Cockney context, making him, however problematically, inseparable from Hunt et al., a contested figure whose appropriation by both the Cockneys and their detractors finally settles Byron as one among the Cockneys themselves, regardless of Lockhart's efforts to extricate him from what, to Lockhart, seemed a pernicious group of scribblers. Lockhart's attempts to sever the Cockneys' ties to Byron finally fails, given the Cockneys' well-publicized links to the age's most famous writer, and given Byron's connections, primarily through Shelley, to Hunt and other members of his circle.

As is the case in his attack on Hunt, Lockhart's attack on Keats masquerades as a review of Keats' poetry—specifically, of *Endymion*. But as in the attack on Hunt, Lockhart's review really functions as an occasion for Z to berate Keats' vulgarity and to remind the public about his "membership" in the by-now notorious Cockney School. To this end, Lockhart mentions near the beginning of the review that "[o]ne of [Keats'] first productions was the . . . sonnet, '*written on the day when Mr. Leigh Hunt left prison.*' It will be recollected, that the cause of Hunt's confinement was a series of libels against his sovereign, and that its fruit was the odious and incestuous 'Story of Rimini'" (90). Lockhart's alignment of Keats with

Hunt provides the reviewer an occasion once again to recount what he regards as Hunt's unforgivable sins—his lack of patriotism and of religion, both of which Lockhart more broadly invokes in terms of the immorality that finds voice in Hunt's "odious and incestuous" *Story of Rimini*. By association, then, Keats' work is similarly attacked as immoral, unpatriotic and blasphemous.

The opening of Lockhart's attack on Keats makes even more sense when it is juxtaposed with two phrases that occur throughout his attack on Hunt. In that review, Lockhart describes Hunt's poetry as "the *unhealthy* and *jaundiced* medium through which the Founder of the Cockney School views every thing," and he characterizes the average reader's response to Hunt's work as "the most *sickening* aversion" (51, 52, emphasis added). By casting Hunt's otherness in terms of illness and disease—and, in particular, in terms of jaundice, an irregularity in skin color that renders illness somatically inscribed[74]—Lockhart attempts to pathologize the writer's vulgarity, to locate Hunt's lack of morals within the material condition of his physical body as separate from, albeit reflective of, his textual corpus. The turn to the body of the other and the exploitative representation of that body as somehow out of control, here because of its diseased condition, functions as nothing more than another version of "La France Républicaine," another image of a bare-breasted mother-whore from whose body the excesses of the revolution are born and at whose breasts so many incestuous, blasphemous infidels are guaranteed both maternal nourishment and erotic gratification.

Lockhart's attack on Keats gives vent to his drive to pathologize the Cockney rhymester in the same manner in which his review of *The Story of Rimini* undoes Hunt. Arguing that Keats' poetry exhibits the symptoms of one of the "manias of this mad age, . . . Metromanie,"[75] Lockhart laments the corruption of Keats' natural talent and comments that "to witness the disease of any human understanding, however feeble, is distressing; but the spectacle of an able mind reduced to a state of insanity is of course ten times more afflicting. It is with such sorrow as this that we have contemplated the case of Mr. John Keats," whose poetic potential "has been undone by a sudden attack of the malady to which we have alluded" (90). Whereas in the attack on Hunt, that writer remained the infector, the agent of transmission for the diseases collectively coded under the general term "vulgarity," here Keats is posed as something of an innocent bystander, as someone who has been "attacked"—acted on and overtaken. Of course, Lockhart's insinuation is clear: the agent of infection is Hunt, and Hunt's influence has resulted in the intellectual decay of one of the age's most promising young writers. In Keats, Lockhart occasions a case study of the dangers of the Cockney School, an exposé about the power of that movement to violate the physical and textual bodies of other writers and thus to ruin them by infecting them with a catalogue of disorders, among them metromania (or, following Roe, "tea-drinking," sedition). This strategic description of Hunt as infector and Keats as infected feminizes Keats and thus codes him as an other, a weak vessel whose frail sensibilities are specifically subject to the most vulgar of influences, a feminized body impregnated by the seed of an even more virile agent of insurrection, Hunt. In contemporary slang, we might say that Keats has been fucked—or, at the very least, "fucked up"—by Hunt, who, symbolically, has taken Keats' weaker body in a kind of rape, depositing his own seditious seed into the body of Keats, which re-produces Hunt's vulgarities in the corpus—the textual bodies—of Keats' "infected" poetry.

In addition to casting his feminization of Keats in the language of disease, Lockhart repeatedly refers to Keats in the language of diminution, reducing the poet to the status of a child, a feminized other who is not-a-man, in passages such as this one: "Mr. Hunt is a small poet, but he is a clever man. Mr. Keats is a still smaller poet, and he is only a boy of pretty abilities, which he has done every thing in his power to destroy" (93). Here, Keats is depicted as a reduced version of Hunt, less powerful for his more limited ability to infect others; in addition, Lockhart's description of Keats' abilities as "pretty" reminds us of the reduction-by-feminization that we saw throughout the attack on Hunt, where Hunt was described, for example, as a "mincing boarding-school mistress" (50). Elsewhere in the attack on Keats, the poet is again diminished as "good Johnny Keats" (91), and Lockhart follows this feminization-by-diminution with an indictment of Keats for wallowing in transgressive pleasures: " . . . it appears, notwithstanding all this gossamer-work, that Johnny's affections are not entirely confined to objects purely ethereal. Take, by way of specimen, the following prurient and vulgar lines, evidently meant for some young lady east of Temple-bar" (92). In this passage, Keats is triply feminized, first in the diminutive form of his name, second in his "prurient and vulgar" subject matter, and third in his imagined audience appeal: Keats, according to Lockhart, writes not only to women but, even more significantly, to women of questionable reputation. Even Lockhart's actual attention to the metrics of Keats' poetry—a turn from the physical to the textual body of Keats—casts matters of style in a vocabulary that connotes literary and erotic transgression: "Mr Keats has adopted the loose, nerveless versification, and Cockney rhymes of the poet of Rimini; but in fairness to that gentleman, we must add, that the defects of the system are tenfold more conspicuous in his disciple's work than in his own" (93). Here, Hunt's name disappears from the text entirely as the mere title of one of his works stands in for him, reminding us that Hunt's notorious textual body functions synecdochally for his personal identity. Further, the casting of Keats as Hunt's "disciple" reminds us of the revolutionary-as-Christ subtext lurking in Clément's "La France Républicaine," so that the problems hypostasized in Clément's nude female body as those inherent to a revolutionary agenda, specifically, licentiousness and excess, are metaphorized here in the subversive and therefore feminine textual bodies to which the members of Hunt's Cockney School have given birth, each work fathered by Hunt's poisonous "seed."

The various binaries that pervade the *Blackwood's* attacks—the same binaries that structure the reactionary discourses of Revolutionary France—coalesce in the pair masculine/feminine, where the former term represents traditional values, and the latter stands for the "other" of revolutionary excess. This equation emerges most clearly in a long passage from Lockhart's attack on Keats: Lockhart bemoans the poetry of the present day, in which good Englishmen like himself are

> . . . reviled by uneducated and flimsy striplings, who are not capable of understanding either their merits, or those of any other men of power—fanciful dreaming tea-drinkers, who, without logic enough to analyse a single idea, or imagination enough to form one original image, or learning enough to distinguish between the written language of Englishmen and the spoken jargon of Cockneys, presume to talk with contempt of some of the most exquisite spirits the world ever produced, merely because they did not happen to exert their faculties in laborious affected descriptions of flowers seen in window-pots, or cascades heard at Vauxhall; in short, because they chose to be wits, philosophers, patriots, and poets, rather than to found the Cockney school of versification, morality, and politics, a century before its time. After blaspheming himself into a fury against Boileau &c. Mr. Keats comforts himself and his readers with a view of the present more promising aspect of affairs; above all, with the ripened glories of the poet of Rimini. (92)

In this passage, the chief concerns that cycle throughout Z's attacks on the Cockney School come to the fore: education, class, subject matter, audience, and a marked disinclination to traditional poetry, philosophy, and politics. Here, we see the emergence of a number of binary pairs in which the first term characterizes the values Z holds dear, and the second describes what the reviewer regards as the sins of Hunt's Cockney School: Englishness/Cockneyism, truth/blasphemy, politics/pleasure, and tradition/innovation. As I have suggested throughout my consideration of the Cockney School attacks, the overarching binary constellation that incorporates all of these anxieties is masculine/feminine, where the former term connotes tradition, privilege, and status-quo values, and the latter, voluptuousness, excess, and revolution. As Lockhart's attack on Keats nears its close, the reviewer adds sarcastically, as if it need be said, that "[w]e had almost forgot to mention, that Keats belongs to the Cockney School of Politics, as well as the Cockney School of Poetry." Clearly, the *Blackwood's* reader is reminded that Keats' poetry embeds an antihegemonic political agenda, and, no less importantly, that in such a subversive context, writing and ideology remain inseparable. And just as

Keats' poetry poses a political threat, by extension, so too must the productions of all other members of the poet's intellectual milieu.

Although Shelley is never specifically named in Z's attacks, his intertextual presence throughout the works of Hunt and Keats situates Shelley as a satellite in the ideological universe surrounding the so-called Cockney School. Distanced from the Cockneys by class, both Shelley and his good friend Byron inhabit the particularly subversive category of the revolutionary aristocrat, that privileged member of society whose political sympathies run counter to the institutions that have empowered him. Like Sade, Shelley and Byron occupy an ideological space that assumes a particular immediacy given their social status: as aristocrats, these men occupy a place of high regard in their country, so that their utterances are likely to bear more weight—at least initially—than those of their "vulgar" compatriots.

The vituperance of Z's attacks on Hunt, Keats, and other members of the Cockney School is matched by Robert Southey's excoriation of Shelley and Byron in the Preface to his 1821 poem, *The Vision of Judgment*. Dripping with venom, Southey's pedantic opening indicts Shelley and Byron as members of what he calls "the Satanic School" and urges readers and writers alike to turn away from the evil influence of such poets and, instead, "to emphasize decency and order."[76] Obviously, the binary Southey erects—Christian/Satanic—aligns Shelley and Byron with the Cockney School by classifying them among the figures whose willing leaps into immorality threaten to mobilize social disorder. The first two cantos of *Don Juan,* for example, received a hostile review from Southey in *Blackwood's*, where the poet laureate referred to the "League of Incest" rumors circling around the Byron-Shelley milieu. More directly, the congruence of the Satanic and Cockney Schools emerges in the *Blackwood's* review of Byron's *Cain*, which laments the influence of Shelley on Byron as well as the inevitability of Shelley's influence of Hunt (232). That Shelley is an atheist and Byron—especially in the guise of the Byronic hero—a sexually transgressive figure reminds us of the ways in which these two writers "fit" the subversive tendencies Lockhart articulates throughout his attacks on Keats and Hunt. Thus, I find it particularly important to understand the place assigned to the Cockney School in the *Blackwood's* reviews because those attacks more broadly outline an ideological space congruent to the one Shelley and Byron are imagined to occupy in the literary and political climate of their day.[77] Like the "Cockney School" of Hunt and Keats, the "Satanic School" of Shelley and Byron must be understood to operate in terms of textual strategies that infuse erotic narratives with revolutionary political agendas, and thus that pose a real threat to "good" readers, a real germ of ideological infection, of textual taint.

∞ ∞ ∞ ∞ ∞

Throughout this book, I investigate the processes of textual seduction as Shelley deploys them through a series of decidedly erotic narratives dedicated to the mapping of a liberated world, to the plotting of utopia. In this way, I expose the mechanisms by which the erotic emerges as a trope for political engagement, all within Shelley's repeated attempts to locate, describe, and bring forth—to plot, in both narrative and cartographic senses—utopia. Where traditional models for reading nineteenth-century British literature have located revolution in the space of an imaginative apocalypse or an artist's thoroughgoing communion with the natural world, my work unveils political engagements within the seemingly apolitical reaches of Shelley's erotic narratives. Ultimately, I argue that the Shelleyan model contributes to the development of a counter-tradition in British literature that situates the erotic as a trope for political discourse, seducing readers with a wide variety of sexual milieux in which pleasure and love are posed as symbols for liberation from oppressive regimes and selfishly invested individuals. Throughout, I demonstrate how the processes of textual seduction model political strategies for displacing larger, oppressive social structures: time and again, Shelley and his inheritors stage the erotic as a device for renegotiating power and privilege, so that every context in which the erotic figures must be understood as a resolutely political one.

Thus far, I have located my argument within the historical context of political pornography and the French Revolution, a signal event William Doyle flags as among "the greatest revolution[s] in the history of the world . . . the first modern revolution, the archetypal one,"[78] and thus a key episode in the long history of social and political upheaval, no less important to Shelley's generation than to Marie Antoinette's. I have considered the influence of post-Revolutionary discourse and iconography on the circles of radical thinkers whose work influenced Shelley, and I have discussed the various mechanisms through which the Shelleyan milieu emerged as a locus of anti-traditional values. Just as my readings of Shelley's erotic narratives locate public interaction (that is, political engagement) amidst representations of private acts, so, too, do the connotations that swirl around Shelley's reputation as a moral and sexual deviant imbricate public sympathies and private indulgences, or politics and pleasure.

Having situated Shelley's work within the context of post-Revolutionary discourse and iconography, I divide my discussion into two sections, "Part One: The Problem," and "Part Two: The Solution." In Part One, I consider three works in which Shelley examines erotic relationships that exemplify inequities in power, where one partner is privileged—and pleasured—at the psychic and, sometimes, the physical expense of others. In Chapter II, I turn to one of Shelley's most-overlooked works, a satire entitled *Œdipus Tyrannus; or, Swellfoot the Tyrant*, to demonstrate how that play injects political commentary into descriptions of erotic acts by lampooning the notorious Queen Caroline Affair. Frequently overlooked in Shelley scholarship, *Swellfoot the Tyrant* provides the groundwork for my argument about the political significance with which Shelley codes erotic scenes, and it offers a firm foundation for the real-world "place" of such engagements by participating in the ongoing public dialogue about one of the most well-publicized scandals of the day.

In Chapter III, I focus on *The Cenci* and *Julian and Maddalo* to consider how Shelley poses erotic relationships as paradigms for alternative social models that dismantle oppressive social structures. I argue that Shelley empowers marginalized figures—specifically, Beatrice and the Maniac—to assert their individual subjectivities by revisiting their erotic histories and altering relationships of power through acts of subversive repetition that mirror the objectifying maneuvers through which they have been disempowered. My interest in negotiations of subjectivity vis-à-vis acts of subversive repetition anticipates the Lacanian psychoanalytic model I develop throughout the second half of my study, and my investigations of the physical and psychological landscapes that mark the worlds of *The Cenci* and *Julian and Maddalo* introduces the concept of "erotic cartography," which I explore in great depth from Chapter III forward.

While I devote Part One to an interrogation of Shelley's investigation of the erotic and its potential to oppress, in "Part Two: The Solution," I consider the place of love in Shelley's model by turning to some of his best-known works to examine how three erotic relationships emerge as paradigms for a new social order. I argue that in these poems Shelley maps out the erotic cartography of a liberated world, a figurative map that draws on the psychology of love and lovers to chart personal relationships and political orders according to the contours of individual love-unions, which the poet sharply contrasts to the inflexibility of oppressive relationships and social structures[79]: as Mark Kipperman has noted, "Shelley's utopianism strives to awaken us unto a world transformed by a dream of love, not a fantasy of power."[80] Throughout the second part of my study, I demonstrate how Shelley eschews the unbending order of tyrannical regimes to peer beyond what I call the "vanishing points" of patriarchy and to imagine a space over the horizon where rigidity dissolves into permeability as oppression succumbs to ecstatic union.

In Chapter IV, I investigate Shelley's development of the liberating potential of what I describe as the "oozy" landscape of *Epipsychidion*, where the poet envisions an erotic union with his idealized lover on a ruined island. Many scholars have read *Epipsychidion* as symbolic of Shelley's ultimate pessimism, but I turn to Lacan's Object/*objet a* model to recuperate the poem's apparent failures as unmitigated victories for Shelley's program of free love. In Chapter V, I consider the incestuous relationship between the eponymous lovers of *Laon and Cythna; Or, The*

Revolution of the Golden City: A Vision of the Nineteenth Century to explain how Shelley's model of the liberation of the world proceeds from his conception of the moist, ambiguous, and pleasurable—indeed, the "oozy"—parameters of the siblings' erotic relationship. Finally, I turn to *Prometheus Unbound* to demonstrate how the selfless erotic engagements of Prometheus and Asia transform political realities, and I discuss the ways in which the physical and psychological landscape that demarcates the lovers' ultimate retreat contributes to Shelley's erotic cartography.

I conclude my study with a review of the model of textual seduction as it is worked out in Shelley, and with a demonstration of how my findings might prove useful in discussions about texts by other writers throughout the century: from the Romantic period, I survey works by Mary Wollstonecraft, William Blake, William Wordsworth, Samuel Taylor Coleridge, John Keats, and Mary Shelley; from the Victorian period, works by Christina Rossetti, Dante Gabriel Rossetti, and Algernon Charles Swinburne; and from the Aesthetic period, works by Oscar Wilde, John Gray, and Aubrey Beardsley, as well as public responses to the so-called Decadent movement in art and literature. In the end, *Shelley's Textual Seductions* explores how and why the Shelleyan counter-tradition of textual seduction may be characterized as politically engaged: while particular texts must be contextualized in terms of their individual historical moments, the works of Shelley and his inheritors participate in the evolution of revolutionary textual strategies wherein the transformation of the world is postulated according to various imbrications of recognizably "public" and "private" concerns by way of the seductive cachet that lies embedded in textual representations of transgressive, erotic engagements, themselves the maps-in-miniature for the liberation of the world through love, plots for—and plottings of—utopia.

Notes

1. Reports of Sade's broadcasts from his prison-cell window are actually based in fact, although the particular story of his activities on 14 July 1789 are pure fiction. Both Simon Schama and Eric Ritter von Kuehnelt-Leddihn discuss Sade's strategy of communication with the world outside his cell by means of a funnel he had been provided for the transmission of bodily waste outside of the Bastille (much could, of course, be made of the figuratively "dirty" messages Sade delivered through that excremental device); see Simon Schama, *Citizens: A Chronicle of the French Revolution* (New York: Alfred A. Knopf, 1989), 392, 399, and Eric von Kuehnelt-Leddihn, "The Age of the Guillotine (Sade, Robespierre, and the Consequences)," in *Reflections on the French Revolution: A Hillsdale Symposium*, ed. Stephen J.

Tonsor (Washington, D.C.: Rignery Gateway, 1990), 73. In his biography of Sade, Maurice Lever confronts what he calls "the grand illusion" about Sade's politics, not only the myths that cast Sade as the literal instigator of the French Revolution, but also the historical misappropriations of Sade that misunderstand the writer as a proto-Surrealist or a proto-Nazi; see Maurice Lever, *Sade: A Biography*, trans. Arthur Goldhammer (San Diego: Harvest), 397-401. In a fascinating examination of Sade's correspondence, Lever proves that far from rejoicing over the triumph of the *sans-culottes*, Sade remained ambivalent about the Revolution, for he understood that while the overturn of the government might guarantee him more personal and artistic freedom, it nonetheless threatened his beloved privileges of class. Lever provides evidence for what he calls Sade's own "class prejudice [that] knew no bounds" (403) and marshals the writer's private letters to prove once and for all that Sade's political sympathies remained at odds with the post-Revolutionary mythology that took hold after his death: for example, in a letter dated 5 December 1791, Sade wrote, "'I am anti-Jacobite, I hate them to death. . . . . I want the luster of the nobility restored, because taking it away solved nothing. I want the king to be the nation's leader. I do not want a National Assembly, but two chambers as in England, which would give the king a tempered authority, balanced by the concord of a nation necessarily divided into two orders; the third [the clergy] is useless, I want no part of it'" (qtd. in Lever 416-417). We see in Sade's own hand, then, the figurative migration of a very different revolution from France to England, a re-placement of the hope for the betterment of his country within the political model of the very nation from which we shall find Shelley and his inheritors imagining a world liberated through a politicized discourse of the erotic.

2. Daniel P. Watkins, *Sexual Power in British Romantic Poetry* (Gainesville: University Press of Florida, 1996), xvi.

3. Francine Du Plessix Gray, *At Home with the Marquis de Sade: A Life* (New York: Simon and Schuster, 1998), 415.

4. See Lever for a full account of the textual history of *Cent Vingt Journées de Sodome*. Of particular interest to me is the fact that in order to make his manuscript easier to hide from the prying eyes of the law, Sade completed the fair copy in what Lever calls "almost microscopic handwriting" on a series of four-inch sheets that were glued together to form a forty-foot long scroll covered with writing on both sides (348-349). In fact, Sade completed this task while imprisoned in the Bastille, and he hid the document in a crevice in the wall of his cell. In the storming of the Bastille, many of Sade's possessions, including his 600-volume library and the text of *Cent Vingt Journées de Sodome*, were destroyed or taken away (352). Sade never recovered this manuscript, and the book did not appear in print until 1904 when it was published by a German psychiatrist, Dr. Iwan Bloch, who procured it from a German collector who had purchased it around 1900 from the Villaneuve-Trans family of France in whose possession the manuscript had remained since being lifted from the Bastille; see Austryn Wainhouse and Richard Seaver, eds., *The 120 Days of Sodom and Other Writings*, by Donatien Alphonse, the Marquis de Sade (New York: Grove Weidenfeld, 1966), 186. Sade continues to figure iconically as an emblem of revolution, sometimes in a political, sometimes in an ideological

context. Man Ray's 1938 portrait of Sade (see Du Plessix Gray, Pl. 18) depicts the beleaguered writer in front of the Bastille, Sade's head emerging from a crack in an egg-like stone structure, the whole of his face scored with lines suggestive of the Bastille's brick exterior. Man Ray thus acknowledges Sade's corporeal link to the institutions of oppressive power—manifested in the physical structure of the Bastille—and exposes that power as written on Sade's body, as somatically inscribed; Lucienne Frappier-Mazur comments on such a function of Sade's body, as well, noting its operation as a register of social and political anxiety; see Mazur, *Writing the Orgy: Power and Parody in Sade*, trans. Gillian C. Gill (Philadelphia: University of Pennsylvania Press, 1996), 6.

5. Ronald Paulson, *Representations of Revolution (1789-1820)* (New Haven: Yale University Press, 1983), 41.

6. Bruce R. Smith, "Premodern Sexualities," *PMLA* 115.3 (May 2000): 323.

7. Robert Darnton, *The Forbidden Best-Sellers of Pre-Revolutionary France* (New York: W. W. Norton and Company, 1995), 100.

8. Jean Grimshaw, "Ethics, Fantasy and Self-Transformation," in *The Philosophy of Sex: Contemporary Readings*, ed. Alan Soble (Lanham: Rowman and Littlefield Publishers, 1997), 182.

9. Penley is quoted in an article by M. G. Lord, "Pornutopia: How Feminist Scholars Learned to Love Dirty Pictures," *Linguafranca* 7 (April/May 1997): 42.

10. *The Compact Edition of the Oxford English Dictionary* [Hereafter *OED*], s.v. "transgression."

11. *The Bulfinch Guide to Art History: A Comprehensive Survey and Dictionary of Western Art and Architecture*, s.v. "sfumato." Bonca's book, which I consider at greater length below, offers a psychobiographical reading of Shelley's investments in Christian models of love; see Bonca, *Shelley's Mirrors of Love: Narcissism, Sacrifice, and Sorority*, SUNY Series in Psychoanalysis and Culture (New York: SUNY, 1999).

12. Shelley, *Rosalind and Helen: A Modern Eclogue*, in *Percy Bysshe Shelley: Complete Poems* (New York: Book-of-the-Month Club, 1993), 699-700.

13. Shelley, *The Triumph of Life*, in *Shelley's Poetry and Prose* [Hereafter *SPP*], ed. Donald H. Reiman and Sharon B. Powers (New York: W.W. Norton, 1977), 410-411.

14. Lucienne Frappier-Mazur, "The Social Body: Disorder and Ritual in Sade's *Story of Juliette*," in *Eroticism and the Body Politic*, ed. Lynn Hunt. Parallax: Revisions of Culture and Society (Baltimore: The Johns Hopkins University Press, 1991), 132.

15. Roland Barthes, *Sade, Fourier, Loyola,* trans. Richard Miller (Baltimore: Johns Hopkins University Press, 1997), 17.

16. The relative positions of language to pleasure—it both precedes and follows pleasure, thus surrounding it completely—underscore the pervasive presence of language in the temporal structure of Sadian theater: everywhere at once, language is, as God Himself claims to be, the Alpha and the Omega, the first and the last, the beginning and the end (Rev. 22:13).

17. Deborah Elise White, *Romantic Returns: Superstition, Imagination, History* (Stanford: Stanford University Press, 2000), 161-162.
18. Eva Lajer-Burcharth, *Necklines: The Art of Jacques-Louis David after the Terror* (New Haven: Yale University Press, 1999), 290.
19. Lynn Hunt, *The Family Romance of the French Revolution* (Berkeley: University of California Press, 1992), 148.
20. Roland Barthes, *Le Plaisir du Texte* [The Pleasure of the Text], trans. Richard Miller (New York: Hill and Wang, 1994), 64.
21. Lynn Hunt notes that the epigraph to *La Philosophie dans le boudoir,* "'La mère en prescrira la lecture à sa fille [the mother will prescribe this reading to her daughter],' is an obvious play on the title page of one of the most pornographic attacks on the queen [Marie Antoinette]: 'La mère en prescrira la lecture à sa fille [the mother will proscribe this reading to her daughter]' [that] adorned the title page of *Fureurs utérines de Marie Antoinette, femme de Louis XVI,* published in 1791"; see Hunt, *The Family Romance of the French Revolution* (Berkeley, Calif.: University of California Press, 1992), 134.
22. Hunt warns against an oversimplification of the similarities between pornography and the libertine tradition; but while such a discussion is important, it remains beyond the real concerns of my own project (138).
23. Evidence of Shelley's ownership of Sade's works so far has remained uncovered, although D. L. Macdonald and Kathleen Scherf write that "Both Byron and P. B. Shelley knew . . . [Sade's] *Justine; or, The Misfortunes of Virtue* (1791)"; see Macdonald and Scherf, eds., *Frankenstein; or, The Modern Prometheus,* by Mary Shelley. (Orchard Park: Broadview Literary Texts, 1994), 93 n 2. Watkins notes that "Sade's writings . . . began to appear during the 1790s, and we know that some of the [R]omantics—Byron, for instance—owned copies of his work" (132 n 7). Many scholars comment on the English "take" on France and all things French as erotic, simply given their French-ness: see, for example, Melanie C. Hawthorne's claim that "what comes from France is always already marked as sexually suspect" in "'Comment Peut-on Être Homosexuel?': Multinational (In)Corporation and the Frenchness of *Salomé*," in *Perennial Decay: On the Aesthetics and Politics of Decadence,* ed. Liz Constable, Dennis Denisoff, and Matthew Potolsky. New Cultural Studies (Philadelphia: University of Pennsylvania Press, 1999), 171; Walter Kendrick's observation that "anything written in French—especially 'French novels'—was suspect. . . . . From a British point of view, radical political opinions went hand in hand with a fondness for things French, especially French fiction," in *The Secret Museum: Pornography in Modern Culture* (Berkeley: University of California Press, 1996), 101; Vernon A. Rosario's claim that "the mystique of *l'amour fou* is the product of a French 'perversification' of sexuality that arose through the circulation of sensual stories, medical ideas, and literary styles among French physicians, novelists, and sexual 'perverts' who populate the pages of post-Revolutionary medical and literary texts," so that by the Victorian age, British physicians regarded perversion as a French disorder, in *The Erotic Imagination: French Histories of Perversity.* Ideologies of Desire, ser. ed. David M. Halperin (New York: Oxford University Press, 1997), 5; and Gary Kelly's observation that,

especially in its representations in England, the French Revolution "itself became gendered," making it a site ripe for the dissemination of sexual politics, in "From Avant-Garde to Vanguardism: The Shelleys' Romantic Feminism in *Laon and Cythna* and *Frankenstein*," in *Shelley: Poet and Legislator of the World*, ed. Betty T. Bennett and Stuart Curran (Baltimore: The Johns Hopkins University Press, 1996), 76.

24. Such a "reading" of the restoration of Charles II dovetails with reactionary readings of contemporary works, such as Sir Peter Lely's portraits and William Wycherley's plays, both of which were imagined to promote, as J. P. Kenyon notes, "a new cosmopolitanism, sensuality, and gaiety"; see Kenyon, *The Wordsworth Dictionary of British History* (Hertfordshire, England: Wordsworth Editions, 1994), 300.

25. For a discussion of contemporary responses to Charles II's controversial private life, see James Turner, "Pepys and the Private Parts of Monarchy," in *Culture and Society in the Stuart Restoration*, ed. Gerald Maclean (Chicago: University of Chicago Press, 1995), 95-110.

26. For a thorough study of media representations of the Queen Caroline Affair, a phenomenon I discuss at length throughout Chapter II, see Iain McCalman, *Radical Underworld: Prophets, Revolutionaries, and Pornographers in London, 1795-1840* (Oxford: Clarendon Press, 1993) and Flora Fraser, *The Unruly Queen: The Life of Queen Caroline* (New York: Knopf, 1996).

27. Marie-Hélène Huet observes that atmospheric turbulence—and lightning in particular—characterized much of the language employed in narrating the political struggles of the late eighteenth and early nineteenth centuries; see Huet, "Thunder and Revolution: Franklin, Robespierre, Sade," in *The French Revolution 1789-1989: Two Hundred Years of Rethinking*, ed. Sandy Petrey (Lubbock: Texas Tech University Press, 1989), 13-32. In the epigraph to *Justine*, Sade observes that "'the prosperity of Crime . . . is like unto lightning, whose traitorous brilliancies but for an instant embellish the atmosphere, in order to hurl into death's very deeps the luckless one they have dazzles'" (qtd. in Huet 27). Mary Wollstonecraft also employed atmospheric metaphors in writing about the political upheavals of her day, comparing the French Revolution to "'hurricanes, whirling over the face of nature'" (qtd. and trans. in Huet 20).

28. John Beer, "Fragmentations and Ironies," in *Questioning Romanticism*, ed. John Beer. (Baltimore: The Johns Hopkins University Press, 1995), 264.

29. Jean Baudrillard, *Seduction*. Trans. Brian Singer. CultureTexts (1979; reprint, New York: St. Martin's Press, 1990), 2.

30. Ernst Bloch, *The Utopian Function of Art and Literature: Selected Essays*. Trans. Jack Zipes and Frank Mecklenburg. (1988; reprint, Cambridge: The MIT Press, 1993), 16, 15.

31. Bloch characterizes representations of utopia as "wish-landscapes," which he describes as taking on the bodily form of a woman (282-283). Vivian Cameron also considers the place of the body in the articulation of desire, and she argues that "images of the body in the French Revolution . . . operate not just on the level of sexuality or the erotic but in fact are polysemous, related to multiple discourses on

morality, on economics, on politics, on reproduction, on rituals such as carnivals, and on a host of other areas"; see Cameron, "Political Exposures: Sexuality and Caricature in the French Revolution," in *Eroticism and the Body Politic*, ed. Hunt, 91. Shelley's landscapes take not the form of any individual body but instead of the bodies of lovers in the act of lovemaking. And while Bloch sees the passage to wish-landscapes in various sorts of openings such as windows and arches (283), Shelley stages openings in the seductive engagement of his readers, in the opening of their minds by way of the sexy appeal of his writing.

32. Ross Chambers, *Room for Maneuver: Reading (the) Oppositional (in) Narrative* (Chicago: University of Chicago Press, 1991), xi.

33. Shelley, "Essay on Christianity," in *Shelley's Prose; Or, The Trumpet of a Prophecy*, ed. David Lee Clark (New York: New Amsterdam, 1988).

34. Geoff King, *Mapping Reality: An Exploration of Cultural Cartographies* (New York: St. Martin's Press, 1996), 41, 174.

35. Ultimately, the model my project articulates suggests a counter-tradition in nineteenth-century literature that is informed by the conflations of erotic scenarios and political commentary, which we see throughout the works of Shelley. This counter-tradition may be held up as an alternative to the standard model of nineteenth-century British poetry that situates Wordsworth (the poet of nature) and Blake (the poet of imagination) as the founders of the tradition and traces the inheritance and perpetuation of each poet's agenda in works by major figures, among them Tennyson and Arnold.

36. The phrase "mix and melt," which I examine at greater length below, comes from Shelley's essay "On Love" in *SPP* 473-474.

37. The term "ooziness" and its derivatives occupy a central position in my argument, even though I recognize their potential to unsettle a number of readers. As I discuss at more length in the chapters to follow, I pose the term "ooziness" in opposition to the term "rigidity," which I derive from the seemingly inflexible or locked systems of order and authority against which Shelley writes. In envisioning an alternative social model in which liberation replaces oppression, Shelley turns increasingly to ooziness—disintegration or liminality, one might also say—as a trope through which hierarchical structures of power and privilege are dismantled, or eroded, through the exchanges of pleasure and love. "Ooziness" thus describes the conditions of seamlessness and reciprocity that underwrite Shelley's social and erotic models, as I demonstrate throughout my project; but for many readers, the term will conjure images of bodily functions. While my connection of ooziness and pleasure clearly suggests erotic imagery (ooziness-as-ejaculation), I am aware of the other bodily functions the term connotes, such as bleeding or the seeping of pus from an infection. In their power to unsettle readers by way of the radically diverse connotations I have named (*viz.* the erotic and the disgusting), the several meanings of "ooziness" lay claim to the ironically seductive potential of the abject, for readers may be both repulsed and fascinated—even titillated—by such imagery. Julia Kristeva discusses abjection at some length throughout her book *Pouvoirs de l'horreur* [Powers of Horror], trans. Leon Roudiez (New York: Columbia University Press, 1982), and she comments on the erotic potential of the abject in an interview

with Elaine Hoffman Baruch included in *The Portable Kristeva*, ed. and trans. Kelly Oliver (New York: Columbia University Press, 1997), 369-380.

38. Elizabeth Grosz traces the evolution of "the body-politic" to seventeenth-century notions about the materiality of space; see Grosz, "Bodies-Cities," in *Sexuality and Space*, ed. Beatriz Colomina. Princeton Papers on Architecture (Princeton: Princeton Architectural Press, 1992), 241-253.

39. Shelley, *A Defense of Poetry*, in *SPP*, 487.

40. Darnton's review of the writings of Louis-Sébastien Mercier and their effects on his readers translates neatly to my ideas about the works of Shelley: Darnton describes the transference of ideology from writer through text to reader as a moment in which the writer's notions are "imprinted in the soul of the reader" (229); I think of the trajectory of thought from Shelley through the text to his readers in an erotic vocabulary, and for me the transferred idea is "impregnated" into the mind of the reader, where it gestates, finally to be "born"—externalized through action, realized and given a life outside the writer-reader intercourse in its effects throughout the society into which it is "born."

41. Bruce Smith, "Premodern Sexualities," *PMLA* 115.3 (May 2000), 326.

42. The flash—the site of titillation—of which Barthes writes anticipates the "ooze" that emerges throughout my discussion, for like the flesh that is revealed in the gape of the garment, the ooze also emerges from an opening, or gape, within which Shelley locates the promises of (sexual) pleasure and (political) liberation.

43. This shift in the "place" of revolution—from public spaces such as the news media and the streets to private spaces such as the bedroom—is, of course, an outgrowth of the libertine tradition to which Sade belongs. Protected and empowered by his position of social prestige and political privilege, the erotic life of the libertine is always politicized.

44. Jürgen Habermas, *The Structural Transformation of the Public Sphere: An Inquiry into a Category of Bourgeois Society*, trans. Thomas Burger with Frederick Lawrence (Cambridge, Mass.: MIT Press, 1994), 14-26.

45. My admittedly elastic definition of "the erotic" echoes Robert M. Polhemus' in *Erotic Faith*: he explains that he uses "the term 'erotic' not in its narrow sexual connotation but to indicate more broadly libidinous desire and a passionate, sometimes romantic, relationship with, affection for, or attachment to another person"; see Polhemus, *Erotic Faith: Being in Love from Jane Austen to D. H. Lawrence* (Chicago: University of Chicago Press, 1990), 1. My inclusion of unpleasure under the rubric of the erotic—experiences and relationships that lead to no affection, in fact to a dis-connection or a desire for disconnection—seems closer to the more general conception of "erotics" which Polhemus defines as "that complicated individual and social tangle of desire that pertains to the various energies of the human libido" (3).

46. Marilyn Butler, *Romantics, Rebels, and Reactionaries: English Literature and Its Background 1760-1830* (New York: Oxford University Press, 1981), 178.

47. Raymond Williams, *Culture and Society 1780-1950* (New York: Harper Torchbooks, 1958), xii, 32, 42.

48. Anne K. Mellor, *Romanticism and Gender* (New York: Routledge, 1993), 65.

Introduction

49. Jon P. Klancher, *The Making of English Reading Audiences, 1790-1832* (Madison: University of Wisconsin Press, 1987), 101.
50. Clifford Siskin, *The Historicity of Romantic Discourse* (New York: Oxford University Press, 1988), 173.
51. Stephen Frosch, *The Politics of Psychoanalysis: An Introduction to Freudian and Post-Freudian Theory* (New Haven, Conn.: Yale University Press, 1987), 149.
52. Judith R. Walkowitz, *City of Dreadful Delight: Narratives of Sexual Danger in Late-Victorian London* (London: Virago Press, 1992), 84.
53. See Roger Shattuck, *Forbidden Knowledge: From Prometheus to Pornography* (New York: St. Martin's Press, 1996), 165-169, 313-321.
54. Lynn Hunt, "Pornography and the French Revolution," in *The Invention of Pornography: Obscenity and the Origins of Modernity, 1500-1800,* ed. Hunt (New York: Zone Books, 1993), 303.
55. Lynn Hunt, "The Bad Mother," in *The Family Romance of the French Revolution,* 105.
56. Lynn Hunt, "The Many Bodies of Marie Antoinette: Political Pornography and the Problem of the Feminine in the French Revolution," in *Eroticism and the Body Politic,* ed. Lynn Hunt (Baltimore: The Johns Hopkins University Press, 1991), 112.
57. Clearly, the effects of the media coverage of the Queen Caroline Affair (which I discuss at great length in Chapter II) parallel those of the pornographic representations of Marie Antoinette in Revolution-era France: both work to dismantle the reputation of the monarchy by drawing on an iconography and discourse of sexual activity in order to participate in anti-hegemonic political rhetoric and, in so doing, to speak sedition.
58. It is important to note that while the media's response to the scandals of Marie Antoinette and Queen Caroline seem rather similar, in each situation the political valences are different. Radicals employed legends about the "Queen Caroline Affair" in their attempts to dismantle the monarchy; on the other hand, both radicals (or revolutionaries) *and traditionalists* resorted to pornographic lampoons of Marie Antoinette, the former in their efforts to attack the institution of monarchy, the latter in their desperate attempts to expose what they regarded as the real problem that must be solved for the institution of monarchy to remain intact.
59. Ronald Paulson, "Burke's Sublime and the Representation of Revolution," in *Culture and Politics from Puritanism to the Enlightenment,* ed. Perez Zagorin (Berkeley: University of California Press, 1980), 245.
60. Evelyne Lever, *Marie Antoinette: The Last Queen of France,* trans. Catherine Temerson (New York: Farrar, Straus, Giroux, 2000), 303. Lever's study, the most recent book-length examination of the place and importance of Marie Antoinette, deals extensively with connections between the body and politics, between private lives and public station, which I examine throughout this chapter.
61. Oliver Bernier, "France's Weak and Frivolous Ruling Couple," in *The French Revolution,* ed. Don Nardo. Turning Points in World History (San Diego: Greenhaven Press, 1999), 52, 54.

62. Bernier notes that amidst growing public anxiety about Marie Antoinette's influence in matters political, "many of the Deputies to the Estates General asked to see the well-known—and wholly fictitious—room at the Trianon [Palace] that had walls covered with emeralds and diamonds" (54). The fantasy of such a room underscores the private/public overlap that coalesce around "the problem" of Marie Antoinette, an overlap that seeks to correct public/political chaos by invading private/erotic space, reminding us, as we shall see throughout the works of Shelley, of cultural fantasies, conscious or not, about the power of private/erotic engagements to alter public/political realities.

63. Linda Dowling, *Hellenism and Homosexuality in Victorian Oxford* (Ithaca, N.Y.: Cornell University Press, 1994), 21.

64. Linda M. Shires, "Of Mænads, Mothers, and Feminized Males: Victorian Readings of the French Revolution," in *Rewriting the Victorians: Theory, History, and the Politics of Gender*, ed. Shires (New York: Routledge, 1992), 145.

65. Bonca notes that one of Shelley's favorite words was "susceptible" (27), and I am reminded in that observation of Shelley's consistently radical language, for just as Burke's connection of revolutionaries to filth and excrement and maternity codes political upheaval in the vocabulary of infectious, feminine influence, so, too, does Shelley's use of the term "susceptible" remind us of his desire to "infect" (and I use a negative term here deliberately, self-consciously) his readers with the revolutionary potential of the texts he produces.

66. Walter Jackson Bate sets up the political context surrounding *Blackwood's Edinburgh Magazine* in a manner quite useful for my readings of the attacks on Keats and Hunt; see Bate, *John Keats* (London: Hogarth, 1979). According to Bate, *Blackwood's* was established by William Blackwood, "a Tory bookseller in Edinburgh" and was conceived "in opposition to the Whig publisher, Archibald Constable, and his *Scots Magazine* and *Edinburgh Review*" (224). Thus, from its inception, *Blackwood's* functioned as an organ of political engagement that sought to counter the liberal claims of Whig publications.

67. Jeffrey C. Robinson, "Passion and Romantic Poets," in *Romantic Passions*. Romantic Circles Praxis Series (http://www.rc.und.edu/praxis/passions/robinson/rbsn.html).

68. Kelly, too, notes the place of the feminine in general, and of women in particular, in cultural fantasies about the spread of revolutionary movements: "By the time [the Romantics] wrote, the condition of women and the figure of woman had long been major topics in the cultural revolutionaries' social critique; for centuries woman had been a figure for the ideological and cultural vulnerability of every class to seduction from above or contamination from below . . . " (75). Although Shelley writes to both female and male readers, his strategies of textual seduction clearly gender the experience of reading, and again, Shelley depends on the perceived femininity—the susceptibility—of his readers to the lure of his sexy texts, finally to ensure the "impregnation" of his ideas in his readers' psyches and, by extension, in the broader cultural imagination.

69. Such instances of intertextuality are numerous, so I shall indicate only a few. Shelley's tragedy *The Cenci* is dedicated to Hunt, and several of the poems in Hunt's collection entitled *Foliage* (1818) are dedicated to Shelley. Hunt's *Story of*

Rimini (1816) is dedicated to Byron, and Shelley's *Adonais* (1821) is composed on the occasion of the death of Keats. Toward the end of his life, Shelley embarked on a plan to launch a new journal, *The Liberal,* with Hunt and Byron, but following Shelley's death by drowning in August of 1822, only four issues of the journal appeared before its publication was discontinued.

70. Dowling goes to great lengths to uncover the conflations of two discursive traditions in Z's attacks. On the one hand, the feminine epithets that Z attaches to the Cockney school derive from a classical republican discourse and have nothing to do with "femaleness in any modern sense but with an absence of privation of value," not to do with "sexual but with civic incapacity" (8, 9). On the other hand, the language Lockhart and Wilson use in slurring Hunt and Keats is clearly tied to contemporary notions about gender as well as to age-old anxieties about the cultural degeneracy incumbent upon the blurring of those roles.

71. My understanding of "the feminine" as the ultimate category of lack is clearly informed by late twentieth-century responses to Sigmund Freud's writings about women, articulated most completely by Luce Irigaray in her book, *Speculum of the Other Woman,* trans. Gillian C. Gill (Ithaca, N.Y.: Cornell University Press, 1985).

72. Nicholas Roe (remark made during an informal seminar sponsored by the Interdisciplinary Group for Historical Literary Study at Texas A&M University, College Station, Tex., 1 April 1996).

73. I place "review" in quotation marks to emphasize the fact that while Lockhart's infamous attack on Hunt was presented as a review of *The Story of Rimini,* any real effort to "review" *The Story of Rimini* was shoved aside as Lockhart criticized Hunt personally.

74. This pathologizing-as-bodily-legibility is remarkably similar to the ways in which French pornography sought to make Marie Antoinette's subversive tendencies and political importance legible at the site of her erotic body.

75. Roe has suggested that in the Romantic era, the French term *"Metromanie"* (metromania) would have had the same sort of political resonance as the names of Mary Wollstonecraft or Thomas Paine; that is, "metromania" would have functioned as a code word for radical political engagements (Roe, informal seminar).

76. Newman Ivey White, *Shelley,* 2 vols. (New York: Alfred A. Knopf, 1940), 2:305.

77. Richard Holmes notes that early in Shelley's career, "[i]n London society [his] name gained currency for atheism and immorality rather than for poetry"; see Holmes, *Shelley: The Pursuit* (New York: E. P. Dutton, 1974; New York: Penguin Books, 1987), 404. Shelley's *Revolt of Islam* was, in fact, negatively reviewed by Lockhart in *Blackwood's* in 1819, but, as Holmes notes, the reviewer went to great lengths to separate Shelley from the Cockney School in terms of poetic style (see Holmes 404-405).

78. William Doyle, "The Revolution in Perspective," in *The Oxford History of the French Revolution* (Oxford: Clarendon Press, 1989), 423.

79. Shelley's erotic cartography depends upon the contingencies between landscapes and the body, much in the way such connections informed Romantic landscape paintings, as Charles Harrison notes: " . . . landscape painting [operated as]

a form of metaphorization of the body and the sensation of the body . . . "; see Harrison, "The Effects of Landscape," in *Landscape and Power*, ed. W. J. T. Mitchell (Chicago: University of Chicago Press, 1994), 226.

80. Mark Kipperman, "Macropolitics of Utopia: Shelley's *Hellas* in Context," in *Macropolitics of Nineteenth-Century Literature: Nationalism, Exoticism, Imperialism*, ed. Jonathan Arac and Harriet Ritvo (Philadelphia: University of Pennsylvania Press, 1991), 98.

PART ONE: THE PROBLEM

CHAPTER II

Shelley's Agenda Writ Large:
Reconsidering *ŒdipusTyrannus; or, Swellfoot the Tyrant*

> Love is . . . the sole law which should govern the moral world.
>
> —Percy Bysshe Shelley, Preface to *Laon and Cythna; Or, The Revolution of the Golden City*

As the epigraph to this chapter suggests, for Shelley, love is the highest law of the universe, an engagement that, ideally, structures and codifies relationships between and among individuals, groups, and nations. Time and again, Shelley invokes love as a revolutionary force capable of dismantling tyranny, and throughout his works, he demonstrates the unique ability of erotic engagements to activate the liberating potential of love. In poems such as *Laon and Cythna; or, The Revolution of the Golden City: A Vision of the Nineteenth Century* (1817) and *Epipsychidion* (1821), Shelley poses decidedly nontraditional erotic relationships to demonstrate their potency in overturning particular social institutions—religion, marriage, law—as well as to examine their potential to rupture the totalizing terrain of "convention," that hegemonic set of attitudes, beliefs, ideas, and behaviors that dominated his historical moment. Throughout his works, Shelley privileges love—the ceaseless and unselfish giving of oneself to another—as the private engagement whose liberating effects may alter the broader sphere of the public world; in Shelley's works, love precipitates the liberation of the world by posing unselfishness and reciprocity as the forerunners of democratic social reform. Ultimately, Shelley's works transfer—or translate, one might say—love into liberty, so that private engagements re-write public policy, transforming tyranny into freedom.

But how, one might ask, can Shelley really believe in the erotic as a political force—and a viable one, at that? To answer this question, we first must consider what Shelley shows to be the diverse ways in which erotic relationships operate, for throughout the works I will consider in this chapter and the three to follow, Shelley describes diverse milieux in which erotic engagements tend toward two completely different ends—liberation and oppression. For example, in *The Cenci* (1819) and *Julian and Maddalo: A Conversation* (1820), Shelley exposes the erotic as an oppressive and destructive force: in both texts, erotic engagements generate oppression because they proceed in a wholly self-interested fashion, because they remain focused exclusively on the self with no more than a cursory regard for any particular other. But in *Prometheus Unbound* (1819) and *Laon and Cythna*, Shelley demonstrates the conditions under which the erotic operates in the interest of liberation: erotic engagements liberate when each lover remains focused on an other—in a narrow sense, on the one who is the particular love object; in a broad sense, on all those who are marginalized by the individuals, institutions, and ideologies empowered by an oppressive hegemonic order. In Shelley's idealized universe, love precipitates liberation when it progresses toward completely unselfish goals—sometimes even to the exclusion of a hero from the utopia his or her self-sacrifice activates.

Facile readings of Shelley obfuscate the poet's complicated understanding of the power (and, to return to an idea I introduced in the Introduction, the *politics*) of love.[1] Such readings misunderstand the apparent incongruities between works that chart Shelley's idealized, revolutionary notions about love and those that lay bare what seem to be love's failures, for in fact, a number of Shelley's works expose the oppressive consequences of "failed" love in order to demonstrate how love devolves into what we might call "love," that is, love-in-quotation-marks, a term that signifies personal engagements evacuated of the meaning and potential Shelley imagines they might have contained, an empty and therefore ironic version of the love Shelley so idealizes. As I shall discuss in Chapter III, Count Cenci's "love" for his daughter Beatrice—a selfish emotion manifested in his desire to rape her—tends toward oppression, not liberation, and at the end of *The Cenci*, the Count's selfish "love" conjures death, the most extreme opposite of liberty, the goal toward which Shelley's idealized notion of love unfailingly leads. In Shelley's model, love fails when it tends toward selfishness, devolving from love into "love" as sexual attacks reinforce social structures of oppression, but love liberates when it dissolves all structures of difference and division in the ooziness of liminality, which is manifested quite literally in the overlapping of bodies during the act of lovemaking. As we will see in my readings of *Laon and Cythna* and *Prometheus Unbound*, when the act of lovemaking rewards the individual with erotic pleasure, the social effect of that act is the production of liberty, for in the giving of the selves to each other, Shelley's lovers activate the liberating potential of love, transmitting its effects far beyond their private intercourse and throughout the public sphere of the world-at-large. For Shelley, love is not only "the sole law which should govern the moral world"; it is also the generative force of the universe, the power by which life is given and individuals are freed from the structures that bind them. A radical reading of Shelley might compare his notion of love to the function Christians accord Jesus Christ: for Shelley, love is the eternal symbol of salvation, the divine figure of intercession who bridges the gap between mortals and the infinite, between man and the universe. Shelley poses love, as Christianity poses Christ, at and as the center of all meaning, rendering it finally the heart of all freedom.

To put matters more simply, for Shelley, love always acts as an agent, and his works chart the maneuvers through which that agent operates toward particular ends, some positive (that is, liberation through love) and others negative (oppression through "love"). Throughout his works, the poet traces these trajectories of love along the contours of erotic engagements to spectacularize the processes of liberty-through-love in representations of sexual relationships; thus, Shelley lures his readers into—seduces them with—a series of deeply political works he disguises, veils, beneath the vestments of dramas, essays, and poems about love. Titillating his readers with descriptions of so many loves that dare not speak their names,[2] Shelley consistently dramatizes the powerful and, moreover, the political significance of love as an agent of social regulation. Ultimately didactic, all of Shelley's works propound a singular doctrine: Love is the Law, both the object of desire and the device for its attainment, at once the means and the end. For Shelley, Love is All.[3]

∞ ∞ ∞ ∞ ∞

In the present chapter, I engage in a lengthy reading of *Œdipus Tyrannus; or, Swellfoot the Tyrant* (1820), one of the most overlooked texts in Shelley scholarship, to argue that its intra- and extra-textual engagements situate the play as a document pivotal to Shelley's articulation of the agenda of liberty-through-love. In a broad sense, this chapter concentrates on Shelley's descriptions of erotic relationships to demonstrate how those engagements function as sites of oppression or liberation. In the next chapter, I map out what for Shelley appears to be "the problem" of love, specifically, the institutions and conventions that divert love from its liberating potential. In Chapters IV and V, I describe "the solution" Shelley poses for that problem—his visionary, intertextual project of liberty-through-love. In each of these chapters, I concentrate on the poet's descriptions of erotic relationships to demonstrate how those engagements function as sites of and models for either oppression or liberation. Throughout my discussion, I underscore the significance of the "other" in Shelley's figurations of liberty-through-love to show how that figure resonates throughout the levels of the private and the public, the personal and the political. For Shelley, love-relationships—schematized in the ideological register of the lovers or the family unit as well as in the physical space of the home—take on an intensely political significance, for in his works we see the personal and the political co-aligned: one's erotic engagements anticipate his or her political commitments. Time and again, Shelley stages the gestation of liberty in the erotic engagements of politicized heroes: oppressors in the bedroom are, by no coincidence, oppressors in the worlds Shelley describes, while unselfishly invested lovers are consistently cast as the agents of liberty. Like voyeurs standing on the outside looking in, peering from the larger world into so many bedrooms, our own erotic acts of pleasure-in-reading take on a particularly political significance as we marvel at the conjuring of liberty in the intercourse of Shelley's heroic lovers: when Shelley's devices succeed, the reader/voyeur is meant to do more than merely enjoy the pleasure of the erotic spectacle; ideally, he or she will engage the political realities of the world in unselfish attempts to redeem that world through the pleasurable power of love.

In the chapters that follow, I discuss a number of works in which Shelley exposes the myriad of problems occasioned by the misdirection of love toward selfishness and isolation, the devolution of love into "love." Throughout these texts, Shelley argues that misguided "love" not only leaves oppressive structures firmly in place, but, ironically, redoubles the power of those structures by confirming their hegemony. I devote the present chapter to a discussion of the centrality of transgression (both erotic and political) to the project of revolution, a strategy Shelley foregrounds in the satire *Œdipus Tyrannus; or Swellfoot the Tyrant*. In the next chapter, I plot the movements of selfish "love" throughout *The Cenci* and *Julian and Maddalo*. Part Two of my project begins with an examination of Shelley's notorious "free-love" poem, *Epipsychidion*, and I consider how that poem articulates the conjoining of Shelley's vision of love to the project of liberty, ultimately to interrogate Shelley's profound pessimism about the ineffectiveness of merely imagining the utopia of erotic liberation. Finally, I turn to *Laon and Cythna* and *Prometheus Unbound* to describe the strategies through which Shelley believes love may release the world from the shackles of tyranny to deliver humankind into the boundlessness of liberty through the movements of seamless, transgressive erotic engagements.

∞ ∞ ∞ ∞ ∞

Shelley's satire of the Queen Caroline affair, *Œdipus Tyrannus; or, Swellfoot the Tyrant. A Tragedy*, stands as a key moment in my reading of Shelley, for it demonstrates the poet's thoroughgoing understanding of the political power of erotic transgression.[4] Significantly, Shelley's satire arises out of a historical moment in which the political ramifications of such transgressions were operating quite visibly in the world around him: *Swellfoot the Tyrant* describes the doomed scheme by which Tyrant Swellfoot attempts to quell public support for the return of Queen Iona to her rightful seat of power—a close parallel to the real-life George IV's desperate attempts to bar his wife, Caroline of Brunswick, from her spousal privilege incumbent upon his accession to the throne. The deep connections between Shelley's satire and contemporary political events cannot be overlooked, for both Caroline of Brunswick and the play's heroine, Iona Taurina, function as highly visible emblems of the mother-whore, that revolutionary icon of the woman-in-public whose very presence threatens to feminize the public sphere and thus to hasten the collapse—the detumescence, as we shall see in Shelley's play—of masculine, patriarchal order.

The collapse of patriarchal order begins, both in the real-life Queen Caroline affair and in the fictitious return of Iona Taurina, with the king's humiliation, which, importantly, registers at both the private and public levels, the former in the Queen's erotic transgressions, real or imagined, and the latter in the public's virtually unanimous support for the king's spoiled spouse, now too his political adversary. Thomas W. Laqueur notes that "[i]n obscure Welsh coastal villages, in rural southwest Hampshire, in hamlets hundreds of miles from London where the people knew 'as little of radicalism as they do of necromancy,' [to borrow a phrase from William Hazlitt,] Caroline found fervent support. Her cause, as William Cobbett said, 'let loose for a time every tongue and pen in England'."[5] In activating "a discourse about the power of the press and the legitimacy of a greatly expanded public opinion" (429), the Queen Caroline Affair demonstrated the power of the press and of public spectacle, as well as the collusion of these forces at the site of political unrest. Laqueur provides an astounding tally of Queen Caroline publications that appeared in 1820 alone—some 500 cartoons and several hundred other items in print in one form or another (429-430)—and concludes that "in no other instance were the radical and the reform networks so effective" (430). Hunt's observation about the French Revolution surely describes the political shocks that jolted Britons in the wake of the Queen Caroline Affair: "[i]n no domain was the invasion of public authority more evident than in family life."[6] But Queen Caroline stood for even more than just a monarch and a wife, a public figure and a private; as Laqueur observes, she stood for all people, as "[e]ach attack on the queen—each irregularity in her trial and treatment—was translated simultaneously into an attack on the liberties of the people" (435). Such a transference of identity is no mere scholarly creation, however; Queen Caroline's own words bear the truth of Laqueur's equation: "'When my honour is attacked, every loyal Englishwoman must feel it as an imputation on her own. . . . The virtues of the great become the property of the people; and the people are interested in preserving them from slanderous contamination.'"[7] The treatment of Queen Caroline *is* the treatment of the people, her abuses symbolic for their own; such, too, are the effects of Iona Taurina, the scorned wife and would-be monarch of Shelley's *Swellfoot the Tyrant*.

Beyond its local political significance, *Swellfoot the Tyrant* draws on a variety of literary contexts, among them Sophocles' tragedy *Œdipus Rex*, Leigh Hunt's drama *The Descent of Liberty: A Mask* (1815), and Shelley's "Ode to Liberty" (1820), a poem that appears as the final selection of the *Prometheus Unbound* volume.[8] In order to make sense of the multiple contexts that inform *Swellfoot*, I will consider each of these literary and political sources at some length before embarking on a close reading of Shelley's so-called "tragedy."

In her 1839 note to *Swellfoot the Tyrant*, Mary Shelley cautions that "[t]his drama . . . must not be judged for more than was meant," that "[i]t is a mere plaything of the imagination, which even may not excite smiles among many, who will not see wit in those combinations of thought which were full of the ridiculous to the author"; yet she concludes that "like everything [Shelley] wrote, it breathes that deep sympathy for the sorrows of humanity, and indignation against its oppressors, which make it worthy of his name."[9] Mary Shelley's well-intended suggestion nevertheless does great damage to her husband's satire, for in fact, the play comments quite earnestly on one of the most culturally significant spectacles of the day— Caroline of Brunswick's return from a protracted Continental tour and her claim to a place beside the soon-to-be-crowned George IV.

Upon her return to England, Caroline was greeted with legal charges of infidelity, and the court case brought against her assumed political significance when Whigs appropriated Caroline as a martyr crushed by the tyrannical regime of the House of Hanover (White, *Shelley* 2:224). But George and Caroline had led completely separate lives for years before George's accession to the throne, and Caroline, as Newman Ivey White explains, "had long been traveling in Mediterranean countries with a fairly complete disregard of decorum" (2:224). Alerted that her name was to be excluded from the reading of the liturgy at her husband's coronation, Caroline returned to England to demand her rightful place in the royal family, whereupon charges of infidelity were brought against her, clearly in George's attempt to distance her from any connections to his new political station.[10] Throughout the scandal, Queen Caroline's actions—actual or merely the stuff of malicious rumor—remind us of Queen Caroline's turn to her erotic body as a political weapon, a phenomenon widely recognized and openly discussed in *The Times*' report of the Queen's landing at Dover on 5 June 1820: "'But this woman comes arrayed only in native courage, and (may we not add?) conscious innocence, and presents her bosom, aye, offers her neck, to those who threatened to sever her head from it, if ever she dared to come within their reach'" (qtd. in Smith, *A Queen on Trial* 30), a description that recalls the eroticization of the final hours of Marie Antoinette's life, and which will appear again in the final moments of Lucretia Cenci's life, as I will discuss in Chapter III. Throughout the scandal, rumors of Queen Caroline's transgressions of private pleasures and public privileges—sex and politics—proliferated, finally finding codification in the Bill of Pains and Penalties, a legal document outlining charges against the Queen, which included the following claim: "' . . . [that] her said royal highness not only advanced the said Bartolomeo Bergami to a high situation in her royal highness's household, and received into her service many of his bear relations, some of them inferior and others in high and confidential situations about her royal highness's person'" (qtd. in Smith 133). And just as a host of beleaguered figures, some real and others the stuff of fiction, collapse into the story of Queen Caroline, the centrality of the so-called Queen Caroline Affair to English life in the early nineteenth century cannot be overestimated: during her trial, the country remained so rapt in the controversy that one of Caroline's defenders, Henry Brougham, "sardonically suggested that certain days should be set apart for the transaction of business" (2:224).[11]

As Michelle Perrot observes, Caroline's trial and the spectacle it engendered represented a wide range of contested terrain in English life: George's treatment of Caroline came to be regarded as symbolic not only of the tyranny endemic to the House of Hanover, but also of the "injustice" of the King's accusations against Caroline for the very indiscretions he had long been rumored to have been enjoying,[12] and finally of the "whole corrupt nature of [the] aristocratic expectations of marriage for which Caroline was unfairly paying the price."[13] Even though Whigs adopted Caroline as a revolutionary hero, her public presence bifurcated rather paradoxically, as outcries of support derived from a centuries-old chivalric tradition in which men fought to save helpless damsels in distress; in other words, in their appropriation of Caroline as a symbol for political resistance to George IV, the Queen's Whig supporters reverted to a hierarchical structure—chivalry—that arose from and perpetuated the hegemony of patriarchal order.[14] Sara Maza characterizes the effects of the Marie Antoinette scandals, which I read as analogous to the effects of the Queen Caroline Affair, as a political rupture: "[f]emale sexuality run amok had, it seemed, taken over the 'sacred center' of the kingdom," and the combined ideological weight of three forces—"the anomalous ascendancy of woman, the privatization of the public sphere, [and] the role of female sexuality" succeeded "in inverting social and political hierarchies."[15] As Anna Clark observes, royal scandals of the eighteenth and nineteenth centuries centered on the connections and disjunctions between and among sex, virtue, and power, and on the ways in which those connections and disjunctions occurred in the space of the text—the cartoon, the editorial, the legal charge, the judicial sentence (47). For all of its initial spectacle, the trial of Queen Caroline came to an end on 10 November 1820 amidst surprisingly lackluster proceedings; Carlos Baker notes that "the Bill of Pains and Penalties was abandoned on November 10, and on the 29th of that month the absolved and impenitent queen, accompanied by a sorry little group of retainers, gave thanks for her acquittal at St. Paul's."[16] After the entire brouhaha faded, Caroline more or less fell from heroic status as English culture began to turn toward what we might recognize today as traditional "family values," and while her life saw the public celebration of one scandal after another, the lack of a similar response to Caroline's death demonstrates her fall from revolutionary icon to has-been, from the spectacle of scandal to a merely distant memory of no particular importance.

The Shelleys were certainly not immune to the Queen Caroline controversy. Newman Ivey White notes that Mary was a strong proponent of the Queen but that Shelley only "technically" supported her, dismissing her as "'a vulgar cook-maid'" and finding the fact that her enemies were so despicable to be Caroline's only redeeming quality (2:225). Shelley certainly regarded the Queen Caroline Affair with some antipathy, as his 20 July 1820 letter to Thomas Medwin indicates: "I wonder what in the world the Queen has done. . . . What silly stuff is this to employ a great nation about. I wish the King and the Queen, like Punch and his wife, would fight out their disputes in person. . . ."[17] Eight days earlier, Shelley wrote at some length about the controversial Queen to Thomas Love Peacock, articulating with greater clarity his appreciation for the complexity of the Queen Caroline Affair. Although he finds it ridiculous, Shelley recognizes the tremendous cultural and political significance of the very public power-struggles that beset the royal couple:

> Nothing, I think, shows the generous gullibility of the English nation more than their having adopted her Sacred Majesty as the heroine of the day, in spite of all their prejudices and bigotry. I, for my part, of course wish no harm to happen to her, even if she has, as I firmly believe, amused herself in a manner rather indecorous with any courtier or baron. But I cannot help adverting to it as one of the absurdities of royalty, that a vulgar woman, with all those low tastes which prejudice considers as vices, and a person whose habits and manners every one would shun in private life, without any redeeming virtues, should be turned into a heroine because she is a queen, or, as a collateral reason, because her husband is a king; and he, no less than his ministers, are so odious that everything, however disgusting, which is opposed to them, is admirable. (*Letters* 2:576)

In his letter, Shelley acknowledges that Queen Caroline not only occupies a central role in the English imagination, but, more importantly, that her very public opposition to King George and his "odious" ministers causes her to figure politically. Queen Caroline emerges as an important political force because of her elevation to the iconic status of oppositional leader through the subversive mechanisms of gossip and the tabloid press, two forces that celebrate the Queen as a dissenting monarch who not only opposes the King but who does so publicly and unapologetically; Queen Caroline thus functions as a transgressor both in the political and erotic senses, for she interrupts the sovereign's claims to power even as she violates—transgresses—contemporary social mores. Queen Caroline's two bodies—her real, physical self, and her textual body which is anatomized, pathologized, and pornographized throughout countless arms of the radical press—coalesce in the image of the symbolic revolutionary whose politicized physicality compromises the constitutional power of King George and his court. In both its physical and textual manifestations, the Queen's oppositional body functions as oppositional narrative, so that in both person and reputation, Queen Caroline interrupts the processes of monarchial order. Throughout the scandal, it is the feminine voice—the voice of the Queen, and the voice of revolt in general[18]—that disrupts an entire household, thereby charging the Queen's physical and textual bodies as catalysts for the radical instability of her husband's political regime and her nation's established order. In Queen Caroline, Shelley recognizes the political implications of sexual transgression, for in her status as an oppositional icon she demonstrates the power of the perverse erotic body to intrude upon the political process by exposing the problematic nature of an entrenched, oppressive regime.[19]

Mary Shelley's note to *Swellfoot the Tyrant* emphasizes the political context out of which Shelley's "tragedy" arose: "[i]n the brief journal I kept in those days, I find recorded, in August 1820, Shelley 'begins Swellfoot the Tyrant, suggested by the pigs at the fair of San Giuliano.' This was the period of Queen Caroline's landing in England, and the struggles made by Geo. IV. to get rid of her claims; which failing, Lord Castlereagh placed the '*Green Bag*' on the table of the House of Commons, demanding, in the King's name, that an inquiry should be instituted into his wife's conduct. These circumstances were the theme of all conversation among the English" (*WPS* 2:350). The plot of Shelley's play hinges on a similar struggle for political power: in *Swellfoot*, the tyrant's long-absent wife, Iona Taurina, is rumored to have engaged in sexual exploits that become the subject not only of much gossip but also of enthusiastic support by the masses of swine, who for generations have been kept in poverty under English monarchial rule. Shelley's play concludes with a green bag episode directly imported from the headlines of his day, a moment in which Iona's purity is cast into disrepute by the contents of that pouch, just as Queen Caroline's sexual indiscretions were purportedly proven by the evidence (much of it trumped-up) that Castlereagh presented to Parliament in the infamous green bag.[20]

Both Newman Ivey White and Kenneth Neill Cameron trace convincing parallels between Shelley's satire and press coverage of the Queen Caroline Affair. White suggests that Shelley's imagery derives from a number of cartoons on the subject of Queen Caroline; specifically, he cites "A Kick Up in a Great House" for its similarity to the conclusion of Shelley's play. Published in August of 1820, the same month during which Shelley completed *Swellfoot the Tyrant*, "A Kick Up in a Great House" lampoons the Queen "riding a snorting, kicking bull and calling 'Justice,' while the Archbishop, King and counselors are fleeing in panic and the table is overturned, spilling the contents of the Green Bag, which are labeled Horse Leech, Italian Dagger, Milan Commission, and Bill of Pains and Penalties" (White, "Shelley's Swell-Foot" 338).[21] The conclusion of Shelley's satire mirrors that cartoon rather closely: as Iona grabs the Green Bag and pours its contents over those who have charged her, her persecutors are transformed into rodents and flee the scene as the triumphant Queen mounts a minotaur named "John Bull" and rides away, savoring her victory.

Popular, inexpensive images of Queen Caroline and others embroiled in her affairs proved increasingly available, and Shelley might well have known of some of these through his correspondence with Hunt and others who remained in England while Shelley traveled on the Continent throughout 1820. Certainly, such images collectively construct some sort of visual and symbolic vocabulary about the royal scandal, and many of them participate in the same vocabulary Shelley employs throughout *Swellfoot the Tyrant*. A sense of the content of such images reminds us of the close links of Shelley's play to contemporary radical propaganda, and it helps us better understand the way in which Shelley's play might have been received in England.

Throughout the Queen Caroline Affair, the city of London operated as a vast textual repository upon which were written, and throughout which were disseminated, a variety of textual matter dedicated to one side of the scandal or the other, as Fraser notes:

> The "general demurrer" against the handling of the Queen was the reason why the walls of London were daubed, "The Queen for ever, the King in the river," why Radical politicians like Dolby and Benbow turned publisher and why their boys, and Hone's, were out with their horns on the street corners, advertising the latest graphic effusion against the Crown and ministers. "No man could go through the streets of London," adverted Sir Matthew Cholmeley, "without having his eyes insulted by the most offensive placards and comparisons of an odious kind between the highest personage and the greatest of tyrants." (Fraser 23)

The depiction of the royal contest as a private struggle between Queen Caroline and George IV finds form in a number of cartoons, among them "Public Opinion!!" of June 1820, which depicts the Queen and King placed on a scale, the Queen sitting calmly, impassively, and alone, and the King struggling to bring down his side of the scale, loading up his seat with "Green Bags" of evidence against his queen and being pulled down by his ministers, one of whom shouts "Confound that Bull! What a row he makes!" as a citizen standing between the King and Queen says, "Well done Caroline! They think to make light of you, but it won't do. I'll see fair play!" (Smith, *A Queen on Trial* 33). Newman Ivey White notes the importance of the symbology of the green bag to Shelley's play as well as to supporters of the Queen in the streets of London, many of whom "carried green bags on long poles in their processions" in support of the Queen.[22] A host of images featuring the Green Bag reveals the public's skepticism about the Crown's manner of investigation and its evidence-gathering techniques in particular, which certainly fueled pro-Caroline sentiments. Laqueur writes that

> ... the bag was used with great virtuosity in demonstrations and in print. Cartoons showed cabinet ministers scooping up John Bull's excrement from the field for the "green bag"; the bag was labeled "foul cloths" or

"foul lies" in scores of popular prints; imps and devils and putrid vapors escaped from it and fluttered around the government's council. It was shown immersed in urinals with Italian witnesses popping out, or as bags of rotten grain with the witnesses inside and ministers as rats gnawing at the tatters .... Liverpool and his colleagues were frequently portrayed as night soilmen and scavengers while their witnesses in the case drank out of chamberpots and slept on dung heaps. Scatology pervaded Caroline propaganda; excrement and the stench of corrupt politics were clearly linked. (436)

Fraser observes that throughout these representations, "the green bag continued to represent repression, conspiracy and, in particular, the perjured evidence of the Italian witnesses" (405). Just as Shelley will employ the green bag as a phallic symbol for political power (in its initial swollenness and then in its limpness), contemporary cartoons recognized the phallic potential in representations of that iconic object. Smith reproduces two images that bespeak the castration anxiety underlying George's contest for power over Caroline. In "Meditations Among the Tombs," George is forced to examine the decapitated body of King Charles, who holds his head to look at George directly as Henry VIII is decapitated before George's eyes (127). Such a moment enacts a displaced castration and forces George to recognize the risk he runs—either he removes his wife, á la Henry VIII, as a source of trouble, or he will "lose his head," so to speak. Another image, George Cruikshank's "Reflection— To Be or Not To Be?", depicts George looking in a mirror and starting at the "spectre of his wife, wearing a crown, looking over his shoulder" (15). That Caroline appears nowhere in the foreground of the picture—that she is not actually in the room with George—reminds us of her function as an embodiment of the King's obsessive fears about the stability of his rule, about the rigidity of his power.

Fraser reproduces a color image by Cruikshank which depicts both Caroline and George contained in green bags, Caroline casting a sly look in George's direction as the King looks anxiously away from her, the "belt" around his green bag pointing downward and ending in a drop-like fob— phallic imagery I read as commenting on the sexual embarrassment Caroline has caused him, which registers as political humiliation: her sash remains neatly tied, while his "belt" hangs limp and dripping, suggesting that perhaps he, not she, is truly the more promiscuous of the two—and certainly the more messy (Fraser, illus. 18). Laqueur reproduces an image entitled "Jack and the Queen Killers," which features the figure of Liberty weighing the Queen's case against the King's; hers, symbolized by a mere dove, outweighs his, symbolized by a heaving, torn bag simply labeled "Green," as Liberty, a sword reading "JUSTICE" leaning against her left shoulder, holds to her left side, atop a book labeled "TRUTH," a shield bearing the image of the Queen (fig. 3).

Paulson reproduces two cartoons that provide an English precedent for representations of the figureheads of an oppressive government in porcine manner: James Gillray's 1806 etching "More PIGS than TEATS; or, the new Litter of hungry Grunters, sucking John Bulls old sow to death"; and the second, Gillray's etching of a year later, "The PIGS Possessed; or, the Broad bottom'd litter running headlong into the sea of Perdition" (*Representations of Revolution* figs. 44 and 45). Contemporary representations of the Queen Caroline Affair followed French Revolution-era cartoons and early nineteenth-century English radical propaganda in depicting various factions as swine. Claudette Hould reproduces two images of the French royal family depicted as, or described in caption in terms of, pigs—"The Family of Pigs Being Led Back to the Sty" (fig. 9), in which the royal family appear in human form but are transported in a pig-cart, and "The Pig Family Being Led Back to the Sty" (fig. 54), in which the family appear as pigs.[23] Similar depictions of oppressors as pigs recur throughout English cartoons excoriating the treatment of Queen Caroline: Fraser writes, "The King came off no better in . . . cartoons. He was the Pig of Pall Mall, with Castlereagh and Sidmouth, again seen as the chief ministers of the theatrical 'piece,' attempting to wash a huge boar with the facial features of the King. It was, Castlereagh gasps, a harder task than cleaning the Augean Stables" (412). As we shall see throughout *Swellfoot the Tyrant*, pigs operate as an embodiment central to Shelley's play, although Shelley will reverse the valences of the representations Hould reproduces to position the pigs as symbolic embodiments of the victims of tyranny.

Shelley might have been familiar with a variety of pro-Caroline pieces from Hunt's *Examiner*, one of the poet's regular sources of English news during his stay in Italy. Cameron cautions against assuming Shelley's knowledge of any of these texts in particular, but he points to one such piece, William Hone's *A New Catechism*, which appeared in *The Examiner* on 30 August 1818 and which drew from Edmund Burke's image of the masses as the swinish multitude to lay bare the miserable conditions under which those masses lived and worked (356); while Hone's piece predates the Queen Caroline Affair by two years, its image of swine nonetheless contributes to the radical vocabulary *The Examiner* made available to Shelley and other English radicals. Cameron also links Purganax's speech to the swine in *Swellfoot* (2.1) to *The Examiner*'s account of Castlereagh's address to the House of Parliament on 6 June 1820: in both scenes, the speakers begin by complimenting the "Boars" whom they address; and Castlereagh delivers his speech just after he presents the green bag that contains evidence of Caroline's transgressions, just as Purganax offers the Green Bag to the Boars as a device that will settle once and for all the question of their hero's innocence or guilt (358, 359). While in *Swellfoot* the Green Bag contains venom and other poisons, in the pro-Caroline

Examiner, the green bags in which Parliament held the evidence against the embattled Queen-to-be are denounced as "'venomous'," and readers are warned that while those bags had long "'infected and nauseated the people, . . . now [they are set] to infect the QUEEN'" (qtd. in Cameron 356). Even Shelley's central device of Iona's consent to the Green Bag test may have been suggested by *The Examiner*'s coverage of Caroline's trials: the newspaper reports that "'With a royal spirit she exclaimed, "Proceed! spatter me with you filth at your own discretion! . . . I defy you."'" (qtd. in Cameron 356). Based on the textual links White and Cameron provide, as well as on the representations I have considered of the French royal family as pigs, Shelley appears to have structured not only the general plot of *Swellfoot the Tyrant* but also its particular incidents around the goings-on of royal scandals as they were publicized in the radical media—specifically, in Hunt's *Examiner*—all of which draw heavily on the representations of political unrest and erotic transgression in French Revolution-era propaganda.

Mary Shelley's note contextualizes the composition of *Swellfoot the Tyrant* in a comic milieu she finds apropos to the absurdity of the real-life political scandal. First, she recalls the incident that inspired Shelley's play: "We were then at the baths of San Giuliano; a friend came to visit us on the day when a fair was held in the square, beneath our windows: Shelley read to us his Ode to Liberty; and was riotously accompanied by the grunting of a quantity of pigs brought for sale to the fair. He compared it to the 'chorus of frogs' in the satiric drama of Aristophanes; and it being an hour of merriment, and one ludicrous association suggesting another, he imagined a political satirical drama on the circumstances of the day, to which the pigs would serve as chorus—and Swellfoot was begun" (*WPS* 2:350). Mary Shelley's note points to the elaborate nests of contexts out of which her husband's satire arises, from the textual interpolation of Aristophanes' *Frogs* to the proximate sounds of pigs that accompanied the poet's performance of his exhortation to liberty. But it is the grunting of those pigs, I argue, that must be regarded far more seriously than Mary suggests, for two reasons: first, one of the most popular anti-monarchial pamphlets of 1820, *A Speech From the Throne*,[24] described the cries for reform as arising from a "swinish multitude,"[25] a phrase originally coined by Edmund Burke as a description for the masses, and which had become radical *lingua franca* by the 1790s (Scrivener 262);[26] second, the *OED* indicates that as late as 1857, the term "pig" functioned as slang for both "a police officer" and "a pressman in a printing office."[27] In Shelley's day, these entities were not as incongruous as they may seem to a twenty-first-century reader: police and pressman regularly engaged in contests for authority as the proliferation of publicity regarding the Queen Caroline Affair exceeded the power of the police to control it. Printers effectively usurped authority from the police, so that just as in Shelley's play, one set of "pigs" displaced another as the keepers of hegemonic order. The swinish multitudes of *Swellfoot the Tyrant,* I believe, *are* those radical pressman who reconstructed Queen Caroline's transgressions as symbolic acts of revolution, those artists and scriveners who assembled the stories about her Continental improprieties into a metanarrative of the struggle for freedom.[28] Along the way, those "pigs" transformed the sexually transgressive monarch into a revolutionary icon by portraying Caroline as both the victim of tyranny and the hope for liberation. In Queen Caroline, we find Revolution hypostatized in an eroticized female body, just as we have seen in a variety of French Revolution-era propaganda, among them Clément's "La France Républicaine. Ouvrant son Sein à tous les Français." Ultimately, Queen Caroline's continental scandals and the political upheavals they threatened to unleash function as an English re-playing of the French Revolution, the migration of that political drama to a new country under the alternative representational mode of the satire.[29] The horror of the French Revolution, one might say, is transformed in the humor of Shelley's play, so that nation and revolution are refined and re-presented, yet still powerfully poised as agents for the re-negotiation of power in the real world; and in Shelley's satire, the significance of the erotic icon is reversed, for where Marie Antoinette was lauded by reactionaries (see note 14), Caroline is adopted as an emblem of revolutionary fervor. The grunting of the pigs at San Giuliano may indeed have suggested the comic element that would inspire Shelley to lampoon the most notorious scandal of 1820, but it was the grunting of those other pigs—the radical pressmen who churned out pamphlet after pamphlet celebrating Caroline of Brunswick's transgressive engagements—that nursed Shelley's satire with the milk of ideological fervor.

As Anna Clark notes, the Queen Caroline Affair, like other royal scandals of the late eighteenth and early nineteenth centuries, "[was] neither anachronistic nor trivial; rather, [it] turned on the relation of virtue to power" (47). Throughout a variety of representational forms, press coverage of the scandal "resonated both with constitutional and class struggles and with domestic sexual politics" (49). Certainly, the Queen Caroline Affair marked a crisis in the public/private split, not only in that a woman was pushed into the spotlight of public scrutiny, but also in that tabloid accounts of her scandalous life abroad brought politics into the private sphere of the home, as "[e]ven 'the Kitchen walls [were] placarded with [accounts] of the Worst description'" (51).[30] The Queen Caroline Affair resonated throughout contemporary debates on the "place" of woman, as Clark observes: "The Caroline affair not only provided an arena for criticism of the double standard [of the separate, gendered spheres]; it opened up possibilities for women's political participation. In the 1810s, male radicals had occasionally scorned women's political efforts, but after over a hundred women and girls were wounded at the Peterloo massacre, they began to take them seriously. The Caroline affair intensified this process by bringing out not only women but women's concerns into the center of the political stage" (58). Clark's language is telling, for she codes the entire event as a drama enacted on "the political stage"; certainly, the division between real life and theatre begins to erode in the spectacle of the Queen Caroline Affair, and Shelley's satire surely participates in that erosion, that transgression.

Hunt's influence upon Shelley's response to the Queen Caroline Affair exemplifies the way in which the radical publisher's friendship with Shelley informed both the poet's political ideology and his textual strategies.[31] In the 9 June 1820 *Examiner*, Hunt charged the Queen's servants with duplicitous conduct on behalf of the King, and he characterized their disloyalty to Caroline as "'gather[ing] poison for one of those venomous Green Bags, which have so long infected and nauseated the people and now are to infect the Queen'" (qtd. in Newman Ivey White, "Shelley's Swell-Foot" 336). Hunt mentions the very device Shelley will pose as pivotal to the reversal of his satire's final scene, and Shelley echoes Hunt's language in describing the bag's "venom" and "perilous liquor" in *Swellfoot the Tyrant*.

Hunt's *The Descent of Liberty: A Mask* (1815) poses a number of ideas Shelley explores throughout his *œuvre*, and I believe that the image Hunt's title conjures may have informed the climax of *Swellfoot the Tyrant*. In both Hunt's mask and Shelley's satire, we see the figure of Liberty, personified as female, descend to earth in an instance of *Deus ex machina* to deliver the world out of bondage and into freedom. Hunt's play announces itself as "A Mask," and Shelley's satire picks up on the *double entendre* of that announcement by dressing the descending Liberty in "a semi-transparent veil" and having her "[pass] unnoticed" through the mob with whose members she forges a temporary alliance. Shelley's "veiling" of Liberty, I argue, is a form of masking, at once an obfuscation of Liberty's presence to the others gathered at the scene and Liberty's removal-by-disguise from the swinish multitude that complicates her return. Shelley's satire echoes Hunt's mask not only in its climactic image, but also in that it recalls the sub-genre of Hunt's text—the mask—by translating that literary form into theatrical costume, by (ad)dressing Hunt's genre in Liberty's veil. Hunt's text reads as pure play—pleasure—and even in its own day, the excessive nature of the mask would certainly have been regarded with some amusement.[32] Nevertheless, Hunt's play does make a number of important points. For example, while the play reads as a glitzy send-up of overwrought mythological dramas, Hunt grounds the mask in a radical utopian message that climaxes with the descent of Peace to Earth. *The Descent of Liberty*, despite its excess, must be understood in the context of Hunt's dedication to subversive politics, for, in the end, the play prophesies a utopia in which the salvation of the world proceeds from the triumph of peace and love over tyranny and oppression—an earnestly political agenda, to be sure, and one that is echoed throughout all of Shelley's work.

In *The Defense of Poetry*, Shelley famously claims that "Poets . . . are the unacknowledged legislators of the world" (*SPP* 508), but Hunt anticipates this figuration five years earlier in *The Descent of Liberty*: his Liberty wears the laurel crown of poets, those figures who " . . . on earth [give] happy voice / To Truth and Right . . . ."[33] For Hunt, as for Shelley, poets articulate truth and righteousness *because* they are the embodiments of Liberty—the very figure Hunt crowns with the laurel that symbolizes poetic achievement. Throughout his play, Hunt refers to the laurel not as the headdress of poets but, more specifically, as " . . . Liberty's crown . . . " (Prologue 36). Hunt's influence on Shelley is obvious, as he pre-dicts a basic tenet of his pupil's own philosophy: Liberty, Truth, Right, and Poetry all work together to bring about the manifestation of Peace on Earth. As we see in a number of Shelley's major works, in Hunt's *Descent of Liberty*, the utopian transformation of the world arises alongside the development of the arts, Music, Painting, and Poetry in particular. Finally, in the "Vision of REAL GLORY" that brings Hunt's mask to a close, we learn that Liberty is conjured by the collective action of peasants, not by the maneuverings of "the palace," Hunt's metonym for all oppressive arms of hegemony, government and the church chief among them. In short, *The Descent of Liberty* must be regarded as an important grounding text for the program of imaginative revolution Shelley develops throughout his career; specifically, I argue that Hunt's title alone may have inspired the key moment in Shelley's *Swellfoot the Tyrant*—the descent of Liberty that precipitates the toppling of monarchial order through the ascent of the erotic transgressor, Shelley's thinly veiled version of the real-life Queen Caroline.

Just as Hunt's *Descent of Liberty* may have inspired the climax of Shelley's satire, Sophocles' *Œdipus Rex* certainly provided the mythic context and the maneuvers across the public/private binary that we see at work throughout *Swellfoot the Tyrant*. Sophocles' play dramatizes the tragedy of a ruler whose domestic and sexual transgressions lead finally to his absolute undoing. Rooted in the densely woven connections between private life (the home and family) and public (social station and reputation), *Œdipus Rex* reminds us of the ultimate consequence incumbent upon any violation of the sanctity of the home: death, either real or symbolic. As the text opens, the blind seer Tiresias reluctantly admits to King Œdipus that the King, once the favorite of the gods, has become the source of all trouble in Thebes, a city gripped by plague and rocked by social unrest. Tiresias characterizes Œdipus' crimes as essentially domestic, for the King, unaware, has murdered his father and married his mother. Horrified by and ashamed of these sins against his family, Œdipus blinds himself by ripping his eyes out of their sockets, and he very publicly removes himself from power by explaining his blindness to his subjects as an appropriately self-inflicted punishment: the consequences of his actions have become too painful for him to see, the narratives of his life too excruciating for him to read.

A simple psychoanalytic reading of Sophocles' tragedy would make sense of the tale in terms of the castration anxiety that arises out of the phenomenon whose name derives from this legend—the so-called Œdipal complex. The boy, jealously harboring affection for the original love-object, his mother, comes to view his father as a rival for her affection and grows to fear being unmanned—castrated—by his father in retaliation for such transgressive desires.[34] Œdipus' self-inflicted blindness functions as a displaced castration, so that the attack on the organs symbolic of masculine power and control, the testicles, is displaced onto the eyes, the organs through which we master the world about us.[35] Œdipus' self-mutilation resonates symbolically as a (self-) castration, the inevitable return of the King's violations of familial relations, the archetypal punishment for his transgressions of domestic order.

Baker characterizes Shelley's apparent borrowings from Sophocles as the poet's "clever use of old materials . . . " (178): Shelley's satire is set in a land plagued by famine, and Sophocles' tragedy begins in a country overcome by plague; and in *Œdipus Rex* a chorus of supplicants seek relief from hunger, while in Shelley's satire a chorus of swine demand relief from oppression. As Baker notes, "the suggestion, as in Sophocles, is that a purgation of the land is in order, and in Shelley as in Sophocles, some business is devoted to the interpretation of an oracular prophecy" (178).

Significant to my understanding of *Swellfoot the Tyrant* is the emphasis in *Œdipus Rex* that Sophocles places on the king's erotic transgressions, "erotic" in the literally sexual penetration of his mother-wife and "transgressive" in the symbolically sexual penetration of his father (in murder, the overcoming of one body by another). These erotic transgressions set in motion the apparatus of social unrest and political instability that marks the tragedy of Sophocles' play, and a congruent set of erotic transgressions marks the processes through which tyrannical rule comes undone throughout *Swellfoot the Tyrant*. For both Sophocles and Shelley, the dismantling of tyrannical order arises out of transgressive erotic relationships whose disruptions of the domestic model resonate throughout the political arena. In Shelley's day, the trajectory of transgression charted throughout Sophocles' play gets re-enacted in the Queen Caroline Affair as a set of domestic quarrels—erotic transgressions—overlaps with contests for public presence and political power. *Œdipus Rex* and the Queen Caroline Affair both demonstrate the political significance of erotic transgression, for each stages the political turbulence incumbent upon the disintegration of the division between the public and private spheres.

Finally, I turn to Shelley's "Ode to Liberty," a poem I regard as a paratext to *Swellfoot the Tyrant* for several reasons. First, Shelley's reading of the "Ode to Liberty" at San Giuliano inspired the composition of the satire, as Mary Shelley's note indicates; second, the "Ode to Liberty" addresses in an outright, political fashion the symbolic figure to whom Shelley returns in his satire—Liberty; third, although contemporary politics might seem tangential to *Swellfoot the Tyrant,* their significance becomes quite clear when that satire is read through the lens of "Ode to Liberty." A careful reading of the "Ode" and an understanding of its contexts provides a useful basis for making sense of Shelley's political position as he sets out to compose *Swellfoot the Tyrant* some two months after he pens the "Ode."

In the "Ode to Liberty," Shelley provides a concise statement of his political principles, a thoroughgoing disquisition about the significance he accords love and liberty in the cyclical struggles between tyranny and freedom. In the "Ode to Naples" he specifically excoriates "the example of revolution set by France,"[36] and in the "Ode to Liberty" Shelley summarily rebukes all practices of tyranny, all programs of political domination. Michael Erkelenz emphasizes Shelley's awareness of the particular context of the generic ode as a public performance (64); not coincidentally, the "Ode to Liberty," as Scrivener indicates, was originally scheduled to be published in a collection entitled *Popular Songs,* a volume that would have included a number of Shelley's most overtly political texts, among them "Lines Written During the Castlereagh Administration," "Song to the Men of England," "Similes for Two Political Characters [originally entitled "To S———th and C———gh"[37]]," "Sonnet: England 1819," and *The Mask of Anarchy* (227). But with the cancellation of that volume, the "Ode to Liberty" first appeared in Shelley's *Prometheus Unbound* volume of 1820, a book pointedly issued one year to the day after the notorious Peterloo Massacre (233), a tragic political misstep in which government troops stormed an unarmed crowd of 5000-8000 protesters in St. Peter's Fields in Manchester, injuring hundreds and killing eleven. Regarded by many in Shelley's circle as a blatant example of the government's disregard for the well-being of its citizens, the Peterloo Massacre marked an important political moment for radical Englishmen like Shelley, and his publication of the *Prometheus Unbound* volume on the first anniversary of that signal event certainly alerted his readers to the volume's radical political engagements.

Scrivener describes Shelley's "Ode to Liberty" as "*A Philosophical View of Reform* in reverse" (239), and Cameron identifies *Reform* (1819) as the first text in which Shelley addresses the significance of the Spanish Revolution (364). Just one year after its composition, the revolution that Shelley predicted in *A Philosophical View of Reform* transformed power throughout Spain in what Cameron describes as a "bloodless triumph" (364). A number of the achievements of the Spanish Revolution paralleled those demanded by English reformers, including the granting of voting rights to all literate men, the introduction of a system of representation, and the biennial election of parliament with the barring of government officers from its seats (364-365). In addition, the Spanish Revolution ushered in a number of progressive rights, including freedom of the press, and it put an end to centuries of state-sanctioned religious tyranny by abolishing the Spanish Inquisition (Scrivener 239). In short, as Scrivener explains, "the Spaniards demonstrated for Shelley that liberty [could] indeed be wrested from a tyrant" (239). The poet thus poses the Spanish Revolution as the triumph of liberty, and he devotes the "Ode to Liberty" as much to praising the Spanish Revolution as to urging his fellow Englishmen to mount similarly bloodless campaigns.

Shelley composed the "Ode to Liberty" between March and July of 1820, and the poem appeared as the final piece in the *Prometheus Unbound* volume, a textual history that contributes significantly to the poem's meaning: the volume's eponymous poem articulates the poet's political vision by recounting the attempts of the lovers Prometheus and Asia to conjure liberty on Earth through their public and private acts, their political and erotic engagements.[38] As I shall demonstrate in Chapter V, *Prometheus Unbound* deals principally with the power of love to undo tyranny. At both the beginning and the end of Shelley's volume, then, liberty is aligned with love, first in the epic poem itself, and finally in the "Ode to Liberty." Throughout the book, Shelley examines the gesture with which he opens the volume, love, as a specifically political one that parallels his call for liberty, so that love and liberty are consistently constructed as "[t]wins of a single destiny," to borrow a line from the Ode, as forces that arise at the same moment and operate in the interest of the same goal (192).

Shelley's "Ode" addresses the personified Liberty in what Donald H. Reiman and Sharon B. Powers characterize as a prayerful fashion (*SPP* 229 n 1), so that throughout the poem, Liberty stands in as a Supreme Being, an agent to whom one appeals for the redemption of the world. The epigraph to the "Ode" is taken from Byron's *Childe Harold's Pilgrimage* (1812-1818), and Reiman and Powers note that Shelley's selection of that passage announces his poem's political commitment, since the lines "begin the last of twenty-one stanzas . . . [in which Byron describes] the struggle between tyranny and Liberty" (229 n 2). Even before its first line, Shelley's "Ode to Liberty" enters into an ongoing political dialogue by establishing its relationship to a text that is politically (and, importantly, erotically) engaged: the tale of the first Byronic hero.

The first line of Shelley's "Ode" introduces an important aspect of the poet's agenda: his belief in the cyclical nature of political struggle. Frequently depicted in the openings of his works, in the "Ode," Shelley suggests that the processes of cyclicality generate the movements of history: "A glorious people vibrated again / The lightning of the nations; . . . " (1-2). The emphasis Shelley places on the word "again" by positioning it at the end of his poem's first line alerts the reader to the centrality of cyclical processes—what we might think of as the condition of "*againness*"—to political struggles: Liberty comes in waves, the poet suggests, so that each onslaught of tyranny eventually succumbs to freedom, and the cycle begins again. As Shelley will suggest in the image of the "eagle and serpent wreath'd in fight" that punctuates the opening of *Laon and Cythna,* the struggle between freedom and oppression proves a never-ending cycle, a dizzying coil from which humankind cannot escape so long as it remains trapped in the symbols and symbology of history, in the self-involving coils of life-as-we-know-it.[39]

In the second stanza, Shelley describes the state of the world without Liberty: it is a sterile place that simply "[Hangs] in the cloud of all-sustaining air", " . . . this divinest universe" that is " . . . yet a chaos and a curse, / For [Liberty] wert not . . . " (21-24). Without Liberty, the natural world reverts to utter disorder:

> The spirit of the beasts was kindled there,
> And of the birds, and of the watery forms,
> And there was war among them, and despair
> Within them, raging without truce or terms:
> . . . .
> The bosom of their violated nurse
> Groan'd, for beasts warr'd on beasts, and worms on worms
> And men on men; each heart was a hell of storms.
>
> (24-30)

Reminiscent of the setting of Byron's "Darkness" (1816), another poem that bemoans the fall of the world into the chaos of a bloody revolution, Shelley's "Ode" describes an Earth torn apart by opposition and despair, a globe devolved into a vast wasteland. In the deepest reaches of the oceans, separated from the warring factions that plague the world, the forces Shelley promotes throughout his works as the instruments of Liberty—art, poetry, and philosophy—lie dormant, their powers reduced to a state of suspended animation by tyranny's numbing effects:

> . . . like unfolded flowers beneath the sea,
> Like the man's thought dark in the infant's brain,
> Like aught that is which wraps what is to be,
> Art's deathless dreams lay veiled by many a vein
> Of Parian stone; and, yet a speechless child,
> Verse murmured, and Philosophy did strain
> Her lidless eyes for thee . . . .
>
> (54-60)

The description Shelley provides for what we might call the "places" of art, poetry, and philosophy under the reign of tyranny remind the reader that even in the worst of times, when nature and man have turned against each other and Liberty seems to have fled the Earth, these children of freedom wait to be (re-)born, even as the cycles of political struggle pave the way for the return of Liberty in the overthrow of tyranny.

But what exactly is this tyranny that grips the earth, drowning its "speechless child[ren]" under waves of contention? Shelley particularizes the instruments of tyranny throughout the "Ode," repeatedly singling out Christianity as the primary force that bars Liberty from the world:

> Like one fierce cloud over a waste of waves
> Hung tyranny; beneath, sate deified
> The sister-pest, congregator of slaves,
> Into the shadow of her pinions wide
> Anarchs and priests, who feed on gold and blood
> Till with the stain their inmost souls are dyed,
> Drove the astonished herds of men from every side.
>
> (39-45)

Here, Shelley aligns political infidels—"Anarchs," or tyrants—with members of the clergy, and thus he implies connections between religious power and political oppression, disparaging the institutions of Church and State as "Twins of a single destiny" (192) who divert the world from Liberty towards oppression, destruction, and physical and spiritual decay.

After musing on the two cradles of Liberty—ancient Athens and Rome, both pre-Christian civilizations—Shelley indicts the force that drove Liberty away from the earth, Christianity, as "The Galilean serpent [that] forth did creep, / And made thy world an indistinguishable heap" (119-120). He characterizes the first millennium of the Christian Empire as

> ... a thousand years
> Bred from the slime of deep oppression's den,
> [Which] Dyed all [Liberty's] liquid light with blood and tears,
> Till thy sweet stars could weep the stain away ....
>
> (167-170)

Next, Shelley aligns tyranny with monarchy by describing that institution as a diminutive form of Christianity: where Christianity is "The Galilean serpent" (119), monarchy is a "reluctant worm" (225), a smaller, less powerful manifestation of the same evil codified in the Christian doctrine. "O, that the free would stamp the impious name / Of KING into the dust!,"[40] Shelley exclaims, reminding us of the political agenda upon which the return to Liberty is contingent—the toppling of all institutions of power, figured here as an act that poses real force ("stamp[ing]") against the power of signification ("the impious *name*").

Shelley's strategy for slaying the twin-monster of Christianity/Monarchy hinges on his ability to subvert the very linguistic codes of Christianity itself, so that in a series of adept figurations, he "stamp[s]" on the "impious name" that galvanizes Christian belief, Jesus Christ—a figure whom Shelley deeply admires, but whose real message, Shelley believes, has been perverted into tyranny by those who call themselves Christians and who thus misrepresent and, in fact, undo Jesus' message of tolerance and love. To this end, Shelley poses Liberty as the object of Christ's mission and thereby evacuates the name "Jesus Christ" of the totalizing significance with which Christianity invests it; in Shelley's vision, Christ's putatively original message of love is revealed to be nothing more—or less—than one mortal man's articulation of the transcendent and eternal project of Liberty.

First, Shelley describes the descent of Liberty to Earth in the language of Biblical rapture, so that Liberty's return is hypothesized as congruent to the second coming of Christ—a correspondence clearly drawn from Hunt's *Descent*—and the sudden and stunned reactions of men parallel those prophesied in the Biblical book of Revelation:

> The eager hours and unreluctant years
> As on a dawn-illumined mountain stood,
> . . . .
> When like heaven's sun girt by the exhalation
> Of its own glorious light, thou didst arise,
> Chasing thy foes from nation to nation
> Like shadows: as if day had cloven the skies
> At dreaming midnight o'er the western wave,
> Men started, staggering with a glad surprise,
> Under the lightnings of thine unfamiliar eyes.
>
> (151-152, 159-165)

Next, Shelley demonstrates the power of linguistic formulations to bring about the very tribulation the descent of Liberty precipitates; specifically, he reminds us that this rapturous moment has been prefigured in "The voices of . . . bards and sages" who call on Liberty's name (80):

> The voices of . . . bards and sages thunder
> With an earth-awakening blast
> Through the caverns of the past;
> Religion veils her eyes; Oppression sinks aghast:
> A winged sound of joy, and love, and wonder,
> Which soars where Expectation never flew,

> Rending the veil of space and time asunder!
> One ocean feeds the clouds, and streams, and dew;
> One sun illumines heaven; one spirit vast
> With life and love makes chaos ever new,
> As Athens does the world with thy delight renew.
>
> (80-90)

The descent of Liberty precedes the cleansing of the earth because her presence chases away those twin-tormentors who have given the world over to chaos and war—"Religion" and "Oppression." Following Liberty's glorious return, peace—anatomized in the "Ode" as " . . . joy, and love, and wonder"—dissolves all markers of difference and division, so that an ailing, fragmented world may be unified and resurrected:

> One ocean feeds the clouds . . .
> One sun illumines heaven; one spirit vast
> With life and love makes chaos ever new.
>
> (89-90)

Finally, the now-awakened Art, yet another earthly manifestation of Liberty, steps in to assume the place of Christ as the "ardent intercessor" (249) between man and nature.

By the end of the "Ode," Liberty has defeated Christianity by dismantling its claim to exclusive power. To prove this victory, Shelley poses Liberty in a symbolic undoing of the Christian doctrine by casting her in the guise of Satan, thus demonstrating the false nature of the merely linguistic division between good and evil and erasing any symbolic differences represented by the signifiers "Christ" and "Lucifer." In the reign of Liberty, all institutions that structure the world according to binary oppositions (represented throughout the poem in the double-binary of good-Christ/evil-Lucifer) are dissolved, so that Shelley alternately cloaks Liberty in the vestments of Christ *and* Lucifer:

> Come Thou, but lead out of the inmost cave
> Of man's deep spirit, as the *morning-star*
> Beckons the Sun from the Eoan wave,
> Wisdom. . . .
>
> (256-259, emphasis added)

As Shelley's readers would certainly have known, the "morning-star" is Venus, the celestial symbol for Lucifer. While Liberty's function throughout the "Ode" is clearly Christ-like, here, Shelley poses Lucifer as the agent who paves the way for Liberty's return. In the system of unity or Oneness that Shelley poses as the antidote for all opposition, Christ and Lucifer are unmasked as inseparable so that, in the end, they may be reconciled as one.

Throughout the "Ode," Shelley makes clear the harsh cost Liberty exacts from those who bar her from the Earth, those warmongers whose investments in political division have fragmented the world and chased Liberty from it:

> And in thy smile, and by thy side,
> Saintly Camillus lived, and firm Atillus died,
> . . . .
> Thou didst desert . . .
> The senate of the tyrants: they sunk prone
> Slaves of one tyrant: . . . .
>
> (97-98, 101-103)

Here, Shelley exposes the evil of single-minded tyrants by counterpoising them to Camillus, a "Roman general [who] rejected the proposal by a traitorous teacher that [he] secure the surrender of Falerii by using the teacher's pupils—the sons of that city's leading men—as hostages" (*SPP* 231 n 6). Liberty smiles on those who resist the tactics of tyranny and oppression, but she destroys those like Atillus whose lives are given over to the pursuit of war for the sake of war itself, to the perpetual maintenance of political division without regard to a greater good. Similarly, Shelley denounces the French Revolution as inimical to the project of Liberty, for in

> . . . Bacchanals of blood
> Round France, the ghastly vintage, stood
> Destruction's sceptered slaves, and Folly's mitred brood!
>
> (171-173)

In Shelley's view, all war, no matter what its purported object, opposes Liberty; consequently, Liberty turns her back against all warmongers and waits for such men to destroy each other, to cancel out each other's evil ways. For Shelley, Liberty arises out of engagements at the level of language—signification—so that in his system, Art, Poetry, Philosophy, and Education function far more effectively as tactics for revolution than physical combat. Shelley's revolution, as countless scholars have observed, is an absolutely imaginative one, an intellectual transformation through which the language of love alone leads the way toward freedom, while physical battle and the discourses of hatred only redouble oppressive structures.

Throughout the "Ode to Liberty," Shelley extols freedom as the mechanism that will transform the world, and he praises a number of nations whose histories demonstrate the power of Liberty to set men free—ancient Athens and Rome, Florence, Spain, and England during the Saxon and Reformation periods. As he does throughout his works, in the "Ode" Shelley metonymizes political conflict in the imagery of landscape to position the physical world as the text in which his abstract notions about Liberty find legibility:

> Spain calls [Liberty] now, as with its thrilling thunder
> Vesuvius wakens Ætna, and the cold
> Snow-crags by its reply are cloven in sunder:
> O'er the lit waves every Æolian isle
> From Pithecusa to Pelorus
> Howls, and leaps, and glares in chorus:
> They cry, Be dim; ye lamps of heaven suspended o'er us.
>
> (182-188)

For Shelley, the physical world is an agent activated by the promise of Liberty; as Liberty prepares her descent to Earth, the physical world howls, leaps, glares, and is split asunder; in short, the changes Liberty promises are figured forth in rapturous alterations of physical and political landscapes.[41]

We see throughout Shelley's "Ode to Liberty" the arsenal of techniques to which the poet turns time and again to articulate his revolutionary vision of the project of liberty-through-love. Posed as the forces that dissolve all binary oppositions into the harmonious One and visualized as the powers poised to reconfigure the very landscape of the earth itself, Liberty and her "[twin] of a single destiny," Love, emerge as the guiding principles of Shelley's philosophy, the master-tropes that inform all of his works. As I will demonstrate in my readings of *The Cenci, Julian and Maddalo, Epipsychidion, Laon and Cythna,* and *Prometheus Unbound,* Shelley continually investigates the motivations and strategies according to which liberty-through-love may be achieved—or diverted. But first, I turn to *Swellfoot the Tyrant* to explore Shelley's interest in the potential for erotic transgression to alter political realities. As in the "Ode to Liberty," in *Swellfoot the Tyrant,* the descent of Liberty brings about rapturous changes in the real world: where the "Ode to Liberty" personifies the physical landscape as leaping, howling, and glaring at Liberty's descent, in *Swellfoot the Tyrant,* the physical bodies of tyrants hypostatize political realities, and their physical transmutations underscore the potential for Liberty to deform all manifestations of tyranny, to chase them from the stage of the world.

The political and literary contexts that inform *Swellfoot the Tyrant* all point to Shelley's deep investment in the struggle for liberty as well as to his understanding that hegemonic authority may be dismantled only through repeated violations of traditional order. In unsettling the binary pairs that underwrite the social order—among them public/private, power/subjection, male/female, and parent/lover—the Queen Caroline Affair, Sophocles' *Œdipus Rex,* and Shelley's "Ode to Liberty" set the stage for the renegotiation of power in the real world. Throughout the works I consider in this chapter and the three to follow, Shelley turns to the disintegration—through transgression, or overlap—of binary divisions as he plots a vision of utopia, a liberated world in which tyranny cedes to freedom as subjection and domination succumb to ecstatic embrace.

∞ ∞ ∞ ∞ ∞

The title page for *Œdipus Tyrannus; or, Swellfoot the Tyrant* raises a number of issues central to the play, beginning with Shelley's naming of the so-called "Tragedy" after its anti-hero. A direct translation of the Greek "Œdipus," "Swellfoot" recalls the origin of the King's name: upon the orders of his father, the infant Œdipus' feet were pierced with a sword to hasten his death-by-exposure on Mount Cithaeron, an ordeal the young child survived to become known for his unnaturally swollen feet, the direct result of a paternally inflicted injury and thus the corporeal register of patriarchal tyranny. But beyond its mere relation to the name of that legendary King, the more general notion of "swelling" informs the whole of Shelley's satire. The *OED* provides a number of definitions for "swell," including an adjectival form that describes one who is "proud or arrogant." Swellfoot's arrogance, his pompous preening and exaggerated self-importance, finds corporeal manifestation in his astonishing girth. The tyrant's narcissistic contemplation of his obesity therefore locates a range of selfish pleasures at the level of the body, each of which symbolizes the tyrant's political station: in other words, Shelley poses Swellfoot's fat as an outgrowth of his selfishly deployed power to expose the relationship between the King's slothfulness and the processes of tyranny. In Swellfoot, we find yet another politicized body, but where the bodies of Queen Caroline and Marie Antoinette were appropriated as desirable images for the promise of revolution, Shelley poses Swellfoot's corpulent body as an undesirable symbol, a disgusting manifestation of the oppressive weight of tyranny.

Shelley's main title brands Œdipus a tyrant, and the subtitle's translation of the King's name functions in a similarly didactic manner. "Swelling" also describes "the rising or heaving of the sea or other body of water in a succession of long rolling waves, as after a storm" (*OED*). In addition to its connotations of excess, arrogance, and girth, "swelling" suggests the temporal nature of power: like waves, power rises and falls, overcoming other powers in its wake only to find itself subsumed under still more powers that loom behind it. The tyrant of Shelley's play metonymizes the broader condition of tyranny, and in the rise and fall of Swellfoot we see the ebb and flow that mark the cyclical nature of power in general. Thus, "Œdipus" names not only a person but a distinguishing physical mark, and "Swellfoot" describes not only Shelley's "Tyrant" but also the cyclical processes—the swelling of the waves of power—that will drag that tyrant down in the turbulence of historical progression.[42]

More generally, Shelley's title alerts his readers to the story of a King whose domestic engagements lead to his undoing. Like his classical analogue, Œdipus, Swellfoot falls victim to the maelstrom of domestic upheaval, here in the return of what we might call the phallicized wife, a Queen who rises ascendant over her King, an "other" ruler who wrests the symbolically phallic scepter from her husband, figuratively castrating him and materially usurping his political power. We find thus embedded in the play's title a wide range of devices that function pedagogically, each instructing the reader how to make sense of Shelley's so-called "tragedy." Taking classical legend for its basis, Shelley's play explores the excesses of tyranny, the cyclicality of power, and the symbolic castration that figure forth any tyrant's inevitable downfall. Shelley's title alone announces a far more serious agenda than most scholars have recognized in his play, and the full texts of the title page and "ADVERTISEMENT" bear out my argument about the play's centrality to Shelley's broader project of liberty-through-love. To demonstrate how Shelley's satire lays bare the model upon which all of his works are structured—the erotic as political engagement—I will consider the play in terms of the following concerns: tyranny (in particular, its relationship to excess, phallicism, the body, and evil), liberty, language, and sexual transgression.

In the center of the title page for *Swellfoot the Tyrant*, Shelley notes that his play is "TRANSLATED FROM THE ORIGINAL DORIC." Shelley's fictitious attribution does not operate primarily to distance him from any political fallout the play might provoke, as some have suggested;[43] instead, by attributing the entire text to an only vaguely identified source, Shelley glosses the satire with his standard writerly agenda of what we might refer to as pluralized authority—the weaving together of (purportedly) mediated narratives.[44] Shelley's attribution of his play to "THE ORIGINAL DORIC" pluralizes the satire's context, displacing it from merely local concerns and thereby implying something about its transhistorical significance: while the play ostensibly recounts a centuries'-old tale, any contemporary reader would certainly have recognized in it the best-known scandal of Shelley's day. Finally, the displacement of the play's origin to antiquity suggests Shelley's self-consciousness about the historical nature of his project: by incorporating the language and imagery of so many contemporary pamphlets, Shelley not only emphasizes their local significance but also demonstrates the political power of domestic struggles in any historical period. Shelley recognizes that the problems posed by Caroline (or, in the play, Iona) are not particular to her historical moment; rather, these figure transhistorically, disrupting power in a wide range of epochs. Although in his letters Shelley derides Caroline as "a vulgar cook maid" and expresses only a tepid enthusiasm for her exploits, *Swellfoot* demonstrates how thoroughly Shelley recognizes the Queen Caroline Affair as an archetypal narrative of tremendous political significance because of the ways in which it traces the relationship between private acts and public station to demonstrate the power of erotic engagements to compromise political stability. The "tragedies" of Swellfoot and Iona and of George and Caroline are identical, for both expose all struggles for political power as domestic upheavals writ large.

The epigraph to Shelley's play, taken from an oracle that predicts Swellfoot's downfall, polarizes the play's principle characters in a traditional self/other opposition by prophesying the reversal of power fulfilled at the play's end:

> ———Choose Reform or civil-war,
> When thro' thy streets, instead of hare with dogs,
> A CONSORT-QUEEN shall hunt a King with hogs,
> Riding on the IONIAN MINOTAUR.
>
> (*WPS* 2:321)

Here, Iona is constructed as *a priori* distanced from power, so that even before the play's beginning, she is posed as an oppositional force, an other who threatens to disrupt the King's rule. In both Shelley's satire and Sophocles' tragedy, the criminalized body is symbolically castrated, so that the threatening body is deformed into a disempowered other: in Sophocles' tragedy, Œdipus' ripping out of his own eyes enacts a displaced self-castration and transforms the once-powerful King into a disempowered other; in Shelley's play, the Queen's assumption of power is marked by her symbolic castration of the King and his relegation to disempowered status. Shelley's play imagines the next step in this progression, but rather than envisioning that step as a utopia in which an emancipatory order liberates the world from oppression, he demonstrates the consequences that are inevitable for a too-sudden transfer of power: in "castrating" Swellfoot, Iona grafts the King's phallus—along with the tyranny it symbolizes—onto her own body, thus perpetuating the very order her domestic transgressions might otherwise have deflated.

Shelley's "ADVERTISEMENT" to *Swellfoot the Tyrant* contributes significantly to the reading of the play I propose. Announcing that "THIS TRAGEDY is one of a triad, or system of three Plays . . . elucidating the wonderful and appalling fortunes of the SWELLFOOT dynasty," Shelley inserts his text into an imaginary dialogue with two other, non-extant plays, which he identifies as "'*Swellfoot in Angaria*' and '*Charite*'" (2:321). This set of plays mirrors the structure and movement of the strophe, antistrophe, and epode of the Pindaric Ode, the poetic form on which Shelley models his "Ode to Liberty," an important grounding text for *Swellfoot the Tyrant*. Each installment in the (supposed) *Œdipus Tyrannus—Swellfoot in Angaria—Charite* triad extends one of the three parts of the Pindaric Ode. The strophe or first installment of the triad, *Œdipus Tyrannus*, celebrates the power and majesty of the Swellfoot dynasty and concludes rather suddenly with the downfall of that regime. The antistrophe or second installment, *Swellfoot in Angaria*, presumably describes the experiences of Swellfoot in forced labor.[45] The epode or third installment, *Charite*, probably describes Swellfoot as he is forgiven and redeemed. Just as strophe, antistrophe, and epode alternate throughout an ode to chart the rises and falls of an individual's fortune (or, more broadly, his power), so, too, does Shelley's imaginary triad document Swellfoot's fluctuating position in the waves of fortune and power, from the heights of the strophe to the depths of the antistrophe to the redemption of the epode. Like waves, strophe, antistrophe, and epode alternate, constantly exchanging primary, secondary and tertiary positions. The literary model of the ode, with its formal emphasis on the cyclical nature of fortune and with its wave-like patterns of might and despair, thus provides a useful model for making sense of Shelley's imaginary triad, for the titles of those plays suggest the precise patterns of cyclicality I have shown the name "Swellfoot" to connote.

Shelley claims throughout the ADVERTISEMENT that his translation remains faithful to the original Doric, with the exception of his own scrupulous "suppressing [of] a seditious and blasphemous Chorus of the Pigs and Bulls at the last act" (321); but by mentioning the unmentionable, Shelley privileges the very material he claims to have purged from his translation. Because Shelley alerts his reader to the content of the censored passages, the semblance of those transgressions remains present throughout the entire play; in other words, by pointing out the suppressed Chorus, Shelley enters blasphemy and sedition into his text under erasure. Further, this entrance-by-omission heightens the relevance of the suppressed Chorus to the play as a whole: where the objectionable Chorus is located in "the last act" of the supposed original, Shelley advertises that material at the beginning of his own translation, so that even before we begin reading *Swellfoot the Tyrant*, Shelley's ADVERTISEMENT infuses the entire text with the blasphemy and sedition he claims to have purged. By entering the Chorus of the Pigs under erasure—that is, by calling attention to the element he claims to have omitted from the play—Shelley ironically recovers the piece within his own expurgation of it, and thus he teases his reader, insinuating a complicity between reader and writer through this transgression of textual propriety. In short, Shelley's inclusion-by-expurgation of the Chorus of Pigs situates his text as a site of pleasure and play, a space in which the intended and the apparent slip around each other's edges, at once acknowledging power and subverting it.

Next, Shelley addresses the issue of the name "Swellfoot" and notes that "The word Hoydipouse (or more properly Œdipus,) has been rendered literally SWELLFOOT, without its having been conceived necessary to determine whether a swelling of the hind or the fore feet of the Swinish Monarch is particularly indicated" (2:321). Casting aside any specific corporeal referent for the tyrant's name, Shelley pluralizes the possible sites at which swelling might find form on the monarch's body. As I will argue throughout my discussion of the play, I read Shelley's images of swelling as phallic, as symbolic of the political control and dominance that contribute to Tyrant Swellfoot's bodily pleasures. Whether the swelling occurs in the

King's stomach, hind feet, or fore feet, Shelley remains clearly aware of the *double entendre* of all swelling itself, so that in each of these locations we recognize the tyrant's displaced penis, for each of the tyrant's swellings metonymizes what we might characterize as the rigid rule of tyranny in which he takes particular pleasure.

Like the title page, Shelley's ADVERTISEMENT functions pedagogically to introduce the political agenda according to which his satire is to be read. However, the critical history of the play suggests that most readers have dismissed the text with laughter, contempt, or, in the case of Mary Shelley, embarrassment;[46] few have looked beyond its surface humor to appreciate what I will show to be *Swellfoot*'s truly important argument. In short, even as we enjoy the humor of Shelley's play, we must not allow that superficial reaction to obfuscate the serious engagements laughter masks; for, as my reading will reveal, *Swellfoot the Tyrant* investigates the possibilities for Shelley's program of liberty-through-love and provides a model for the sorts of literary/political overlappings he explores throughout his works.

Shelley's *Dramatis Personæ* have been the subject of some speculation, but the principal guide I will follow is Newman Ivey White's exhaustive excursus on the matter in his 1921 *PMLA* article. Put simply, Tyrant Swellfoot is meant to stand for King George, and his Ministers Purganax, Dakry, and Laoctonos represent a number of George's own minions, among them Sidmouth and Castlereagh (White, "Shelley's Swellfoot" 340). While I have already reviewed the prevalence of the Gadfly, the Leech, and the Rat in contemporary radical propaganda, in Shelley's play the Gadfly assumes particular significance because of its relationship to the play's hero, Iona Taurina, Shelley's thinly disguised representation of Queen Caroline. As Stuart Curran explains, the name "Iona" derives from the classical Io (or Isis), the daughter of Prometheus, another of Shelley's important revolutionary heroes.[47] According to Greek myth, Zeus enraged his wife Hera by falling in love with the beautiful maiden Io. In some versions of the legend, Hera transformed Io into a cow in order to protect her and to quash her husband's infidelity; other versions of the myth claim that Zeus caused Io's transformation in an attempt to deceive Hera about their affair.[48] Whichever the case, Shelley's nomenclature preserves the basic plots of both legends, since Iona's last name, "Taurina," recalls her bovine heritage. The language of Shelley's play points out the connection between Queen Iona and the mythical Io quite explicitly: as Purganax expresses his hatred for the Queen, he is interrupted by the chorus of swine, and in their truncation of the Queen's name, we hear the unmistakable articulation of her mythical analogue:

> Aroint ye! thou unprofitable worm!
> And thou, dull beetle, get thee back to hell!
> To sting the ghosts of Babylonian kings,
> And the ox-headed Io—
>
> (1.1.272-275)

Curran remarks on traditions that link Io to Venus as well as to "the Hebrew Isha, the ancient name for woman" (215 n 24). He notes that Isha is a cognate for Asia, the name of Prometheus' lover, the woman who activates that hero's triumphant release (215 n 24). Thus, Iona embodies physical beauty (as Venus), represents all women (as Isha), and figures importantly in the tradition to which all of Shelley's heroes belong, since her eroticized body emerges as crucial to the project of revolution. As my discussions throughout this book will demonstrate, all of Shelley's heroes—female and male—are feminized, so that each must be understood in terms of their oppositional (or what I will discuss as their specifically feminine) relationship to established order. The politicization of Iona's body poses her as a particularly significant touchstone in the more general cast of feminized heroes we see throughout Shelley's works, for even though she will be shown ultimately to depart from the project of liberty, the various devices that mark her body as oppositional, as other—femininity and sexual transgression—re-emerge in the bodies of all of Shelley's heroes.

Of equal significance is the fact that while Iona Taurina does not appear until act 2, her presence looms throughout the progress of the entire play, for even before the play begins, Shelley's epigraph positions the Queen as an important player in the tragedy's negotiations of power. Clearly, Iona figures as the central force of the play, one so powerful that throughout the entire act preceding her appearance on the stage, Shelley constructs her as the primary catalyst for the instability of Swellfoot's tyrannical reign, the central character around whose presence-in-absence the anxiety of Swellfoot's regime coalesces.

Tyranny

I. Excess

The setting that opens *Œdipus Tyrannus* provides a spectacular referent for the play's (supposed) audience,[49] and Shelley's use of that set demonstrates the prescience he accords visual tableaux: "*A magnificent Temple, built of thigh-bones and deaths'-heads, and tiled with scalps. Over the Altar the statue of Famine, veiled; a number of boars, sows, and sucking-pigs, crowned with thistle, shamrock, and oak, sitting on the steps, and clinging round the Altar of the Temple*" (2:323). Shelley visualizes the physical space of Swellfoot's rule as a temple to lack, a shrine to the denial of bodily needs and the physical suffering such denial incurs. Made up of the body parts of the dead, the temple's figure of "Famine" embodies the very condition that affords the King's excesses—the terminal suffering of his subjects throughout the British Empire: the thistle, shamrock, and oak represent Scotland, Ireland, and England.[50] To underscore Swellfoot's willful blindness to that condition, Shelley directs him to enter the stage " . . . *in his Royal robes, without perceiving the Pigs*" (2:323) and, shortly later, to address them thus:

> . . . Ha! what are ye,
> Who, crowned with leaves devoted to the Furies,
> Cling round this sacred shrine?
>
> (1.1.18-20)

Shelley returns to the play's opening set in the final scene: "*The interior of the Temple of* FAMINE. *The statue of the Goddess, a skeleton clothed in party-coloured rags, seated upon a heap of skulls and loaves intermingled. A number of exceedingly fat Priests in black garments arrayed on each side, with marrow-bones and cleavers in their hands. A flourish of trumpets*" sounds as Swellfoot enters, accompanied by his Ministers and "IONA TAURINA *guarded*" (344). At the play's end, Shelley's stage directions solidify the connection the opening setting implies between tyranny (represented by Famine), monarchy (Swellfoot and his minions) and religion (the Priests); and in the play's final moment, Shelley poses the figural embodiments against Iona, who enters the stage "guarded," her body marked clearly as an oppositional site/sight, as a force of potential rupture.

The play's final scene opens with a Chorus of Priests whose song disrobes the figure of Famine to expose the particular mechanism of tyranny she embodies: "Goddess bare, and gaunt, and pale, / Empress of the world, all hail!" (2.2.1-2). The Priests' celebration of Swellfoot's tyrannical rule exposes the wedding of Fortune (excess) and Famine (lack) in the phrase "Empress of the World," a conventional apostrophe for Fortune, here directed to the image of Famine. Thus, Shelley lays bare the technology of tyranny his play has exposed and reminds his audiences that excesses of power (coded as fortune) depend upon the maintenance of oppression (famine). The Tyrant Swellfoot, Shelley argues, rules by forced labor (angariation), and he maintains his power through exploitation.

Next, The Chorus of Priests names the forces that participate in the maintenance of tyranny:

> Thro' thee, for emperors, kings, and priests and lords
> Who rule by viziers, sceptres, bank-notes, words,
> The earth pours forth its plenteous fruits,
> . . . .
> Those who consume these fruits thro' thee grow fat,
> Those who produce these fruits thro' thee grow lean.
>
> (2.2.7-12)

While we might imagine that all four of these guises of tyranny—emperors, kings, priests, and lords—rule through the range of devices Shelley lists, the parallel placement of two nouns in lines 7 and 8—kings and sceptres—suggests other such interline pairings. Of special significance is the interline connection between "priests" and "bank-notes." With this coupling, Shelley aligns two institutions, the Church and paper money, that he consistently attacks throughout his works, again reminding us of the central place *Swellfoot* occupies in his larger corpus.[51]

The Chorus of Priests that opens the final act returns us to my observations about the play's subtitle:

> Through thee [Famine] the sacred SWELLFOOT dynasty
> Is based upon a rock amid that sea
> Whose waves are swine—so let [the dynasty] ever be!
>
> (2.2.17-19)

The Priests recognize the cyclical nature of power and acknowledge the precarious place the Swellfoot regime occupies as it bobs on the currents that threaten to overcome it, the waves of swine who prepare to rise in revolt. And by the play's end, even the Priests recognize the inevitability of the tyrant's downfall in the growing unrest of the swinish multitude, so that as the play draws to a close, Shelley invokes exactly the connotations of the name "Swellfoot" I have suggested. But even after the Chorus of Priests alerts him to the swells of historical progression, Swellfoot remains as oblivious to the rancor of his subjects as he was in his opening speech: when the Arch-Priest Mammon warns Swellfoot that "Mighty events are hastening to their doom!" (2.2.66), the tyrant refuses to acknowledge the situation, remarking that "I only hear the lean and mutinous swine / Grunting about the temple" (2.2.67-68). By the end of the play, the proud, slothful Swellfoot has become no more aware of the inevitability of his downfall than he was at the beginning. In displaying his ignorance about the cyclical nature of historical progression, Swellfoot reminds us of the ways in which pride blinds all tyrants to political realities, and he remarks unselfconsciously on his own blindness to the needs of his subjects, a condition he has demonstrated since his initial appearance on the stage.

In the speech that opens Shelley's play, the King celebrates not only his life of excess, but also Famine, upon whose reign he knows his luxurious life depends:

> Thou supreme Goddess! by whose power divine
> These graceful limbs are clothed in proud array
>   [*He contemplates himself with satisfaction.*]

> Of gold and purple, and this kingly paunch
> Swells like a sail before a favouring breeze,
> And these most sacred nether promontories
> Lie satisfied with layers of fat; and these
> Bœotian cheeks, like Egypt's pyramid,
> Nor with less toil were their foundations laid,
> Sustain the cone of my untroubled brain,
> That point, the emblem of a pointless nothing!
>
> (1.1.1-10)

In his initial speech, the King praises the force that brokers his excesses and abuses of power, the Goddess of Famine who transubstantiates the weakness and hunger of the swinish multitude into the excess that is the King's corpulent body. The opening speech exposes excess as the King's nourishment, his fat cheeks emblematic for the hoarding, the excessive consumption, that symbolizes the swollen nature of tyrannical rule.[52]

In recounting Mammon's culinary recommendation to the King, Shelley exposes selfish waste as symptomatic of tyranny:

> Allow me now to recommend this dish—
> A simple kickshaw by your Persian cook,
> Such as is served at the great King's second table.
> The price and pains which its ingredients cost,
> Might have maintained some dozen families
> A winter or two . . . .
>
> (2.2.22-27)

Mammon's description of the meal is important for two reasons. First, it indicates the attitude of tyrants toward the well-being of their subjects: Mammon is conscious of the use to which the expense of this lavish meal might otherwise have been put—to "[maintain] some dozen families / A winter or two"—but nevertheless he recommends this feast for the King's exclusive enjoyment. Second, Mammon's speech pluralizes the location of tyranny and broadens its "place" beyond the Swellfoot dynasty to suggest that it circulates throughout all strains of monarchy; after all, that great feast Mammon describes was served at another King's table—and a second (lesser) one at that. Shelley offers Mammon's dinner-table conversation with the tyrant as a reminder of the gross excess that characterizes all forms of monarchial rule.

Purganax understands the pathology of excess, and he describes its development in a manner that makes his recognition of the links between excess and tyranny quite clear. He proposes impaneling "A jury of the pigs" (1.1.299) to sit in judgment of Iona, and he masterminds a plan (later rejected) which proceeds from the assumption that the pigs' exposure to luxury will corrupt them and trick them into serving tyranny (or selfishness) rather than liberty (or justice)[53]:

> Or fattening some few in two separate styes,
> And giving them clean straw, tying some bits
> Of ribbon round their legs—giving their sows
> Some tawdry lace, and bits of lustre glass,
> And their young boars white and red rags, and tails
> Of cows, and jay feathers, and sticking cauliflowers
> Between the ears of the old ones; and when
> They are persuaded, that by the inherent virtue
> Of these things, they are all imperial pigs,
> Good Lord! they'd rip each other's bellies up,
> Not to say help us in destroying her.
>
> (1.1.300-310)

In Purganax's scheme, excess nourishes selfishness, quieting each pig's hunger for liberty and justice. The plan demonstrates Purganax's understanding of the pathology of tyranny: it grows out of overindulgence, such a complete leap into selfishness that all others come to be regarded as hostile factions jealously jeopardizing one's life of luxury. For the tyrant, the division between self and other must be terrifying, for in his selfishness, the tyrant not only elevates himself to the status of All while relegating all others around him to the status of the other—as his mere minions or, worse, his slaves—but he also removes himself completely from the rest of civilization, constructing himself in opposition to all others and therefore rendering himself the lone embodiment of worth, the singular locus of power. Completely self-interested, the tyrant's power thus remains under the threat of attack, for he can trust absolutely no one.

Like Purganax, the Leech understands the power of excess to turn honest people into selfishly invested tyrants. Shelley poses the Leech as a figure whose allegiance is crucial to the maintenance of Swellfoot's rule, for he recognizes the "disease of the state" (read, of the throne) as "plethory" or excess, the very condition he is " . . . so fit to reduce . . . " (1.1.267). But the Leech announces that he " . . . will suck / Blood or muck!" (1.1.264-265), admitting his own lack of allegiance to one mode of sustenance or another, since blood and muck may be conceptualized as opposing pairs, the former the stuff of life, the latter the dregs of decay. Purganax recognizes and rejects the turncoat potential of the Leech and, fearing his disloyalty, orders the "dull beetle . . . back to hell!" (1.1.273). His anxiety over the threat the Leech poses both underscores the importance of single-mindedness to the maintenance of tyranny and remarks on the political consequences that derive from transgression, from the overlapping of allegiance from one order to another.

II. Phallicism

The language of the play's opening speech occasions what I read as the first of many phallic references to Swellfoot's power, the plentiful passages through which the King's empowerment-by-law registers at variously phallic sites on his swollen body.[54] As Swellfoot admires his own

> ... kingly paunch
> [that] Swells like a sail ...
> ... [his] most sacred nether promontories
> [that] Lie satisfied ...
>
> (1.1.3-6)

we recognize a variety of pleasures that take form in a range of corporeal signifiers: gustatory pleasure is symptomatized in Swellfoot's obesity, and the erotic pleasure he gains from the control he wields over others is manifested in a variety of displaced phallic symbols, among them his "kingly paunch" and, much more transparently, his "sacred nether promontories." Both sites transport swelling away from the tyrant's feet, so that from the first few lines of the play, Shelley alerts us to the fluctuating manifestations and phallic overtones of the tyrant's name. What is swollen throughout the play is not really the tyrant's foot at all, but tyranny itself—the model of complete domination Shelley metaphorizes in corporeal displacements of erection.

Psychoanalysis aligns language with phallic privilege and argues that the phallic components of mastery and order are always encoded into language, particularly in proscriptive forms such as religion and law. The power of speech, the power of a name, always echoes phallic (masculine) privilege. Mammon's hostile response to Dakry, Swellfoot's minister whose name derives from his notorious reputation for breaking into tears,[55] reveals the importance of masculinity to power in the play's model of tyranny. After Dakry's admission that he has appealed to the swine through a speech extolling the virtues

> Of delicacy, mercy, judgment, law,
> Morals, and precedents, and purity,
> Adultery, destitution, and divorce,
> Piety, faith, and state necessity,
> And how I loved the Queen! ...
>
> (1.1.332-336)

he recalls that he " ... wept, / With the pathos of my own eloquence" (1.1.336-337). Thus, Dakry admits that his emotion arose not from his fellow-feeling for the suffering of the swine and their heroine but from the power of his own language to elicit a bodily response. Mammon berates Dakry both for his rhetoric and for his narcissism, replying that "I wonder that grey wizards / Like you should be so beardless in their schemes" (1.1.344-345). Beardlessness, obviously, tropes unmanliness, which Mammon counterpoises to the greyness of Dakry's hair, a color symbolic of aged (and traditionally masculine) wisdom. By pointing out the incongruity between Dakry's physical and mental states (old and wise) and his mode of rhetorical engagement ("beardless," womanish), Mammon marks Dakry as a problematic body, a half-man, half-woman figure whose combination of intelligence and weakness renders him an unstable figure, a dangerously weak link in the chain of Swellfoot's order. In his transgressions of gender, his overlappings of mannishness and womanishness, Dakry poses a threat to Swellfoot's rule: like all of Shelley's revolutionary figures, Dakry's transgressions interrupt tyranny's stronghold.

The prevalence of phallicism to the maintenance of tyrannical order appears even more clearly in an early exchange between Mammon and Purganax. Mammon expresses his anxiety about the revolutionary sentiments the return of Iona might provoke, but Purganax quells Mammon's fears, thereby psychically re-empowering—re-phallicizing—him, saying,

> I have taken good care
> That shall not be. I struck the crust o' the earth
> With this enchanted rod, and Hell lay bare!
> And from a cavern full of ugly shapes,
> I chose a LEECH, a GADFLY, and a RAT.
>
> (1.1.150-154)

Figuratively copulating with Hell by inserting the tyrant's (displaced) phallus into that archetypal space of evil, Purganax's striking of the earth with his "enchanted rod" is, of course, a symbolic sex act undertaken to perpetuate Swellfoot's tyrannical order, a pleasurable exchange between a Minister and Hell that leagues tyranny and evil against Iona, the play's embodiment of the Other who stands in opposition to their hegemony. In this figural copulation, we see phallicism employed as a motif through which tyranny and evil conceive their own regeneration. An earlier moment in the play anticipates such a phallic engagement when Swellfoot orders his butcher to come "[o]ut with your knife" and to "cut close and deep" into those swine who beleaguer him (1.1.75, 1.1.82). Like Purganax, Swellfoot relies on symbolically phallic devices of empowerment—knives, in this case—to perpetuate his tyrannical regime.

III. The Body

The bodies of Tyrant Swellfoot and his subjects schematize the play's oppositions between empowerment and disempowerment, or possession and lack, and the play's registration of political relationships at the site of the body—a recurring trope throughout Shelley's works—finds form in the oppositional pair of erection/emaciation. While we have seen the symbology of erection in the various devices that represent the tyrant's swollenness of power, emaciation emerges in the following exchange as a corporeal signifier for the disempowerment or oppression of the pigs:

> *First Sow.* My pigs, 'tis vain to tug!
> *Second Sow.* I could almost eat my litter!
> *First Pig.* I suck, but no milk will come from the dug.
> *Second Pig.* Our skin and our bones would be bitter.
> *The Boars.* We fight for this rag of greasy rug,
> Though a trough of wash would be fitter.
>
> (1.1.52-57)

The condition of oppression is written upon the bodies of Swellfoot's subjects, somatically inscribed on bodies so drained of potential that they tend toward anti-productivity and cannibalism, exemplified most dramatically in the Second Sow's marked anti-maternalism, which invokes the diametric opposite to maternal nurturing—cannibalism: the mother eats her children rather than nourishing them with milk from her breasts. The Semichorus of Swine call attention to this phenomenon in their plea to the King to relieve their general state of suffering:

> I wish that pity would drive out the devils
> Which in [Swellfoot's] royal bosom hold their revels,
> And sink us in the waves of thy compassion.
>
> (1.1.60-62)

Here, the Swine locate the evil of tyranny at a particular site on the King's body and, significantly, they describe that evil as an alien force from which the body may be purified. Swellfoot, too, demonstrates his understanding of the body as a site for the mediation of politics when he recalls the attempts he has made to maintain political order:

> Moral restraint I see has no effect,
> Nor prostitution, nor our own example,
> Starvation, typhus-fever, nor prison—
>
> (1.1.76-78)

Even the pigs turn to the body in their revolutionary schemes, as one Minister reports to the King:

> What is still worse, some sows upon the ground
> Have given the ape-guards apples, nuts, and gin,
> And they all whisk their tails aloft, and cry,
> "Long live Iona! down with Swellfoot!"
>
> (1.1.324-327)

In moments such as these, we see throughout the play the turn to the body and its physical and psychological needs—for food, for sex, for freedom— as a site where politics may be mediated in the purchasing of allegiance through the satisfaction of basic corporeal cravings.

The denial of bodily needs, however, contributes to a much more complicated model of political control, because it participates not in the purchasing of allegiance but in the generation of a state of chaos from which allegiance vanishes completely, as starved individuals turn against all others who share in their miserable condition. This phenomenon is observed by an old Sow:

> A wretched lot Jove has assigned to swine,
> Squabbling makes pig-herds hungry, and they dine
> On bacon, and whip the sucking-pigs the more.
>
> (2.1.135-137)

Hunger, as the Second Sow's anti-maternalism demonstrated, starves compassion, exiling one from any sense of loyalty to a larger community. Hunger—the denial of a physical need, the bodily manifestation of oppression—overtakes the spirit of generosity, which Shelley situates as pivotal to his campaign of liberty-through-love; and selfishness, the psychic manifestation of hunger, leads only to a redoubling of oppression, to a multiplication of the effects of tyrannical gorging. On the other hand, extreme hunger can be pressed into the service of liberty, as those held in real or imaginary prisons starve to such extremes that their emaciated bodies slip between the bars that hold them, freeing them from their place of containment. Such is the case of Purganax's rat, who is "So thin with want, . . . [that it] can crawl in and out / Of any narrow chink and filthy hole" (1.1.181-182). The denial of bodily need participates primarily in the maintenance of tyranny, but when it reaches a vanishing point in the completely emaciated body, the trajectory of hunger reverses, and that body is thrust into oppositional engagements that enable it to "break out" of (the symbolic prison of) oppression.[56] Throughout Shelley's play, oppression and freedom are thus consistently linked to the denial of bodily needs and to the physical condition of the oppressed, most clearly with regard to nourishment: tyrants gorge, and subjects starve.

Finally, the body functions throughout *Swellfoot the Tyrant* as a register of political instability. When Swellfoot realizes his rule is in danger of being usurped, he laments his sudden loss of appetite, saying,

> . . . After the trial,
> And these fastidious pigs are gone, perhaps
> I may recover my lost appetite.
>
> (2.2.28-30)

Swellfoot's loss of appetite *is* his loss of power, so that just as his empowerment has been metonymized in swollenness, in the "erections" of his corpulent body, his impending disempowerment now finds form in hunger's antithesis, in the complete evacuation of his appetite. As the inevitability of

Swellfoot's fall becomes clear, Mammon turns to another symbolic body, that of the Goddess Famine, and reads her corporeal instability as metonymic for the state of Swellfoot's regime:

> I hear a crackling of the giant bones
> Of the dread image, and in the black pits
> Which once were eyes, I see two livid flames.
> These prodigies are oracular, and show
> The presence of the unseen Deity.
> Mighty events are hastening to their doom!
>
> (2.2.61-66)

Mammon recognizes in this collapse of the Goddess of Famine the new narrative of the play, the reversals of power that will be figured on the bodies of Shelley's *Dramatis Personæ*. Throughout the play, Shelley consistently poses the body as a register for politics according to a binary model of excess and lack: the swollen (or erect) body metonymizes power; the collapsed (or emaciated) body, oppression.

A moment from early in the play emphasizes the particular power of the body to serve as a site for the mediations—or, here, re-mediations—of politics. In act 1, Swellfoot orders the butchering of a particularly vocal hog, but Zephaniah, the Pig-Butcher, warns,

> Your Sacred Majesty, [that pig] has the dropsy;
> We shall find pints of hyatids in's liver,
> He has not half an inch of wholesome fat
> Upon his carious ribs.
>
> (1.1.86-89)

The irony of tyranny is its inevitable second coming, its negative return to those who have employed it in the service of their own power. Here, Swellfoot finds that one of his own commodities, the pig, has been reduced to no value whatsoever; moreover, that completely emaciated pig now poses an alarmingly immediate threat to Swellfoot's safety, for its diseased body, had it been butchered, would have returned the effects of Swellfoot's tyranny to the tyrant himself. If Swellfoot had consumed the pig's meat, he would have been infected with dropsy, a disease that causes unquenchable thirst, and thus he would have been delivered by illness to the condition of lack or emaciation that the play poses as symbolic of disempowerment—the very condition through which Swellfoot has held his subjects at bay. Ultimately, Shelley demonstrates in Swellfoot's gustatory near-misstep the potential for tyranny to turn against itself, for the selfish wielders of power to be stung with their own venom, for Swellfoot's undoing would have begun with his the act of eating—the very pleasure he so narcissistically celebrates in the play's opening lines.

IV. Evil

A number of passages throughout the play remind readers of the yoking of tyrannical government to religion, which Shelley regards as the institutionalization of evil. For example, we learn that the oracle structuring the play's action—the play's epigraph—was uttered by the Arch-Priest of Famine, Mammon, but his account of the less-than-religious circumstances in which that oracle was delivered suggest the hypocrisy of religion in general. When Purganax queries him about the oracle, Mammon admits that it may have grown out of a fit of drunkenness:

> And whether I was urg'd by grace divine,
> Or Lesbian liquor to declare these words,
> Which must, as all words must, be false or true;
> It matters not: for the same power made all.
>
> (1.1.123-126)

The play's religion of Famine has no closer tie to truth than drunkenness, yet the centrality of the play's oracle reminds us of the power of language, particularly when it is spoken by a figure invested with the institutional power of the church.

When the pigs appeal to the King for better treatment, Swellfoot lambastes them as "Seditious hunks! . . . " (1.1.85), and when the Semichorus of Swine begs him to provide better quarters, the tyrant cuts off their speech, pronouncing it " . . . sedition, and rank blasphemy!" (1.1.70). Swellfoot thus regards himself not only as a political ruler but as a God, so that any subjects who question his rule violate the political and religious hierarchies that guarantee his power and are branded as transgressors, political threats. Similarly, Mammon's description of the games his grandchildren enjoy reinscribes the play's conflation of religious and political power: the Arch-Priest of Famine brags about

> . . . my little grandchildren, the gibbets,
> Promising children as you ever saw,—
> The young playing at hanging, the elder learning
> How to hold radicals. They are well taught too,
> For every gibbet says its catechism,
> And reads a select chapter in the Bible
> Before it goes to play.
>
> (1.1.215-221)

Shelley's stage directions underscore his equation of religion and tyranny by calling for the entrance of " . . . *MAMMON, the Arch-Priest; and PURGANAX, Chief Council of Wizards*" (326). Mammon, the leader of the State church of Famine, represents the ecclesiastical arm of Swellfoot's regime; but the *à deux* entrance of this "Priest" and a "Wizard" reminds

Shelley's readers of the baselessness of the religion of Famine, of its status as nothing more than mere superstition lately institutionalized under Swellfoot's rule. Elsewhere, Purganax is unmasked as a manifestation of deceit or treachery in general and of Satan in particular; the Semichorus of Swine notes that he " . . . has plainly shown a / Cloven foot and jack-daw feather" (2.1.126-127).[57] Swellfoot's subjects, like the play's readers, see through the power his regime grants to the religion of Famine, for the play unveils that religion as a mere mask for tyranny, a disguise for systematic oppression.

The play's central device, the Green Bag, which contains the poisonous liquor to be poured over Iona's head, also participates in Shelley's yoking of tyranny and evil. First, Shelley exposes the bag's color as a trope for evil. Upon its presentation to the masses, the Second Boar exclaims,

> Oh! no GREEN BAGS!! Jealousy's eyes are green,
> Scorpions are green, and water-snakes, and efts,
> And verdigris, and—
>
> (2.1.74-76)[58]

While the language of the Boar's response may seem amusing in its odd declension from human traits to the natural world to "verdigris," the underlying point of that decline should be quite seriously regarded, for the inclusion of "verdigris" in the Second Boar's list of green items may not be as incongruous—or comic—as it seems: among its other uses, verdigris functions as a fungicide or insecticide.[59] Thus, we find that the Second Boar's speech poses an opposition between tyranny and the natural order, between the fatal liquor (insecticide) and (aspects of) the natural world. In short, the Second Boar's odd declension from jealousy to scorpions to verdigris reminds us that Swellfoot's subjects recognize the threat specific to the device Purganax offers: the swine regard the bag as an instrument of evil, not as the repository of truth and liberation Purganax claims it to be. The introduction of the bag into the play bears quoting at length, for it constructs that device in a manner pivotal to my reading of the play's alignment of tyranny and religion. It is Mammon, the Arch-Priest of Famine, who first introduces the device to Swellfoot's ministers, and he describes the bag as follows:

> . . . for here
> The Gadfly's venom, fifty times distilled,
> Is mingled with the vomit of the Leech,
> In due proportion, and black ratsbane, which
> That very Rat, who, like the Pontic tyrant,
> Nurtures himself on poison, dare not touch;—
> All is sealed up with the broad seal of Fraud,

> Who is the Devil's Lord High Chancellor,
> And over it the primate of all Hell
> Murmured this pious baptism:—"Be thou called
> The GREEN BAG; and this power and grace be thine:
> That thy contents, on whomever poured,
> Turn innocence to guilt, and gentlest looks
> To savage, foul, and fierce deformity.
> Let all baptised by thy infernal dew
> Be called adulterer, drunkard, liar, wretch!
> No name left out which orthodoxy loves,
> Court Journal or legitimate Review!—
> Be they called tyrant, beast, fool, glutton, lover
> Of other wives and husbands than their own—
> The heaviest sin on this side of the Alps!
> Whither they to a ghastly caricature
> Of what was human!—Let not man nor beast
> Behold their face with unaverted eyes!
> Or hear their names with ears that tingle not
> With blood of indignation, rage and shame!"
> This is a perilous liquor; . . .
>   . . . beware
>   . . . the fatal liquor—
>
> (1.1.355-383)

Mammon's speech exposes what we might think of as the play's Trinity of Oppression: the green bag's potential to ruin all those loved by " . . . orthodoxy . . . /Court Journal or legitimate Review" situates religion, law, and criticism as the institutional manifestations of evil exposes Shelley's play (1.1.371-372). Mammon introduces the Green Bag as an instrument of Satan's blessing and describes its powers as so corrupting that they reverse innocence into guilt: the innocent, doused by the bag's "fatal liquor," become guilty, while the gentle are transformed into the "savage, foul, and fierce." Mammon's speech reminds us of the power of language to serve tyranny in its description of Satan's call for the ultimate transformation of innocence into guilt at the level of language;[60] that is, those who hear the names of the innocent will respond to such signifiers "'With blood of indignation, rage, and shame!'" and thus will re-construct those names as the signifiers of guilt, or evil. The "fatal liquor" of the green bag acts not only as a metaphor for tyranny, but, more generally, as an agent in the play, a veritable character whose transgressive movements bring about radical transformations in the world. From the beginning, then, the bag is recognized as a locus of transgression, for its contents reverse the valences of the innocence/guilt binary; thus, the bag poses a threat to hegemonic power, a threat finally raised in the play's last turn, as we shall see.

Liberty

Tyranny is the overarching force that structures Shelley's play: it is the brand of power that Swellfoot wields over his commodity-subjects, and, as I will demonstrate, it is the model to which Iona and her revolutionaries revert upon their apparent triumph over Swellfoot and his minions. Tyranny's opposite, Liberty, also figures in Shelley's play, primarily to dissuade the swine from violent revolution, as Scrivener notes (266), but her apparitional status underscores the ultimate disappearance of Liberty in the aftermath of Iona's defeat of Swellfoot. Personified as a female spirit, Liberty appears on stage only for a brief moment in the play's final scene: "*A graceful figure in a semi-transparent veil passes unnoticed through the Temple; the word LIBERTY is seen through the veil, as if it were written in fire upon its forehead. Its words are almost drowned out in the furious grunting of the* Pigs, *and the business of the trial. She kneels on the steps of the Altar, and speaks in tones at first faint and low, but which ever become louder and louder*" (347). Significantly, Shelley presents Liberty as veiled, her half-exposed body establishing her place among Shelley's larger cast of eroticized heroes. The inscription of "Liberty" upon her forehead suggests the dedication of her body to the forces of good, or, more specifically, to the will of God Himself, an odd move for Shelley the atheist, but one consistent with the oppositions he has posed throughout the play between tyranny and liberty: where the former is blessed by Satan, the latter, by extension, is aligned with good and, here, stands branded by the fiery hand of God. Of equal significance is the fact that Liberty's first words are ignored by the Pigs, who heed her message only momentarily before drowning her out again with even more "furious grunting" as they topple the tyrant, only in the end to embrace the very model Liberty urges them to reject.

Liberty's appeal to the emblem of tyranny, the Goddess of Famine, articulates an agenda congruent to Shelley's own; thus, we see in Liberty's descent the potential for the imaginative revolution, the utopia Shelley plots throughout his works: Liberty charges Famine to

> . . . wake the multitude,
> Thou can lead them not upon the paths of blood.
> The earth did never mean her foizon
> For those who crown life's cup with poison
> Of frantic rage and meaningless revenge—
> But for those radiant spirits, who are still
> The standard-bearers in the van of Change.
>
> (2.2.91-97)

Liberty poses an alliance with Famine to advance an agenda she hopes the pigs will endorse, and she stoops to Famine only because Famine's corporeal effects may move the swine to action.⁶¹ Clearly, Liberty's call echoes Shelley's support for bloodless revolutions: like Shelley, Liberty counterpoises the natural order of the world to the unnatural forces of tyranny by showing how tyranny perverts the "foizon" (abundance) of earth's gifts into selfishness and rage,⁶² and in her descent to Famine, Liberty invokes the image of "the van of Change," implying her desire for Iona's triumph to transform power into some form other than tyranny. To press her point, Liberty calls directly on Iona, imploring her to "Remit, O Queen! thy accustom'd rage! / Be what thou art not! . . . " (2.2.100-101). Shelley-like, Liberty appropriates a tool of domination—in the case of Shelley, language; in the case of Liberty, Famine—and redeploys that tool in the service of freedom. Liberty thus aligns her mission with the emblem of oppression, Famine, solely in the anticipation of a radical transformation in power. Such a transformation is fully activated by Famine's descent and subsequent resurrection as the Minotaur, John Bull; however, the transformation Liberty poses from tyranny to freedom is blocked by Iona's ultimate reversion to her "accustom'd rage." In the end, the possibility of freedom Liberty offers is quashed by the tyranny of Iona's selfishness, so that by the conclusion of the play, Shelley's would-be revolutionary hero is unmasked as another Swellfoot.

While tyranny draws on the transformational powers of the Green Bag to destroy Iona, Liberty employs similar forces to infuse the loaves of bread that adorn the altar to Famine with the powers of transubstantiation: "*. . . all those who eat the loaves are turned into Bulls, and arrange themselves quietly behind the altar. The image of FAMINE sinks through a chasm in the earth, and a MINOTAUR rises*" (348). Liberty—"Freedom," as she once calls herself (2.2.102)—joins forces with her "eternal foe" (2.2.102), Famine, in order to quash tyranny, and she reverses the symbology of the adornments of Famine's altar, transforming them from emblems of lack into devices of sustenance. Finally, Liberty's transformation topples the altar to Famine and raises in its place not a static symbol but a kinetic being, the Minotaur, who, according to myth, is the child of Pasiphæ and a bull, the issue of the same transgressive (human-beast) erotic union of which Iona stands accused. Momentarily ascendant over both the religion of Famine and the politics of Tyranny, this offspring of sexual transgression reveals himself as "JOHN BULL," or England (2.2.110), and he offers to assist Iona in her pursuit of her persecutors:

> And if your Majesty would deign to mount me,
> At least till you have hunted down your game,
> I will not throw you.
>
> (2.1.114-116)

The Minotaur's offer is triply transgressive, for not only does it propose an act of bestiality, but in that "mounting," the valences of the masculine/feminine binary are reversed (Iona is constructed as active, and the Minotaur, mounted, as passive), and the self-feminized Minotaur advances his offer in the interest of toppling the hyper-phallicized Swellfoot's political power. In the important figure of the Minotaur, Shelley demonstrates the potential for sexual transgression to operate in the service of Liberty.

By announcing his "Ionian" ancestry, the Minotaur aligns himself with the name of Shelley's heroine, attaching his lineage to hers; in this way, the bodies of Iona and the Minotaur collapse into each other, hers in the ancestry they share, his in Iona's symbolic act of bestiality from which one of his kind may have been born. The rising of the Minotaur—his erection—is, I would argue, the tumescence of the phallus Iona has snatched from Swellfoot in her stunning reversal of the Green Bag test. Finally, the Minotaur's request that Iona "deign to mount" him reminds us of the reversals of gender that hypostatize the reversals of political power at the end of Shelley's play: just as Iona has seized power from Swellfoot, so, too, has she emerged as the play's New Man, the phallicized figure whose order will codify Bœotia's new law. Castrated, Swellfoot is relegated to the realm of the Other, while the newly phallicized Iona ascends to the position of privilege he has lost. At this point, Shelley dramatizes the problem inherent to such a sudden move from disempowerment to privilege: as soon as she is freed, Iona renounces the cooperation of Liberty by turning to the devices of physical domination and oppression and by pursuing Swellfoot and his minions with the same jealousy and hatred that motivated their capture of her. Symbolically armed with the phallic power of Swellfoot's rule, Iona has, in the end, been transformed by her own greed and lust for power into just another Swellfoot, so that the play closes on a world whose new ruler is, in effect, no different from the one she has deposed.

Language

As we have seen, Shelley foregrounds tyranny throughout *Swellfoot*, but he also devotes some attention to the mechanisms of liberty, and in so doing he demonstrates how both of these orders operate at and through the level of language. Richard Cronin observes that the play exposes language as "a conservative force [that] is one of the means by which established authority maintains its power,"[63] and Gold agrees, commenting that Shelley's play demonstrates Swellfoot's "[deliberate] . . . abuses [of] language" (65). While Swellfoot's pride and complete self-indulgence blind him to the hostility of his subjects, in fact he remains cognizant of the nature of his relationship to them: they are his commodities. When asked by the Semichorus of Swine "What should we yield to thee?" (1.1.38), Swellfoot misunderstands the irony of the question and answers flatly, " . . . skin and bones, and some few hairs for mortar" (1.1.39). A bit later, when ordering the execution-by-butchery of one of his hogs, Swellfoot justifies the exploitation of his commodity-subjects by recuperating the act in the service of his own power:

> He'll serve instead of riot money, when
> Our murmuring troops bivouaque in Thebes' streets;
> And January winds, after a day
> Of butchering, will make them relish carrion.
>
> (1.1.90-94)

Swellfoot's subjects are of use to him only when they serve to bolster his sense of power and security, and those he oppresses recognize the depths of insignificance to which they have been pushed: " . . . only now the name / Of pig remains to me," moan the Semichorus of Swine, clearly recognizing that they have been stripped of all possessions except their names (1.1.34-35). But the pigs will come to realize—and draw upon—the power of that very impoverishment, since, under tyranny, the only thing of which they cannot be dispossessed is language, coded in this passage as "the name." Although they can claim nothing except their names as their own, it is their ability to call—to speak—that will serve the pigs well at the play's end, where Iona's triumph over her persecutors results from her careful linguistic maneuvers, from her use of language to interrupt power. But while in other poems, such as *Epipsychidion*, Shelley explores the liberatory potential of language, in *Swellfoot the Tyrant*, the poet focuses primarily on how language may be appropriated by tyranny. For example, the cleavers and marrow-bones displayed by the Priests in the play's final scene serve as more than mere instruments of physical attack: the scene opens with the Chorus of Priests accompanied by the "Court Porkman" who plays music upon the bones and cleavers. In this moment, Shelley aligns physical domination (the cleaver as weapon) with linguistic tyranny (the cleaver as mechanism of speech) in order to demonstrate how the Priests' Chorus maintains Swellfoot's order just as effectively as the cleavers dissuade any who would question Swellfoot's rule.[64]

Earlier in the play, the Gadfly's account of his attacks against Iona underscore his understanding of the powerful nature of language:[65]

> I have stung her and wrung her,
> The venom is working;—
> And if you had hung her
> With canting and quirking,
> She could not be deader than she will be soon.
>
> (1.1.254-258)

The Gadfly compares the power of venom, the device he uses to harm Iona, to that of the scaffold. In doing so, he conjoins a corporeal effect and a legal mechanism, aligning his body with one of the instruments of (so-called) justice that carry out Swellfoot's orders. Significantly, the Gadfly considers the important role language plays at the scene of a hanging: the Gadfly poses two speech acts, "canting" ("affected speech, monotonous or mechanical discourse, or hypocritically pious language" [*Webster's II*, s.v. "canting"]) and "quirking" ("verbal trickery; assailing with quirks or quips" [*OED,* s.v. "quirk"]), as agents that carry out the judicial process of hanging. The product of the Gadfly's body, venom, operates in the interest of justice, killing the accused criminal Iona in the same way that a convicted criminal might be killed by hanging *and the language* that accompanies it, the "canting and quirking" by which it is marked. Language, the Gadfly cleverly observes, may be employed as an agent of tyranny at the site of the physical body; thus deployed, it may bring about consequences as dire as death.

Mammon acknowledges the coercive power of language when he proposes his grand scheme for deceiving the swine. His speech is significant because of the particular end to which its coercive devices lead—the security of tyranny through the eradication of Iona, the play's apparent agent of liberty:

> ... We must entice
> Her Majesty from the stye, and make the pigs
> Believe that the contents of the GREEN BAG
> Are the true test of guilt or innocence.
> And that, if she be guilty, 'twill transform her
> To manifest deformity like guilt.
> If innocent, she will become transfigured
> Into an angel, such as she is;
> And they will see her flying through the air,
> So bright that she will dim the noon-day sun;
> Showering down blessings in the shape of comfits.
> This, trust a priest, is just the sort of thing
> Swine will believe. . . .
>
> (1.1.390-402)

Mammon's speech highlights the power of language to guarantee political stability. It is, of course, Mammon who masterminds the scheme meant to ensure the maintenance of Swellfoot's regime, a plan that is nothing more than an elaborate design to exploit the pigs' enthusiastic support for Iona and, in so doing, to trick them into endorsing the Green Bag test.

Purganax addresses "*The* BOARS *in full Assembly*," (337), and his speech deserves some consideration for its demonstration of the power of language to serve tyranny. Addressing his audience as "Gentlemen and Boars" (2.1.1), Purganax attempts to sway the masses by playing to their egos, calling them

> Ye, by whose patience under public burthens
> The glorious constitution of these styes
> Subsists, and shall subsist.
>
> (2.1.2-4)

While appearing to compliment the pigs by acknowledging their contributions to the "glorious" conditions in which they live, Purganax ironically reveals the true state of affairs: the pigs' suffering and misery result directly from what he politely terms their "patience," that is, their disinclination to revolt against the conditions that oppress them. Next, he alludes to one of the institutions with which Shelley aligned tyranny at the play's beginning—money—by speaking of taxes as " . . . the true source of piggishness" (2.1.6). According to Purganax, taxes measure and mark the meaning of piggishness, so that as the meaning (that is, the stature or importance) of piggishness increases, so too must taxes. He goes on to praise the system of taxation as a device that bespeaks the pigs' power and might, and he asks them

> . . . How can I find a more appropriate term [than taxes]
> To include religion, morals, peace, and plenty,
> And all that fit Bœotia as a nation
> To teach other nations how to live? . . .
>
> (2.1.6-10)

Finally, Purganax reverses the hierarchy of government (those who tax) and citizens (those who are taxed) by claiming that

> . . . the revenue [from taxes], that great spring of all
> The patronage, and pensions, and by-payments,
> Which free-born pigs regard with jealous eyes,
> [Is diminishing], till at length, by glorious steps,
> All the land's produce will be merged in taxes,
> And the revenue will amount to—nothing!
>
> (2.1.12-17)

Purganax argues that taxation empowers citizens—those very pigs whose high tax rates relegate their lives to squalor and want. It is the pigs, Purganax insists, who are the true heroes of the country, for not only are the taxes they pay "that true source of piggishness" (an argument that recalls Swellfoot's regard for his subjects as mere commodities, since the "meaning" of a commodity derives from the amount of income it generates), but the taxes are also the coffers that ensure the supremacy of Bœotia over other countries. Finally, Purganax claims that because the tax-paying pigs are the guardians of the supremacy of Bœotia, the free (untaxed) regard the oppressed (taxed) with a jealous eye. Purganax thus reverses the relationship between the oppressed (the pigs) and the oppressors (the government) that Shelley has exposed throughout the play.

In yet another rhetorical sleight-of-hand, Purganax attempts to reverse the pigs' response to the conditions in which they live by appealing to their egos—which he has stroked in the first part of his speech—in an effort to release Swellfoot from any particular blame for the physical discomforts the pigs endure. First, Purganax claims that the pigs' living conditions are borne of economic and political necessity, and he assures them that those discomforts are only temporary:

> ... that the population of the pigs,
> Instead of hog-wash, has been fed on straw
> And water, is a fact which is—you know—
> That is—it is a state-necessity—
> Temporary, of course.
>
> (2.1.21-24)

In the next passage, Shelley exposes one of the mechanisms that guarantee the success of Purganax's coercive rhetoric—the sudden insertion of a threat into a speech that otherwise addresses its audience as reasonable individuals and powerful political players:

> ... Those impious pigs,
> Who, by frequent squeaks, have dared impugn
> The settled Swellfoot system, or to make
> Irreverent mockery of the genuflexions
> Inculcated by the arch-priest, have been whipt
> Into a loyal and an orthodox whine.
>
> (2.1.25-30)

Purganax deploys the rhetoric of tyranny, but because he couches it in a speech that lauds the pigs as the true keepers of power, his audience offers no resistance to his subtle threat. However, when Purganax mentions the name of their hero, Queen Iona, Shelley indicates that there is "*A loud cry from the* Pigs" (338) who exclaim "She is innocent! most innocent!" (2.1.32). Purganax, ever the master of coercive rhetoric, echoes the pigs' enthusiasm and continues his speech as follows:

> That is the very thing that I was saying,
> Gentlemen Swine; the Queen Iona being
> Most innocent, no doubt ....
>
> (2.1.33-35)

Purganax de-emphasizes his articulation of a threat by returning to the subject of the pigs' hero, whom he pretends to support; in this way, the moment in his speech in which tyranny is spoken directly—rather than ironically, as it is throughout the play's series of coercive, mock-complimentary passages—vanishes in Purganax's echoing of the pigs' enthusiasm for Queen Iona. He goes on to claim that the Swellfoot regime shares the pigs' high regard for the Queen, and he insists that all rumors to the contrary were started by those who wanted to keep the government and the pigs at odds so that they might hoard

> ... that hog-wash, which has been
> Your immemorial right, and which I will
> Maintain you in to the last drop ....
> (2.1.41-43)

Here, Purganax returns politics to the site of the body and its needs by arguing that those who attack Iona's reputation do so to gain "hog-wash" and by reminding the pigs that as their political partner, he intends to recover that same source of nourishment from the rumor-mongers who would steal it.

Swayed by his speech, the pigs regard Purganax as an important political player in their revolutionary scheme, and they question him about the accusations that have been raised against Iona. Purganax admits that while no one has made

> ... *any* positive accusation; ...
> There were hints dropt, and so the privy wizards
> Conceived that it became them to advise
> His Majesty to investigate their truth;—
> Not for his own sake; ... [but in the interest of the pigs].
> (2.1.45-49)

Purganax distances the crown from an oppositional relationship to the Queen and aligns it instead with the pigs' cause by claiming that Swellfoot's decision to investigate those trumped-up accusations was made entirely on their behalf:

> ... he fears the morals of the swine,
> The sows especially, and what effect
> It might produce upon the purity and
> Religion of the rising generation
> Of sucking pigs, if it could be suspected
> That Queen Iona—
> (2.1.52-57)

Purganax's rhetoric returns us to the language that characterized reactionary portrayals of Queen Caroline: his narrative constructs the revolutionary woman as a particularly dangerous figure, given her influence over the domestic sphere and the generations she will produce. Thus,

Purganax justifies Swellfoot's investigation by arguing that rumors of Iona's transgressions—baseless though they are—might incite *sows* to bad behavior, giving rise to a generation of pigs whose morals would be tainted by the degenerate practices of which Iona stands accused and who would thus threaten the continued supremacy and security of Bœotia. Once again, we see how the play uncovers the ideological link between domestic relationships and political realities, and how these links find real-life equivalents in the scandal surrounding Queen Caroline: in both instances, the presence of a woman-in-public interrupts hegemonic authority, feminizing the public realm and politicizing the private.

At this point, the pigs demand to be told of the crimes for which Iona stands accused. Rather than answering them directly, Purganax responds by allusion: he recalls Iona's relationship to Pasiphæ, the legendary lover of a bull, but he stops short of accusing Iona of a similar transgression, emphasizing only that while others gossip, " . . . *I* say nothing . . . " (2.1.67). Following Purganax's accusation-by-allusion, the First Boar pronounces Iona "Most innocent!" (2.1.73), and Purganax proposes the Green Bag test to prove that innocence, which he insists " . . . both you and I, and all assert" (2.1.72).

The pigs recoil from the Green Bag Purganax produces, responding to it as if it were a character in the play, an agent who threatened to harm them in some way; as I have discussed, they declaim its color for its connections to jealousy, treachery, and danger. Once again, Purganax unleashes his manipulative rhetoric to address the pigs as reasonable and rational individuals. To calm them, he commends their purity and goodness:

> . . . Honourable swine,
> In piggish souls can prepossessions reign?
> Allow me to remind you, grass is green—
> All flesh is grass;—no bacon but is flesh—
> Ye are but bacon. This divining BAG
> (Which is not green, but only bacon colour)
> Is filled with liquor, which if sprinkled o'er
> A woman guilty of—we all know what—
> Makes her so hideous, till she finds one blind,
> She never can commit the like again.
> If innocent, she will turn into an angel,
> And rain down blessings in the shape of comfits
> As she flies up to heaven. Now, my proposal
> Is to convert her sacred Majesty
> Into an angel, (as I am sure we shall do,)
> By pouring on her head this mystic water.
>
> [*Showing the Bag.*]

> I know that she is innocent; I wish
> Only to prove her so to all the world.
>
> (2.1.76-93)

Purganax describes the bag as a representative of the pigs themselves and rhetorically resurrects the bag as a device that will ensure their heroine's vindication. Further, he articulates the conceit of the Green Bag test, of which Shelley's audience is already well aware—the lie that its liquids have the power to transform one into vile or angelic form, when in fact anyone baptised by the liquids will be hideously deformed. Purganax concludes his speech by assuring the pigs of his confidence in Iona's innocence, re-emphasizing the congruence of his political sympathies and their own.

Both of Purganax's speeches in act 2 underscore what Gold describes as the "linguistic tyranny" that *Swellfoot the Tyrant* exposes—that is, the ability of language to enforce an oppressive agenda, particularly through the device of the ironic claim.[66] Significantly, Shelley exposes the operation of tyranny at the level of language, the very device he poses elsewhere as the instrument of liberty. Thus, language remains for Shelley an always-empowered device, but the trajectory of its empowerment—toward tyranny or liberty—depends entirely upon the motives of the interlocutor: the selfishly invested speaker employs language in the service of tyranny; the unselfish speaker, in the service of liberty. Iona's consent to the Green Bag test hints at her agenda for the use of language, for she agrees only because she has already plotted to reverse that test's goal. While she states directly that

> ... I!—
> Lord PURGANAX, I do commit myself
> Into your custody, and am prepared
> To stand the test, whatever it may be!
>
> (2.1.180-183)

the "*(aside)*" that closes the scene reminds the reader of the irony of her consent: " . . . I, most content of all, / Know that my foes even thus prepare their fall!" (2.1.191-192). Shelley thus exposes Iona's consent to the Green Bag test as coercive rhetoric: she appears to bow to the device posed to judge her, but she reminds us in her aside of the irony of her consent, her already-formulated plan to turn that device against her would-be oppressors.[67] In so doing, Iona unmasks herself as the agent of freedom, the figure who, in appearing to consent to the maneuvers of tyranny, uses language to turn tyranny's device against itself, finally to destroy Swellfoot's regime. As we shall see, however, Shelley's turn to Iona as a revolutionary hero is undone by the play's end when Iona's victory devolves into her blind assumption of tyrannical power.

Sexual Transgression

As the putative hero of *Swellfoot the Tyrant*, Iona Taurina figures significantly throughout the text from the epigraph right through to the end, where she is the last major character to exit the stage. Although Iona does not appear on stage for the first two-thirds of the play, Shelley transforms her absence into a formidable presence, so that even before the play begins, the reader is aware of Iona's great significance as the satire's oppositional force. In act 1, scene 1, Mammon makes the first mention of the renegade Queen by speaking her name and alluding to her transgression: " . . . This Iona— / Well—you know what the chaste Pasiphæ did" (1.1.138-139). The play's first direct invocation of Iona contextualizes the Queen according to a specific mode of sexual transgression—bestiality. This reference might have reminded Shelley's readers of the parallels between the play's rumors about Iona and those circulating in the real world about Queen Caroline, but to make that parallel doubly clear, Shelley re-emphasizes the overlappings of those transgressive Queens as the play comes to a close: Dakry advises Swellfoot that

> . . . In a crisis
> Of such exceeding *delicacy*, I think
> We ought to put Her Majesty, the QUEEN,
> Upon her trial without delay.
>
> (2.2.68-71, emphasis added)

Any contemporary reader would have understood the prosecution of Iona as Shelley's analogue for the so-called "Delicate Investigation" that culminated in the trial of Queen Caroline.

Throughout the play, Shelley poses Iona as a representation of what I have been describing as the figure of the other; that is, Iona functions as an emblem for the swelling masses who cry out for an end to the order that oppresses them. While Mammon agrees that Purganax's scheme to quiet Iona by persecuting her with a horse-leech " . . . might suffice . . . " (1.1.196), he adds that " . . . 'tis the swinish multitude I fear" (1.1.197) and, additionally, that in his anxiety about the toppling of power he has

> . . . Disinherited
> My eldest son[-in-law] Chrysaor, because he
> Attended public meetings, and would always
> Stand prating there of commerce, public faith,
> Economy, and unadulterate coin,
> And other topics, ultra-radical.
>
> (1.1.198-203)

Mammon's speech contributes significantly to the play's construction of Iona, primarily because it aligns her with the oppositional force of the "swinish multitude" whose power he clearly fears. Further, Mammon's domestic intervention demonstrates the power family relationships wield over political stability, since he disinherits his own son-in-law for speaking publicly against the regime that empowers the Arch-Priest. We must, I argue, read Mammon's anxiety over Chryasor's political engagements as a parallel to Swellfoot's regard for Iona: Iona is empowered—phallicized— by virtue of her membership in the royal family, and that phallic privilege makes doubly dangerous the public spectacle she has become. While Chryasor, Mammon's son-in-law, is threatening because he is a man who speaks oppositional politics in a public space, Iona is equally threatening because her royal status accords her the same public place that both Swellfoot and Chryasor occupy as well as the (masculine) power that enables her to make her sentiments known outside the confines of the home. Just as Chryasor so threatens his father-in-law's public station that Mammon is driven to disinherit him, so, too, do Iona's transgressions so threaten Swellfoot's public station that he agrees she must be disinherited— that is, tried, convicted, and disenfranchised from Swellfoot's political power.

Iona's power to reconfigure the political landscape of the play draws directly from the phallic privilege she enjoys as an effect of her royal station. We see, for example, that even before she "castrates" her husband in the play's final moments, that act is prefigured in the rumors about her that succeed in embarrassing the throne. Upon hearing of his wife's return to Thebes, Swellfoot exclaims that "Swellfoot is wived! . . . ", and he commands his guards to be "Off with her head!" (1.1.291), to

> . . . bring [me] the head and body,
> If separate it would please me better, hither
> Of Queen Iona.
>
> (1.1.312-314)

Clearly, Swellfoot recognizes the reversals of power that his wife's return to public visibility forebode, and he articulates those reversals in terms of gendered maneuvers: the *OED* defines the verb "wive" as "to act as a wife"; thus, the King's exclamation that "Swellfoot is wived!" codes Iona's return as his symbolic castration. Fearing this reversal of power, he calls for the only action he believes able to trump that reversal—the displaced castration of the Queen by way of her beheading. Swellfoot's desire for Iona to be taken into custody and brought to him, dismembered, underscores his anxious need to reassert his phallic authority over Iona, to take comfort in the sight of his phallic power as it is registered at the site of her "castrated" body.[68] Another, albeit less direct, call for the "castration" of Iona comes in Mammon's endorsement of " . . . the ceremony / . . . of the uglification of the Queen" (1.1.413). Like Swellfoot's demand for Iona's decapitation, Mammon's proposal for her "uglification" privileges the sight/site of her physical body as the place at which power may be mediated: because it is desirable, her body is empowered; but if it is made undesirable—"uglified"—then her body will be disempowered. The "uglification" of the Queen serves as her symbolic castration, and the Green Bag test assumes importance as the gesture that will re-erect Swellfoot's phallic dominance.

Throughout the play, each time the swine laud Iona as their hero, they codify the Queen's power. At one point, they call for "Iona for ever! . . . ", and elsewhere they carry her into the city as their conquering hero, guarding her safety with their own bodies:[69]

> . . . the swine . . . in a hollow square
> Enclosed her, and received the first attack
> Like so many rhinoceroses, and then
> Retreating in good order, with bare tusks
> And wrinkled snouts presented to the foe,
> Bore her in triumph to the public stye.
>
> (1.1.318-323)

The chorus of Swine becomes so completely invested in Iona's heroic potential that they are willing to sacrifice their bodies in the protection her own; truly, they regard her as a member of their community, as the other who will deliver all of the swinish multitude into the realm of privilege, the disempowered monarch whose transgressive acts will release all other others from oppression. The pigs address her thus, exhorting her to

> Place your most sacred person here. We pawn
> Our lives that none a finger dare to lay on it.
> Those who wrong you, wrong us;
> Those who hate you, hate us;
> Those who sting you, sting us;
> Those who bait you, bait us;
> The oracle is now about to be
> Fulfilled by circumvolving destiny;
> Which says: "Thebes, choose *reform* or *civil war*,
> "When through your streets, instead of hare with dogs,
> "A CONSORT QUEEN shall hunt a King with hogs,
> Riding upon the IONIAN MINOTAUR."
>
> (2.1.146-157)[70]

Clearly, the pigs have adopted the very strategies of corporeal opposition that Iona has modeled: in posing her transgressive body against the authority of her husband, Iona has taught the swine how to negotiate power at the site, or location (as well as through the sight, or spectacle) of the body. The pigs appropriate Swellfoot's regard for them as commodities and turn that position of powerlessness around, so that they become, to borrow a phrase from Luce Irigaray, "commodities among themselves,"[71] dispossessed beings whose refusal of the very market that exploits them improvises a new market in which they are empowered as brokers—a complete reversal of their positions as mere commodities. Pawning their safety for the Queen's, the pigs graft their political convictions onto their bodies, reminding us of the play's consistent imbrications of politics and corporeality. Transforming their bodies into registers of political power, the pigs conceive their bodies as metonyms for the body of Iona, so that any who harm, hate, sting, or bait her royal body do the same to the emaciated bodies of the swine who support her. Iona articulates their relationship of communal corporeality and assures the pigs that she, too, is one of them; in her first speech in the play, she speaks of herself in the third person and addresses the swine, saying:

> The tender heart of every boar acquits
> Their QUEEN . . .
> . . . and she reposing
> With confidence upon the grunting nation,
> Has thrown herself, her cause, her life, her all,
> Her innocence, into their hoggish arms . . . .
> (2.1.159-164)

Aligned both physically and symbolically, Iona and the swine demonstrate the structure of the revolutionary market: commodities act as individual agents for the good of the larger community; they engage freely in the interest of liberty, so that all exchanges are based not on selfishness and the maintenance of tyranny but, to the contrary, on community and the advancement of liberty. Where traditional monarchy conceives a King's two bodies as earthly and spiritual, in the liberated market, the Queen's two bodies are both decidedly fleshy—her own and the collective body of her (egalitarian) subjects.

The swine's cries for victory over Swellfoot's tyrannical regime give voice to the political function they accord Iona's presence: "Hail! Iona the divine," they shout, "We will be no longer swine, / But bulls with horns and dewlaps" (1.1.277-279). Just as Iona's potential to disrupt Swellfoot's regime arms her with phallic power, so, too, do the swine anticipate the specifically gendered transformations their "divine" hero will deliver: freed from Swellfoot's tyranny by Iona, the swine will be transformed into bulls, their newly grown horns the outgrowth of the phallic transaction Iona has brokered. When Iona seizes Swellfoot's phallus to claim it as her own, she promises to distribute the power of that phallus equally among the commodities-among-themselves, the freed pigs-*cum*-bulls.

As the play suggests time and again, Iona's transgressive status threatens the stability of Swellfoot's reign; through the figure of Iona, Shelley poses sexual transgression as a means for political subversion. In the logic of the play, Iona is cast as a politically dangerous figure because of her (so-called) perverse erotic engagements, although Shelley wisely never particularizes the full range of Iona's perversity. For example, in addressing the swine, Purganax does not specify the crimes for which Iona stands accused but instead refers to the Queen as "A woman guilty of—we all know what—" (2.1.83). Similarly, Mammon avoids naming Iona's crimes by retreating instead to allusion: "Well—you know what the chaste Pasiphæ did" (1.1.139). Lastly, Purganax contextualizes Iona's perversity within a history of sexual transgression by referring to Pasiphæ as "Iona's grandmother" (2.1.71). In these ways, Iona's actual "crimes" are never stated directly; further, the ultimate crime that all of Iona's transgressions metaphorize—Swellfoot's "castration"—is punished even before it is committed, since Swellfoot calls for the beheading of the Queen even before she confronts him directly with her demand for political power. Finally, the political significance of sexual transgression is suggested in the maneuvers of the Gadfly who, sent out to torment the returning Queen, accomplishes his overtly political mission in the sexually symbolic space of the boudoir:

> All inn-doors and windows
> Were open to me;
> I saw all that sin does,
> Which lamps hardly see
> That burn in the night by the curtained bed,—
> The impudent lamps! for they blushed not red.
> Dinging and singing,
> From slumber I rung her,
> Loud as the clank of an ironmonger!
> . . . .
> With the trump of my lips, and the sting at my hips,
> I drove her—afar!
>
> (1.1.233-245)

First, the Gadfly reminds us of Iona's reputed lasciviousness by locating her activities in a bedroom and characterizing them as sinful—they should, he remarks, embarrass even the bedlamps. Next, he appropriates the more general space of pleasure, the inn, as a metaphor for Iona's lusty body, so that its "inn-doors and windows / . . . open to me" suggest the ready availability of her body to any who would purchase "entrance" into it. Finally, the Gadfly eroticizes his political mission by describing his attack in terms undeniably coital: he trumps her with his lips and stings her at his hips. The sexual pleasure of the Gadfly's political mission is also suggested in the only pair of internally rhymed lines we find in his entire speech— "Dinging and singing, / From slumber I rung her"—lines whose language apes the rhythm of the bawdy limerick, an aural *double entendre* I am certain Shelley expected his audience to appreciate.

Because Iona's erotic body functions as the site of her political power, it seems only logical that her political triumph at the play's end would be manifested in that very body; and in fact, this is exactly the case. As I have already suggested, Iona's mounting of the Minotaur—John Bull, or England—not only spectacularizes her political power but also marks that power in terms of a gendered transaction. Rumored throughout the play to have been sexually engaged, Pasiphæ-like, with a bull, here we see Iona's sexual transgression celebrated even as its political valences are reversed, so that now her once-criminalized transgression metaphorizes her defeat of Swellfoot and her ascension to his seat of power:

> Hoa! hoa! tallyho! tallyho! ho! ho!
> Come, let us hunt these ugly badgers down,
> These stinking foxes, these devouring otters,
> These hares, these wolves, these anything but men.
>   . . . my loyal pigs,
> Now let your noses be as keen as beagles',
> Your steps as swift as greyhounds', and your cries
> More dulcet and symphonius than the bells
> Of village-towers, on sunshine holiday;
> Wake all the dewy woods with jangling music.
>   (2.2.117-126)

In the play's final moments, Iona emerges as Shelley's revolutionary hero, albeit only temporarily. Seizing power from the hands of a tyrant, she redistributes it among those whom tyranny had oppressed, and she demonstrates her God-like transformative powers by calling for the beautification of the swine, so that their grunts—throughout the play symbolic of oppression—now burst forth as beautiful music. Finally, Iona displaces religion with liberty as the instructive device of the world: she encourages the pigs' newly beautiful voices to replace the bells in village (church-) towers, lilting through the landscape and acting as agents for re-establishing the harmonious connections between the liberated kingdom and the larger natural world.

Unfortunately, all of Iona's revolutionary goals—which, so far, parallel Shelley's agenda—are decidedly dashed in the next line when the Queen indulges her selfish need for revenge in a move that unmasks her as nothing but another Swellfoot, another ruler whose pride and arrogance take form in excesses deployed at the site of the body—specifically, in domination and murder:

> Give them [the beasts that the newly empowered pigs are hunting] no law
> (are they not beasts of blood?)
> But such as they gave you. Tallyho! ho!
> Through the forest, furze, and bog, and den, and desert,
> Pursue the ugly beasts! tallyho! ho!
>
> (2.2.127-130)

Iona's language effectively dissolves her potential as a revolutionary hero, for her words show how by putting on his power, Iona has assumed Swellfoot's phallus, too: her rule is no different from his, and she prepares to hunt her persecutors with the same avidity Shelley attributed to Tyrant Swellfoot and excoriated throughout his play.[72]

Swellfoot closes with Iona joining the chorus of swine in a call for war as all "*Exeunt, in full cry;* IONA *driving the* SWINE, *with the empty* GREEN BAG" (349).[73] The play's finale thus resuscitates the tyranny of Swellfoot's reign, since the Queen calls on the pigs to pursue her enemies in the same way Swellfoot employed the Gadfly to sting Iona. Finally, the Green Bag re-emerges as an agent in the play, now drained of its contents but no less symbolic of evil than it was in the hands of the play's first Tyrant. Yoked to jealousy, envy, and selfishness—suggested by both the bag's color and its historical function as a mechanism for solicitors' puffed-up self-display[74]—that instrument of containment and deception closes the play as a representative for the phallus Iona has assumed as well as for the one she has not: symbolic of Swellfoot's selfish excesses, the Green Bag remarks the transfer of Swellfoot's tyranny into Iona's hands; and visually invoking tyranny's defeat—its emptying or evacuation—the bag reminds us of the potential Iona holds even as its limpness underscores her failure to erect a new order in place of the old. At the close of the play, the Green Bag returns us to the satire's first image of tyranny, Swellfoot's kingly paunch, for both sites call our attention to the selfish pleasures that metonymize tyranny: the paunch, overeating; the bag, revenge.

∞ ∞ ∞ ∞ ∞

My reading of *Œdipus Tyrannus; or, Swellfoot the Tyrant* has demonstrated Shelley's engagement with the central pattern that marks all of the works I consider throughout this study—specifically, the overlapping of political and erotic engagements. In *Swellfoot the Tyrant,* Shelley satirizes a contemporary political controversy, the Queen Caroline Affair, to demonstrate the potential for sexual transgression to figure politically. Throughout the satire, Shelley employs the same devices he poses as the instruments of revolution in his so-called visionary works—language, the body, and sexual transgression; but in *Swellfoot,* he demonstrates how these devices may be appropriated by tyrants just as potently as by revolutionaries. Shelley's play poses these instruments in a manner inconsistent with his broader agenda of liberty-through-love in order to demonstrate their innate political power; that is, by exposing the tyrannical uses to which these devices may be put, Shelley departicularizes them from what might otherwise be dismissed as naïve idealism. Instead, Shelley demonstrates how language, the body, and sexual transgression affect change at the level of politics and, consequently, in individual lives—whether for good or for bad, whether in the interest of oppression or of liberation. In *Swellfoot the Tyrant*, Shelley begins to justify his belief that love is, to paraphrase this chapter's epigraph, the law that governs the universe; that is, his satire remarks on the ways in which both Iona Taurina's transgressive engagements and her relationship with her husband function to affect the tenor of Swellfoot's regime and, in a broader context, how those engagements (fail to) reconfigure the political landscape of the play. In short, *Swellfoot the Tyrant* spectacularizes the processes through which intimate relationships inform political realities, privileging the realm of the erotic as the experiential space from which the moral law of the universe might be re-written.

Notes

1. Here, I am thinking of narrowly sentimental accounts of Shelley as the "ineffectual angel beating his wings against the wind," which were introduced in the generation after his death by Matthew Arnold, and which have been perpetuated throughout the twentieth century in novelistic "biographies" such as André Maurois' *Ariel: A Shelley Romance* (London: John Lane, 1924) and Laura Benét's *The Boy Shelley* (New York: Dodd, Mead and Company, 1964), as well as in a collection of poetry by Robert Cooperman entitled *In the Household of Percy Bysshe Shelley* (Gainesville: University Press of Florida, 1993).
2. "The love that dare not speak its name," a fin-de-siècle euphemism for homosexuality, was coined by Lord Alfred Douglas in the poem "Two Loves," which appeared in *The Chameleon* in December, 1894. I paraphrase (and, in terms of chronology, anticipate) Douglas' formulation for two reasons: first, because the subversive erotic milieux Shelley describes—such as the brother-sister incest between Laon and Cythna—would have held the same kind of resonance in his day as homosexuality did in Douglas'; second, because a number of reviewers hostile to Shelley's sexy representations attacked him on the grounds of having gone too far, of having offended public morals by giving voice to the kinds of love that should remain unspoken.
3. Although in the Preface to *Prometheus Unbound* Shelley claims to abhor didactic poetry, I believe the poet nevertheless fails to recognize the didactic nature of the majority of his own work, which propounds the singular doctrine of liberty-as-love, a concept I explore throughout this book.

4. Steven E. Jones appreciates the importance of *Swellfoot* to Shelley's *œuvre*, and he regards the satire " . . . as a transitional work in Shelley's career, as he moves away from the confident, exhortative energies of *The Mask of Anarchy* and toward the darker, more deeply ironic vision of *The Triumph of Life*"; see Jones, *Shelley's Satire: Violence, Exhortation, and Authority* (DeKalb: Northern Illinois University Press, 1994), 148.

5. Thomas W. Laqueur, "The Queen Caroline Affair: Politics as Art in the Reign of George IV," *Journal of Modern History* 54 (September 1982): 417.

6. Lynn Hunt, "How the Revolution's Divorce Laws Affected Private Life," in *The French Revolution. Turning Points in World History* (San Diego: Greenhaven Press, 1999), 112.

7. "The Queen's Answer" as printed in *The London Times*, 17 August 1820, and quoted in E. A. Smith, *A Queen on Trial: The Affair of Queen Caroline* (Dover: Alan Sutton, 1993), 104. As explained in the Introduction, I follow cultural codings of all threats to established authority as feminine, as, symbolically, "women," so in rendering Queen Caroline's words, I suggest we read "every loyal Englishwoman" to mean something more like "every oppressed English citizen," every person who, for whatever reasons and in whatever forms, remains barred from liberty.

8. Kenneth Neill Cameron provides a useful reading of *Swellfoot* as an anti-Malthusian statement. While the object of Cameron's inquiry is slightly different from mine—he treats economic theory, while I consider the political function of the erotic—I will return to some of his ideas throughout my reading of the play; see Cameron, *Shelley: The Golden Years* (Cambridge: Harvard University Press, 1974).

9. Mary Shelley, note to *Œdipus Tyrannus, or Swellfoot the Tyrant*, by Percy Bysshe Shelley. In *The Works of Percy Shelley in Ten Volumes* [Hereafter *WPS*], ed. Roger Ingpen and Walter E. Peck, 10 vols. (New York: Charles Scribner's Sons, 1928), 2:350.

10. Jones remarks on the congruence of Queen Caroline's situation to the Shelleys', and he suggests that since "Shelley is in a position analogous to Caroline's," his composition of *Swellfoot the Tyrant* "may have served in part to mask an uncomfortable realization that he shared something with the whole affair: Shelley, too, was in exile and the focus of a marital scandal, accused of mistreating his wife Harriet. . . . As a poet who would be a 'legislator,' he was outside looking in, hoping to move those within the circle of power" (125). Jones points to one of Mary's letters that directly aligns the Shelleys' situation with Caroline's in its observation "that spies might well be preparing to present a green bag of 'scandal' against them" (145).

11. A number of scholars have remarked on the importance of the Queen Caroline Affair to early nineteenth-century British culture: see Anna Clark, "Queen Caroline and the Sexual Politics of Popular Culture in London, 1820," *Representations* 31 (Summer 1990): 47-68; Thomas Laqueur, "The Queen Caroline Affair: Politics as Art in the Reign of George IV," *Journal of Modern History* 54 (September 1982): 417-466; John Stevenson, *London in the Age of Reform* (New York: Oxford, 1977); Iain McCalman, *Radical Underworld: Prophets, Revolutionaries, and*

Pornographers in London, 1795-1840 (New York: Clarendon Press, 1993), 163-173; and Fraser, *passim*.

12. Roger Fulford reproduces a contemporary caricature that demonstrates the public's recognition of the hypocrisy of George's charges against his wife; see Fulford, *The Trial of Queen Caroline* (New York: Stein and Day, 1968), 210.

13. Michelle Perrot, *A History of Private Life: From the Fires of Revolution to the Great War*, ed. Philippe Ariès and Georges Duby, trans. Arthur Goldhammer, 4 vols. (Cambridge: The Belknap Press, 1990), 4:48.

14. This "chivalrous" construction of Queen Caroline as a political icon mirrors—meaning that it reflects and reverses—Edmund Burke's defense of Marie Antoinette in *Reflections on the Revolution in France* (1789-1790). Burke laments the indignity of the fall of the royal couple during the Revolution by invoking a chivalric code which, as J. G. A. Pocock argues, "had . . . the ideological effect of explaining how noblemen and gentlemen could play their part in the polite modern Europe of the *ancien regime*. A chivalrous nobility and a learned and charitable clergy belonged to the same historical process as the enlightened townsmen of the age of commerce. It was the decline of all three that Burke was lamenting when he described chivalry crumbling under the impact of revolution"; see Burke, *Reflections on the Revolution in France*, ed. J. G. A. Pocock (Indianapolis: Hackett Publishing Company, 1987), xxxiii. Burke laments the fall of the royal family in a passage that aligns the Revolution with the death of chivalry: "Oh! what a revolution! . . . little did I dream that I should have lived to see such disasters fallen upon [Marie Antoinette] in a nation of gallant men, in a nation of men of honor and of cavaliers. I thought ten thousand swords must have leaped from their scabbards to avenge even a look that threatened her with insult. But the age of chivalry is gone . . . and the glory of Europe is extinguished forever. Never, never more shall we behold that generous loyalty to rank and sex, that proud submission, that dignified obedience, that subordination of the heart which kept alive, even in servitude itself, the spirit of an exalted freedom" (66). Burke's bizarre language co-aligns freedom and oppression, for only in the "chivalrous" age of subordination and hierarchy, he insists, are men truly free. Pocock argues that Burke's chivalrous defense of Marie Antoinette—his descriptions of the Queen's "piety," "courage," and "dignity," his memory of the "great lady" "glittering like the morning star, full of life and splendor and joy" (66)—"is the occasion of a complex piece of conservative thinking, in which tradition and progress find themselves reconciled" as Burke simultaneously laments the fall of the age of chivalry and calls for its resuscitation (xxxiii).

15. Sara Maza, "The Diamond Necklace Affair Revisited (1785-1786): The Case of the Missing Queen," in *Eroticism and the Body Politic*, ed. Hunt, 68, 69.

16. Carlos Baker, *Shelley's Major Poetry: The Fabric of a Vision* (New York: Russell and Russell, 1961), 175.

17. *The Letters of Percy Bysshe Shelley* [Hereafter *Letters*], ed. Frederick L. Jones, 2 vols. (New York: Clarendon Press, 1964), 2:220. One speech by the Semichorus of Swine in *Swellfoot* echoes Shelley's sentiments rather closely:

> I vote Swellfoot and Iona
> Try the magic test together;
> Whenever royal spouses bicker,
> Both should try the magic liquor.
> (*WPS* 2.1.128-131)

18. As in the Introduction, here I follow traditional binary distinctions in coding revolution as feminine since it is deployed in opposition to hegemonic, or masculine, authority: in patriarchal societies, authority is always masculine, and alternatives to authority must, by their very oppositional status, figure as feminine.

19. Jones points to Shelley's letter of 30 June 1820 to the Gisbornes as "the germ of *Swellfoot the Tyrant,* including all the salient topics—the perceived financial crisis, the carnivalesque violence, the display of the royal domestic dispute, . . . and the seriousness of the people's plight . . . incongruously mixed in with the ridiculous events" (128).

20. Melanie C. Hawthorne has pointed out to me that the significance of the name of Shelley's heroine holds more than just mythological associations, which I discuss below: "Iona" is a partial anagram of the real-life Queen's first name (Caroline), and Iona's second, or patronymic name, "Taurina," underscores the heroine's familial heritage to remind the reader that not only does she symbolize but also that she descends from Taurus, the Bull—John Bull, or England.

21. It is worth noting that the last images described in White's quote find equivalents in real life as well as in Shelley's satire: the "Italian dagger" symbolizes the witnesses from Italy who testified against Caroline; the "Milan Commission" was the name of the committee that convened to investigate rumors about Caroline's Italian dalliances; the "Bill of Pains and Penalties" was the legislation that sought to punish Caroline for her exploits and to bar her from royal power were she found guilty; and the "Horse Leech" appears, re-invented, in Shelley's satire as Swellfoot's minion, "The Leech." Both "Horse Leech" and "Leech" derive from the name of Sir John Leach, the official appointed to chair the Milan Commission, which was convened "to gather evidence [against Caroline] systematically" (Cameron 355).

22. See Newman Ivey White, "Shelley's Swell-Foot the Tyrant in Relation to Contemporary Political Satires," *PMLA* 36 (1921): 332-346.

23. Claudette Hould, *Images of the French Revolution* (Québec: Musée de Québec/Les Publications du Québec, 1989).

24. Newman Ivey White reports that *A Speech From the Throne* went through an astonishing 50 editions in 1820 ("Shelley's Swell-Foot" 339).

25. The sheer popularity of the pamphlet suggests that Shelley probably knew it. In addition to its use of the phrase "swinish multitude," the following lines from the pamphlet resonate throughout Shelley's satire:

> Reform, reform the swinish rabble cry,
> Meaning of course, rebellion, blood and riot.
> Audacious rascals! you, my Lords, and I
> Know 'tis their duty to be starved in quiet.
> (qtd. in White, "Shelley's Swell-Foot" 339)

26. White points to an article in the 30 June 1820 *Examiner* in which a chorus of pigs "was used as an instrument of satire against George IV by Professor Porson" (*Shelley* 2:225).

27. The use of the pig as a symbol for the abuse of power is not specific to the nineteenth century, however; George Orwell's novel *Animal Farm* (1945) employs pigs to the same end.

28. The sedition trials involving a number of radical pressmen—among them William Hone, Thomas Jonathan Wooler, and Richard Carlile—were topics of much discussion in early nineteenth-century radical circles, and Shelley would certainly have been aware of these well-publicized contests between the government and the radical press. His decision to pit pressmen against the government in *Swellfoot the Tyrant* may have arisen from contemporary contests for authority.

29. Baker suggests that satire often functions as a response to political oppression in the form of comic relief to tyranny, and he notes that "the queen's precipitate return to England and the uncrowned king's abortive efforts to divorce her on grounds of adultery were a comic substitute for the tragedy of Peterloo Fields" (174). Elise M. Gold also recognizes the particular power of satire "to rid the world of . . . oppression": she argues that "the satirist, in effect, initiates a different type of imaginative reform . . . [by] teaching readers to be more discriminating judges of the deceptive actions and speech which give rise to political and social inequities"; see "*King Lear* and Aesthetic Tyranny in Shelley's *The Cenci, Swellfoot the Tyrant,* and *The Witch of Atlas*," *English Language Notes* 24 (September 1986): 66. Jones considers Shelley's decision to write about the Queen Caroline Affair in the form of satire rather than, say in pantomime or burlesque, and concludes that "[satire] is set in an imagined public arena of discourse, where genres and groups could interact in that virtual (or generic) space Bakhtin called 'the public square where the folk gather'" (134).

30. Here, Clark quotes a letter from George Wells of Weston, 16 September 1830.

31. Although in *Shelley,* Newman Ivey White includes only two of Hunt's literary texts among his list of "Shelley's Reading"—*The Story of Rimini* (1816) and *Foliage* (1818)—Shelley was certainly better familiar with his friend's literary productions than White suggests. As Shelley's letters demonstrate, while in Italy he was kept apprised of the goings-on around Queen Caroline by Hunt as well as by Thomas Love Peacock.

32. Because it demonstrates the operation of the theatrical form of the mask as a spectacularization of the masquerade, *The Descent of Liberty* participates in the playfulness of the masquerade itself—the suspension of identity, the erotic draw of the uncertain or ambiguous. Jeffrey N. Cox argues that Hunt and his associates turned to mythological subjects " . . . in pursuit of the cultural power to address and perhaps to liberate an audience when the forces of liberation had been routed and their positions—in exile or on the Cockney borders of official culture—were defined by a certain powerlessness"; see Cox, "Staging Hope: Genre, Myth, and Ideology in the Dramas of the Hunt Circle," *Texas Studies in Language and Literature* 38 (Fall/Winter 1996): 245. Cox points to *The Descent of Liberty* as a work that sets the course for some of the most interesting of the dramatic

experiments of the second-generation Romantics, and he locates in Hunt's mask "a first attempt to answer the question of what form the drama should take as culture enters the post-Napoleonic, potentially post-revolutionary era. Hunt's surprising answer is that the imprisoned radical writing after the fall of Napoleon turns to a courtly form which flourished before the rise of Cromwell: he offered *The Descent of Liberty* as 'A Mask'" (245).

33. Leigh Hunt, *The Descent of Liberty: A Mask* (London: James Cawthorn, 1815), 3.472-473.

34. For more on castration anxiety and the Œdipal complex, see Sigmund Freud, "The Infantile Genital Organization," in *The Complete Psychological Works of Sigmund Freud,* trans. and ed. James Strachey with Alix Strachey and Alan Tyson, 24 vols. (London: The Hogarth Press, 1986), 19:141-145.

35. The psychoanalytic re-figuration of the eye-as-phallus follows this logic: just as psychoanalysis poses the penis as the closest corporeal referent to the phallus—that transcendental signifier of law, control, and order—so, too, might the eye be said to fulfill this function, since it is a primary device by which (generic) man orders the world about him. This displacement of the phallus/penis to the eye problematizes the patriarchal agenda of psychoanalysis, however, for it empowers women to claim equal access to the embodied phallus, stripping men of their essentially constructed (i.e., baselessly figured) superiority. Such a quagmire of gender politics is addressed quite interestingly in Georges Bataille's 1928 novel *Histoire de l'oeil* [Story of the Eye] in which a man is quite overcome by his lover's unusual power over him—the eye inside her vagina that watches him, mastering/castrating him through the force of its (displaced) phallic power.

36. Michael Erkelenz, "Unacknowledged Legislation: The Genre and Function of Shelley's 'Ode to Naples,'" in *Shelley: Poet and Legislator of the World,* ed. Betty T. Bennett and Stuart Curran (Baltimore: The Johns Hopkins University Press, 1996), 70.

37. Michael Henry Scrivener notes that the title of Shelley's poem was changed by Thomas Medwin to "Similes," apparently in an attempt to distance the poet from the fallout a more blatant attack on powerful political figures (here, Sidmouth, the Home Secretary, and Castlereagh, the Foreign Secretary) would incur; see Scrivener, *Radical Shelley: The Philosophical Anarchism and Utopian Thought of Percy Bysshe Shelley* (Princeton: Princeton University Press, 1982), 239.

38. Of course, as I have already suggested, the public/private distinction proves a false one; inevitably, as Shelley's works show, political commitments metonymize erotic relationships, and vice-versa.

39. My use of the phrase "self-involving coils" gestures toward my discussion of *The Cenci* in Chapter III: Shelley uses this image to describe a situation of oppression in which one seems helplessly trapped, and which encloses one more and more tightly, finally suffocating liberty in its firm tension and unyielding grasp.

40. Cameron notes that Shelley gave his publishers license to substitute asterisks for any expressions in the "Ode" the public might find offensive. Thomas Love Peacock, who delivered the manuscript to the publisher, dutifully inserted four asterisks in place of the word "KING" in the line quoted above. But in the

Quarterly Review's account of the "Ode to Liberty," Peacock's four asterisks were changed to six, so that many of the journal's Tory readers misread Shelley's line as calling for the stamping of the name of "CHRIST" into the dust (369). Although the *Quarterly Review* deliberately manipulated Shelley's original passage, that misrepresentation remained quite true to the argument underlying the entire "Ode," since Shelley consistently aligns all institutions of tyranny—naming the government and the church as chief among these—and calls for the overthrow of them all; throughout the "Ode," "KING" and "CHRIST" are meant to stand in for each other in exactly the same way that the *Quarterly Review*'s malicious misrepresentation of the "Ode to Liberty" suggests.

41. My use of the term "rapturous" is meant to suggest the turbulent revolution of the Biblical rapture as well as the state of erotic pleasure to which that term loosely refers. I return more fully to the function of landscape in Shelley's intellectual revolution in my readings of *Epipsychidion*, *Laon and Cythna*, and *Prometheus Unbound*, which comprise the second half of this book.

42. My sense of Shelley's notion of historical progression is informed by Scrivener, who argues that Shelley's " . . . political anarchism establishes a political ideal, a utopia, toward which society is moving in stages; it rejects a millenarian logic whereby utopia could be achieved immediately; it accepts politics as a process of gradual reforms and compromise, as well as ethical idealism" (xii).

43. Gold misreads the ADVERTISEMENT as if Shelley meant for his readers to take seriously the frontmatter of an overtly satirical piece: she suggests that the role Shelley assumes in the ADVERTISEMENT functions as "an apt but conventional mask for the satirist behind which he can comfortably attack such tyrannical abuses [as the play exposes], particularly those of language . . . " (65). Gold's misreading of Shelley's "place" in the front matter divorces the satire from the broader project of pluralized authority, which I have discussed above.

44. Other examples of such a writerly agenda include *Laon and Cythna*, which Shelley claims is dictated to him after he is transported to a visionary other-world, and the sonnet "Ozymandias," whose mediated narrative begins "I met a traveler in an antique land / Who said— . . . " (*SPP* 103, lines 1-2).

45. "Angariate" is an obsolete verb meaning "to exact forced labor from; to press into service" (*OED*, s.v. "angariate").

46. For example, Newman Ivey White dismisses "the revolting setting" of the satire as encouraging "most readers [to] regard the poem as a failure even when taken for no more than was meant," *viz.* pure play ("Shelley's Swell-Foot" 332).

47. Stuart Curran, *Shelley's Annus Mirabilis: The Maturing of an Epic Vision* (San Marino: The Huntington Library, 1975), 215 n 24.

48. Edward Tripp, *The Meridian Handbook of Classical Mythology* (New York: New American Library, 1970), 319.

49. "Supposed" because *Œdipus Tyrannus* was never meant to be performed. Thus, any references I make to (anticipated) audience responses are purely hypothetical and are based on clues Shelley provides throughout the text about the kind of reaction he expected his (similarly inclined) readers/viewers to experience. The initial publication of Shelley's closet drama made "a considerable impact," as

Holmes notes, for the text was "immediately seized by the politically motivated Society for the Suppression of Vice who threatened to prosecute [Shelley's publisher, James] Johnson" (611).

50. Scrivener, following Cameron, notes that the religion of the play is Maulthusianism, a dedication to the economic theories of Thomas Malthus (1766-1834) who advocated castrating the poor in order to prevent their perpetuation (263, 264).

51. For example, in *The Cenci* we are told that Count Cenci's crimes—among them the murder of his sons—are forgiven because of the substantial sums he contributes to the Church.

52. Certainly, the sharp economic discrepancy between the monarchy and the masses in Shelley's day gave particular force to his representations of poverty-as-oppression in *Swellfoot the Tyrant*. The excesses of wealth stood in marked contrast to the pangs of poverty that many Englishmen suffered throughout the first quarter of the nineteenth century: during the massive crop failures of 1815-1817, for example, the regent continued construction on an elaborate castle, an indulgence the impoverished English surely resented. In one sense, Famine really was the official domestic policy of Shelley's day, as the gulph between the "haves" and the "have-nots" threatened to swallow any of those radicals who would question the inequity of riches. "Mammon," as we know from Spenser's *The Færie Queene*, is a summary figure for the pursuit of earthly goods. Aurally, the name invokes the Biblical figure of Ammon, who gave in to selfishness and lust and raped the Princess Tamar, only afterwards to realize that the experience so perverted him that, for Ammon, all love was turned to hate (2 Sam. 13:1-19). Echoed in "Mammon," "Ammon" thus remarks the reversal of love into hate, a microcosmic representation of the reversal of liberty into oppression. The name "Mammon" may also derive from a perversion of "manna" or "spiritual nourishment from a divine source" (*Webster's II: New Riverside University Dictionary*, hereafter *Webster's II*, s.v. "manna"), so that the name of the Arch-Priest of Swellfoot's religion reminds us of the perverted nature of all religion under tyranny: rather than providing spiritual nourishment, religion-under-tyranny starves believers of all hope. Here, Swellfoot's unchecked indulgence remarks on the economic situation in England from about 1815-1820: surely, Shelley's description of Swellfoot's gustatory indulgence comments on the poverty and malnourishment from which many Englishmen suffered as the monarch "[lay] satisfied with layers of fat. . . ." Jones argues that in describing Swellfoot's obesity, Shelley would have been "well aware [that] Leigh Hunt had been imprisoned for writing a similar libel . . . calling the Regent 'this Adonis in loveliness,' a 'corpulent gentleman of fifty!'" (136).

53. Shelley may also be commenting on the then-notorious process of jury-rigging, in which the government would hire citizens to sit on a jury and rule in favor of the crown. Among Shelley's circle, such a practice was considered yet another example of the unchecked power of tyrannical rule, another manifestation of what in the play Shelley codes as swollenness.

54. I follow Freudian psychoanalysis and its Lacanian and feminist revisions in aligning phallicism with patriarchal authority or tyranny; see Freud, "Female

Sexuality," in *The Complete Psychological Works of Sigmund Freud*, 21:225-243; Jacques Lacan, "The Meaning of the Phallus," in *Feminine Sexuality: Jacques Lacan and the école freudienne*, ed. and trans. Juliet Mitchell and Jacqueline Rose (New York: W. W. Norton, 1982), 74-85; Nancy J. Chodorow, "Feminism, Femininity, and Freud," in *Feminism and Psychoanalytic Theory* (New Haven: Yale University Press, 1989), 165-177; Irigaray, *Speculum*; Irigaray, "Psychoanalytic Theory: Another Look," in *This Sex Which Is Not One*, trans. Catherine Porter (Ithaca: Cornell University Press, 1985), 34-67; Jane Gallop, "Writing Erratic Desire," in *The Daughter's Seduction: Feminism and Psychoanalysis* (Ithaca: Cornell University Press, 1982), 92-112; Gallop, "Beyond the Phallus," in *Thinking Through the Body* (New York: Columbia University Press, 1988), 119-133; and Susan Gubar, "'The Blank Page' and the Issue of Female Creativity," in *The New Feminist Criticism: Essays on Women, Literature, and Theory*, ed. Elaine Showalter (New York: Pantheon Books, 1985), 292-313.

55. Dakry's real-life counterpart, Lord Eldon, became notorious for his tendency to burst into tears in public.

56. I return to the concept of the "vanishing point" and develop its relationship to ideological structures far more fully in my reading of *The Cenci* in Chapter III.

57. As a noun, the word "daw" is "[a]pplied contemptuously to persons" and may signify a simpleton or fool, a lazy person or sluggard; as a verb, "daw" means "to daunt, subdue, or frighten," implying the daw figure's coercive power (*OED*, s.v. "daw"). More specifically, the word "jackdaw" denotes a bird that lives in old buildings and churches—themselves Shelleyan emblems of oppressive orders, as we shall see in the chapters to follow, and the jackdaw functions most famously in fables as a figure of deceit (*OED*, s.v. "jackdaw"). In early nineteenth-century radical discourse, the term "jack-daw" was applied to "a propagandist for the church against the theorists of radical reform"; see *The Black Dwarf*, ed. Peter Garside (New York: Columbia University Press, 1993), 255. William Blake employed the same image for the clergy in a poem entitled "The Human Abstract" in *Songs of Innocence and of Experience Shewing the Two Contrary States of the Human Soul* (1794), and the jack-daw is lampooned in an 1818 poem, "The Three Bulls and the Jackdaw. A Fable," which appeared under the name "Philo Taurus" in *The Black Dwarf* in 1818 (Garside 254-255).

58. Not insignificantly, Shelley compares the plight of Beatrice Cenci and her similarly oppressed mother and siblings to that of "scorpions ringed with fire," a metaphor I discuss in much detail in Chapter III. The Cencis remain so enmeshed in the traps of tyranny that they can find no way out; at each turn, their progress is blocked, and in the end they have no real recourse except to react as scorpions ringed with fire—to destroy themselves before the tyrannical forces symbolized by fire do so. Shelley completed *The Cenci* about a year before *Swellfoot the Tyrant*; quite possibly, he may be alluding to the earlier play in this invocation of scorpions, and, if so, his self-referential intertextuality underscores the ultimately serious nature of the satire's agenda. The image of a scorpion stinging itself to death also appears in Byron's poem *The Giaour* (1813) and in a gothic drama by Francis

North entitled *The Kentish Barons* (1791) which, as Cox notes, suggests its "liberal or democratic tendencies" in its attack on despotic power; see *Seven Gothic Dramas 1789-1825*, ed. and intro. Jeffrey N. Cox (Athens: Ohio University Press, 1992), 86.
59. *Webster's II*, s.v. "verdigris."
60. While Shelley explores the operation of language in the service of tyranny throughout *Swellfoot the Tyrant*, in other works, such as *Prometheus Unbound* and *Epipsychidion*, he investigates the potential of language to work in concert with liberty. *Swellfoot* stands as an important text since, like *The Cenci*, it bifurcates the effects of language, acknowledging its potential to be appropriated in either the service of oppression or of liberation.
61. Such a move underscores the revolutionary inevitability of oppression, for those deprived of the most basic human need—nourishment—have no choice but to revolt in the interest of self-preservation. Shelley's belief in the tendency of revolution to emerge from the experience of extreme oppression anticipates Karl Marx's argument in his *Economic and Philosophical Manuscripts* (1844) that the proletariat—those disenfranchised from power—is the very group that will bring about radical change, the group that will initiate revolution, safe in the assurance that, having nothing invested in the system of order, there is absolutely nothing to lose.
62. Jones adds that just as Shelley's voice was drowned out by the grunting of pigs as he read the "Ode to Liberty" at San Giuliano, so too is Liberty's voice drowned out by the grunting of pigs, who seem oblivious to her speech (139).
63. Richard Cronin, *Shelley's Poetic Thoughts* (New York: St. Martin's Press, 1981), 6.
64. Clark notes that marrow bones and cleavers function as "devastating insults against George IV's manhood and intelligence" (66 n 57).
65. Newman Ivey White observes that "the only instance noted in which the word ['Gadfly'] seems to have a significance in the satires of the times is an allusion to Sidmouth as 'the devil of traps and beaks and gadflies and eavesdroppers'" in a piece called *A Slap at Slop* ("Shelley's Swell-Foot" 343).
66. Gold uses the phrase "linguistic tyranny" to describe the "abuses [of] language" Shelley models on *King Lear*, a play she reads as the paratext for *Swellfoot the Tyrant*, *The Cenci*, and *The Witch of Atlas* (65).
67. Shelley's marriages, first to Harriet Westbrook and then to Mary Wollstonecraft Godwin, offer other examples of such a moment of transgressive reinscription, of the purely performative miming of a cultural act, ultimately in the service of some end other than the heteropatriarchal imperative, the tradition that Western culture enshrines.
68. The psychoanalytic connections between castration and decapitation have long been recognized. For a reading of decapitation as the symbolic castration of women, see Hélène Cixous, "Castration or Decapitation?" trans. Annette Kuhn, *Signs* 7 (Fall 1981): 41-55. I return to (figural) castration as a mode for spectacularizing relationships of power in my reading of *The Cenci* in Chapter III.
69. Cameron notes the real-life precedent for this moment: "[Queen Caroline's] progress from the seacoast to London turned into a triumphal procession.

According to *The Examiner*, she was cheered at every step of her way by tumultuous crowds, the women crying out, 'God bless her . . . she must be innocent!' and the men unharnessing the horses from her carriage and pulling it through the flag-decked streets" (355).

70. Jones notes that the addressees of the oracle (here, the people of Thebes) vanish in Shelley's epigraph; he argues that while the satire points to the political instability that besets Bœotia (itself "a proverbial site of stupid citizens" [138]), the dropping of the addressees in the epigraph pluralizes the potential audiences to whom it might have been directed. Ultimately, Jones concludes that while in the play the oracle is directed to the citizens of Thebes, the epigraph re-directs that oracle—and its promise of reform or civil war—to all of Shelley's readers (143). Such a move lends credence to the extratextual, real-life engagements of *Swellfoot* I have suggested throughout.

71. See Irigaray, "Commodities Among Themselves," in *This Sex Which Is Not One*, 192-197.

72. Scrivener's reading of the play's ending reminds us of Shelley's comic intention: "imagining Iona Taurina on top of the bull, shouting 'tallyho,' dissolves the Queen Caroline Affair into the farce that it actually was" (267). However, Cameron reads the play's final scene more satirically, unmasking the comic in terms of Shelley's understanding of the political reality that faced England—despotism or revolution (360)—a reading not unlike Jones' (142, 143). To prove his point, Cameron parallels the swine's ironic praises to Famine with "the peasant vision of Thomas Spence in his *Constitution of a Perfect Commonwealth*—the vision that Shelley reiterated, warningly, in *A Philosophical View of Reform*" (361). Finally, Cameron argues that Shelley's final scene "was indebted to the conclusion of the young Coleridge's *Letter of Liberty to Her Dear Friend Famine* in the *Conciones ad pupulum* volume (1795)" and suggests that Shelley probably "assumed . . . his more literate readers would perceive the reference. Coleridge's argument was that unless the rulers of England changed to more liberal policies, they would be overwhelmed by the forces of revolution generated by economic distress (famine)" (361). Jones notes that Coleridge's piece introduces Despotism as a harlot with "MYSTERY" written upon her forehead (141), a probable precedent for Shelley's textualized body of Liberty.

73. Jones argues that Iona's exit "suggests that any deeper and more extensive [political] change is yet far in the future" (143). His reading of the satire's end aligns *Swellfoot the Tyrant* with what I later describe as the political pessimism that pervades Shelley's so-called "visionary" works.

74. In 1785, Francis Grose glossed the phrase "green bag" as follows: "An attorney; those gentlemen carry their clients' deeds in a *green bag*, and, it is said, when they have no deeds to carry frequently fill them up with an old pair of breeches, or any other trumpery, to give themselves the appearance of business"; see Grose, *Classical Dictionary of the Foreign Tongue* (London: Routledge and Kegan Paul, 1963), s.v. "green bag."

CHAPTER III

Tyranny and Liberation, or Rigidity and Ooziness:
Physical and Psychological Landscapes in *The Cenci* and *Julian and Maddalo*

> How wonderfully I am changed! Not a disembodied spirit can have undergone a stranger revolution! I never knew until now that contentment was any thing but a word denoting an unmeaning abstraction. I never before felt the integrity of my nature, its various dependencies, & learned to consider myself as an whole accurately united rather than an assemblage of inconsistent & discordant proportions. Above all, most sensibly do I perceive the truth of my entire worthlessness but as depending on another. And I am deeply persuaded that thus ennobled, [I shall] become a more true & constant friend, a more useful lover of mankind, a more ardent asserter of truth & virtue—above all more consistent, more intelligible[,] more true.
>
> —Percy Bysshe Shelley, on his relationship with Mary Wollstonecraft Godwin in a letter to Thomas Jefferson Hogg, 4 October 1814

Love, Landscape, and Revolution

Shelley's love for Mary Wollstonecraft Godwin marked nothing less than a revolution in the development of his thought, for that relationship demonstrated the profound effects of love the poet had but theorized in *Queen Mab* (1812-1813) and other early works. The emphasis Shelley places on what he describes in his letter as the ennobling power of love functions as a leitmotif throughout his works from 1814, the year of his meeting and elopement with Mary Godwin. As these works make clear, this primary erotic relationship concretizes Shelley's "unmeaning abstraction[s]" and allows the poet for the first time to consider himself a unified, complete being, to recognize "the integrity of [his] nature." That Shelley's whole identity coalesces in his love for Mary is spelled out earlier in the same letter: "I speak thus of Mary now—& so intimately are our natures now united, that I feel whilst I describe her excellencies as if I were an egoist expiating upon his own perfections—" (1.402). Collapsing each into the other, love functions as an ennobling and, even, a democratizing force: it dissolves all manner of individual difference and erases all modes of division; it strengthens both lovers, uniting them as one and purifying their individual and collective engagements with the world around them.

Clearly, Shelley's estimation of his love for Mary as a "revolution" is no exaggeration.

Four years after his elopement with Mary, Shelley composed a prose fragment entitled "On Love" (1818), an essay in which he charted love's psychological trajectory between the self and the beloved, a theoretical rumination that derives from the sentiments conveyed in his letter to Hogg. For Shelley, love always grows out of an absence, a longing for the complement to one's inevitably fragmentary nature: "*Thou* demandest what is Love. It is that powerful attraction towards all that we conceive or fear or hope beyond ourselves when we find within our own thoughts the chasm of an insufficient void and seek to awaken in all things that are, a community with what we experience within ourselves" (*SPP* 473). Love begins in the experience of longing, the realization of a psychic disconnection and the anxious urge to cover over that lack; for Shelley, love is the means for bridging that gap, for leaping from the disappointments of the real world to the hope of utopia.

As the language of "On Love" suggests, Shelley's description of love anticipates exactly the traditional psychoanalytic model of the self/other opposition. Put simply, this opposition, or binary division, poses an intrinsic separation between the individual (the self) and all others in the world. The individual's engagements maneuver him through a vast sea of perpetual unfamiliarity, so that even among the multitude, the self remains psychologically isolated from all others, each of whom seems so very unlike him. Shelley describes this condition in "On Love" by recalling how, even in the midst of social interactions, he remains painfully aware of his state of psychological exile: "I know not the internal constitution of other men, or even of thine whom I now address. I see that in some external attributes they resemble me, but when misled by that appearance I have thought to appeal to something in common and unburthen my inmost soul to them, I have found my language misunderstood like one in a distant and savage land. The more opportunities they have afforded me for experience, the wider has appeared the interval between us, and to a greater distance have the points of sympathy been withdrawn. With a spirit ill fitted to sustain such proof, trembling and feeble through its tenderness, I have every where sought, and have found only repulse and disappointment" (473). This acute sense of dislocation marks the psychological condition of the exile, the stranger in a strange land, a figure whose psychology Shelley investigates throughout his works, particularly in *Alastor, Julian and Maddalo,* and *Epipsychidion.* According to this model, the exiled self is overcome—or rescued—by the discovery of the beloved, who returns to the self a fullness and satisfaction, the very absence of which marks the exilic state. As Shelley notes, in exile, ". . . we find within our own thoughts the chasm of an insufficient void . . . " and we look about us in search of the one who will rescue us from that condition of despair or, as both of the Shelleys refer to it elsewhere, that complete lack of sympathy.[1]

According to Shelley's model, the beloved acts as an agent under whose spell the exiled self emigrates into the world at large; accordingly, the lover promotes the psychic health (or fulfillment) of the self and invigorates each of his diverse engagements. Shelley describes the effect of the beloved in terms of what we might think of as a purifying lens, or mirror:

> We are born into the world and there is something within us which from the instant that we live and move thirsts after its likeness. . . . . We dimly see within our intellectual nature a miniature as it were of our entire self, yet deprived of all that we condemn or despise, the ideal prototype of every thing excellent or lovely that we are capable of conceiving as belonging to the nature of man. Not only the portrait of our external being, but an assemblage of the minutest particulars of which our nature is composed: a mirror whose surface reflects only the forms of purity and brightness: a soul within our soul that describes a circle around its proper Paradise which sorrow and evil dare not overleap. (473-474)

Shelley argues that the individual seeks out the purified version of himself, and once he finds it, he repeats that physiological convergence in his other engagements in the world about him, the contemplation of which mirrors back to him the trajectory of lover and beloved, thus ensuring him of his "place" in a world from which he only recently stood removed in psychic exile. The loss of love, Shelley concludes, functions with equal but opposite magnitude: where love enlivens the individual and rescues him from psychic exile, "so soon as this want or power is dead, man becomes the living sepulchre of himself, and what yet survives is the mere husk of what once he was" (474). The loss of the beloved destroys the self, rendering him an exile (or other) once again, a dramatic double-reduction that registers corporeally in the individual's mental and physical decline, in psychic fragmentation and somatic disorder.[2]

Shelley's description of love suggests love's role in political matters, for not only does the voice of the lover infuse the natural world with new sound and new meaning, but it enlivens the individual with a force Shelley likens to "patriotic success" (474), or pride-in-nation. Thus, even while he seems to devote "On Love" to the more esoteric concerns of the psychological maneuvers of love and their effects on the individual, throughout the essay Shelley alludes to the contingencies between the love's movements and the individual's engagements with the world about him.

Throughout "On Love," Shelley articulates his model of love's trajectory in terms of the language of landscape, a strategy to which he returns throughout his works, and which is key to understanding the model of erotic cartography I explore in the second half of this book. Shelley begins by describing the individual's condition of solitude as a "chasm" in the psyche, and he writes that upon the location of the beloved, the individual hears his lover's voice in the physical world around him, in "the tongueless wind," "the flowing of brooks," and "the rustling of the reeds" (474). The model Shelley poses throughout "On Love" suggests not only a collapse of the self/other binary, so that the individual and the beloved, as Shelley says, "mix and melt" into each other (473), but also what Freud describes as "the oceanic sense," the individual's perception and sensation of a complete connection with the natural world. Freud points to the oceanic sense as the psychic complement to religious faith: in "Civilization and Its Discontents" (1930), he describes an experience about which a friend had written to him, "a sensation of 'eternity,' a feeling as of something limitless, unbounded—as it were, 'oceanic.' One may, [Freud's friend] thinks, rightly call oneself religious on the ground of this oceanic feeling alone, even if one rejects every belief and every illusion."[3] While Freud admits that he "cannot discover this 'oceanic' feeling" in himself, he does understand the experience in theory, and he suggests that it arises from the epiphany of one's "indissoluble bond" with the earth, "of being one with the external world as a whole" (21:65). Freud concludes that the "oceanic sense" derives from the same psychological and intellectual need that gives rise to religious belief, "another way of disclaiming the danger which the ego recognizes as threatening it from the external world" (21:72). Shelley's model of love externalizes Freud's oceanic sense, so that the pleasure (or the sense of wholeness) an individual experiences as a result of covering over the vast and yawning psychic chasm gets metonymized in Shelley's notion of erotic relationships: finding ourselves in the beloved, we recognize our vitality amidst all of those about us, enabling us finally to achieve a divine union with the whole of the universe, which reveals itself as the projection of our desires, the reflection of our pleasures.

As I suggested in Chapter I, Shelley's notion of Love as All situates love as a replacement for religion; in short, Shelley elevates love to the metanarrative of truth, posing the act of love as a means of salvation from the disappointments of the world at large. Shelley's model of love anticipates Freud's notion of the oceanic sense as a transcendental state congruent to religious faith. Freud locates "the origin of the religious attitude" in "the feeling of infantile helplessness" that prompts one's desire to become a part of the world-at-large (21:72). Freud's postulation of the oceanic sense as a compensation for the human drive for religious faith—itself an outgrowth of the helpless infant's adoration of its father—finds a parallel in Shelley's notion of love as emerging from the exiled self's feelings of helplessness in psychic solitude. Freud's infant seeks the security of the (biological) father and, later, transfers that adoration and trust to its (spiritual) Father, God; Shelley's exiled self, like the infant, looks for its likeness, but it turns neither to its parent nor to the Supreme Being but to the beloved who, in Shelley's scheme, fulfills both of those functions within the context of the erotic union and through the processes of commingling, both psychically and sexually. The relationships Shelley describes between and among lovers thus replicate both domestic and religious models, so that lovers and beloveds assume the roles of caretakers and saviors in their erotic engagements. In addition to anticipating Freud's oceanic sense, Shelley's model exemplifies Romantic pantheism, the early nineteenth-century belief that "God is everything and everything is God"[4]—perhaps an odd formulation to attribute to the atheist Shelley, but one which nevertheless encompasses the divine, salvific potential the poet locates in the elements of the natural world as well as in the erotic unions of lovers and beloveds.

By broadening the description of love's effects and incorporating elements of the landscape, Shelley's 1819 poem "Love's Philosophy" suggests the particular links between his views of love-as-oneness and the oceanic sense Freud would describe almost a century later:

> I
>
> The fountains mingle with the river,
> And the rivers with the ocean;
> The winds of Heaven mix for ever
> With a sweet emotion;
> Nothing in the world is single;
> All things by a law divine
> In one another's being mingle—
> Why not I with thine?
>
> II
>
> See the mountains kiss high Heaven,
> And the waves clasp one another;
> No sister flower would be forgiven
> If it disdained its brother;
> And the sunlight clasps the earth,
> And the moonbeams kiss the sea;
> What are all these kissings worth,
> If thou kiss not me?
>
> (WPS 3:299)

Throughout the poem, Shelley's description of the wholeness of the natural world replicates his model of love—the melting (or convergence) of lovers into beloveds and the collapsing of all bans (or restrictions) placed around love by social convention. In this simple poem, which Hunt described as a "delicious love song,"[5] Shelley gestures toward perhaps the most controversial component of the erotic model he develops in a number of his visionary works: incest. In exalting the erotic exchange between the "sister flower" and "its brother," Shelley categorizes incest rhetorically and ideologically among the many models of love that find form in the natural world. In short, Shelley naturalizes this highly fraught form of erotic transgression, not, I think, to provoke attacks by conservative thinkers but rather, and more importantly, to quash them.[6]

Acutely aware of the effects of social convention on the progress and expression of love, Shelley bemoaned love's reduction, under the bans of propriety, to what he recognized as a criminalized condition. While still married to Harriet Westbrook, Shelley wrote to James Henry Lawrence and decried the miserable state of love under convention, arguing that true love is forced to seek institutionalized legitimation in a moment of bad faith simply to avoid the stigma of social censure:

> I am a young man, not yet of age, and have now been married a year to a woman younger than myself. Love seems inclined to stay in the prison, and my only reason for putting him in chains, whilst convinced of the unholiness of this act, was, a knowledge that in the present state of society, if love is not thus villainously treated, she, who is most loved, will be treated worse by a misjudging world. In short, seduction, which term could have no meaning, in a rational society, has now a most tremendous one; the fictitious merit attached to chastity has made that a forerunner of the most terrible of ruins, which . . . would be a pledge of honour and homage. If there is any enormous and desolating crime, of which I shudder to be accused, it is seduction.—I need not say how much I admire "*Love*"; and little as a British public seems to appreciate its merit, in never permitting it to emerge from a first edition, it is with satisfaction I find, that justice has conceded abroad what bigotry has denied at home. (*Letters* 1:323)[7]

In this account, Shelley defends his decision to marry Harriet on the grounds that to have pursued his affection for her outside of the culturally sanctioned bonds of marriage would have brought undue censure upon her reputation. Just a few years later, Shelley would defend his marriage to Mary Godwin with the same logic, explaining that while he remained opposed to the institution of marriage, he nevertheless gave in to convention because he feared he would never regain custody of his children by Harriet if he and Mary Godwin pursued what would have been regarded as an improper—or, to borrow his own language, a "seductive"—relationship. Shelley remained keenly aware of the ways in which both of his marriages seemed to compromise his ideas about love, but what appear to be his bowings to convention may be reconstructed as calculated political gestures, as performative rituals through which the poet attempted to subvert the cultural hegemony of marriage;[8] in short, Shelley gave in to the "act" of marriage in full consciousness of the meaninglessness he accorded that gesture. In his marriages, Shelley stages what post-structuralist theorists might refer to as "the performative" or as "transgressive reinscription": he enters into an oppressive structure in good faith and in complete self-consciousness of his apparent ideological compromise, all in the interest of appropriating that structure and subverting it in the interest of his own gain.[9] Shelley's marriages, to be sure, were nothing less than the "seductions" his culture sought to criminalize, but by disguising them under the cloak of marriage, he conferred legitimacy and respectability upon both unions. In short, Shelley's ritualistic "acts" of marriage functioned covertly to move the poet and his wives away from the pit of disrepute, the void of seduction, as Shelley mimed these rituals to completely oppositional ends—the protection of his wives from social censure and, in the case of his marriage to Mary Godwin, the recovery of his children from Harriet Westbrook Shelley's family.[10] For Shelley, the institution of marriage operated always and only as nothing more than a jail, and seduction—though he declaimed the meaning that convention had attached to the term—functioned as the only possible alternative to that system. In Shelley's view, lovers have no real options, because seduction had been criminalized by an unreasonable society, and marriage, the only alternative to seduction, was instituted *a priori* as a trap. The marriage of the revolutionary does not signal, as some might argue, the acquiescence of the radical; rather, it marks his maneuver into a protected cultural space from which he may operate covertly, as a member of "proper" society—a "family man," as we might say in twenty-first-century parlance.

For Shelley, love is the agent that incites men to action, but often it is misunderstood by those who have no real sense of its progress, no ideological commitment to its trajectory; as he writes to Hogg, "Love makes men quicksighted, & is only called blind by the multitudes because [love] perceives the existence of relations invisible to grosser optics" (*Letters* 1:401-402). Shelley's less sophisticated contemporaries' "blindness" to his grand project of love certainly contributed to the poet's sense of psychic dislocation from his age; consequently, his relationship with Mary must be regarded as a "revolution," for its effects extended beyond the couple's intimate engagements to impinge upon all other intimate relationships in Shelley's life, as well as on the myriad of political engagements upon which the poet systematically embarked. Like his relationship with Mary, Shelley's literary engagements operate covertly on the level of the seductive: as works that displace politics into erotic narratives, they trick us out of the discursive realm of the public (politics) and into the discursive realm of the private under the representational form of narratives about love (the erotic), or, to speak less metaphorically, they move us from the world-at-large to the bedroom. Carefully concealing politics beneath the veil of the erotic, Shelley seduces readers with texts that revel in transgressive concepts and unions, for while he appears to focus on erotic engagements (such as one family's tragic history, or two friends' philosophical debate), all of Shelley's erotic texts overlap with social criticism and political engagement, as my readings of *The Cenci* and *Julian and Maddalo* will demonstrate.

The model of erotic engagement Shelley describes in "On Love" foregrounds the unselfish privileging of the beloved in its celebration of the social effects of any lovers' ecstatic union. In this chapter and the two to follow, I demonstrate how that model remains integral to the poet's ongoing project of liberty-through-love, a phenomenon Shelley believes codifies and activates not only the erotic gratification of the individual subject but also the well-being of all people through the occlusion of tyranny. Throughout his works, landscape metaphors prove pivotal to the development—and the location—of Shelley's notion of erotic revolution: time and again, his construction of physical landscapes derives from the psychological maneuvers each work explores, so that through those landscape metaphors, Shelley demonstrates how an individual's erotic engagements equip him to navigate the fragmented topographies of a world shattered by the political collapse that is the legacy of the French Revolution.

In the present chapter, I examine the family dynamics that mark *The Cenci* to understand how those dynamics contribute to a set of psychological chasms from which the tyrant's family seeks to escape, as well as how the family's inability to navigate the landscape of tyranny exiles them from the patriarchal order in which they live, finally forcing them to improvise an alternative model I will describe as a "feminine community." Similarly, I will turn to *Julian and Maddalo* to consider how Shelley draws on images of physical landscape to suggest—one might say even to gloss—the psychological engagements recounted in the relationships between and among all of the poem's characters. The rigid structures of power in *The Cenci* replicate the phallic certainty of patriarchalism Shelley's drama deconstructs, and the watery shorelines of *Julian and Maddalo* gesture toward an alternative space where erotic connections—absorptions—work to decenter larger social structures. By reading *The Cenci* and *Julian and Maddalo* together, I will suggest that Shelley counterpoises the rigidity of oppression to the ooziness of liberation, and I will consider how Shelley demonstrates the ways in which these conditions replicate models of personal and political engagement. While the rigidity of *The Cenci* oppresses, the ooziness of *Julian and Maddalo* liberates, and the latter work's moist landscapes duplicate those that structure *Epipsychidion, Laon and Cythna,* and *Prometheus Unbound,* three of Shelley's visionary poems, which I discuss throughout the second half of this book.

In both *The Cenci* and *Julian and Maddalo*, Shelley lures his readers into redemptive portrayals of suffering, confident in the notion, as Baudrillard has said, that "[t]he odious and the abject can seduce" (127). Kristina Straub notes that representations of pain lure the reader/spectator into the action, incorporating the reader within the text in exactly the manner I have described as key to Shelley's textual seductions; Straub writes:

> The spectacle of the player's body and mind in pain marks discursively the power associated with spectatorship—power based on differences of sex, gender, class, and race—to demand or relieve suffering. It also exposes the raw edges of that power, the messy effects of spectatorship on specularized bodies and minds. The specularization of players in eighteenth-century popular theatrical discourse evinces an ongoing, unresolved hegemonic struggle, not the static structure of the "gaze.". . . . [T]he discursive line

between the two is not always so clear; the language of pain, used by both the specularized victim and the spectator, exposes the incompleteness of the struggle, the places where the subjection of the other reveals not a "natural" hierarchy, but the traces of ideological work. Within this context of struggle and ambiguity, the picture of individual resistance to oppression is complex but . . . finally a heartening one.[11]

In the cases of *The Cenci* and *Julian and Maddalo*, Shelley examines relationships neither based on nor directed toward pleasure, but pain, ultimately to interrupt the deployments of tyranny, to open spaces through which we may see and perhaps pass to a different order, to imagine and perhaps even to arrive at the site of liberty.

∞ ∞ ∞ ∞ ∞

> You haven't vanished.
> The letters of your name are still a scar that doesn't heal,
> a tattoo of disgrace on certain faces.
> Comet with a ponderous phosphorescent tail: reasons-obsessions,
> you cross the nineteenth century with a grenade of truth in your hand,
> and explode on arrival at our times.
> —Octavio Paz, *An Erotic Beyond: Sade*

Based on the real-life history of a sixteenth-century Italian family, Percy Shelley's five-act tragedy *The Cenci* investigates the contiguities between the home and the world at large, between domestic struggles and social structures, between the private and the public, to demonstrate how erotic engagements negotiate power and privilege in each of those spaces, and to show, as Polhemus recognizes, how representations of "family relationships . . . [offer] unfolding erotic narratives in themselves" (5). Tied to the narrative of one family's tragic demise, Shelley's play, from the outset, remains limited to the historical record, and for that reason alone, we must dismiss all charges against the piece as inconsistent with Shelley's broader project of liberty-through-love. Critics who point to the play's protagonist, Beatrice, as a failed Shelleyan revolutionary (given her turn to the violence of parricide rather than to tolerance and love) not only misunderstand the factual limitations of Shelley's drama, but also fail to take note of the more subtle moments in the plot that replicate Shelley's larger ideals, such as Beatrice's innovation of what I shall discuss as an alternative social model, the "feminine community" she envisions and describes to her fellow survivors.[12]

The Vanishing Points of Patriarchy

Shelley structures *The Cenci* around two crimes, Count Cenci's incestuous rape of his daughter, Beatrice, and the murder-plot she masterminds in retaliation against her father's act. These central transgressions, which I will argue are mirror images—that is, reversals—of each other, are framed by two other sets of murders: the deaths of two of Cenci's sons, which the Count gleefully announces during a banquet in act 1, and the executions of Beatrice and her step-mother, which close act 5.[13] Interestingly, the first pair of murders enters the play in the guise of a public altercation that gets dismissed as a private matter—Cenci says to his guests, "Good night, farewell; I will not make you longer / Spectators of our dull domestic quarrels"[14]—while the executions at the play's end publicize one culture's response to domestic crisis. The drama thus opens and closes with images of murder that symptomatize domestic disharmony, the first in a father's very public celebration of the assassination of his sons, the last in one family's execution for parricide.

Shelley's development of plot in *The Cenci* mirrors the ideological device that structures the play's historical moment: patriarchal rule. Even as the play seems to "vanish" in both directions in deaths—by this I refer not only to rape and parricide but also to the other offstage deaths that frame the play's action, *viz.* the murders at the beginning of the play and the executions at the end, all of which occur outside of the play and are merely recalled (in the first instance) or anticipated (in the second) by the play's language—so, too, does patriarchal hegemony "vanish" around the characters themselves.[15] I draw the metaphor of "vanishing" from the terminology of drafting, not magic, for while both disciplines employ the term to signify disappearance, I speak of vanishing with regard to perspective: just as parallel lines—railroad tracks, for example—appear to join near the horizon, to overlap and, so it appears, to continue forth undivided, or doubly enforced, so, too, do the "lines" of patriarchal power overlap throughout Shelley's play, coming together and continuing beyond the visible "ends" of the earth, so that the limits of—the gaps in—parallel powers, the room for maneuvering between and around them, cannot be seen and, thus, remain unimaginable. Shelley scores the psychic landscape of *The Cenci* with lines of patriarchal authority whose vanishing points enclose the entire world of the play in a hermetic system—a virtual prison—of tyranny, leaving Beatrice desperately to wonder, ". . . Ah, wretched that I am! / Where shall I turn?" (1.2.29-30).[16] That Shelley's text is a drama reminds us of its theatricality, its intention to be performed on the stage, a three-dimensional physical space whose edges are bound by darkness and death, the former in the actors' inability to see beyond the edges of the stage to the other world that exists just beyond its perimeter, and the latter in the characters' understanding that the space offstage, symbolically, encodes the space of death, as *The Cenci* shows at its beginning in Count Cenci's celebration of the murders of his sons, at its mid-point in the rape of Beatrice and in murder of Count Cenci, and at its conclusion in the (displaced) deaths of Beatrice and Lucretia. Hunt's study of French Revolution-era iconography demonstrates that figures of great symbolic value cannot simply be killed; they must be completely disintegrated, vanished from view,[17] as must be Count Cenci, given his embodiment of the diverse manifestations of oppression, and as must be Beatrice, given her interruption of the structure of tyranny. For Beatrice, as we shall see, death seems the only escape from the vanishing points of tyranny, but even death is a kind of vanishing, a disappearance from stage of the world, the erasure or reduction to zero, as the mathematical usage of "vanish" suggests (*OED*, s.v. "vanish").[18]

In *The Cenci*, the vanishing points of patriarchy function on three levels to inform the play's thematics, space, and constructions of individual identity. Thematically, the vanishing points of patriarchy derive from the system I have discussed, that interlocking grid of patriarchal order in which each level, or block, replicates and enforces the power of the previous one and anticipates the power of the one to follow. As in the classic sense of perspective, the vanishing points of patriarchy proceed in every direction, so that whether one looks ahead or behind, above or below, systems of regulation and order all conspire to maintain a grid-like lock that vanishes into the horizon, a system from which there seems no visible means of escape. Such a model suggests a striking parallel to the oppressive function of Sadean libertinism; as Octavio Paz observes, "[e]ach of Sade's erotic descriptions turns into a geometry lesson and a circular demonstration that traps us" (82). In *The Cenci*, the Roman Catholic Church, the play's intermediary of tyrannical order, repeats and institutionalizes the power Count Cenci wields in his home, even as it proceeds according to the traditional concept of God as an unbending patriarch. The Church, as an intermediary, constructs both the father and the Father as the repositories of power and privilege, able to save or condemn anyone they wish, and it cements the privileges of that power in its own institutional form.[19]

Spatially, the vanishing points of patriarchy structure all of the action within—as well as outside of—the play. The tragedy's central acts, the rape of Beatrice and the murder of Count Cenci, both occur offstage and thus vanish from the play's action, only to appear after-the-fact in its language. While we do not witness Cenci's rape of Beatrice, we know exactly when that violation occurs, because we read the symptomology of that act in Beatrice's discombobulated ravings at the beginning of act 3. Similarly, the death of Count Cenci occurs offstage, but the report that Beatrice receives from Marzio and Olimpio in act 4 scene 3 mediates the act for us in language, so that through their conversation we are able to "see" the violation Shelley vanished from our view. Cenci's rape of Beatrice demonstrates his unchecked patriarchal privilege, and even her complicity in his death will, at the play's end, resuscitate the patriarch's power, as I shall demonstrate; in this way, Cenci's original violation and the act Beatrice undertakes in response to it both vanish into the overarching structure from which the Count's power derives—patriarchal order: where parricide is meant to cancel out rape, the executions of Beatrice and Lucretia cancel out their fleeting victory, erasing any sort of power they may temporarily have held over the Count and reinscribing it in the continuing narrative of patriarchal order, which dictates the sentence of death for each, and into which all interruptions, all narratives of alternative orders, vanish, or disappear.[20] Similarly, the moments that shape the play's beginning and end, the actions into which the opening and closing of the play disappear, or vanish, witness the murders of Cenci's family—two of his sons before the play opens, and his wife and daughter after the play closes. The thematic development of *The Cenci* depends upon acts that appear only offstage, violations vanished from our view, and we understand that all of these, including Beatrice's act of retaliation, vanish into the singular narrative of patriarchal order and privilege.

Finally, the vanishing points of patriarchy inform all constructions of identity throughout the play, since each character's actions—for example, complicity in the murder of Count Cenci—derive from the strategies of patriarchal privilege the tyrant enjoyed. All of these concerns—space, thematics, and the construction of identity—coalesce at the play's end, where the (off-stage) executions of Beatrice and Lucretia point to the ultimate power of patriarchal tyranny in the vanishing of any individual whose actions threaten its certainty. To borrow from the language of Paz's understanding of Sadean eroticism, Count Cenci's erotic acts "[erase] the world: nothing more real surrounds [his victims] except [their] ghosts" (18), the vanished traces of those oppressed to the point of absolute extreme—to disappearance.

Private and Public, Family and Society

At the most local level, patriarchy is manifested in the Cenci household, where the Count sets policies, controls transactions, and charts what we might think of as the emotional landscape of that family's dynamics.[21] More broadly, Cenci's power is repeated in the patriarchal structure of the Roman Catholic Church, whose absolution the Count purchases time and again by paying fines for his many crimes. Cenci's acts of transgression against Church law are repeatedly recuperated within the apparently limitless power of patriarchal rule in two ways: first, in that the Count derives pleasure from his crimes as he watches others suffer; second, in that the Church, ironically, benefits from the Count's every transgression of law, since the Count transfers a portion of his wealth (an exclusively patrilineal privilege) to the Church in return for absolution. In this completely hermetic patriarchal system, all acts of transgression—including parricide—are recuperated as contributors to the exponential growth of patriarchy, which is manifested in the play's social order and institutionalized in its most visible and far-reaching repository of patriarchal law, the Roman Catholic Church. Amidst the vanishing points of patriarchal tyranny that mark the perimeter of *The Cenci*, all acts, benevolent and wicked, liberating and oppressive, bespeak the Church's authority and perpetuate its hegemony.

We witness the play's first patriarchal exchange in the Count's transfer of money and property to the Church, which guarantees forgiveness for his most recent crime, murder: as the play opens, Cardinal Camillo assures the Count that "[t]hat matter of the murder is hushed up" (1.1.1). Thus, we see that at patriarchy's vanishing points, traditional notions of right and wrong break down only to be reassembled into the singularity of (incontestable) patriarchal authority, so that Cenci's crimes underwrite the Church's religious and legal mission. Throughout the play, patriarchy is elevated to the status of truth in the meta-narrative of the Christian belief, which functions as a moral compass for all members of the Cenci family: when Beatrice is raped by her father, whose crimes are, however indirectly, condoned by the Catholic Church, her decision to turn to God for help indicates the degree to which she is, to borrow Shelley's language, a " . . . [scorpion] ringed with fire," (2.2.70) a living being so completely trapped in the coils of oppression that her only options are to burn—to be overcome by the circumstances that entrap her—or to commit suicide.[22] Which of these options Beatrice ultimately chooses might pose a matter of some debate: in my reading, her act of parricide *is* her act of suicide, because in killing her father, Beatrice sets into motion what she knows will be the processes of her own demise; we could say that in speaking her resistance to patriarchal hegemony, Beatrice dictates the sentence of her own execution.[23] At patriarchy's vanishing points, the deaths of the Count and his long-suffering daughter collapse into a single narrative that warns against any and all transgressions of patriarchal power, so that violation and retribution disappear into patriarchal hegemony.[24]

The plot of *The Cenci* centers around a series of erotic engagements—intimate relationships, some pleasurable and others unpleasurable, between and among individuals. These engagements assume political importance because they function as the means by which power is mediated throughout the play.[25] Shelley's tragedy begins in what I consider an always erotic space, the family home, where individuals retreat from public life and, ideally, find solace and comfort in familial relationships. But when the home is a castle and the family a microcosm of patriarchal tyranny, these idealistic assumptions are compromised: the Cenci palace both is and is not a private space, for in addition to functioning as a home for the family, it serves as the location of Cenci's court, the place that bears witness to his spectacles and schemes; thus, the public-private nature of the Cenci palace suggests the first of many overlaps in the parameters I have delineated.[26] For example, Beatrice's erotic engagements overlap with her opposition to the laws that govern her historical moment; consequently, all of her acts of resistance may be classified as erotic, because through them she repeats her refusal of her father's amorous advances and metaphorically recalls her "place" within the family's erotic milieu.

More narrowly, the plot of Shelley's tragedy coalesces around two acts of transgression, Cenci's rape of his daughter and Beatrice's arrangement for the murder of her father. Throughout the play, each time Beatrice rebukes her father for his dark desires, she complicates Cenci's jealously guarded subjectivity. Beatrice's response to her father's attempts to take control of, to master, her takes most dramatic form in the obliteration of Count Cenci's body. Rape and parricide thus vanish into a singular act, the struggle for power, which the play's ideological order has already tilted in favor of patriarchy in general, and of fathers—Count Cenci—in particular. Beatrice's act of parricide repeats the refusals with which she has persistently rebuked her father: physically violated, her rebukes take corporeal form, so that her resistance, initially coded in oppositional language, emerges as, or translates oppositional language into, a physical act. Ultimately, it is the Count who must shoulder the blame for all of the transgressions we see throughout the play; indeed, because she is the victim of circumstance, because she is trapped at every turn, Beatrice responds to rape in the only way she knows how: she replicates the physical violations her father has staged time and again before her. In the end, Beatrice "wins," but the Count does, too, for where Beatrice's victory comes in her defeat (however problematic) of her tormentor, the Count's greater triumph emerges in Beatrice's act of parricide, by means of which she mirrors back to him the very kind of behavior he has encouraged. In this way, Beatrice is not unlike Sade's Juliette, whom Frappier-Mazur positions as the figure "who most clearly embodies the symbolic dimensions of parricide, the outright rejection of the law," largely because of and through her "only mediated access to the established power structure" (*Writing the Orgy* 172). In both Sade and Shelley, parricide operates as a woman's response to patriarchal dominance, an interruption of "the established power structure" that Frappier-Mazur describes, a rupture that derives from erotic inequities and which takes some sort of erotic form, some sort of visitation of pain/pleasure on the body of the oppressor. In parricide, Beatrice stages her collapse as her father's other and unwittingly devolves into the displaced image of Count Cenci himself.

In her first act after the murder, Beatrice bestows the spoils of the Count's wealth upon the assassins and thereby assumes the symbolic place of her father as the head of the household. Vanished by way of death, Count Cenci stands invisibly throughout this transaction as Beatrice quite transparently steps into the figurative space—the void—his death has opened:

> Beatrice (giving them a bag of coin). Here, take this gold,
>   and hasten to your homes.
> And Marzio, because thou wast only awed
> By that which made me tremble, wear thou this!
>   [*Clothes him in a rich mantle*]

> It was the mantle which my grandfather
> Wore in his high prosperity, and men
> Envied his state: so may they envy thine.
> Thou wert a weapon in the hand of God
> To a just use. Live long and thrive! And, mark,
> If thou hast crimes, repent: this deed is done.
>
> (4.3.48-56)

Beatrice's patriarchal privileges here are many. With the death of her father, she believes herself freed from oppression, which enables her to articulate her subjectivity unchallenged. As the "man" of the house,[27] Beatrice commands Cenci's riches as her own, and she earmarks them to "pay" for her own transgression in exactly the same way her father paid Cardinal Camillo to "hush up" the matter of murder in the play's opening lines. Finally, Beatrice replicates her father's tendency to regard himself as God,[28] for here she speaks as if she were God in forgiving the crime of murder she has willed. An act undertaken at her direction and deployed on her behalf, Beatrice, God-like, declares parricide a non-crime, an exception to the laws that govern the action of Shelley's play. Both in her act of violent retaliation against her father's systematic oppression and through her negotiations around that act, we see that Beatrice, in effect, becomes Count Cenci. This transformation marks Beatrice's failure as a Shelleyan revolutionary, but that failure marks only one moment in the trajectory of her development throughout the play, and to telescope Beatrice's status at and around that problematic transgression is, as I will demonstrate, to misunderstand her ultimate station at the play's end.

The curse of the Cenci family, first named and diagnosed as "self-anatomy" at 2.2.110, arises out of a complex of conditions that pins the family beneath the grid-like structure of patriarchal oppression, in which every level replicates those above and below, before and after it.[29] The power dynamics of large social structures, such as the Church, appear to vanish into smaller units, such as the family, where they are replicated ideologically. Self-anatomization can best be explained in terms of the self/other opposition, for it is the absorption, or vanishing, of the subject/object split into the self, a form of narcissism in which one takes oneself as the erotic object and discounts the subjectivity of all others. For Shelley, this kind of psychological singularity, this inability to look beyond the self to recognize the needs and desires of an other, always leads to mortal destruction. On this score, Count Cenci is merely another version of the Poet of *Alastor*, whom Shelley mourned for his inability to escape the limits of his own fantasy and to re-integrate into the world about him. Like that Poet, whose death becomes inevitable from the moment he falls in love with his idealized vision, the inward-turned Count Cenci must die, for his complete blindness to the needs and desires of others—that principle characteristic of self-anatomization—leads first to his psychic exile and then to his death. Where self-anatomizing begins by vanishing all others as the self is raised to the pinnacle of power and meaning, it ends in the vanishing—the death—of the self, because, as Shelley argues, without connections to other human beings, without sympathy, the individual withers and dies, a phenomenon we see not only in many of Shelley's works but also in Mary Shelley's *Frankenstein,* perhaps the period's most eloquent assessment of the problems of self-anatomy, given its investigation of the destruction incumbent upon the failure to find sympathy, the failure to situate oneself among others in the world.

Throughout Shelley's tragedy, Count Cenci functions as the paradigm of self-anatomy, and his overbearing presence in the lives of his family and in the symbolic structures of his culture erases any alternative model that might be deployed against him; Cenci's enemies are thus left to counter his narcissistic assumptions of power and pre-eminence through mimetic displays of his own tyranny. Beatrice's attempt to escape her father's domination through the act of parricide replicates exactly the structures of patriarchal authority Count Cenci embodies, for it repeats the selfishly deployed pursuits of power and pleasure the Count has modeled for his family, and on the structural level it enables the continuation of Cenci's agenda—the carrying out of patriarchal law, which underscores the sovereignty of any father's unchecked power over his entire household. For Beatrice, parricide is a Pyrrhic victory, since even as her father vanishes from the scene, the effects of his power over her reappear in the social, legal, and religious structures under which her acts are scrutinized. In Beatrice's trial, we see the re-staging of her rape, the reappearance of her father in the form of institutionalized order—the translation or transubstantiation of his power into language and punishment—as well as the re-violation of Beatrice's body in the act of execution. The contests for power between Beatrice and Count Cenci vanish at the play's end as Cenci's triumph is quashed by Beatrice's, whose victory is punished by her father's re-emergence in law.

In "Beyond The Pleasure Principle" (1920), Freud observes that "the feelings of pleasure and unpleasure . . . predominate over all external stimuli."[30] Certainly, such negotiations characterize the family dynamics of the Cenci household, and these psychic conditions are repeated in the laws that institutionalize patriarchal rule throughout sixteenth-century Italy: the pleasure/unpleasure binary mirrors that of innocence/guilt, or, in the case of the Count, who certainly derives pleasure from the crimes he commits, (purchased) forgiveness/condemnation. One would be hard-pressed to argue convincingly that Beatrice takes pleasure in her father's murder, for in fact, were she not on some level penitent for the actions into which the mechanisms of patriarchal oppression have forced her, Shelley undoubtedly would have left her unremarked.[31] Beatrice's act of unpleasure, her rejection of her father's lusty advances, leads ultimately to her condemnation. In other words, while the Count's desire to rape his daughter functions as an articulation, a manifestation of his agenda of pleasure, Beatrice's call for the murder of her father must be figured as an agenda forced upon her by her condition of misery. A direct contrast to the pleasure that her father advances, parricide is Beatrice's articulation of unpleasure.[32]

Count Cenci locates pleasure at and through the visible sight—the somatic and psychological evidence—of his unchecked mastery and power; specifically, he exults in viewing the effects of his supremacy as it is registered on the bodies of others:

> . . . I delight in nothing else. I love
> The sight of agony, and the sense of joy,
> When this shall be another's, and that mine.
> . . . .
> . . . —yet, till I killed a foe,
> And heard his groans, and heard his children's groans,
> Knew I not what delight was else on earth,
> Which now delights me little. I the rather
> Look on such pangs as terror ill conceals,
> The dry fixed eye ball; the pale quivering lip,
> Which tell me that the spirit weeps within
> Tears bitterer than the bloody sweat of Christ.
> I rarely kill the body which preserves,
> Like a strong prison, the soul within my power,
> Wherein I feed it with the breath of fear
> For hourly pain.
> (1.1.81-83; 1.1.106-117)

As other critics have observed, Cenci's pleasure derives from its representation—and reversal—as pain on the bodies of others; thus, we see the self/other dynamic at work from the first act of *The Cenci*, where Shelley makes clear the psychological processes of reflection and reversal that mark the relationship between the Count and his daughter.[33] In short, Cenci's pleasure depends upon and is registered in his victims' pain. Significantly, torture rises ascendant over murder in the Count's hierarchy of pleasures, because his ultimate goal is not to kill his victims but to keep their "soul[s] within [his] power" "[l]ike a strong prison . . . " (1.1.115). The collapse of Cenci's hierarchy of pleasures is telescoped to the play's end when those who planned the Count's assassination are confined, tortured, and executed as the mechanisms of law and order reinscribe the Count's (patriarchal) power over his family and repeat, in reverse ascendancy, the two technologies from which he derived pleasure—torture and murder. Thus, even from his grave, Cenci succeeds in his project of pleasure-through-domination: jailed and sentenced to execution, his survivors continue to feel the effects of Cenci's empowerment at the site of their physical and psychological selves. In the ultimate assertion of patriarchal privilege, this reinscription of the Count's power over others is perpetuated in the narratives that recall the family's demise, a phenomenon Beatrice recognizes in the play's final act:

> Think . . . what it is to slay
> The reverence living in the minds of men
> Towards our antient house, and stainless fame!
> . . . .
> . . . Think
> What 'tis to blot with infamy and blood
> All that which shows like innocence, and is,
> Hear me, great God! I swear, most innocent.
>
> (5.2.144-152)

As Beatrice understands, the pronouncement of her guilt underscores the Count's power over her, for it derives from, contributes to, and makes quite visible the vanishing points of patriarchy in which the special circumstances of her case hold absolutely no sway; thus, Beatrice is bound to be pronounced guilty, and she is bound—trapped—by that very pronouncement, the judicial sentence yet another demonstration of the effects of language on the physical body. And even in the narratives she imagines her family's tragedy will inspire, the Count's original violation of her body will be repeated time and again. Following her rape, Beatrice complains that " . . . —My brain is hurt; / My eyes are full of blood . . . " (3.1.1-2); in the posthumous family histories she imagines, her family's reputation—and Beatrice's own story—will bear the same marks of domination, those streaks of blood that return us to the violence of the rape. Thus, Beatrice's physical and textual bodies dissolve into each other as she is doubly violated, first in rape and finally in the histories of her family's domestic struggles that have yet to be written. Such a collapse of her physical and textual presences reinscribes the Count's perpetual power over Beatrice and demonstrates his ability to act even after his death: earlier in the play, Cenci told Lucretia that

> . . . and when dead,
> As she shall die unshrived and unforgiven,
> A rebel to her father and her God,
> Her corpse shall be abandoned to the hounds;
> Her name shall be the terror of the earth;
> Her spirit shall approach the throne of God
> Plague-spotted with my curses. I will make
> Body and soul a monstrous lump of ruin.
>
> (4.1.88-94)

In both person and reputation, body and history, Beatrice remains subject to the Count's power over her, a power that takes the form of—and in—language. Appropriately, Beatrice construes the effects that the pronouncement of her guilt will have on her family's history in terms of language: she will, over and over again, be spoken of as a father-killer rather than exculpated as a victim of circumstance. Beatrice's sentence bespeaks her perpetual suffering, for in the narratives of the Cenci tragedy that are sure to follow her death, Beatrice will be denied subjectivity—violated, raped—over and over again. Here we see yet another example of the ways in which parricide and rape overlap throughout the play: Beatrice's response to rape is parricide, but her culture's containment of that response is another kind of rape—the violation of both her physical body (in execution) and her body-as-text (in reputation, in narrative). Rape leads to parricide, which leads to another rape (in Beatrice's execution) and another parricide (in the "staining" of the Cenci family name), and so on. Ultimately, rape and parricide—one an explicitly sexual, the other a more broadly familial transgression—vanish into each other.

While Cenci's pleasure derives from the appearance of pain on the bodies of his victims, Beatrice's unpleasure similarly must be written upon the body of her victimizer, since throughout the play she functions as her father's other, reflecting his strategies in her designs. This problematic relationship makes clear the reversals Shelley stages in these two pivotal characters: pleasure in one is reflected as unpleasure in the other, and just as the Count "writes" his authority, his pleasure, on the bodies of his victims, Beatrice inscribes her unpleasure, her response to oppression, on the body of her victimizer. After he has violated Beatrice, the Count gleefully tells his wife that he hopes the rape will bring forth a child, so that in the

> . . . hideous likeness of herself, . . . as
> From a distorting mirror, she may see
> Her image mixed with what she most abhors,
> Smiling upon her from her nursing breast.
>
> (4.1.146-149)

Shelley thus underscores the Count's need to externalize his desires, to find an object upon whose body the evidence of his mastery may be rendered visible, somatically inscribed. The Count's curse on Beatrice participates in the privileges of patriarchy, for not only will their child bear the Count's name, but it will also hold up to its mother the likeness of the crime from which she can never escape: the body of her child will transubstantiate the narrative of patriarchal oppression. Further, that child/text will be empowered by patriarchal privilege, for, since it will inherit the name of its father and the mixed likenesses of both its parents, it will survive them to carry into the next generation the visible reminder—the spectacular narrative—of the Count's ultimate triumph of pleasure-power over Beatrice.[34] Finally, the Count's curse on his daughter reminds us of the always-erotic nature of his power, since it is from her breast that the monstrous reminder of his tyranny will loom: just as Shelley was taken with Beatrice's eyes in the portrait he saw of her in Rome, so, too, will Beatrice be mesmerized by the gaze of her own brother-son, whose face will mirror back—repeat—for her the traumatic moment of her union with her father-tormentor from a site on her body that is, importantly, symbolic of both the maternal and the erotic.

Torture, Retaliation, and Eroticism

In the Count's fantasy of psychological torture, both Beatrice's erotic body and the fantasized body of her child vanish into each other to reinscribe the overdetermined relationship that her father-lover-tormentor has inscribed upon her body-text. Cenci poses the bastard-child as the device through which the invisible may be transubstantiated as the visible (and, indeed, as the corporeal) in two ways. First, the offspring's features, an amalgamation of the Count's and Beatrice's, spectacularize its parental history. Second, while illegitimate children traditionally take the names of their mothers rather than their fathers, the extraordinary circumstances of this child's parentage circumvent such an erasure of the father from this child's history so that, ironically, its mother vanishes amidst the transaction of the family name from father (the Count) to son (*his* child). The birth of the child thus accomplishes Cenci's goal in torturing his daughter: just as he seeks to erase Beatrice's subjectivity by way of repeated physical and psychological violations, the birth of the bastard and the conditions that will prevent Beatrice from claiming that child as her own will result in her erasure—her vanishing—from the child's family history.

Beatrice's act of parricide invokes the complicated processes of mirroring that mark the central conflict of *The Cenci*, for in repeating her father's crime, in taking his body as the material upon which she inscribes her oppositional narrative (however limited the power of that narrative may be), Beatrice repeats her father's systematic exploitation of her body. Freud notes that " . . . repetition, the re-experiencing of something identical, is clearly in itself a source of pleasure" ("Beyond the Pleasure Principle" 18:42), and Lacan revises Freud's view in a manner particularly relevant to my reading of *The Cenci*: he notes that repetition always occurs at the same time as the "resistance of the subject."[35] Further, he adds that the German term for repeating (*wiederholen*) is related to the terms for hauling (*holen*) and remembering (*erinnerung*) (49, 67), so that in Lacanian psychoanalytic formulations, the three processes are always related: repetition connotes the labored recall of trauma. In remembering such an act, one repeats that act in symbolic rather than literal form, Lacan argues, for repetition never functions as true reproduction, but rather as reproduction-in-effigy (50, 128). Beatrice's act of parricide thus repeats—reproduces in effigy—her father's act of rape and arises alongside her attempt to re-assert the subjectivity of which the Count had robbed her. Similarly, the Count's desire for his child by Beatrice to appear not as a mirror image of himself but as a "hideous likeness" of his initial crime also plays into Lacanian notions of repetition, of labored recall. In the play, the psychodynamics that mark the relationship between Beatrice and her father remain complicated: at one level, each character is the opposite of the other, but, at another remove, we see how the play's principle pair vanish into each other, since each articulates subjectivity in the same way—by violating the body of the other.[36] As I have argued, amidst the vanishing points of patriarchy in which Beatrice remains trapped, even her attempt to escape patriarchal oppression contributes to the totality of that system, for in its most simple terms, parricide repeats the violence and selfishness that characterize all of the Count's crimes: in murdering her father, Beatrice wraps herself in the cloak of her father's selfish pleasures, in the mantle of patriarchal oppression her father paraded before her. But because her act robs the Church of an important source of income, Beatrice interrupts patriarchal certainty and therefore must be made to disappear—to vanish—from the stage of authority; thus, her execution functions as the repetition of (here, compensation for, or cancellation of) the death of her father. Beatrice's attempts to frustrate her father's agenda emerge as acts of subversion that threaten the homogeneity of patriarchal rule, but as the play makes clear, the cloak of patriarchal privilege is a garment no daughter is ever allowed to wear, and she who so dares must be stripped (raped) and disciplined (executed) for her transgression.

Whether Beatrice should be considered a revolutionary figure or whether she succeeds or fails as a Shelleyan hero remains a matter of scholarly contention.[37] While her response to patriarchal oppression at the local level—parricide—complicates arguments that cast her as a true Shelleyan hero (since that crime demonstrates her tendency to repeat her father's narcissism rather than to turn to the Shelleyan strategies of tolerance and love), her response to patriarchal oppression at the broader level lends credence to those readings, like mine, that would save her from such attacks. Part of the plot of *The Cenci*, I would argue, focuses on Beatrice's education in revolution. Her first response to oppression is to deploy exactly the strategies that have been directed against her, so that in reacting to her father's violation, she exerts her authority over him in a perverse re-enactment of his mastery over her body. In revisiting the scene of the crime, so to speak, Beatrice reverses the narrative of power that marks their relationship. But because her response fails to see beyond the vanishing points of patriarchy, because parricide mirrors—repeats, in a Lacanian sense—rape, Beatrice's act of revolution must be recognized as a selfish one, and, accordingly, the play finds her disciplined by the larger structures of patriarchal power that repeat, at the macrocosmic level, her father's domestic tyranny. In short, Beatrice's attempt to undo patriarchal privilege disappears as the institutionalized forms of that privilege punish—and erase—her act of retaliation. Beatrice's failure is, in fact, the failure of the French Revolution: relative positions of power shift, but power and its uses continue unchanged and unexamined, and so revolution leads, finally, to a reinscription of the status quo (the relative positions of the empowered and the disempowered simply reversed) and, thus, to no real change whatsoever.

Beatrice's response to incarceration, however, operates quite differently. First, she successfully subverts the language of law and order, thereby turning from an act of physical oppression to the alternative strategy of revolutionary narrative. As she refuses to confess to the crime of which we know she is guilty, Beatrice's eloquence persuades even the assassin she has hired to declare her innocent of the crime, and it leads Cardinal Camillo, who, according to Shelley's stage directions, is *"much moved"* (5.2.59), to express uncertainty about her guilt:

> What shall we think, my lords?
> Shame on these tears!
> I thought the heart was frozen
> Which is their fountain. I would pledge my soul
> That she is guiltless.
>
> (5.2.59-62)

Beatrice's subversion of language, her ability to manipulate truth by means of eloquent discourse, transports her across the lines of subjectivity from the place of the other to that of the self, from disempowerment to might: as he is made to face her, Marzio exclaims,

> . . . Oh!
> Spare me! My brain swims round . . . I cannot speak . . .
> . . . .
> Take me away! Let her not look on me!
>
> (5.2.87-90)

and a bit later, he pleads,

> . . . Oh, spare me! Speak to me no more!
> That stern yet piteous look, those solemn tones,
> Wound worse than torture.
>
> (5.2.108-110)[38]

Beatrice's physical body, ironically empowered even as she sits in judgment for parricide, assumes control of the entire scene, so that the keepers of order (represented by Camillo) waver in their convictions against her, and even the figure who knows the truth (Marzio) comes undone, unhinged by

Beatrice's extraordinary affect. Marzio's response to Beatrice's "solemn tones" and her "stern yet piteous look" recalls Shelley's: like the assassin, Shelley obviously knew of Beatrice's complicity in parricide, but, like Marzio, Shelley was moved by her defense and, as he indicates in his Preface, by the disturbing power of her gaze, which arrested him in Rome and, in effect, charged him to write the narrative of her guilt-as-innocence.[39]

The Feminine Community

In the end, Beatrice emerges as a Shelleyan hero, for she articulates an alternative social model that responds to patriarchal oppression by conceiving of another order whose parameters are demarcated by compassion, tolerance, and love. Beatrice's utopia derives from the psychological structure of Shelley's model of idyllic love—the mixing and melting of lover and beloved into one. In this way, the psychological parameters of Beatrice's model anticipate the physical parameters—the watery borders, the indeterminate beginnings and endings—of the utopic spaces of liberation Shelley describes in his visionary works, among them *Epipsychidion, Laon and Cythna,* and *Prometheus Unbound.* In sum, the physical and psychological landscapes of these works all follow from Shelley's celebration of liminality, or ooziness, as the master-trope of freedom—a trope that derives, as I have argued, from the transgressions, the overlappings, of the bodies of lovers during the act of lovemaking. The psychological landscape of *The Cenci*—the unforgiving rigidity of the patriarchal order and the oozy embrace of the alternative, "feminine" community that Beatrice describes—anticipates the physical landscapes Shelley plots elsewhere as the particular spaces from which freedom will be generated as tyranny vanishes from the face of the earth.

In her penultimate speech, Beatrice adjures her brother, Bernardo, who recognizes Beatrice as his "perfect mirror" (5.4.130), to ". . . Err not in harsh despair, / But tears and patience. . . . " (5.4.144-145). Near the play's end, Bernardo's description of his sister re-casts Beatrice as the positive contrary to the tyrant Cenci, as the nurturing Mother who stands in opposition to the sadistic Father. In psychoanalytic terms, Bernardo's speech codes Beatrice as the keeper of life (eros) and their father as the keeper of death (thanatos). Elsewhere, Beatrice's language re-casts her not as Bernardo's sister, but as his mother:

> . . . One thing more, my child,
> For thine own sake be constant to the love
> Thou bearest us; and to the faith that I,
> Though wrapped in a strange cloud of crime and shame,
> Lived ever holy and unstained. . . .
>
> (5.4.145-149)

Earlier, Beatrice assumed a maternal role in comforting Lucretia, urging the inconsolable woman to " . . . put your gentle head / Upon my lap, and try to sleep a while" (5.3.119-120). Beatrice's self-consciously doubled relationships to other members of her family—she is Bernardo's sister-mother and Lucretia's daughter-mother—repeat the double role (of father-lover) that Count Cenci forced upon her, but since Beatrice has turned from vengeance to love, her doublings inscribe comfort rather than oppression. The Count's acts concretized dysfunctional relationships between and among members of his family; Beatrice's language—which, for Shelley, figures always as an agent of revolution—re-sets those familial relationships, substituting love for hate, softness (or compassion) for rigidity, embrace for violation. Beatrice has learned, and through her Shelley reminds his readers, what Kipperman observes about the use of language: language *is* power, but the direction that power takes depends entirely upon the motivation behind the utterance, so that, finally, language can liberate or it can oppress (58). When Beatrice's language seals the pact for her father's murder, her language oppresses; but when it describes an alternative to life under the rule of patriarchal order, her language liberates.

Inspired by Beatrice's love for her family, Bernardo articulates the model Beatrice will expand in the play's final lines, the feminine community Shelley envisions as an alternative to the tyranny of patriarchal order:[40]

> *Bernardo.*   To see
> That perfect mirror of pure innocence
> Wherein I gazed, and grew happy and good,
> Shivered to dust! To see thee, Beatrice,
> . . . .
> Thee, light of my life . . .
>   . . . and thou, Mother,
> Whose love was a bond to all our loves . . .
> Dead! The sweet bond broken!
>   *Enter* CAMILLO *and* GUARDS.
>   They come! Let me
> Kiss those warm lips before their crimson leaves
> Are blighted . . . white . . . cold. Say farewell, before
> Death chokes that gentle voice!
>   (5.4.129-140)

Bernardo's speech reminds us of the groundwork Shelley has established throughout *The Cenci* for the articulation of this alternative order. First, the speech returns us to the notion of the beloved Shelley discussed in "On Love"—"a mirror whose surface reflects only the forms of purity and brightness" (474); next, it contextualizes love according to familial roles, particularly with regard to the sister and the mother, the traditional keepers of domestic order; third, it aligns the bodies of Beatrice and

Lucretia with nature, thereby contrasting them to the Count's body, whose pleasures Shelley has indexed throughout the play as anti-natural;[41] finally, it returns our attention to the significance of speech to individual subjectivity, for it is Beatrice's "gentle voice" that "Death [will choke]": Beatrice's life *is* (in) her language, and the silencing of her voice, of course, is coterminous with her murder, so that the failure of her narrative to dissuade those who judge her functions as (the proximate cause of) Beatrice's death. As *The Cenci* moves to its close, the distinctions between language and acts continue to vanish, culminating in their complete disintegration by the play's end.

Appropriately, it is to Beatrice that Shelley gives the play's final speech, in which she particularizes the alternative order Bernardo began to describe:

> Give yourself no unnecessary pain,
> My dear Lord Cardinal [Camillo]. Here, Mother, tie
> My girdle for me, and bind up this hair
> In any simply knot; aye, that does well.
> And yours I see is coming down. How often
> Have we done this for one another; now
> We shall not do it any more. My Lord,
> We are quite ready. Well, 'tis very well.
>   THE END.
>   (5.4.158-165)

Beatrice's speech, I argue, marks the climax of Shelley's tragedy: it makes space for the articulation of the alternative model that replaces oppression with love and suffering with care,[42] so that in the play's final moment, we see the ascendance of a feminine community over the patriarchal order as Beatrice willingly eases into the arms of Death, to whom she refers as an "... all-embracing ... / ... mother ... " (5.4.115-116). Beatrice begins by comforting Camillo who, as the Pope's emissary, has worked as a co-conspirator in her execution, and then she turns to the more local register of the family to comfort her mother, whose blind loyalty to patriarchal rule led her to betray Beatrice's murderous intention earlier in t he play.[43] Beatrice's careful attention to her mother's hair and clothing—modeled after Lucretia's act of arranging Beatrice's girdle and hair—repeats (*pace* Lacan) the Count's attacks on the bodies of his victims, reproducing in effigy his acts of self-interested domination as triumphant gestures of love and respect. The tying up of the hair proves particularly significant to Beatrice's articulation of an alternative order, for we must read that act as an oppositional re-enactment of the gesture Count Cenci threatened to carry out several times in the play—the dragging of his daughter-victim by her hair.[44] In the play's final action, then, a father-tormentor's physical violations vanish into a daughter-mother's gentle care for the physical well-being of her own mother-daughter. Mirror-like, Beatrice reverses the image of Count Cenci's crimes and, through an act of transgressive reinscription, transfers their effects to her mother, thereby translating paternal oppression into maternal love. Finally, Beatrice draws on the privilege of speech to take control of the play's final moment, for although she remains subject to execution, it is she who declares that "We are quite ready," she who deems that her fate is "Well, 'tis very well." As the play ends, we see Beatrice and Lucretia—significantly, a daughter and a mother—led away toward death, and we are left understand their execution as the only threshold leading out of, the only gap offering room for negotiation between the tyrannical structures that encode the vanishing points of patriarchal oppression.[45]

Of course, to argue that the feminine community described in Beatrice's final speech offers some sort of solution to the problem of *The Cenci* is to leap headlong into naïveté, for the history of the Cenci family reminds us of the real-life ramifications that followed that final speech—the executions of Beatrice and Lucretia. While the alternative order Beatrice envisions remains, for her, merely a theoretical construct, Shelley returns to that model time and again in his visionary works, where sexual and familial relationships affect political realities as love ushers in a new age of peace. Indeed, the final moments of *The Cenci* participate in Shelley's ongoing strategy of textual seduction with which my larger study is involved: drawing on the individual reader's sympathy for the plights of these "scorpions ringed with fire" (2.2.70), Shelley elicits the reader's engagement with the ideological maneuvers the play investigates. While Beatrice's articulation of a feminine community fails to exculpate her from certain death, the model she describes may in fact prove one that Shelley's readers will embrace. Repeating—mirroring—the history of a family whose demise grew out of patriarchal oppression, Shelley asks his reader to turn from the rigidity of tyrannical order to the ooziness—the uncertainty—of a new model, of a space that exists just beyond the vanishing points of patriarchy in an/other world where freedom waits, its arms open in patient maternal embrace.

The Cenci stands as a signpost for Shelley's uses of the erotic, for it demonstrates how such engagements always concern the negotiations of power between and among individuals and groups; thus, *The Cenci* justifies the political significance Shelley reads—and writes—into all of his representations of erotic engagements. In short, the tragedy maps out the power of the erotic to complicate social structures by gesturing either toward oppression (when love devolves through selfishness and tyranny to "love") or toward liberation. Although the central erotic act of *The Cenci* inscribes oppression, the play does not fail to demonstrate the ultimately liberating potential of any and all erotic engagements, for it shows how such investments may be directed (or re-directed) toward an alternative social model even from within the tightly woven grid, the virtual prison, of patriarchal order: in love, Shelley demonstrates, the endlessly self-replicating systems of patriarchal oppression vanish as tyranny is eclipsed by freedom and violation disappears into embrace.

∞ ∞ ∞ ∞ ∞

Two years before he composed *The Cenci*, Shelley explored a similar mix of eroticism and social critique in *Julian and Maddalo: A Conversation* (1819), which Reiman has argued voices Shelley's key statement about human nature.[46] *Julian and Maddalo* describes the philosophical debates of the title characters as they journey to a madhouse-tower where they are deeply affected by the ravings of a lunatic. According to the Maniac's tale of woe, his misery and apparent insanity derive from what I shall consider an erotic crime: the Maniac's abandonment by his lover. Traditionally, *Julian and Maddalo* has been read autobiographically, with the idealistic Julian interpreted as Shelley and the cynical Maddalo as Byron.[47] Certainly, we know that the poem's Venetian setting and occasion recall Shelley's long walks and rides with Byron, whom he visited in Italy in 1816 and again in 1818. We know, too, that the Maniac, around whose disjunctive narrative the poem's progress depends, is at least in part modeled on the figure of Tasso, about whom Shelley began—and abandoned—a play in 1818 just before composing *Julian and Maddalo*. Tasso, a sixteenth-century Italian court poet, was imprisoned for falling in love with Princess Leonora—for an erotic desire that transgressed the boundaries of class.[48] As Timothy Clark observes, "the origin of the maniac in Tasso clearly refutes any naïve biographical reading of *Julian and Maddalo*. Shelley's study of Tasso's life and madness in an Italian city-state re-emphasizes the close relation he saw between the psychology of poets and their social and political contexts" (184). The connection of Tasso to Shelley's Maniac—who was actually named "Tasso" in an early version of *Julian and Maddalo*[49]—underscores the political significance of the poem's theme, for as the case of Tasso makes clear, any act of erotic transgression is subject to discipline in the forms of psychic and physical oppression; or, to frame the problem in the language of this study, the relationship of love to power reinscribes the perpetual overlappings of erotic and political engagements.[50]

Landscape, Psychology, and Unconnectedness

My reading of *Julian and Maddalo* will focus on the poem's representations of psychic and physical landscapes, prospects that function as metaphoric registers for the potential of the erotic to operate as an instrument for mediating power between and among individuals. Like *The Cenci*, Shelley's conversation poem situates the erotic as a political device: on the one hand, it demonstrates the potential for the erotic to oppress, while on the other, it anticipates an imaginary landscape in which the breakdown of all boundaries—both physical and psychological—gestures toward complete liberation from the constraints of social convention.

While the connection of Shelley's Maniac to Tasso glosses the political component that undergirds what appears to be a poem about philosophy and love, the connection of the Maniac to Beatrice Cenci underscores Shelley's ongoing investigation of the imbrication of sexual and political tyranny. As Curran notes, both Beatrice's rape and the Maniac's abandonment demonstrate that, regardless of the nature of any particular act, "violation is itself the point, suddenly and totally altering one's past relations with the world, substituting a vacuum, the profound sense of loss, of existing within negation" (139).[51] In the Preface to *Julian and Maddalo*, Shelley makes clear his intention of posing the Maniac as an instructive device, and within the poem, Maddalo reiterates the Maniac's pedagogical function: Shelley writes that "[The Maniac's] story, told at length, might be like many other stories of the same kind: the unconnected exclamations of his agony will perhaps be found a sufficient comment for the text of every heart" (*SPP* 113); likewise, Maddalo anticipates their meeting with the Maniac by assuring Julian that

> " . . .'Ere [the sun] fade,
> . . . I will shew you soon
> A better station' . . . ."
> (85-87)

Ultimately, Shelley conjures the Maniac as a fleshy representation for the bodies of his readers, as a composite for the whole human condition. However, his decision to leave the reader uncertain about the complete story of the Maniac—at the end of the poem, Julian refuses to tell the truth he has uncovered—underscores the dialectical processes, or paratextual conversations, that surround the poem itself: instructive but not heavy-handed, *Julian and Maddalo* provides an occasion for Shelley to construct a set of circumstances that encourage the reader, Julian-like, to look inward and to examine his or her own philosophies of life. In fact, the ultimate conversation in *Julian and Maddalo* lies not between the title characters, whose exchanges Shelley leaves unfinished, but between the reader and the text, within the resonance between the conversation piece and, to borrow a phrase from Shelley's own language, the "text of every heart" (113): as the hinge that joins reader and author in a relationship of contingency, a textual commingling, this poem offers perhaps the key example of Shelley's model of textual seduction.

The final lines of Shelley's Preface point to the central problem of *Julian and Maddalo*, the condition of unconnectedness, a concern that Julian's actions underscore near the poem's end. Julian's sudden departure from and much-delayed return to the madhouse-island repeat exactly the abandonment the Maniac suffered at the hands of his inconstant lover.[52] Claiming he has been deeply moved by the Maniac's tale of woe, Julian observes that

> If I had been an unconnected man
> I, from this moment, should have formed some plan
> Never to leave sweet Venice . . .
> . . . .
> But I had friends in London too . . . .
>
> (547-549)

Even though he realizes that were he to remain in Venice he might " . . . reclaim [the Maniac] from his dark estate," (574), Julian's personal obligations—his webs of connectedness—force him to abandon such a sympathetic program. Unsurprisingly, Julian learns upon his return "many years" later (583) that the Maniac has died, apparently from the heartbreak of his lover's second return and abandonment, her act symbolically prefigured in Julian's own.

Throughout *Julian and Maddalo*, connections and disconnections structure the relationships between and among characters, and the poem's physical landscapes mirror those interpersonal formations. *Julian and Maddalo* thus constructs something of a textual mirror, for its emotional engagements are reflected in the natural formations that surround them, and vice versa.[53] In the end, what we see throughout the psychic and physical landscapes of *Julian and Maddalo* are so many "chasm[s] of an insufficient void," as Shelley called them in "On Love" (473), so many "gulph[s] of Hell," as Beatrice described them to her father-tormentor in *The Cenci* (4.1.98-99); like Shelley's tragedy of the "sad reality" of the Cenci family (*SPP* 237), *Julian and Maddalo* offers only a theoretical way out of such oppression, so that the effects of liberation remain unfelt by those who continue to bear the weight of misery and confinement. Maddalo accuses Julian of "talk[ing] Utopia" (180); we might similarly regard the poem's vision as utopia deferred, as a mere gesture toward the plotting of liberation.

The opening lines of *Julian and Maddalo* alert us to Shelley's overlappings of landscape and psychology, for even though the poem is subtitled "A Conversation," a phrase seemingly signifying an equitable transaction, we see in the first set of speeches the wave-like maneuvers through which each friend attempts to dissuade the other from what he perceives to be a faulty—a fragmented, un-connected—philosophy. The initial exchange between Julian and Maddalo demonstrates the potential for liminality to be punctured by contention, for even as each expresses his ideas to the other, the reader remains aware that this "conversation" is really a competition: each friend engages in linguistic combat in an attempt to dismantle the system of the other. Throughout their discussion, Julian and Maddalo drift increasingly apart as each becomes more completely entwined in his own logic and more distanced from the system—and the sympathy—of the other. Perhaps inevitably, their conversation tends toward contention and psychic dissonance, aspects reflected in the physical landscape—

> This day had been cheerful but cold, and now
> The sun was sinking, and the wind also.
> Our talk grew somewhat serious....
>
> (34-36)

—and which Shelley re-invokes synecdochally in the Maniac's physical and mental condition.

The twin landscapes that mark *Julian and Maddalo*—one psychic, the other physical—mirror the central problem the poem confronts: the recurring Shelleyan trope of love and the reciprocally purifying engagement between the self and the beloved.[54] In fact, the Maniac's miserable condition derives from the rupture of Shelleyan love; the central figure of the poem thus embodies the breakage—the chasms or gulphs—in Shelleyan love that leave an individual floating through misery and self-involvement toward inevitable destruction.[55] Similarly, we might think of Julian and Maddalo as embodying these same sorts of fault lines, for Shelley describes each figure as philosophically incomplete, Julian erring on the side of idealism and Maddalo on the side of cynicism. Like the Maniac, both Julian and Maddalo are fragmented beings, embodiments of extremes, and when each attempts to convince the other to adopt his own outlook, he calls attention to the faulty philosophy—the psychic fragmentation—the other embodies. In Maddalo, Julian recognizes the danger to which unchecked cynicism will lead, and Maddalo, Julian's complement, or mirror, exposes the inevitable disappointment toward which Julian's unbridled optimism tends. As the poem progresses, we observe the maneuvers through which each friend attempts to talk the other into acquiescence, until Maddalo poses the Maniac as the emblem of Julian-to-be, the manifestation of the despair to which Julian's optimism is bound to lead. By the poem's end, Julian, his idealism dashed, becomes just another Maddalo, for his inability—or unwillingness—to provide the Maniac with the support he craves emerges as symptomatic of the cynicism in Maddalo that Julian initially rejects. In short, Julian vanishes into Maddalo as idealism collapses into cynicism at the poem's end.

In fact, at the poem's end we find the complete reversal of the psychologies with which we began: Julian, the defeated idealist, betrays the Maniac by returning to his obligations in London, and Maddalo, the would-be cynic, is revealed as the caregiver whose acts of benevolence ensure that the Maniac's final years pass as comfortably as possible. This reversal reminds us of the many ways in which Julian and Maddalo must be read as complementary figures, for even as the personality of each is mirrored in that of the other, so, too, does each friend continue to remark on and to reflect upon his companion's unhealthy psychology. Connectedness and unconnectedness—dedication and refusal, engagement and abandonment—figure throughout the poem as the diverse poles from which Julian and Maddalo swing, pendulum-like, throughout the course of their friendship and, indeed, throughout their conversations. Similarly, connectedness and unconnectedness mark the physical landscape of Shelley's poem, both repeating the psychic dialecticism in which Julian and Maddalo engage and anticipating the chaotic swings—the pauses, shrieks, and emotional reversals—that punctuate the Maniac's speech.[56]

The poem's opening lines anticipate the myriad overlappings we observe throughout Julian's encounter with the Maniac. Julian describes riding with Maddalo along the sea-shore, that place where the back-and-forth, to-and-fro patterns of the tide obliterate any sort of clearly demarcated boundaries between land and sea. The poem's first "scene" thus sets the liminal conditions that structure the relationships the poem explores. Throughout *Julian and Maddalo*, we see that in every place our characters move—the city of Venice, the ocean, the island, and the tower—traditional boundaries are suspended, and moistness, ooziness, functions as a trope for the various overlappings of love and power the poem investigates.

The geographic phenomenon that structures the opening of the poem finds a psychic referent in the Maniac's maudlin story: coming and going, the tide erodes the determinacy of the shoreline, just as the abandonment of the Maniac by his lover leaves that wretched figure devoid of any sense of boundaries, evacuated of the well-regulated sense of self we recognize as "sanity." Similarly, the psychic resolution upon which the poem's end depends—Julian's return—remains unfixed, indeterminate, displaced by "many years" (583). Both the geography of the poem's opening and the emotional interpenetrations of its conclusion replicate the Maniac's vanished position, his presence-in-absence, which Shelley describes throughout the poem and which is echoed in the oozy architecture of the odd structure in which the Maniac resides. The ooziness, the indeterminacy that structures so much of *Julian and Maddalo*, also finds a place in *Rosalind and Helen*, where the span of time during which the title characters relate their histories duplicates exactly the span of time taken by the Maniac to tell his story—from dusk to dawn, the tale beginning and ending in moments of transition, of liminality. Too, *Rosalind and Helen* offers a moist geography whose oozy landscapes read much like those that demarcate *Julian and Maddalo*, and, finally, as in *Julian and Maddalo*, in *Rosalind and Helen*, the natural world echoes back the sighs and cries of the speaking subjects, so that the voices of humans and the music of nature mix and melt into each other, reinforcing the liminal conditions of both poems, the oversaturations of all physical forms.

The Maniac's body, like his surroundings, may be likened to the bodies of Sade's victims which, as Lajer-Burcharth notes, seem "porous," "afloat" (290), conditions that remind us of the place of all of these bodies in an erotic context, for "[w]etness and flow are inseparable from the erotic imagination" (Polhemus 168). Moist, the Maniac's body floats dangerously near disintegration; porous, his body models for us the condition of receptivity so central to real communication, so key to the intercourse Shelley encourages throughout his deployments of textual seduction. In the Maniac, we surely find a corrective to Count Cenci, whose rigid embodiment of patriarchal tyranny offers a direct contrast to the fluid nature of the Maniac's body; and while " . . . the imposition of rigid cartographies can be a way of securing or maintaining the domination of the powerful" (King 49), moisture, receptivity—nearly disintegration, nearly vanishings—operate in the way King, following Gilles Deleuze and Félix Guattari, describes the process of "deterritorialization," a "letting loose of flows and desires," in which "the surface map is rendered blurred and slippery," a sinking into an apparent miasma only to be "followed by . . . 'reterritorialization'" (57-58), in which a new order may be inscribed, opening the potential for a shifting away from tyranny, for an escape from beneath the grids of power, for a move beyond the vanishing points of patriarchy. Such movement, such shifting, remains one of Shelley's goals in *Julian and Maddalo*, and he achieves this goal largely through representations of variously moist, wet, teary, oozy bodies, spaces, and engagements.

Catherine Ingraham notes that "architecture situates, and then represses, sexuality in the line and wall."[57] The unusual architecture of *Julian and Maddalo*, which the poem localizes in the madhouse-tower and repeats in the landscape and psychologies that surround it, completely erases both the integrity and the function of the architectural line. The madhouse-tower thus figures as the space in which repression comes undone as boundaries completely break down.[58] In the several locales that chart the progress of the poem, neat divisions of space—inside and outside—dissolve into the ooziness of indeterminacy. Julian's original perception of the Maniac anticipates these conditions of liminality and permeability exactly:

> I heard on high,
> Then, fragments of most touching melody,
> But looking up saw not the singer there—
> Through the black bars in the tempestuous air
> I saw, like weeds on a wrecked palace growing,
> Long tangled locks flung wildly forth, and flowing,
> Of those who on a sudden were beguiled
> Into strange silence, and looked forth and smiled
> Hearing sweet sounds.—
>
> (220-228)

Julian's description encodes the condition of liminality that surrounds the entire poem: he receives only "fragments"—disconnected portions—of the Maniac's melody; at first he sees not the singer but "black bars" around the tower itself, which signify not only the mournful music the Maniac produces but also the physical restraints on the window casements. While the tower at first appears to be overgrown with vegetation, those "wild locks"—the noun in that phrase evocative of the devices of imprisonment—gradually come into focus as the unkempt hair of the Maniac, who leans out of his window to sing his song, to loft his message to the world about him and, perhaps most importantly, to complicate the inside/outside boundary that traditionally sets the conditions of confinement. Both inside the tower and (leaning) outside of it, both enclosed and set free, the Maniac emerges as the center of meaning and the origin of production in this oozy, liminal, constantly shifting setting. As he raises his voice to the winds, the Maniac complicates the boundaries that demarcate incarceration and inwardness by transmitting his tale of woe beyond the space of his cell and into the world at large. It is the Maniac's song that sets him free, for his narrative situates him at and as the complicated origin of representationality—the keeper/releaser of all meaning, the jailer/liberator of all thought.

Shelley invokes the most spectacular register of the poem's collapse of binary systems when Julian approaches the Maniac's cell:

> [Maddalo] led
> To an apartment opening on the sea—
> There the poor wretch was sitting mournfully
> Near a piano, his pale fingers twined
> One with the other, and the ooze and wind
> Rushed through an open casement, and did sway
> His hair, and starred it with the brackish spray.
>
> (271-277)

Both the Maniac's physical body and his architectural location remind us of the conditions of liminality that code the entire scene: although he sits inside his apartment, his body is "starred . . . with the brackish spray" of the ocean that lies outside the tower and surrounds the island, peppering the space, certainly, breaking again the boundaries of shore and water, one and the other, and so on. Even though the Maniac is confined inside the tower, his body functions as a register of the outside world; and where the madhouse-tower seems to enclose the Maniac, the open window provides him with what Chambers might call the room for maneuver, that indeterminate space in which meaning may be made and remade over and over again.[59] While the tower is situated on an island beyond the borders of Venice, its watery boundaries repeat the canals that problematize the rigidity of the perimeter of that city;[60] therefore, the madhouse-island may be read as the displaced text of the city, the microcosm of the whole range of self/other negotiations we see in the "real" world—the "sane" space—of Venice. The island is enclosed—enveloped, embraced—by water, so that ultimately the Maniac resides at the center of concentric circles, the most local of which is the tower, and the most remote of which is the world that surrounds the entire poem. Although he is marginalized by both his psychic state and his physical location, the Maniac emerges as the locus of the poem's entire meaning, the center of the universe that conspires to enclose him. The landscape of the poem suggests as much, for as Julian and Maddalo approach the island, the sun disappears behind the tower (96-106), and that architectural structure, emblematic. of course of the Maniac himself, re-places the sun at the landscape's horizon. Sun-like, the Maniac hovers at the center of the universe as the poem's anchor of order, its maker of meaning. The Maniac's ability to navigate through the permeable boundaries of these concentric circles—these coils[61]—is manifested in the effect of his narrative on those who hear it: Julian and Maddalo exit the tower, leave the island, return to Venice and to London, and take with them this "text of every human heart," thereby transmitting—repeating—the message, meaning, and effect of the Maniac's ravings far beyond the physical boundaries that presume to contain him. As Levinson observes, their encounter with the Maniac demonstrates the poem's movement from individual to social concerns (155), for even though they appear to approach the space of isolation, the significance of that encounter shifts the emphasis of the poem away from Julian and Maddalo's self-involved wordplay to the ravings of the lunatic, which operate as a metanarrative for the human experience.

Somatic Inscription (Body, Text, Madness)

Upon Julian's initial sight of him, the Maniac, completely self-involved, detached from the rest of the world, assumes an oddly onanistic posture. Shelley interprets this posture and the misery it metonymizes as warnings against unconnectedness:

> His head was leaning on a music book,
> And he was muttering, and his lean limbs shook;
> His lips were pressed against a folded leaf
> In hue too beautiful for health, and grief
> Smiled in their motions as they lay apart—
> As one who wrought from his own fervid heart
> The eloquence of passion, soon he raised
> His sad meek face and eyes lustrous and glazed
> And spoke—sometimes as one who wrote and thought
> His words might move some heart that heeded not
> If sent to distant lands; and then as one
> Reproaching deeds never to be undone
> With wondering self-compassion; then his speech
> Was lost in grief, and then his words came each
> Unmodulated, cold, expressionless;
> But that from one jarred accent you might guess

> It was despair made them so uniform:
> And all the while the loud and gusty storm
> Hissed through the window, and we stood behind
> Stealing his accents from the envious wind
> Unseen. I yet remember what he said
> Distinctly: such an impression his words made.
>
> (278-299)

We see in Julian's description of the Maniac the image of the Romantic Poet *par excellence*, he who falls in love with his own vision, rejecting the outer world for the inwardness of narcissistic pleasure. The Maniac's slumped posture, his kissing of the music book, his self-directed conversation, all metaphorize a masturbatory pleasure in which one takes the self as the object of affection. Just as his conversation is monologic (and therefore autocratic), so, too, in kissing the music, the Maniac kisses himself, for it is he who has composed it. Our first impression of the Maniac leaves us with an image of the self-in-exile, the erotic body turned away from the world and enclosed in an hermetic loop of narcissistic gratification; in short, we witness a desiring subject so completely inwardly turned that all external realities vanish from his view. Narcissism, devolved to melancholy, registers at the sight of the Maniac's physically and psychically debilitated body, a literal embodiment of the perils borne from such an engagement. Outside the tower, nature heaves in revolt, the hissing winds signaling "the loud and gusty storm" (295). This meteorological condition underscores the poem's consistent overlappings of landscape and psychology, and it comments on the philosophical objections Shelley holds to the Maniac's posture of self-involved narcissism, which are metaphorized in the landscape that marks the perimeter of the scene: the howling storm glosses the Maniac's mental discord and unhealthy posture as symptomatic of the turning of nature against itself.

Throughout his narrative, Julian emphasizes the extraordinary power of the Maniac's eloquence: even though he sets this tale down years after the fact, Julian remembers the madman's entire story—disjointed as it is—exactly as it was delivered. The Maniac's 210-line ejaculation must certainly offer "the text of every heart" if Julian is capable of remembering it more than a decade later.[62] Like Julian, who follows the precedent set by Maddalo, and like Shelley, who emphasizes the madman's educatory function in the poem's Preface, the Maniac understands the pedagogical potential of his narrative. Near the end of his story, he exclaims, "'I live to shew / How much men bear and die not!'" (459-460), and in so saying he repeats what Shelley, Julian, and Maddalo all recognize—that the Maniac's tale speaks "the text of every heart" to construct the trope for all human misery. During his lamentations, however, the Maniac confronts the problem of his pedagogical mission as he considers the limits of language. "'How vain are words!'" he cries, anticipating Shelley's denouement in

Epipsychidion, yet still the Maniac remains unable to stop himself from speaking:

> "But from my lips the unwilling accents start
> And from my pen the words flow as I write,
> Dazzling my eyes with scalding tears . . . ."
>
> (475-477)

In this passage, Shelley explores the erotic component of suffering and melancholy, for even though his pain and sorrow are multiplied by his recognition of the limits of signification, the Maniac continues, unable to stop himself from speaking and writing. Just as the blood in Beatrice Cenci's eyes represented her violation and (the repetition of her father's) perverse pleasure, the Maniac's tears register the trace of his primary violation only to reproduce that violation as melancholic pleasure. While Beatrice regarded the blood in her eyes as the reverse inscription of her father's pleasure—that is, as the evidence of her pain—the Maniac, too, reads his tears as markers of the reinscription of oppression and of its transformation to melancholic joy. In weeping, the Maniac repeats his initial response to an erotic violation, but in forcing himself to remember and to repeat that narrative of abandonment, he collapses the division between self and other into his own corpus (both physical and narrative), so that in telling his story, the Maniac appropriates agency for the very violation he has suffered.

Throughout his speech, the Maniac complicates his place with regard to the mediations of self and other. For example, in castigating himself, he displaces his attack against the lover who has abandoned him, so that instead of attacking the woman he adored and thereby admitting her failure as an ideal love object, he redirects his hatred toward himself, preserving his lover as an innocent ideal and locating the cause of love's failure in his appearance and behavior. While he begins his attack by laying blame at the feet of the lover, the Maniac ultimately recuperates that blame and heaps it on himself, so that the violence his speech proposes is deflected away from the body of the other and redirected toward his own:

> "That you had never seen me—never heard
> My voice, and more than all had ne'er endured
> The deep pollution of my loathed embrace—
> That your eyes ne'er had lied love in my face—
> That, like some maniac monk, I had torn out
> The nerves of manhood by their bleeding root
> With mine own quivering fingers, so that ne'er
> Our hearts had for a moment mingled there
> To disunite in horror—"
>
> (420-428)

Betrayed by his beloved, the Maniac self-consciously manipulates the lines of subjectivity to rebuke his own erotic body as the object of his loathing. Perhaps the only way he can gain control of his condition is by internalizing the erotic crime, so that he becomes both its subject and object, both its perpetrator and its victim, while his lover disappears completely from the reaches of innocence or guilt. By means of this recapitulation, the Maniac repeats his abandonment by the lover, jettisons her out of the entire psychic transaction, and, finally, empowers himself with the ability both to act and to react, to construct both the meaning of and the response to that torturous violation.[63]

Similarly, the Maniac's odd description of himself as a self-castrating monk functions to recuperate pain as pleasure: where the hypothesized monk forecloses upon any prospect of erotic gratification by ripping his penis from his body, the Maniac's fantasy of that act transforms pain into pleasure, melancholy into joy, for the ripping off of the penis repeats and returns us to the beginning of the Maniac's "scene" in this poem, where his inwardly turned posture, his murmuring to himself as he kisses the sheets of the music he has written, encodes isolation and suffering as masturbatory pleasure. In the Maniac-as-monk fantasy, castration functions as the melancholic repetition of masturbation, so that even this self-inflicted punishment of the (rejected) erotic body provides an opportunity for the staging of self-pleasure.

The Maniac's vanishing from the world at large operates according to the mental and physical constraints that separate the Maniac from the rest of humanity, *viz.* his misery and imprisonment, the first a psychological condition and the second a physical one. The Maniac's overflowings of woe—a reverse representation of the ejaculation of pleasure—articulate his condition of indeterminacy, the state of uncertainty and misery borne from his complete loss of control. The Maniac's incarceration makes doubly clear the psychological processes of his erotic condition: rejected by his ideal other, he has been transferred across the lines of subjectivity to stand alone in complete objectivity, reduced, at least seemingly, to utter powerlessness. Just as Count Cenci repeatedly abused Beatrice until she vanished in the repetition,[64] so, too, does the weight of oppression cause the Maniac to vanish, first in the inconstancy of his lover and ultimately in Julian's repetition of that primary violation. And just as Beatrice Cenci finds herself trapped in the vanishing points of patriarchy, so, too, does the Maniac find himself trapped by the circumstances that conspire in his misery, his psychic and physical oppression.

Vanishings

The vanishing points that score the physical and psychological landscapes of *The Cenci* find form in the offstage murders that frame the play's action as well as in the play's representations of patriarchal tyranny. Similarly, the vanishing points that mark *Julian and Maddalo* function both structurally and representationally: the poem begins and ends in the space from which the Maniac has been vanished/banished, the city of Venice, so that the opening and closing introduce the central figure of the poem only apparitionally, as the ghost in the machine of the Julian-Maddalo negotiation; and as throughout *The Cenci*, in *Julian and Maddalo* Shelley critiques systems of order, which are exemplified in the conditions of incarceration (the Maniac's) and mobility (Maddalo's and, in particular, Julian's) and repeated in the spaces in which these characters are situated. Julian and Maddalo, the poem's free and "sane" men, are capable of navigating the divide between the "real" world and the madhouse-island, and so they may appear in either place as they please, but the Maniac vanishes from all perspectives: his incarceration prevents him from moving into the "real" worlds of Venice and London, and even his presence on the island vanishes in the intangible forms into which he dissolves, the sound of his music and the silhouette of the tower in which he is confined.

Appropriately, Julian's initial impression of the Maniac is mediated through displaced representations, the synecdochal markers of the Maniac's unkempt hair, which snakes like vines around the tower, and his plaintive song, which punctuates the silence of this no-space, this carefully constructed lacuna whose ambiguous status as both the margin and the center of the poem collapses all boundaries and dissolves any clear demarcations between freedom and constraint, finally problematizing all structural representations of order and power. Where the rigidity of tyranny functions above and below, before and after, in front and in back of Beatrice Cenci and extends to the vanishing points of patriarchy at the ends of her world, the harsh disappointment of a (broken) erotic relationship surrounds the Maniac, disappearing into his body, erasing (him) from the concentric circles that entrap him and vanishing into the permeable boundaries—the indeterminate spaces—that demarcate the landscape of *Julian and Maddalo*. In the end, the Maniac's body, physically and mentally self-involved, yet "starred . . . with the brackish spray" (277), reminds us of the problems he poses to systems of order: both cynic and idealist, both jailed and set free, both miserable and joyous, both masturbatory and productive, the Maniac embodies the collapse of all contraries, thus standing as the repository of all possibilities; and so it is into the figure of the Maniac that all dissonance, discord, and division vanish, only to reappear as a chaotic pastiche.

As the poem draws to a close, Julian comments on the special condition that draws him to Venice. While in the opening of the poem he observed the barrenness of the landscape and noted that " . . . I love all waste and solitary places . . . " (14-15), at the poem's end, he revisits the psychological allure of the region by conceptualizing it in the very terms I have been considering:

>   —for to me
> It was delight to ride by the lone sea;
> And then, the town is silent—one may write
> Or read in gondolas by day or night,
> Having the little brazen lamp alight,
> Unseen, uninterrupted; books are there,
> Pictures, and casts from all those statues fair
> Which were twin-born with poetry, and all
> We seek in towns, with little to recall
> Regrets for the green country. . . . .
>
>   (549-558)

Julian's description of Venice recuperates the observations I have made about the Maniac's body as the locus of the production of meaning, for even as his body metonymizes the oozy borders of the city, we see in the psychological effect of Venice a condition that repeats the processes of breaking down—or melting—the Maniac embodies. Julian regards Venice as a magic space, a zone of liminality and endless production where even the movements of the earth cease to have meaning and "little brazen lamps" allow one to continue the practices of artistic creation beyond day into night. Finally, while Julian opened the poem by noting his fondness for barren landscapes (because they encourage self-knowledge), at the poem's end he reconsiders his love for Venice in terms of the irony of that barren space: it is, he notes, the birthplace of art, of "books," "pictures," and "casts," all of which are "twin-born with poetry." Just as the Maniac's body stands as the poem's origin of meaning, so, too, does the city his body metonymizes stand as the space of the production of meaning—or at least of its highest representational forms. Shelley thus constructs the variously "broken" spaces of the poem—the shoreline, the borders of Venice, the island, and, finally, the Maniac—not as symbols of mourning and loss, but rather as emblems of the pleasures of unlimited productivity.

∞ ∞ ∞ ∞ ∞

In both *Julian and Maddalo* and *The Cenci*, Shelley explores the dismantling of oppressive orders by posing erotic relationships as paradigms for alternative social models. In these works, Beatrice and the Maniac complicate the subject/object split according to which power relationships are traditionally defined, for both figures traverse relationships of power by asserting their subjectivities in response to the objectifying maneuvers through which they have been confined and oppressed. At the end of *The Cenci*, Beatrice turns to her mother to articulate an alternative social model, the feminine community in which love and care counter—repeat, in the Lacanian sense—the oppression and tyranny that resound throughout the world of the play. Likewise, throughout *Julian and Maddalo*, the Maniac articulates and embodies an alternative social model in which the recuperation of erotic disappointment as masturbatory pleasure counters the primary erotic transgression of the lover's abandonment. In both works, Shelley counterpoises the rigidity of tyrannical order—in the Cenci home, in the social structures that govern sixteenth-century England, and in the Maniac's confinement—with the ooziness of discombobulation and the ambiguity of exile. In these works, dissonance, discord, liminality, and death—all agents of separation from the world at large—resituate disenfranchised individuals at the center of alternative social models whose meaning and power originate from those marginalized figures themselves. As we shall see in the second half of my study, Shelley explores the ooziness that marks the physical and psychological landscapes of these new worlds more thoroughly in *Epipsychidion*, where he envisions an erotic union with his idealized other on a ruined island, and in *Laon and Cythna* and *Prometheus Unbound*, where lovers' ceaseless, selfless erotic engagements bring about the transformation of political realities. Eschewing the unbending order of tyrannical regimes, Shelley looks beyond the vanishing points of patriarchy to imagine a space over the horizon where love and liberty reign—and, together, plot utopia.

Notes

1. "Sympathy," as its etymology suggests (the Greek *sumpatheia* derives from *sum-* [like] and *pathos* [emotion]), simply means fellow-feeling, or like-mindedness, concepts Shelley develops in *Alastor* and Mary Shelley explores in *Frankenstein; or, The Modern Prometheus* (1818). In "On Love," Shelley opposes sympathy to solitude, which he describes as "that deserted state when we are surrounded by human beings and yet they sympathize not with us" (*SPP* 474).
2. Shelley explores this phenomenon most clearly in *Alastor*: upon his realization that he will never locate a real-world embodiment of the ideal beloved of whom he has dreamed, the Poet resignedly floats down a river to his death, all the while undergoing marked physical changes, such as the thinning of his hair, the loss of his color, and, in the end, the experience of visual and auditory hallucinations.
3. Sigmund Freud, "Civilization and Its Discontents," in *The Complete Psychological Works of Sigmund Freud*, 21:64.
4. *Benét's Reader's Encyclopedia*, 4th ed., s.v. "pantheism."
5. Hunt published "Love's Philosophy" in the 22 December 1819 *Indicator* (*Letters* 2:152 n 5).
6. As we shall see in Chapter V, Shelley returns to the theme of incest as a crucial component to the model of liberation he charts in *Laon and Cythna*.
7. In particular, Shelley writes to compliment Lawrence on his four-volume *The Empire of the Nairs; or The Rights of a Woman*, which the poet describes as helping him "to perceive the greatest argument against [marriage], . . . prostitution both

legal and illegal" (*Letters* 1:323): prostitution is the "bigotry" to which Shelley refers in the letter as having been "conceded abroad" but "denied at home."

8. I use the term "performative" here in a poststructuralist sense to suggest that in marrying Harriet Westbrook and, later, Mary Godwin, Shelley acted out a socially sanctioned ritual in order to shield those relationships from attacks against their legitimacy. Like all performative acts, Shelley's marriages operate as highly self-conscious enactments of traditions, in which the poet has no belief or ideological investment whatsoever.

9. On the performative, see Judith Butler, *Bodies That Matter: On the Discursive Limits of "Sex"* (New York: Routledge, 1993), 12-16; on transgressive reinscription, see Jonathan Dollimore, *Sexual Dissidence: Augustine to Wilde, Freud to Foucault* (New York: Clarendon Press, 1991), 33-35, 285-286, and 307-325.

10. I place the term "acts" in quotation marks to emphasize the artificiality of both of Shelley's marriages, the self-consciously oppositional nature of both unions to the restrictions placed upon the progress of love by hegemonic codes, or social regulations. I use the verb "mime" in the French feminist sense to describe an ironic gesture that subverts the hegemonic ideal it seems to reproduce. Such processes of mimicry are best explained in Toril Moi's reading of Irigaray's *Speculum*, which I will quote at some length; replacing "Irigaray" and "*Speculum*" with "Shelley" and "his marriages" makes the correlation clear and, I think, demonstrates the oppositional strategy through which his apparent bowings to convention operate:

> Thus the academic apparatus of the doctoral thesis, still perceptible in *Spéculum*, may be an ironic gesture: coming from a woman arguing the case Irigaray is presenting, her impeccably theoretical discourse is displaced and relocated as a witty parody of patriarchal modes of argument. If as a woman under patriarchy, Irigaray has, according to her own analysis, no language of her own but can only (at best) imitate male discourse, her own writing must inevitably be marked by this. She cannot pretend to be writing in some pure feminist realm outside patriarchy: if her discourse is to be received as anything other than incomprehensible chatter, she must copy male discourse. The feminine can thus only be read in the blank spaces left between the signs and lines of her own mimicry.
>
> Moi, *Sexual/Textual Politics: Feminist Literary Theory* (New York: Routledge, 1985), 140.

In the same way, Shelley, an oppositional figure and therefore a feminized one, as I have argued) may only respond to the overarching structures of patriarchal order by subverting its unbending codes, since he cannot effectively speak outside of them. In his own life, Shelley thus "gives in" (but only *apparently*) to the act of marriage—even as he supports the notion of free love—purely in the interest of gaining custody of his children and protecting his wives from social censure; and in his work, Shelley describes liberation from within the hegemonic discourse he so deplores by reverting to age-old models of the bower of bliss and the love-union, two absolutely conventional tropes for artistic representations of Elysium, or paradise.

11. Kristina Straub, *Sexual Suspects: Eighteenth-Century Players and Sexual Ideology* (Princeton: Princeton University Press, 1992), 172.

12. In particular, I reject arguments by Michael Worton and Suzanne Ferris that fail to incorporate the local "failures" of *The Cenci* into Shelley's larger project. See Worton, "Speech and Silence in *The Cenci*," in *Essays on Shelley*, ed. Miriam Allot (Liverpool: Liverpool University Press, 1982), 78-94, and Ferris, "Reflection in a 'Many-Sided Mirror': Shelley's *The Cenci* through the Post-Revolutionary Prism," *The Wordsworth Circle* 23 (Spring 1992): 134-144. I am grateful to Charles Stahmer for pointing out these references in "A Language That Both Is and Is Not Their Own: Another Look at the Efficacy of Language in Shelley's *The Cenci*," a paper presented at the "Re-Reading Romanticism" conference at Duke University, 13 November 1993.

13. Stuart Curran observes that Shelley emphasizes the importance of mirroring to the whole of the tragedy in the play's first two scenes. These scenes—"in which strong evil contrasts with weak good" (the first) "then weak evil with strong good" (the second)—provide what Curran calls a "theatrical chiasmus" that underscores the structural basis for the numerous instances of mirroring throughout the play. See Curran, *Shelley's "Cenci": Scorpions Ringed With Fire* (Princeton: Princeton University Press, 1970), 263. Saint-Amand, quoting Marcel Hénaff, notes that throughout the works of Sade, "the victim's body necessarily appears instead of and in the place of the missing mirror" (121), so that, as we see in Count Cenci's sadistic treatment of Beatrice, the body of the victim reflects—mirrors back—the oppressor's power, and so in seeing his victim in pain, the oppressor reads that pain as a reflection of his own power and/in pleasure.

14. Percy Shelley, *The Cenci: A Tragedy in Five Acts*, in SPP 1.3.162-163.

15. Many critics have discussed the problems that contribute to what I describe as the "vanishing points" of patriarchy. Among the most useful of these accounts are those by Curran (105), Michael Henry Scrivener (193-196), and, in particular, Jerrold E. Hogle, *Shelley's Process: Radical Transference and the Development of His Major Works* (New York: Oxford University Press, 1988), 147-162.

16. Colette Guillaumin discusses the inescapable structures—grids—of power that constitute and perpetuate all forms of identity, grids outside of which nothing exists but which are nevertheless *not* natural, even though their stronghold over the all of the universe makes them seem so. Guillaumin's image offers another useful mode for making sense of the trap in which Count Cenci's victims lie, helpless; see Guillaumin, "Race and Nature: The System of Marks," rpt. in *French Feminism Reader*, ed. and trans. Kelly Oliver (Lanham: Rowman and Littlefield, 2000), 97. M. Christine Boyer also considers grids as effective maps for "the hyperspace that simulates the whole from the characteristics of its parts," just as the universe of *The Cenci* may be viewed from the bottom up, from the most local register of power, the father/Count Cenci, to the most abstract and total, the Father/God; perhaps the reason Beatrice cannot see beyond the vanishing points of patriarchy, the edges of the grid of power beneath which she remains trapped, has something to do with what Boyer observes about "the aesthetics of fragmentation [underwriting the grid itself, which allow] the erasure of contextual memory [and instead] facilitate immersion into small zones and parts"; see Boyer, *The City of Collective Memory:*

Its Historical Imagery and Architectural Entertainments (1994, Reprint, Cambridge: The MIT Press, 1996), 491.

17. Hunt writes, "As if to ensure the return of this particular throne [of Louis XV] to dust, the severed head and body of the king were immediately deposited in a deep grave in the Madeleine Cemetery and covered with quicklime. All remaining traces of the king's physical presence were effaced"; see Hunt, *The Family Romance of the French Revolution*, 1.

18. My use of the term "vanish" as a transitive verb follows the fourth definition provided by the OED, a rare form meaning "to cause to disappear; to remove from sight." My unusual and perhaps maddening use of a generally intransitive verb will, I hope, draw attention to the highly fraught processes through which language may be used to provoke a particular response from a reader, as well as through which any individuals who question patriarchal authority are vanished—reduced to nothing, made to disappear (discomfort marking the first twinge of imminent disappearance, the first stage of reduction, of vanishing).

19. Hould reproduces three images that remind us of the collusion of institutions at the site of shared power, images that predate and predict Shelley's representation in *The Cenci* of the overlappings of patriarchal power shared by Cenci, the state, and the Church/God; see "The Uniting of the Three Orders; or, Perfect Harmony" (Pl. 22), "A Three-Headed Monster Representing the Three Aristocratic Orders Devours the Remains of the People . . . " (Pl. 43), and "Chimera by M. Desprez" (Pl. 44).

20. Such power of language reminds us, too, of its links to oppressive systems of rule: in the legal sentence, language's power of incarnation is manifested most dramatically, and, as *The Cenci* suggests, language always reflects and reinforces the systems of power that authorize its use; conversely, the transgressive text, in which language is used surreptitiously and forced to turn back against itself, offers one means for dissolving the links that suture language to hegemony and, as Shelley shows in the visionary works I examine in the chapters to follow, for re-directing language away from its oppressive uses. In this way, as we shall see, Shelley maps language in and through the plots of utopia, which he unfolds in variously transgressive narratives.

21. Appropriately, Beatrice invokes landscape imagery in describing and responding to her relationship with her father: she reacts to her father's physical presence by covering her face and exclaiming, "Oh, that the earth would gape! Hide me, O God!" (2.1.111), and she sends a message to her father that she " . . . see[s] the gulph / Of Hell between us two . . . " (4.1.98-99), that she " . . . see[s] a torrent / Of his own blood raging between us" (4.1.113-114).

22. Shelley's image certainly proves consistent with my description of the play's vanishing points of patriarchy: where Shelley imagines oppression as a ring inside of which one lies trapped, my notion of patriarchal oppression extends in front of and behind, before and after, above and below Beatrice to enclose her in a kind of box—the flattening out of a coil, a three-dimensional version of Shelley's ring and of Guillaumin's grid—in which she may be contained and, later, disposed. Charles J. Rzepka, following Deleuze and Guattari, offers another interesting model for

making sense of power-relations in Romantic writing: "blockage," a process which forces a subject to confront the threat of absorption, annihilation, fragmentation, and subsequent reintegration (read "vanishing" in my senses of the term), a process that may only be corrected—reversed—through intercourse, through communication that allows for the exchange of sentiments and, thus, shifts in perspective; see Rzepka, "Re-collecting Spontaneous Overflows: Romantic Passions, the Sublime, and Mesmerism," in *Romantic Passions,* Romantic Circles Praxis Series (http://www.rc.umd.edu/praxis/rzepka/rzp.html).

23. This construction of parricide-as-suicide derives from the many readings of the play that describe Beatrice and her father as mirror-images of each other. See, for example, Earl Wassermann's reading of Beatrice's reproduction of her father's God-like narcissism in *Shelley: A Critical Reading* (Baltimore: The Johns Hopkins University Press, 1971), 87; Cox on "Shelley's *The Cenci*: The Tragedy of 'Self Anatomy'," in *In The Shadows of Romance* (Athens: University of Ohio Press, 1987), 139-169; and William Ulmer's discussion of the play's characters as "only looking-glass selves" in *Shelleyan Eros: The Rhetoric of Romantic Love* (Princeton: Princeton University Press, 1990), 115. Such readings locate in the death—or rape—of one character the same (self-) violation of the other, so that in raping Beatrice the Count acts out his own self-violation, and in killing her father Beatrice stages her own execution.

24. At the play's literal vanishing point—its end—we are left only to imagine the executions of Beatrice and Lucretia. I regard these deaths as metaphorical rapes on two bases, first because sex and violence vanish into each other throughout the play, and second because Mary Shelley's copy of the "Relation of the Death of the Family of the Cenci" (*WPS* 2:159-166) provides a textual basis for understanding the contextualization of murder as an erotic act. The manuscript she reproduces describes the execution of Lucretia as follows: "The first who came down to die was Lucretia, who, being fat, found difficulty in placing herself to receive the blow. The executioner taking off her handkerchief, her neck was discovered, which was still handsome, although she was fifty years of age. Blushing deeply, she cast her eyes down . . . " (2:164). The removal of the handkerchief, the acknowledgment of the comeliness of her neck, and Lucretia's involuntary response—her blush—code the occasion of her execution as an eroticized transaction, so that the severing of her head from her body symbolizes the penetration of her body by the phallic power of law.

25. Others who recognize the politicized nature of the familial relationships in the Cenci household include Cameron (399), Curran (*Shelley's "Cenci"* 99, 259, and 273), and Wassermann (85).

26. The architecture of the Cenci palace reinscribes its complicated relationship to public and private space: Shelley notes that "Cenci himself built a chapel in the court of his Palace, and dedicated it to St. Thomas the Apostle, and established masses for the peace of his soul" (*SPP* 241). Cenci's castle not only represents but schematizes the institutionalization of patriarchal rule, which the tragedy exposes time and again as corrupt and oppressive.

27. The moments that precede Cenci's death underscore Beatrice's ability to cross the lines of binary oppositions, so that she renounces her womanhood and becomes, figuratively speaking, "a man." When the assassins descend from Cenci's chamber and announce that "We dare not kill an old and sleeping man" (4.3.9), Beatrice asserts her supremacy over them by rebuking them as "Miserable slaves," "Base palterers," "Cowards and traitors," (4.3.22, 4.3.25, 4.3.26), and then she stages her ascendancy over them by "[*Snatching a dagger from one of them and raising it*" (4.3.31). Beatrice thus wields the phallus, the emblem of patriarchal privilege, as she hoists the (obviously phallic) dagger and objectifies the would-be assassins through the force and mastery of language, a process we see repeated near the play's end when one of the assassins, Marzio, cowers at Beatrice's "solemn tones" (5.2.109). Consequently, the assassins are shamed—and frightened—into committing the act as commanded, in part because they fear Beatrice's clearly masculine, undeniably Cenci-like wrath, not to mention her typically masculine use and control of language.

28. Cenci codes himself as God-like throughout the play, specifically at 1.3.96-98, 2.1.162, 4.1.50, 4.1.90, and 4.1.103-111. Beatrice envisions her father as God-like as well when she confronts the horrible possibility of dying only to find him waiting for her as the keeper of eternity; see 5.4.63-75.

29. Cox treats the curse of the Cenci family at length; see "Shelley's *The Cenci*," 139-168.

30. Sigmund Freud, "Beyond the Pleasure Principle," in *The Complete Psychological Works of Sigmund Freud*, 18:29.

31. Shelley's description of Beatrice, which comes near the end of his Preface to *The Cenci*, bears quoting in full:

> The portrait of Beatrice at the Colonna Palace is admirable as a work of art: it was taken by Guido during her confinement in prison. But it is most interesting as a just representation of one of the loveliest specimens of the workmanship of Nature. There is a fixed and pale composure upon the features: she seems sad and stricken down in spirit, yet the despair thus expressed is lightened by the patience of gentleness. . . . the lips have that permanent meaning of imagination and sensibility which suffering has not repressed and which it seems as if death scarcely could extinguish. . . . her eyes . . . are swollen with weeping and lustreless, but beautifully tender and serene. . . . Beatrice Cenci appears to have been one of those rare persons in whom energy and gentleness dwell together without destroying one another: her nature was simple and profound. The crimes and miseries in which she was an actor and a sufferer are as the mask and mantle in which circumstances clothed her for her impersonation on the scene of the world. (*SPP* 242)

32. Ulmer's discussion of the power of legal discourse proves instructive here, for he points out what I have remarked in note 20 and what I will indicate below, that Beatrice's fate is delivered in the form of a "sentence" (122). Ulmer thus recognizes the crucial contingencies between power and language throughout the play and the ways in which any real distinctions between acts and articulations dissolve at

the vanishing points of patriarchy. Throughout the play, language overtakes action and ascends to truth; thus, when he hears Beatrice's impassioned assertion of her innocence, Marzio, whom Beatrice hired as an assassin, becomes convinced of Beatrice's innocence in the scheme (5.2.157).

33. A number of scholars comment on the play's self/other formulations, but the most thorough and useful of these are Hogle (148-152), Cox (143-146 and 158), and Ulmer (115). Again, the connection between the psychology of Count Cenci and the psychology of the Sadean libertine cannot be overemphasized: "The libertine is a solitary who cannot ignore the presence of others. His solitude does not consist in their absence, but rather in establishing a negative relation with them. In order to realize this paradoxical relationship, the erotic object must enjoy a sort of conditional consciousness, to be dead in life or an automaton"; see Octavio Paz, *An Erotic Beyond: Sade*, trans. Eliot Weinberger (New York: Harcourt Brace and Company, 1998), 53.

34. As we have seen elsewhere, this dual response to a situation reminds us of the ways in which Beatrice and her father serve as reflections of each other: Beatrice dreads the narratives that will perpetuate her misery, while the Count takes pleasure in anticipating them.

35. Jacques Lacan, "Of the Network of Signifiers," in *The Four Fundamental Concepts of Psycho-Analysis*, ed. Jacques-Alain Miller and trans. Alan Sheridan. (New York: W. W. Norton, 1981), 51.

36. Ulmer notes that the crux of the play's self/other maneuvers hinges on each character's attempts to validate him- or herself as a subject (115); Hogle argues that the central conflict of the tragedy arises from Beatrice's refusal to mirror back to her father the desires he projects onto her (151); Cox discusses Cenci's rape of Beatrice as the most dramatic example of the play's central concern, the negotiations of self and other ("Shelley's *The Cenci*" 154).

37. See, for example, Cox ("Shelley's *The Cenci*" 152), Scrivener (163), and Wassermann (103-104 and 111).

38. This exchange repeats the moment earlier in the play when Beatrice used language and the threat of the raised dagger/phallus to assert her dominance over the assassins Marzio and Olimpio (see note 27).

39. Marzio is the first of two characters into whom I would argue Shelley himself vanishes, for, like the assassin, Shelley reconstructs Beatrice's guilt-as-innocence in his representation of the "sad reality" of the Cenci family, thereby exculpating Beatrice of any real responsibility for her action (*SPP* 237). The second character into whom Shelley vanishes is Bernardo, whom Beatrice charges to preserve her memory, to compose the true narrative of her (guilt-as-) innocence.

40. My notion of the feminine community hinges not on gender but on power relations: under patriarchal rule, men are assumed to be empowered and/as women are disempowered. But as we see in *The Cenci*, such an essentializing formulation does not hold, for in the vanishing points of patriarchy, some men (the Count) oppress others (his sons). The "feminine community" thus moves beyond essentializing notions of gender to include all who are oppressed under patriarchal rule, all individuals who are somehow disenfranchised from power. Shelley's notion of such an

order mirrors Mary Wollstonecraft's description of the madhouse community in *The Wrongs of Woman: Or, Maria. A Fragment* (1798), which suggests to me that his development of an alternative social model based on the ethic of love rather than oppression may be the legacy of his mother-by-marriage.

41. Shelley suggests the anti-natural component of Cenci's desires and acts in the Count's language, when the tyrant argues that his vices are natural (1.3.12-13), in Beatrice's rebuke of her father as an "Unnatural man" (1.3.54), and in Giacomo's description of his father and Nature as rejecting each other (3.1.286-288).

42. Significantly, in these replacements, members of the feminine community become actors rather than merely passive victims: "love" and "care" describe reciprocal engagements, while "oppression" and "suffering" connote inequalities.

43. Lucretia's betrayal of Beatrice comes at 4.1.32-37, although at 4.1.70-72 she recants her admission and claims she was lying "but to awe [Count Cenci]" (4.1.72). Until the last moments of the play, Lucretia functions as the third element in the Beatrice-Cenci relationship, the triangulating point whose loyalties between the play's principle "couple" remain divided. But at the play's end, Lucretia's loyalty is secured by the maternal care that Beatrice bestows upon her.

44. See *The Cenci*, 4.1.6 and 4.1.30.

45. The final moments of *The Cenci* recall the closing moments of *Rosalind and Helen: A Modern Eclogue*, which appeared in print a year earlier. In that poem, the reunion of Rosalind and Helen and the succor they offer each other anticipates the feminine community Beatrice describes, an existence whose ethic is based on comfort and compassion rather than on mastery, control, and excoriation. In this utopia, Rosalind's child, Lilla, the product of an incestuous union, plays a key role in ensuring the happiness of her mother and her mother's dear friend, and so in this feminine community we see the product of incest functioning not as a blight, a curse, as Count Cenci would have his child with Beatrice function, but instead as an embodiment of love, an instrument of liberty.

46. See section III of Reiman's chapter "Shelley and the Human Condition," in *Shelley: Poet and Legislator of the World*, 3-13.

47. Chief among these are readings by Newman Ivey White (*Shelley* 2:42-43, 2:558-559, 2:560-562) and Holmes (449-451). Desmond King-Hele describes the poem as "a memento of [Shelley's (Julian's)] talks with Byron (Count Maddalo) in Venice that summer"; see King-Hele, *Shelley: His Thought and Work* (Rutherford, N.J.: Fairleigh Dickinson University Press, 1960), 103. For debates on the identity of the Maniac—some argue he is Shelley, others Byron—see Charles E. Robinson, *Shelley and Byron: The Snake and Eagle Wreathed in Fight* (Baltimore: The Johns Hopkins University Press, 1976), 91.

48. Significantly, Shelley first introduced the figure of Count Maddalo in the *Tasso* fragment and then imported him directly into *Julian and Maddalo*; see Holmes (425) and Timothy Clark, *Embodying the Revolution: The Figure of the Poet in Shelley* (New York: Oxford University Press, 1989), 181.

49. For the naming of the Maniac in Shelley's MS, see Clark (182). Clark also considers the Maniac as a portrait of Rousseau (205, 209).

50. Clark notes that "Tasso's life became an instance of the dangers of excessive imagination" (179); thus, one can see how the Maniac-as-Tasso might offer a corrective to Shelley's/Julian's idealism.

51. Others who read the Maniac in terms of Beatrice Cenci include Marjorie Levinson, who observes that "the Maniac, abandoned by his lover, in turn forsakes his friends and thus betrays his social obligation; he is as compromised by the evil originally imposed upon him as is Beatrice Cenci possessed by her exploitation"; see Levinson, *The Romantic Fragment Poem: A Critique of Form* (Chapel Hill: University of North Carolina Press, 1986), 155. Wasserman finds in Beatrice's "derangement" the traces of Maddalo's "resignation to despair" as well as "the blot of 'falsehood' . . . [that] violation has fixed upon . . . [the] pure mind" of the Maniac (99). Wasserman argues that both *Julian and Maddalo* and *The Cenci* "are to be read in the same way, in terms of two independent forces meeting in conflict, and the author [concealing] his 'own conceptions of right or wrong, false or true,' in order that we, as readers or spectators, may know ourselves by seeing ourselves reflected in the unresolved conflict" (118). In his exhortation of the pedagogical value of *Julian and Maddalo,* Wasserman echoes Shelley, whose Preface situates the Maniac as a catalyst for the reader's self-knowledge.

52. Julian's mirroring of the lover's act of betrayal reminds us of another of the concepts I have been developing throughout my argument, the collapsing of amorous, familial, and friendly relationships into the broad category of the erotic: in betraying him by way of abandonment, Julian repeats the lover's erotic crime and thus incorporates (the vestiges of) an amorous transgression into the realm of (an inconstant) friendship.

53. Cronin remarks on the congruence of the poem's landscape to its title characters' psychologies (117). Wasserman also recognizes landscape as Shelley's gloss on Julian and Maddalo's personalities; he writes that "the major unifying control over the poem is its atmospheric symbolism . . . " (67); see especially 62-75.

54. Hogle provides a dense and useful reading of *Julian and Maddalo* in terms of its various self/other negotiations; see 112-134.

55. Such an image of a poet as the victim of his own imagination returns us to Shelley's sympathetic yet critical treatment of the protagonist of *Alastor.*

56. Levinson notes that "the Maniac's discourse is riddled with lacunae" (158). While I describe the relationship between Julian and Maddalo as a dialectical one, Levinson's image of lacunae—holes, or what Shelley might call gulphs, given his penchant for landscape imagery—offers another effective way of thinking about the spatial implications of the poem's interpersonal engagements and the philosophical chasms that separates the poem's eponymous characters.

57. Catharine Ingraham, "Initial Properties: Architecture and the Space of the Line," in *Sexuality and Space,* ed. Colomina, 267.

58. Levinson notes that from the beginning of the poem, Julian's description of the landscape underscores its "radical instability—literally, the rootlessness—of existence" (151).

59. In *Room for Maneuver,* Chambers discusses this concept in terms of irony and seduction: "[irony] simultaneously negates the discourse of power it cites in its

'narrative function' and appropriates it for the purposes of an educational demonstration. . . . . a negation necessarily appropriates the affirmation that it mentions, in order to turn it into an 'other' purpose" (240); " . . . a shift from the 'ironic' to the 'seductive' model of textual oppositionality is mediated by the 'melancholic'" (16). According to Chambers' definitions, Shelley's mode—the narrative—is seductive (27), and his works resound with ironic appropriations: repeatedly, Shelley stages representations of hegemonic power only to question the legitimacy of that power by exposing its machinations, as we have seen in both *Swellfoot the Tyrant* and *The Cenci*. Time and again, Shelley's works narrate the experience of melancholy in order to activate the room for maneuver.

60. Elsewhere in his work, Shelley returns to the notion of the watery boundaries of Venice as emblematic of the breakdown of rigidity: in "Lines Written among the Euganean Hills," Shelley refers to Venice as "Ocean's nursling . . . " (*SPP* 103-112), and in the "Ode to Naples," he writes of "The Sea which paves the desert streets of Venice" (*WPS* 4:51-56).

61. With the word "coils" I deliberately invoke and thus suggest a spatio-ideological connection to the "self-involving coils" that overtake the Cencis, the conditions that render the family "scorpions ring'd with fire."

62. I date Julian's (hypothetical) composition of the poem in terms of the only chronological clue he provides: at the poem's beginning, Maddalo's daughter is an infant with whom Julian plays, but upon his return, she " . . . had now become / A woman . . . " (588-589). Thus, we can assume that more than a decade passes between Julian's initial visit and his return.

63. Hogle discusses at some length the problems incumbent upon the Maniac's mediations of the self/other relationship and his reinscription of the primary violation, and my thoughts here echo his; see 125-130.

64. Contemporary discussions of pornography consider the function of repetition at some length: see Susanne Kappeler, "Pornography: The Representation of Power," in *Pornography: Women, Violence, and Civil Liberties*, ed. Catherine Itzin (New York: Oxford University Press, 1993), 88-101; see also chapters by Susan Gubar ("Representing Pornography: Feminism, Criticism, and Depictions of Female Violation"), Richard B. Miller ("Violent Pornography: Mimetic Nihilism and the Eclipse of Differences"), and Linda Williams ("Fetishism and Hard Core: Marx, Freud, and the 'Money Shot'"), in *For Adult Users Only: The Dilemma of Violent Pornography*, ed. Susan Gubar and Joan Hoff (Bloomington, Ind.: Indiana University Press, 1989), 47-67; 147-162; 198-217.

PART TWO: THE SOLUTION

CHAPTER IV

Revolutionary Landscapes and the Politics of Love:

Epipsychidion as Erotic Cartography

> Woe is me!
> The winged words on which my soul would pierce
> Into the height of love's rare Universe,
> Are chains of lead around its flight of fire.—
> I pant, I sink, I tremble, I expire!
>
> —Percy Bysshe Shelley, *Epipsychidion*

> To neglect this dimension—to overlook the power that words or spoken phrases have to influence the body, and hence to modulate our sensory experience of the world around us—is to render even the most mundane, communicative capacity of language incomprehensible.
>
> —David Abram, *The Spell of the Sensuous: Perception and Language in a More-Than-Human World*

Shelley's observation in *The Defence of Poetry* that "Poets are the unacknowledged legislators of the world" (*SPP* 508) reminds us of the profound political engagement that characterizes all of the poet's works, from the most timely, such as *Œdipus Tyrannus; or, Swellfoot the Tyrant,* to the most visionary, such as *Prometheus Unbound* and *Laon and Cythna.* We find in Shelley's works a constant shift in the space of political engagement as it moves from the realm of the explicitly political to the intimate space of the bedroom, that sometimes literal and sometimes figurative location in which Shelley unveils the erotic and heroic engagements his poems recount. In Chapter III, I began considering the ways in which Shelley's descriptions of revolutionary spaces coincide with his idealized notion of erotic relationships. I argued that the language through which Shelley describes idyllic love provides a template for understanding the psychic and physical landscapes he charts throughout the visionary works, where he describes the generation of new worlds as older, oppressive orders are overturned by the power of love.[1] In their various processes of mixing, melting, dissolving, and absorbing, these spaces—which I referred to as Shelley's "oozy" landscapes—replicate erotic relationships to participate in the poet's vision of a world liberated by love. In short, I argued that Shelley deliberately maps his radical politics according to an agenda of pleasure, so that, in the end, the cartography of those spaces must be understood as a specifically erotic one.

Thus far in my study, my notion of the erotic has remained rather elastic. In my reading of *Swellfoot the Tyrant,* I used the term "erotic" to refer primarily to sexual relationships, but I broadened that definition by demonstrating how just as Iona's relationship to her husband must be classified as an erotic one (given their marital history), so too must her relationship to her culture at large, since her lusty reputation loomed foremost in the minds of Swellfoot's subjects. In my reading of *Swellfoot the Tyrant*, I began to expand the model of the erotic beyond the explicitly sexual to consider how political relationships might be similarly categorized, and I justified the expansion of that category by examining the simultaneously public-private (political-domestic) nature of Iona's struggle with Swellfoot. Thus, I attempted to explore the ways in which both relationships—one private/domestic (husband and wife) and the other public/political (King and Queen)—could be classified as "erotic." My readings of *The Cenci* and *Julian and Maddalo* centered around a concept I described as the "vanishing points" of patriarchy, a model in which each system of oppression repeats all others, unmasking the contingencies that link domestic tyranny with religious and political tyranny, as my reading of *The Cenci* demonstrated. Further, I argued that just as Count Cenci's original violation of his daughter takes the form of an undeniably sexual—and therefore erotic—crime, Beatrice's retributive action, the assassination of her father, might also be unveiled as an erotic episode because it mirrors—repeats, in a Lacanian sense—her father's crime by the transgressive reinscription of her (un)pleasure as evidence of her *power* upon the body of the other. In my reading of *Julian and Maddalo,* I returned to a more narrowly sexual notion of the erotic to describe the relationship between the Maniac and his inconstant lover, but again I expanded the category of the erotic to include the fellow-feeling offered by the poem's title characters in response to the Maniac's tale of woe. In this, the second half of my study, I narrow such an my elastic model of the erotic to examine the sexual relationships Shelley explores in three visionary poems, *Epipsychidion* (1821), *Laon and Cythna* (1817), and *Prometheus Unbound* (1819). Throughout my discussion, I keep in play the notion of the political significance of these erotic relationships by demonstrating how Shelley privileges acts of love—erotic engagements—as mechanisms for renegotiating power and privilege in the world.

Specifically, I will interrogate the congruence of the language and imagery Shelley uses to describe the twin agendas of pleasure and politics (or eroticism and revolution) in *Epipsychidion, Laon and Cythna,* and *Prometheus Unbound*. It is, after all, in searching the barren vista of his own mind that the hypothesized figure in "On Love" discovers his great longing for a beloved and thus is inspired to embark upon an erotic quest to smooth the broken landscape of his fragmented psyche, so that he may rescue himself from solitude by locating and communing with his beloved.

Just as Shelley theorizes love as an experience of complete union that obliterates all social structures separating, categorizing, and hierarchializing individuals, so, too, does he emphasize the centrality of the processes of commingling and absorption to his project of erotic revolution by charting revolutionary scenarios according to a psychological topography whose contours are determined by Shelley's representations of idealized erotic relationships; thus, Shelley plots utopia according to a resolutely erotic cartography.

David Abram argues that "our own speaking ... does not set us outside of the animate landscape but—whether or not we are aware of it—inscribes us more fully in its chattering, whispering, soundful depths."[2] Similarly, my readings of Shelley's poems do much to show how "... speaking bodies are generative sites, vortices where the [vast, topological] matrix itself is continually being spun out of the silence of sensorial experience" (84). Speaking bodies create—and re-create—the physical realities they inhabit; and just as Beatrice Cenci's pleas to a higher patriarchal power locked her into the system she sought to escape, the alternative orders Shelley describes in *Epipsychidion, Laon and Cythna,* and *Prometheus Unbound* are generated by and through the very act of articulation. God-like, Shelley demonstrates his powers of incarnation, relying on his Word to bring about the material conditions that will activate his vision of a liberated world. But the relationship between articulation and change proves a reciprocal one, for just as articulation brings about material revolutions, so, too, do those revolutions affect the speaking bodies from which they proceed: "Our sensing bodies respond to the eloquence of certain buildings and boulders, to the articulations of dragonflies. We find ourselves alive in a listening, speaking world" (Abram 86).

In this chapter and the next, I investigate the conversation between speaking bodies and the worlds they inhabit to explore the potential for that dialogue to activate human liberation. To this end, I consider how and to what effect Shelley displaces the free-love community of *Epipsychidion* to an island dedicated to the celebration of absolute freedom, just as he locates the retreats of both Prometheus and Asia and Laon and Cythna in utopic "other-spaces" whose oozy perimeters are marked by waterfalls. As my readings of these works will demonstrate, Shelley's revolutionary landscapes recuperate difference into wholeness by deconstructing socially imposed boundaries within topographies marked by moisture, absorption, and productivity. In all three poems, fluid, permeable boundaries separate Shelley's idealized lovers from the "real" worlds they have escaped, which Shelley exposes as hostile to the revolutionary agenda each pair of lovers exemplifies.

The notion of landscape and the uses of mapping underwrite much of my work throughout the second half of this study, because I find such experiences and representations of modes of perception and creation central to Shelley's efforts to plot utopia. By "landscape," I mean the natural world as it is presented in representational forms; by "map" I mean those forms themselves. The use of landscape to offer a dream of stability that proceeds from a harmony among all its elements informs Shelley's plottings of utopia; in both cases, a representational form draws on elements from the real world to offer a possibility for that world perfected, for utopia realized. Such a function resounds throughout the landscape tradition, which, as Ann Bermingham observes, operates as a mode of political discourse.[3] Stephen Daniels notes the tendency in landscape paintings from the eighteenth and nineteenth centuries to "[search] out pleasing harmonies of form and material between nature and culture, between the cottage and the hillside, the bridge and the crag. Such landscapes epitomized a stable, secure way of life, all the more so for seeming so isolated from the main currents of modern life."[4] W. J. T. Mitchell recognizes that the term and concept "landscape" functions as far more than just a mode of painting, that landscape is "an instrument of cultural power" "by which social and subjective identities are formed."[5]

Shelley's utopic wonderlands offer the poet's representations of his fantasy of the world perfected, an image that draws on the real world about him, yet overcodes reality with the dream of liberty-through-love. Charles Harrison recognizes the potential for landscape painting to offer "a form of metaphorization of the body and of the sensation of the body" (Harrison 226); in just this way, Shelley's maps plot utopia according to the contours of erotic bodies—of the lovers' embrace, in particular. King notes that "the imposition of rigid cartographies can be a way of securing or maintaining the domination of the powerful" (49), and certainly Shelley aligns rigid cartographies—harsh landscapes—with loci of tyrannical control, as we have seen in the world of *The Cenci*, a play whose landscapes—not merely natural, but psychological and political, as well—score fragmentation and dysfunction upon the bodies of its players, as well as throughout the regions they inhabit. Shelley's utopic yet unfinished *Triumph of Life* centers on a vision induced by the pleasure the poet takes in the natural world, which lulls him into a dream-like state from which the vision is born—a period of meditation, contemplation, reminiscent of Wordsworth's famous description of poetry as "the spontaneous overflow of powerful feelings . . . recollected in tranquillity," in particular the tranquility of the natural world.[6] The process of a lulling-by-landscape is replicated later in *The Triumph of Life* in Rousseau's description of the magical cave to which he retires, where the trickling of eternal waters lulls him into forgetfulness like the waters of Lethe and which, having induced such a state of receptivity, ushers an understanding of truth. Shelley ends his career by reminding us throughout *The Triumph of Life* what *Epipsychidion*, *Laon and Cythna*, and *Prometheus Unbound* suggest: that the pathway to enlightenment appears in the contemplation of the natural world, which takes representational form in the oozy landscapes of Shelley's utopias.

In the present chapter and the next, I conclude my discussion of Shelley's use of the erotic by reading the revolutionary landscapes the poet describes in *Epipsychidion, Laon and Cythna,* and *Prometheus Unbound* according to an erotic cartography I deduce from the relationship each poem's pair of idealized lovers enjoy. I thus make sense of the various processes of mixing, melting, dissolving, and absorbing as both psychological and topographical strategies through which systems of oppression are overcome through erotic unions, which model and engender strategies for the liberation of the world: in these variously oozy spaces, revolutionary landscapes metonymize erotic relationships to activate Shelley's politics of love. The processes of plotting utopia prove particularly important in my readings of *Epipsychidion, Laon and Cythna,* and *Prometheus Unbound,* for in charting the physical landscapes of these poems according to Shelley's model of idyllic erotic union, I demonstrate how the effects of love are manifested in the physical world, so that psychology and topography—psychic and physical landscapes, as I also describe them—melt into one as the earth replicates the lovers' embrace, thus guaranteeing the protection—the veneration, even—of the idyllic model of love that underwrites Shelley's *œuvre.* While *Epipsychidion* fails to transport its subjects to the fantasized other-space of complete freedom, the lover-heroes of *Laon and Cythna* and *Prometheus Unbound* do succeed in ascending to such oozy utopias; in the end, it seems that Shelley endorses sexual intimacy as a powerful agent of revolution when—and only when—it is accompanied by a deep dedication to liberty, a visionary agenda that leaps beyond the confines of the real world. Beer recognizes in Romanticism "a constant aspiration toward wholeness" (257), and for Shelley, wholeness begins in the lovers' embrace and proceeds outward, replicating that embrace throughout the larger world. In this chapter and the next, we shall see that *Laon and Cythna* and *Prometheus Unbound* complement *Epipsychidion* by elucidating the conditions under which that poem's collapses, or failures, may be resuscitated and, indeed, invested with transnational, transhistorical political significance. Just as I began the first half of this book with a chapter-length reading of *Œdipus Tyrannus; or, Swellfoot the Tyrant,* I begin the second with a chapter-length reading of *Epipsychidion,* a poem I find crucial to Shelley's articulation of the model of idyllic love and, by extension, to his plottings of utopia. I conclude my focus on Shelley by investigating the more optimistic potential of Shelley's model that emerges from *Laon and Cythna* and *Prometheus Unbound.*

∞ ∞ ∞ ∞ ∞

In my readings of *The Cenci* and *Julian and Maddalo,* I examined Shelley's descriptions of oozy landscapes as spaces that offer potential for the realization of the revolutionary power of love. I counterpoised those spaces to the rigidity of the structures governing the worlds of both poems: in *The Cenci,* Shelley describes a world locked at every juncture with the figural Father at its center, a tyranny symbolically embodied across the vanishing points of patriarchy in God, the Church, Law, and the eponymous Count; in *Julian and Maddalo,* Shelley describes a world that gives way to ooziness with the Maniac at its center, a figure whose emotional traumas have effectively vanished him from the oppressive and exclusionary world at large. Near the end of the twentieth century, Grimshaw called for readers "to democratize desire; to learn to eroticise sameness, equality, and mutuality" (177), and he recognized the place of erotic fantasy in the evolution of a liberated human race; almost two hundred years earlier, in 1821, Shelley offered an alternative to these two models in a poem entitled *Epipsychidion,* an erotic fantasy whose investigation of the processes of decentering follows from Shelley's belief that all systems of order and hierarchy must be dismantled if his own ideology is to be saved from collapse. Throughout the poem, the techniques of decentering emerge neither as acts of vanishing nor of oozy disintegration but instead as pathways to liberation.[7] The transportation of the poem's lovers beyond the bounds of social convention—beyond the limits of the world, as we shall see—situates them in a utopic no-space that is at once the beginning and the end of time, a frontier whose open shores suggest infinite potential.[8]

The well-documented friendship the Shelleys shared with Teresa Viviani in late 1820 inspired the poet to compose what is perhaps his greatest love poem, *Epipsychidion.*[9] At the time the Shelleys met Teresa, the daughter of the governor of Pisa, the nineteen year-old was being held in a convent as part of her father's effort to force her into an arranged marriage. Triply victimized by patriarchy, economics, and the marriage-contract, Teresa was, as Cameron notes, the image of the Shelleyan heroine *par excellence*—Beatrice Cenci come to life (276). Unsurprisingly, Shelley was moved by Teresa's story of oppression, and as he fell more and more in love with her, he sought to find a way for their love to overcome the literal and figurative structures that separated each from the other—the Convent of St. Anna in which Teresa was being held, and Shelley's marriage to Mary, which prevented him from giving in completely to his *amour* for the governor's daughter. *Epipsychidion* developed as the fruit of Shelley's dilemma, a *paean* to unrequited love in which the local triangle of Percy-Teresa-Mary is transformed into a mythic narrative of an unnamed poet, his beloved "Emily," and the others in their orbit who join them on an imaginary island consecrated to political freedom and unbridled sexuality. As Diane Long-Hoeveler notes, "*Epipsychidion* suggests that in a totalizing love relationship the male comes as close as he can on earth to experiencing the fiction of redemptive oneness with another person."[10] In *Epipsychidion,* Shelley confronts the Symbolic Order, that space of reason, language, and law traditionally regarded as a masculine sphere in which the rigid structures of power and the myriad restrictions placed on pleasure excoriate *a priori* the models of love Shelley advances, in part for their failure to endorse the heteropatriarchal imperative as well as for their inherent opposition to systems of hierarchy and exclusion, two structures endemic to the patriarchal infrastructure that undergirds the Symbolic Order.[11] Baudrillard describes the effects of seduction as proceeding from "*mastery over the symbolic universe*" (8), and surely *Epipsychidion* marks Shelley's initial triumph over the Symbolic Order, for his union with Teresa (impossible in the Symbolic Order) is displaced into the poem's account of the poet's intimacy with Emily (realized in the Imaginary); more importantly, the pseudonymous pair's flight beyond the edges of the world—and beyond the grasp of law and order—demonstrates their triumph over the Symbolic Order, which conspires to keep the real-life Shelley and Teresa forever separated.

But even the high-flown language of *Epipsychidion* proves insufficient to remove the poem from Symbolic indictment; ironically, its very language redoubles the forces that break the poem. To draw on Shelley's language, " . . . honey'd words betray," so that language reveals the power of the Symbolic Order over the poet, his beloved, and their dream of refuge and escape (*Epipsychidion* 270). Ulmer admits that "*Epipsychidion* retains the one as the unrealizable paradox" (137), and Hoeveler points to the poem as Shelley's "final expression of the disillusionment he had found in idealizing women" (143); indeed, *Epipsychidion* reveals the problems incumbent upon the model Shelley posed in "On Love," since his idealization of an other, his elevation of the beloved to the status of all, dooms her to failure, so that even her representational ascent to the space of perfection is weighed down by the chains of signification, dragged back towards impermanence and lack.

Whereas *The Cenci* and *Julian and Maddalo* revolve around a single figure, *Epipsychidion* oscillates between two couples—Shelley and Emily and the poet and the poem. The integrity of the document thus dissolves as the poem vanishes at its beginning and end, in its Advertisement and its conclusion, where Shelley unwrites—deconstructs—the larger poem. By way of highly self-conscious opening and closing devices (an Advertisement in which Shelley disavows authorship to create an elaborate fantasy about the "real" poet, and an *envoi* in which he turns to the poem and admits its mastery over him, acknowledging his own entrapment within the self-involving coils of signification[12]), *Epipsychidion* vanishes into ambiguity and utopia, into what we might think of as the writerly equivalent of Shelley's oozy landscapes. In short, in its flight to utopia, *Epipsychidion* appears to veer toward textual disintegration, or complete collapse.

Throughout my discussion of *Epipsychidion*, I focus primarily on two issues: the political component of erotic engagement and the significance of ooziness and collapse to the progress of Shelley's poem. In making sense of these issues, I turn to Lacanian psychoanalysis, for such a model enables me to take into consideration not only the relationship of the individual experience to larger social structures, but also the function of (the failure of) signification in the articulation of Shelley's ideal. In short, the Lacanian model demonstrates the reciprocal relationships between individual experience and the larger social order that Shelley remains so invested in uncovering, and it accounts for the apparent failure of *Epipsychidion*'s visionary ideal in the poem's final lines.

Terence Allan Hoagwood points to Shelley's father-in-law, William Godwin, as an important influence on Shelley's understanding of the links between personal experience and social structures, for Godwin argued that any hegemonic order "insinuates itself into our own personal dispositions, and insensibly communicates its own spirit to our private transactions."[13] With regard to "the reciprocal efficacy of social relations and mental phenomena,"[14] Hoagwood reads both Godwin and Shelley as arguing that "[a] political order not only manifests an ideology or way of knowing; it also constitutes and engenders such a structure of thought and feeling. Morality (concerned with individuals) and political science (concerned with collectives) are inextricably involved . . . " (140). Certainly, I am not the first scholar to turn to psychoanalysis for a theory that describes the imbrications of personal and political phenomena, for such a turn is an obviously valuable one in making sense of the individual's "place" in the world, and vice versa. Peter Gay, for example, finds psychoanalysis particularly useful in historical-literary studies because it allows one to apply "a set of methods and of propositions designed to wrest from the past its recondite meanings and to read its full orchestrated score."[15] Stephen Frosh insists that psychoanalysis, " . . . simply the body of theories that deals with the formation of the unconscious, and hence with how social and personal worlds interpenetrate," "is *always* politically relevant precisely because it always deals with the way experiences with the social become engaged with as if they are deeply personal, and because it searches out the unrecognized forces that give pattern to our desires, dreams, and neuroses" (270, 269). Frosh explains that psychoanalysis "contains the possibilities for an approach that analyses the mechanisms by which the social world enters into the experience of each individual, constructing the human 'subject' and reproducing itself through the perpetuation of particular patterns of ideology. This is analysis of the bourgeois condition, but potentially of other conditions as well—of all conditions under which personality is formed. As such, psychoanalysis can be more than a portrayal of 'a class in decline'; it can also provide insights into how we may be constituted under changed circumstances, and possibly into how those changes may be brought about" (11). Frosh draws from Herbert E. Marcuse's *Eros and Civilization* (1955) and from Wilhelm Reich's *The Function of the Orgasm* (1942) and *The Mass Psychology of Fascism* (1946) to demonstrate the connections between personal experiences and social models (or sexual and political engagements), and he follows these thinkers in arguing that any successful political revolution depends upon a prior sexual revolution. Because the sexual impulse is weakened and repressed by oppressive social structures, only in its release from repression will the structures that have dominated it come undone (147-155): as Frosh argues, "it is love that provides the subversive possibilities" in an oppressive social system, so that in periods of political domination, love is the only real path to revolution (166).

Such an emphasis on the "place" of sexual revolution in the larger political landscape is not merely a twentieth-century phenomenon, however. In his reading of William Blake's *Songs of Innocence and of Experience, Shewing the Two Contrary States of the Human Soul* (1794), Paulson locates the radical argument that "political repression is related to (or equated with, or reducible to) sexual repression" (*Representations of Revolution* 115).[16] Blake's belief may conceivably have been passed to Shelley, for his participation in the so-called Johnson circle—the group of radical thinkers, writers, and artists who converged around the publisher Joseph Johnson during the early part of the Romantic period—put him in contact with William Godwin and Mary Wollstonecraft, two important influences on Shelley's understanding of the human condition, as I have discussed.[17]

While Paulson points to Blake as an important early Romantic influence on models that collapse the effects of personal and political engagement, the late twentieth-century scholar Eugene Wolfenstein turns to a hybrid methodology—psychoanalytic-Marxist theory—to make sense of the psycho-politics of such imbrications. Wolfenstein argues that "[the desire] to construct a groundwork in psychoanalytic-Marxist theory . . . arises from an interest in human emancipation."[18] He places psychoanalysis in "the category of social action at the level of individuals[,] . . . . an epistemologically distinct type of social action, namely, emancipatory praxis" (351), and he co-aligns psychoanalysis and Marxism because he believes that both regard reality as dialectical, that both methods aim for the same goal of "overcoming the falsification of consciousness and alienation of life-activity that [their] critical and phenomenological methods reveal" (8). Marxism, "a theory of interests rooted in work-activity" (5), cannot alone account for the concatenation of "familial and economic relationships[,] which] are interpenetrative and mutually conditioning" (9), nor can it "adequately illuminate the psychological experience of sex and gender" (138); thus, Wolfenstein grafts Marxism onto psychoanalysis in order to construct a hybrid theory that accounts for phenomena at both the individual and the social levels in order to demonstrate how these phenomena construct and affect each other. Where Wolfenstein expands the simple psychoanalytic model to take into consideration the place of economics and class in social structures and individual experiences, my more narrow focus on the political effects of psychological formations dictates my use of the psychoanalytic model, as I have argued.

To some degree, my turn to a Lacanian psychoanalytic model follows Slavoj Zizek's application of that methodology to his understanding of Eastern European democratic movements. Zizek's investment in the connections between politics and theory finds form in his own institutional practices, for not only is he a respected member of what Ernesto Laclau describes as "the Slovenian Lacanian School," one of the most important movements behind "the so-called 'Slovenian Spring'—that is to say the democratization campaigns that have taken place in recent years," but Zizek also serves as the principle political columnist for the weekly paper *Mladina,* "the most important mouthpiece of this movement."[19] Zizek points to Lacanian theory as demonstrating the importance of language in the mediation of social structures, for Lacanian theory demonstrates that "the performative character of naming is the precondition for all hegemony and politics" (xiv), an assumption crucial to making sense of the project of *Epipsychidion.*[20]

By following a Lacanian psychoanalytic model, my close reading of *Epipsychidion* engages a variety of categories that contribute to the erotic by way of a series of collapses—physical, emotional, and linguistic—which, collectively, activate the melting or merging of lover and beloved into the Shelleyan One. Specifically, I consider five categories that contribute to the poem's erotic model: love, the other, the female and the feminine, androgyny, and the rejection of the Imaginary. Approaching *Epipsychidion* thematically rather than "reading" the poem through from beginning to end enables me more easily to separate and thus more deeply to investigate the five categories that inform what I will describe as the poem's erotic cartography, its map of a world liberated by love, its plot(ting) of utopia.

Cameron points to *Epipsychidion* as exemplary of "the very essence of romantic love poetry," and he argues that the fantasy is "not an exercise in escapism but a passionate expression of need and longing" (288). Following a reading suggested by Robert N. Essick, Ulmer underscores the centrality of the poem to Shelley's ongoing project, for "in *Epipsychidion* the interdependence of language and desire in the Shelleyan imagination achieves definitive illustration" (131).[21] Desmond King-Hele points to a letter Shelley wrote to Mary on 15 August 1821—after he had completed *Epipsychidion*—in which he admits that "my greatest content would be utterly to desert all human society. I would retire with you and our child to a solitary island in the sea . . . and shut upon my retreat the floodgates of the world" (*Letters* 2:339). Shelley's letter gestures toward the autobiographical significance of *Epipsychidion* by emphasizing the centrality of the poem to his personal program of liberation—escape—from the oppressive structures of the world. The exilic model that structures *Epipsychidion* seems an appropriate vehicle for Shelley's articulation of his ideas about happiness and liberation, and while the flight into exile might *prima facie* seem a leap away from the political realities of the world Shelley wants so desperately to redeem, we shall see in the Conclusion how exile operates in concert with activism, so that "flight" signifies neither escape nor retreat but a rather powerful textual strategy that encourages the reader to affect the real-world change Shelley's works may seem, in their leaps into exile, to abandon.

Following Cameron, Essick, Ulmer, and King-Hele, I argue that *Epipsychidion* occupies a central position in Shelley's canon; for me, this centrality hinges on the links the poem demonstrates between erotic and political engagements. In my reading, *Epipsychidion* encodes a three-fold political significance. First, the poem's elevation of a real-life relationship to the level of myth moves personal history to the space of metanarrative, rendering social or public what initially seem a series of merely personal or private interactions. Second, the poem's multiplication of an erotic relationship to include more than two individuals raises the personal, private nature of that engagement to a social or public level, breaking the shackles of the heteropatriarchal imperative and ushering in a radical democratization of love by prophesying the emergence of a community of like-minded thinkers who share not only in the philosophy of free love but, more tangibly, in the intercourse enjoyed by the poem's central pair of lovers. Finally, the poem's displacement of the ideal to a completely imaginary space underscores the political component of the poem's flight of fancy, for it admits the failure of the real world to support Shelley's revolutionary notion of the limitlessness and the democratizing potential of free love.[22]

In his first (and later rejected) preface to *Epipsychidion*, Shelley situates the poem's supposed author in relationship to architectural structures—specifically, to the biblical Tower of Babel: "He had framed to himself certain opinions, founded no doubt upon the truth of things, but built up to a Babel height; they fell by their own weight, & the thoughts that were his architects, became unintelligible one to the other, as men upon whom confusion of tongues has fallen. . . . " (qtd. in Holmes 634). *Epipsychidion* might well be considered the poet's own Tower of Babel, for just as the Symbolic Order obliterates the poem beneath the weight of its rigid, oppressive systems, so, too, did a jealous and angry God strike down the legendary Tower of Babel :

> 6 And the LORD said, Behold, the people *is* one, and they have all one language; and this [the building of the tower] they begin to do: and now nothing will be restrained from them, which they have imagined to do.
> 7 Go to, let us go down, and there confound their language, that they may not understand one another's speech.
> 8 So the LORD scattered them abroad from thence upon the face of all the earth: and they left off to build the city. (Gen. 11:6-8, *KJV*)

Just as the Tower of Babel is destroyed by God for the threat of linguistic and political unity it symbolizes, so, too, is *Epipsychidion* broken because of one poet's sacrilege—his attempt to locate and to commune with his beloved, his dream of overcoming difference and division, his fantasy of melting into the One. As I suggested in Chapter III, Shelley's notion of love places the beloved in the space traditional Christianity reserves for Christ, thus transforming the beloved into a redeemer, or savior; in *Epipsychidion*, Shelley elevates his ideal to the status of the All and then attempts to approach her on the wings of poesy, only to be struck down for his arrogance by language—the Symbolic Order—as the poem collapses all around him. In the end, Shelley is left to abandon his vision of an erotic utopia and to admit his enslavement to the chains of signification that bind him: "Weak verses, go, kneel at your Sovereign's feet, / And say;—'We are the masters of thy slave . . .'".[23] By the poem's conclusion, the idealized love object, Emily, emerges as supremely powerful, while the poet who so positions her is borne down by the weight of his own words, which master him even as they mouth enslavement to his idealized other. Shelley's *envoi* to *Epipsychidion* reverses completely the circumstances that originally prompted the poem's composition: the poet is now jailed, and Emily is set free as the God of language in Shelley's (still) Symbolic, oppressive universe. In their exchange of relative positions, the reconfiguration of the would-be lovers demonstrates the failure of *Epipsychidion* to alter the structures of power that confine them, for although the lovers can alter their positions within the system (of entrapment, separation, and exclusion), they cannot obliterate the literal and figurative presence of the jail, which is manifested both in the actual structure where Emily is held captive as well as in the language—the Symbolic Order—that prevents Shelley from actualizing utopia.[24]

Lacanian psychoanalytic theory offers explanations for both the problems and the successes of the vision of love Shelley describes in *Epipsychidion*. My reading of the poem follows such a model, as I suggest that the idealized object of *Epipsychidion*—"Emily"—emerges as one of many of Shelley's attempts to embody what Lacan designates as the *objet a*, that ultimate object of desire that lies beyond all modes of signification, entirely outside of articulation. Next, I suggest that Shelley's description of Emily as well as his displacement of the beloved to an island, a space (ambiguously) defined by fluid borders, demonstrate that the poet may be struggling to discover the pre-Œdipal other in a realm that corresponds to the Lacanian Imaginary, an alternative sphere that exists just beyond the perimeter of the Symbolic Order, just beyond tyranny's vanishing points at the edges of the known world. Finally, I discuss Shelley's apparent entrapment within language—an issue with which the poet grapples obsessively throughout *Epipsychidion*, as well as in many of his other works—and I make sense of the device through which Shelley temporarily escapes the Symbolic Order in terms of the French feminist model of *jouissance*.

Lacan's notion of the function of desire, that longing for what one wants, or lacks, sets the terms that inform my model for reading *Epipsychidion*. For Lacan, desire is a kind of grid in which three terms—subject, object, and *objet a*—overlap. Lacan invokes the concept of "the other" to account for the development of a subject's knowledge about the world. Following the mirror stage, in which the infant mis-recognizes himself as a whole and complete being who is separate from his mother, the subject is plunged into the Symbolic Order, where he devolves from what Lacan calls the "specular I" to the "social I."[25] This move marks a crucial moment in the subject's development, for here he learns to mediate his place in the world—and to understand his worth—in terms of the other; Lacan writes: "It is this moment that decisively tips the whole of human knowledge into mediatization through the desire of the other, constitutes its object into an abstract equivalence by the co-operation of others, and turns the I into that apparatus for which every instinctual thrust constitutes a danger . . . " (5). In short, the other functions as and offers the space from which the subject is produced, the means through which one recognizes himself and evaluates his place in the world: "The Other is the locus in which is situated the chain of the signifier that governs whatever may be made present of the subject—it is the field of that living being in which the subject has to appear."[26] Now a self-conscious participant in the realm of language and law, the subject mediates his place in the world by way of his relationships to a variety of others, first his mother and later his fellow human beings.[27]

Shelley's description of his desire for the beloved—his ideal other—corresponds to the Lacanian psychoanalytic model I have reviewed. In "A Defence of Poetry," Shelley calls love "the greatest secret of morals . . . an identification of the beautiful which exists in thought, action, or person" (*SPP* 487). In "A Discourse on the Manners of the Ancients," he describes love as "the universal thirst for a communion not merely of the senses, but of our whole nature."[28] The focus of love, the beloved, is "this object . . . [which] forever exists in the mind, which selects among those who resemble it, that which most resembles it and instinctively fills up the interstices of the imperfect image in the same manner as the imagination moulds and completes the shapes in clouds, or in the fire, into the resemblances of whatever form, animal, building, &c., happens to be present to it" (220). For Shelley, the beloved is never more nor less than an approximation of an ideal, a manifestation of the fantasy the subject truly desires. Shelley's most concise definition of the beloved may be found in "On Love," which I have examined at some length already: "We dimly see within our intellectual nature a miniature as it were of our entire self, yet deprived of all that we condemn or despise, the ideal prototype of every thing excellent or lovely that we are capable of conceiving as belonging to the nature of man . . . . a mirror whose surface reflects only the forms of purity and brightness; a soul within our soul . . . . the voice of one beloved singing to you alone" (*SPP* 473-474). Shelley describes the beloved as a perfect match for its perceiver; in idealizing the other, the lover conceptualizes the beloved as a purified reflection, a mirror of the most desirable qualities of himself. Having located the beloved, one externalizes one's best qualities and grafts them onto the fantasy, the ideal other one so desperately desires. Shelley's model of the beloved draws on what Freud considers the hallmarks of narcissism; a person who loves "according to the narcissistic type" sees in his beloved one or more of the following projections:

> (a) what he himself is (i.e. himself),
> (b) what he himself was,
> (c) what he himself would like to be,
> (d) someone who was once part of himself.[29]

In Freud's scheme, the narcissist who loves according to the first three of these descriptions becomes fixated upon himself, while the one who loves according to the fourth description becomes fixated upon the lost part of himself. Freud locates that lost element in the figure of the mother, and while Shelley's description of Emily as the agent who transports him to a space beyond the Symbolic Order may code her as his psychic mother, Emily's place in Shelley's model of love situates her as the poet's other half, the complement to his fragile, fragmented nature. In loving Emily, Shelley mends the psychic rift that exiles him from happiness. Whether she functions specifically as his lost mother or as himself-projected proves less significant, it seems to me, than the generally narcissistic manner in which Shelley constructs her.

Shelley's concepts of love and desire locate his notion of the beloved in a female-identified figure. Yet a reader can easily discern from Shelley's remarks that the beloved, the ideal other, is really only a construction of the masculine gaze; that is, she must correspond to her perceiver's ideal, and thus she is evacuated of any intrinsic value, any subjectivity. Shelley's notion of the other robs her of any identity apart from the one her perceiver assigns to or recognizes in her, as his comments in "On Love" suggest: " . . . we would that another's nerves should vibrate to our own, that the beams of their eyes should kindle at once and mix and melt into our own, that the lips of motionless ice should not reply to lips quivering and burning with the heart's best blood. This is love" (473). Shelley's insinuation that the beloved merely embodies its perceiver's ideal might be expressed in linguistic terms: the beloved operates as a signifier, the ideal as a signified. Significance, Toril Moi notes, is "a question of positioning" (161), for signification, or naming, is an act or power that "reveals a desire to regulate and organize reality according to well-defined categories" (Moi 160). Moi upbraids such a desire as phallocentric (159), and the phallocentrism inherent to *Epipsychidion* appears as an array of symptoms, chief among them the gender-specificity of the poet's object of desire. According to Freud, a female usually serves as the desired object because she guarantees the security and mastery the male fears losing; in this way, Lacan adds, woman represents the phallus, that signifier without a signified, that concept of mastery and order which, in a patriarchal system, is imagined to be manifested in the organ (mis-recognized as) symbolic of male productivity—the penis (132).[30] Both Freudian theory and its Lacanian recapitulation confirm the primary condition Shelley's model of love suggests: just as Shelley's other must correspond to—and therefore validate—the perceiver's idealized self-image, Freud's understanding of the female evaluates her desirability according to her ability to represent to the male his means of access to the thing he most fears losing—the phallus. In sum, as the mirror of himself-perfected, Shelley's idealized other confirms his own supremacy and (self-) idealization.

In recounting his erotic history, Shelley admits that he has been unable to "unburthen [his] inmost soul" to another: he laments, "I have everywhere sought, and have found only repulse and disappointment" ("On Love," *SPP* 473). Lacanian psychoanalysis would diagnose Shelley's disappointment as the condition that gives rise to demand. Frustrated, demand develops into desire, which by its very nature remains unfulfilled; were it satisfied, it would be transformed into something else, perhaps satiation, perhaps disappointment. To put it simply, desire describes a condition in which would-be love is frustrated by its lack of fulfillment or satisfaction.[31] Since his quest for the ideal proves ultimately unsuccessful, the speaker of *Epipsychidion* is unmasked as a victim not of love but of desire. But from what want has this desire developed? What, in other words, has been repressed?

Lacan argues that what one always wants, or lacks, is the Imaginary. Hoeveler sees desire in much the same way: "The end of desire . . . can only be death, escape from the Symbolic altogether" (51). Perhaps, then, what is repressed by the speaker of *Epipsychidion* and what becomes the true object of his desire is a complete escape from the Symbolic Order and a return to the Imaginary; in fact, Shelley calls for such a problematic flight in *Epipsychidion* when he heralds the erotic couple's

> . . . one death,
> One Heaven, one Hell, one immortality,
> And one annihilation . . . .
>
> (585-587)

I will make sense of this troubling nihilism by arguing that the poet experiences a temporary escape from the Symbolic Order through the experience of *jouissance*, a moment of psychic transcendence during which a subject overleaps the bounds of the Symbolic Order to obtain a glimpse of the lost realm of the Imaginary.

But in the end, the poet and Emily fail to be transported to the utopic other-space Shelley envisions, and one is thus left to ponder the causes for the ultimate failure of the poem's erotic ideal. If we were to articulate Shelley's conundrum according to a linguistic model, we might argue that just as signifiers are nothing more than arbitrary connections for representing signifieds, the object of desire Shelley articulates, poses, and pursues throughout his love poem will inevitably prove an arbitrary and insufficient approximation of his ideal. Moi argues that the entire notion of attempting to "capture" a signified within a signifier is "always in part doomed to failure, for it is the nature of meaning to be always already elsewhere" (160). Like the signifier, any human embodiment will, at best, provide nothing more than a close match for an ideal, or so Moi's formulation suggests. One can sense Shelley's uncertainty about the processes of signification in his essay "On Life," where he describes the relationship of words to things as a metaphor for the relationship of the ideal to the physical: ". . . [it is] vain . . . to think that words can penetrate the mystery of our being . . . the difference is merely nominal between those two classes of thought which are vulgarly distinguished by the names of ideas and of external objects."[32] Hoeveler reads another of Shelley's idealized females, the Witch of Atlas, as a character completely evacuated of "ontological reality": she is, Hoeveler claims, "an absent referent in an endlessly meaningless chain of signifiers" (57). My reading of Emily will correspond to Hoeveler's account of the Witch of Atlas, and I will explain the inevitable shortcomings of *Epipsychidion*'s ideal other, the "failure" of Shelley's Emily, in terms of Lacan's model of the *objet a*.[33]

Triangulated among the subject who desires, the person or thing who is desired by the subject, and the larger, unobtainable object that is the true end toward which all the subject's desires tend, desire is bound to go unfulfilled, Lacan argues, since the object upon whom a subject fixes his gaze mis-represents the ultimate object of desire, the *objet a*, which Zizek describes as "the chimerical object of fantasy, the object causing our desire and at the same time—this is its paradox—posed retroactively by this desire" (65), "a void in the center of the [S]ymbolic [O]rder" (185), "the pure void which functions as the object-cause of desire" (163).[34] Mesmerized by the object, the subject loses sight of his larger ideal as he falls into a scopic trap from whose center the object beckons. In "The Eye and the Gaze," Lacan describes this process at length:

> . . . The gaze may contain in itself the *objet a* of the Lacanian algebra where the subject falls, and what specifies the scopic field and engenders the satisfaction proper to it is the fact that, for structural reasons, the fall of the subject always remains unperceived, for it is reduced to zero. In so far as the gaze, *qua objet a*, may come to symbolize this central lack expressed in the phenomenon of castration, and in so far as it is an *objet a* reduced, of its nature, to a punctiform, evanescent function, it leaves the subject in ignorance as to what there is beyond the appearance, an

ignorance so characteristic of all progress in thought that occurs in the way constituted by philosophical research.[35]

Hypnotized by the beloved, the subject misperceives her as the ideal, and his scopophilic obsession with the object blinds him entirely, concealing from his perception and view the *objet a* he truly desires.

According to Lacan, the beloved, that physical being upon whom the subject gazes, is not the real point of desire; rather, she is merely an approximation of the subject's true ideal, and so all objects are interchangeable, since none of them truly signifies what is desired. All objects—in Shelley's poem, Emily chief among them—are, consequently, doomed to failure, bound to be recognized as insufficient markers for the ideal. One truly desires the imperceptible, unobtainable *objet a,* and the various and individual objects any subject perceives—and even adores—will ultimately be unmasked as futile attempts to locate and embody that *objet a.* In this theoretical model, individual objects can never be anything more than insufficient versions of the *objet a,* for every object of desire will prove infinitely replaceable by all others, each an inexact representation of the ideal other. Consequently, Shelley's drive to locate the embodiment of the elusive *objet a* is destined to result in disappointment and frustration. Zizek describes the *objet a* as an element with "no positive consistency . . . an objectification of a void, of a discontinuity opened in reality by the emergence of the signifier" (95). Unable to fix the *objet a* in any mortal form, Shelley is forced to look for a means of escaping the Symbolic Order, a way of leaping beyond the bounds of signification which prevent him from uniting with the ultimate end of his desire, the *objet a* which/who exists in the uncharted void outside of all signifying systems.

Following Lacan, both Irigaray and Kristeva point to *jouissance* as one means of transport beyond the Symbolic Order. During the experience of *jouissance,* a subject escapes the limitations imposed by the Symbolic Order to obtain a fleeting glimpse of the Imaginary. I argue that such a rupture punctuates the transcendent flight in *Epipsychidion* when the poet frees himself from the boundaries of his world to glimpse an alternative order that exists just before and after—at the very ends of—the Symbolic Order. The place of birth and death, the cradle and the grave, the Imaginary hovers around the Symbolic Order as the maternal or "other" realm that envelops and caresses the edges, the borders, of the patriarchal regime. In *Epipsychidion,* Shelley poses a female figure—Emily—as the break between the subject and what must seem, to a patriarchal order, complete chaos, that area beyond the Symbolic Order that marks its limits and remarks its end(s). Appropriately, the figure who transports the subject beyond the limits of the Symbolic Order—the one who facilitates the poet's *jouissance* and activates his escape from oppression—is Shelley's idealized and unobtainable companion, his mother-sister-lover, Teresa "Emily" Viviani.

∞ ∞ ∞ ∞ ∞

> Faithfulness is to the emotional life what constancy is to the
> life of the intellect—simply a confession of failure.
> —Oscar Wilde, *The Picture of Dorian Gray*

Epipsychidion begins with Shelley's patent denial of authorship: the first line of the Advertisement reads, "The Writer of the following Lines died at Florence . . . " (*SPP* 373). Quite to the contrary, however, Shelley's personal correspondence encourages the autobiographical readings of the poem that dominate its critical heritage, a tradition I shall follow.[36] Although in *Epipsychidion* Shelley claims that he "never thought before [his] death to see / Youth's vision thus made perfect" (41-42), Emily, Shelley's pseudonymous representation of Teresa Viviani, appears to signify the ideal being Shelley had been pursuing since his early youth. Shelley calls her "A divine presence" (135), and he describes an imaginary island, "a far Eden of the purple East" (417) to which the lovers may escape and upon which the pair may celebrate their love free from the threats leveled against them by the forced system of monogamy the Symbolic Order demands, manifested at the local level in Teresa's real-life confinement under patriarchal proscription.

This brief synopsis may suggest that I read *Epipsychidion* as an optimistic love poem, but that is not at all the case. While Shelley's poem does attempt to decenter the structures that govern and restrict human lives, the vision of love the poem provides proves ultimately unsatisfactory, for *Epipsychidion* fails to articulate a reliable means of escape from the restrictions of the Symbolic Order. In sum, *Epipsychidion* merely serves as Shelley's flight of fancy, for while it reveals the poet's desire to escape the restrictions of social convention, it fails to describe any viable means for realizing such unlimited freedom and pleasure. Nevertheless, I situate *Epipsychidion* at the crux of my investigation of Shelley's ongoing project because the poem most completely delineates the poet's model of ideal love and most clearly sketches the erotic cartography of liberation, a figurative map upon which the poet plots personal relationships and political orders according to the contours of individual love-unions, which Shelley sharply contrasts to the inflexibility of oppressive relationships and tyrannical social structures.

Love

I return to Shelley's essay "On Love" to underscore the poet's model of love's trajectory: he describes the love's quest as the search for " . . . a mirror whose surface reflects only the forms of purity and brightness; a soul within our soul . . . . the voice of one beloved singing to you alone" (*SPP* 474). Three years later, the notorious "free love" passage in *Epipsychidion* (149-189) multiplied Shelley's image of the "one beloved" by calling for a decidedly polyvalent harmony:

> I never was attached to that great sect,
> Whose doctrine is, that each one should select
> Out of the crowd a mistress or a friend,
> And all the rest, though fair and wise, commend
> To cold oblivion . . . .
>
> (149-154)

Shelley deliberately opposes his creed of free love to what he describes as "the code / Of modern morals," which demands marriage even of those who fail to find true love (153-154). In Shelley's view, the heteropatriarchal imperative of a marriage-driven society forces some individuals into completely loveless unions since their culture demands that "one *should* select / Out of the crowd a mistress *or a friend*" (153-154, 150-151, emphasis added). Caught in the normative trap of the marriage-plot, men and women become "poor slaves . . . with weary footsteps" who find themselves "chained" to a "friend" apt to develop into a "jealous foe" (155-156, 158). Shelley rejects such a constrained notion of morality outright, for he believes that it condemns humankind to travel the wretched road of matrimony to what he insists is its inevitable end—misery.

Happily, Shelley notes that all social conventions—marriage chief among them—are limited by time, and he imagines that when what he dismisses as "modern morals" are replaced by a less restrictive system, the heteropatriarchal imperative will collapse, allowing men and women finally to experience "true love" (154). Shelley grounds his system of free love—an alternative to the oppressive system of "modern morals"—in the belief that the sharing of love leads not to its diminishing, but, conversely, to its increased abundance:

> If you divide pleasure and love and thought,
> Each part exceeds the whole, and we know not
> How much, while any yet remains unshared,
> Of pleasure may be gained, of sorrow spared.
>
> (180-183)

Shelley justifies free love by insisting that man's knowledge, understanding, and experience of the power of love will remain impeded until love is released from all restrictions. "True love"—love unshackled from social convention—"in this differs from gold and clay, / That to divide is not to take away" (160-161); in short, the more lovers one has, the greater one's capacity for love: "Love is like understanding, that grows bright, / Gazing on many truths" (162-163). For Shelley, love always tends toward equality (early in the poem, he reminds the reader of his faith in the democratic potential of love when he insists that " . . . I know / That love makes all things equal" [125-126]), and he argues that when love is allowed to function freely, when it is released from the code of modern morals that so severely curtails its potential, love invariably tends toward liberation, redemption and purification to

>   make free
> The limbs in chains, the heart in agony,
> The soul in dust and chaos.
>
> (405-407)

As I have observed, Shelley's model of love replaces both God and religion as the generative power and symbolic code of the universe.

Shelley argues that marriage is evil because it forces people together and prohibits the individual from expressing love for infinitely many others; by contrast, he insists that any unrestrained union of the self and the beloved must be good. Interestingly, the system of coupling which the marriage-contract encourages is not the notion Shelley wants to dismantle; rather, he takes to task a system in which the couple is elevated exclusively to the status of "all" and any other configurations are excoriated as aberrant. The forced loyalty of marriage prevents one from expressing true love for others because it insists that love must be unnaturally curbed, limited to just one object; in short, under the strict and artificial limitations enforced by and contributing to the hegemony of heteropatriarchialism, love is allowed expression only in the configuration of the monogamous couple:

>   Narrow
> The heart that loves, the brain that contemplates,
> The life that wears, the spirit that creates
> One object, and one form, and builds thereby
> A sepulchre for its eternity.
>
> (169-173)

Shelley speaks for all people—not only for those who might really desire such an exclusive, narrow love but also for those who are forced into monogamy by the inclusion of marriage among the code of modern morals, and he exposes what he regards as the ironic nature of the institution of marriage—that its supposed basis, true love, can never reach its potential as long as love is subjected to the limitations of matrimony, the symbolic union exalted by mainstream culture as love's highest expression. In Shelley's view, this symbology of love is all wrong, for it values most highly the very manifestation of love that imposes so many limitations on the individual, and it leads to the excoriation of any other erotic configurations—such as the free-love community lauded later in *Epipsychidion*—whose boundless potential comes to be regarded not as emblematic of (the) infinity (of affection, of understanding, of power) but instead as the brink of chaos, as the devolution from "proper" human behavior to animalistic, orgiastic delight.

In justifying his philosophy of free love, Shelley compares love to the imagination, which gains its power not from one source but from infinitely many:

from earth and sky,
And from the depths of human phantasy,
As from a thousand prisms and mirrors.

(164-166)

Imagination projects what Shelley describes as its "light" on all things, filling the entire universe "with glorious beams" (163, 167). Just as imagination gains its substantial powers only by drawing on unlimited sources, so, too, will the individual realize the true nature of love only when love is divorced from monogamy and other similarly restrictive conditions. One could say that Shelley's concept poses free love as exponentially generative, for once his heroes realize love, they reproduce—multiply—love in and through their relationships with all other human beings. In Shelley's model, love feeds on diversity; once nourished, love re-invigorates and re-empowers the lot of lovers in any given erotic orbit.

Shelley believes there are some "sages" like himself who understand the need for free love and who recognize the present state of the world encumbered by modern morals as "a garden ravaged" (184, 187). His account of the "far Eden of the purple East," that place to which he hopes to escape with Emily and other members of their free-love community, describes the space as an avenue of return to a time before the onset of modern morals, a time when love was unrestrained by social codes and boundaries (417). But the invention and codification of unnatural laws, like marriage, ravaged this paradisiacal "garden," de-forming it into the strife-ridden society from which Shelley seeks respite (187). No mere escapist, Shelley offers a notion of the cyclicality of historical progression that looks forward to the dawn of a new age in which oppression will cede to liberation: man's present unhappiness, caused in no small measure by forced monogamy, "Tills for the promise of a later birth / The wilderness of this Elysian earth" (188-189).

In its dedication to confounding social convention, in its insistence on polygamy over monogamy, in its radical divergence from the heteropatriarchal imperative as the centerpiece of its trajectory, Shelley's model of love challenges the "code of modern morals" according to which human behavior is regulated—or policed. I believe Shelley's radical utopia must be located in that realm outside the space of language and law, in the Lacanian Imaginary, a pre-Œdipal (and certainly pre-Symbolic) space where limitation gives way to abundance and restriction cedes to possibility as rigidity dissolves into ooziness. The means of access to this place—located at once before and after the Symbolic Order, enveloping hegemony, embracing it, even—is the subject's experience of *jouissance*, that primarily erotic avenue of return to the realm of the Imaginary. Shelley encodes *jouissance* in *Epipsychidion* at the moment he articulates the space of the ideal, that "far Eden of the purple East" to which he wishes to fly with Emily and his community of siblings-lovers. Yet Shelley's flight to the Imaginary must, by its very nature, remain brief and highly problematic, so that his fantasy emerges finally as a failure, given the poet's admission that he cannot defeat the Symbolic Order even at the microlevel of his poetic language. Ultimately, I will offer an alternate strategy for making sense of the poem that will exculpate Shelley from the local failures, or collapses, through which the poem's "honeyed words" seem to "betray" him (270): *Epipsychidion* finally demonstrates the inability of language to provide access to the place Shelley has experienced and thus underscores the insufficiency of language to the project of liberation, rather than the impossibility of the ideal. The poem's "weak verses" indict the Symbolic system in which Shelley operates, which the poem finally unmasks as the real source of the apparent flaws in Shelley's philosophy of the liberatory power of love: were the poet able to break free from the constraints of signification, his vision might indeed succeed in its ascent to the "far Eden of the purple East" *Epipsychidion* describes.

The Other

While Shelley reveals that he first envisioned *Epipsychidion*'s ideal other in his youthful imagination, he admits that he never expected his fantasy to materialize: "There was a Being whom my spirit oft / Met on its visioned wanderings," he admits, but he " . . . never thought before [his] death to see / Youth's vision thus made perfect" (190-191, 41-42). Acutely aware of the purely fantastic nature of the beloved whom he has idealized, Shelley finally comes to recognize the failure of the whole world to correspond to his vision. But even as he finds himself trapped in the loneliness and isolation that symptomatize the world's failure to engender his ideal, he continues to pursue his vision through a number of intimate relationships, all of which eventually prove false.

Following a series of ill-fated unions, Shelley discovers one whom he mis-perceives as the genuine embodiment of his ideal:

> At length, into the obscure Forest came
> The Vision I had sought through grief and shame.
> Athwart that wintry wilderness of thorns
> Flashed from her motion splendour like the Morn's,
> And from her presence life was radiated
> Through the grey earth and branches bare and dead; . . . .
> . . . .
> . . . this glorious One
> Floated into the cavern where I lay,
> And called my Spirit . . . .
> (321-326, 336-338)

Shelley recognized the figure immediately, saying, "I knew it was the Vision veiled from me / So many years—that it was Emily" (343-344).

Emily merely stands for—signifies—Shelley's ideal. Jacques Derrida points to the inevitable "slippage" between signifier and signified that forces the whole process of signification toward collapse;[37] certainly, the apparent correspondence between Shelley's youthful vision (the signified) and Emily (the signifier) finally proves false. Hoeveler's observation about Shelley's Witch of Atlas might also be made of Emily, for although she clearly contains what Hoeveler refers to as "ontological reality," the poem exposes Emily, like the Witch, as "an absent referent in an endlessly meaningless chain of signifiers" (57). Merely an immediate embodiment of Shelley's fantasy, Emily—like the many other women the poet has pursued—is unmasked as a false manifestation of the poet's ideal.[38] The inevitable failure of any of Shelley's lovers to "match" his idealized vision may well inform the free-love philosophy the poet continues to advocate throughout *Epipsychidion* even after he believes he has found the embodiment of the ideal in Emily, which should, initially, strike Shelley's readers as odd: if Emily were truly the embodiment of the ideal Shelley glimpsed in his youth, why would he expound a doctrine that frees him to pursue other lovers, too?

From the beginning of the poem, Shelley trumpets the erotic freedom that forms the centerpiece of his relationship with Emily. Although he believes her to be the physical embodiment of his ideal, and although he certainly desires an intimate union with her, Shelley refuses to narrow his attention to Emily as his only *objet d'amour*.[39] Even though he assures the reader that Emily has replaced the lover he most recently mistook for the embodiment of his ideal—*Epipsychidion*'s Moon, whom many critics agree represents Mary Shelley[40]—Shelley refuses to exclude his former lover from his relationship with Emily. Rather than jettisoning that false embodiment out of the idealized community of lovers, Shelley recuperates her into an alternative erotic register, casting her primarily in the role of sister and only secondarily in the role of lover. Still, in proposing that his former lover remain a part of the love-community, Shelley situates the Moon as a sisterly love object for both himself and Emily: "Sweet Spirit! Sister of that orphan one, / Whose empire is the name thou weepest on" (1-2), he cries,

> Would we two had been twins of the same mother!
> Or, that the name my heart lent to another
> Could be a sister's bond for her and thee.
>
> (45-47)

Any distinctions in the relationships between and among the triad of lovers dissolve into permeability and flux, so that Mary appears first as Emily's sister and then, by connection, as Shelley's, while Emily, at first Shelley's lover, eventually emerges as his sister, as well. Radically democratizing the free-love community by destabilizing traditional notions about the fixed nature of identity and relationships, the sibling model Shelley poses as an alternative to the monogamous couple insinuates the erotic in its familial milieu and multiplies the possible combinations of lovers-siblings by re-envisioning sexual relations in terms of a sibling structure across which love is distributed equally. Yet even in this triangulated relationship, Shelley foregrounds the sexual component of his model as he declares his wife, Mary, to be his "one *lawful*" lover, Emily his "one *true*" (49, emphasis added).

Shelley complicates the dynamics of triangulation even further when he describes an imaginary island to which the lovers will retreat, a stage for "a pleasure-house / Made sacred to [an Ocean-King's] sister and his spouse," another triangulated relationship that mirrors the one Shelley has proposed (491-492). Like the island, which I have described as a frontier-space, at once pre- and post-historical, the relationship between the Ocean-King, his sister, and his spouse anticipates and repeats—comes before and after—the one that Shelley proposes to Emily and to (the absent) Mary. The function of the triangle in these relationships remains significant, for it interrupts—or breaks—the linear trajectory of power that defines the limits of the heteropatriarchal couple, in which one is empowered at the expense of the other, by introducing a third element against—or toward—whom power is deflected.[41] The sibling eroticism of the ideal Shelley describes thus may be read as consistent with this triangulation, for the double valence of erotic relationships in the triangular model—they take sometimes sexual, sometimes familial forms—complicates the rigidity of power that proliferates in systems of linear eroticism, where an unbroken line extends exclusively from one lover to another.[42]

Finally, Shelley introduces yet another satellite into this erotic universe, the "Comet," whom many have argued is Mary's step-sister, Claire Clairmont, and he invites her, too, to join the lovers on the island.[43] This fourth erotic partner serves not to break the democratic triangulation I have described into a kind of rectilinear box, in which power might travel from one point to another and so on, but simply to activate the multiplication of the original triangular model, for with the introduction of the Comet, Shelley's erotic universe tends toward a multiplicity of erotic choices and a final breakdown of the linearity and singularity of the conventional marriage-plot. Together, the disintegration of "proper" sex roles and the blurring of personal identities and positional relationships in Shelley's erotic community (where one is both sibling and lover, just as one's lover is now the Moon, now the Comet, and so on) establish a high sexuality in which each partner fulfills some sort of exalted yet distinctly separate role. The island's erotic inclusiveness thus replaces the exclusive privilege of the marriage-contract in the Symbolic Order; in Shelley's fantasy, none of the lovers is left out or degraded, and all of them—all members of his erotic "family"—constitute a single, indivisible, democratic unit.

Shelley's radically democratic model of free love flies in the face of the social conventions of his day, but still, the poet searches for an earthly location where such a community might flourish, for surely he cannot move beyond that world in which he lives to situate his erotic model in a truly "other" space outside of the confines of his lived reality and its conventions, regulations, and laws—in short, beyond hegemony in all of its manifestations. One could say that Shelley's utopia simply is not "far out" enough, because it is displaced onto an island—a real-world, geographic formation—and, like the vanishing points of patriarchy I discussed in Chapter III, the rigid rules of the Symbolic Order reach around the ends of the earth to contain even this utopic no-space, this frontier that seems to be so far removed from the world Shelley rejects. Shelley's drive to name the beloved and to fix his erotic model in a particular location tie his project to the Symbolic Order, and his investment in signification emerges as an ironic compulsion that snatches him back into the very system he wishes to escape. By expecting a "real," flesh-and-bones woman to match his ideal, Shelley demonstrates his desire to restructure reality according to the fantasies he has been unable to realize in the real world. Time and again, the poet proves unable to reconcile the Symbolic Order and the Imaginary, to jump back and forth between the space of naming, regulation, and law and his fantasy of erotic utopia. With each of these great leaps, *Epipsychidion* teeters more and more precariously on the verge of complete collapse.

The Female and the Feminine

Shelley's location of his ideal in a female form fits neatly, albeit disturbingly, with Freud's understanding of the "place" of woman: always defined through the male, the female is only—and never more than—what the male makes of her.[44] Any reader's understanding of Emily depends completely upon Shelley's portrayal of her, especially since the poet conceals her real identity beneath the veil of metaphor. Pseudonymizing Teresa Viviani as "Emily," Shelley alters reality according to his imaginative agenda, so that she who is confined by her father is liberated by the poet (only) in order to participate in his own elaborate plotting of erotic utopia. Even Shelley's words point to Teresa's thoroughgoing obfuscation: "She met me, robed in such exceeding glory, / That I beheld her not" (199-200). Vanished into the metaphorical form of Emily, Shelley's Teresa is elevated throughout the poem to the status of a goddess-like figure whose love secures the poet's physical empowerment and emotional well-being. Teresa's/Emily's life radiates through all things, undoing barrenness with vitality and waking the spirit of the Endymion-like Shelley from its deep slumber. Her initial effect on Shelley is all-consuming—she "call[s] [his] Spirit" (338); but even as she alters his imagination, the physical world in which he lives remains in stasis, thus compromising the spiritual awakening Shelley experienced upon his first extraordinary encounter with her.

Because Emily/Teresa remains removed from him, cloistered in a convent and promised in an arranged marriage, Shelley's access to this (mistaken) embodiment of his ideal remains severely and tantalizingly limited, and *Epipsychidion* operates as the poet's only means for circumventing their separation. Even if she were to prove the true embodiment of Shelley's ideal, Teresa/Emily would remain unobtainable, so that Shelley's pursuit of her could never amount to anything more than an exercise in the futility of desire, that lack or inability to "unburthen" himself to an other of which he complained throughout "On Love" (*SPP* 473) and which galvanizes *Epipsychidion*'s desperate fantasy. Ironically, her very confinement and inaccessibility cause Teresa/Emily to function as Shelley's truly "ideal" other, for even though she can unite with him emotionally and intellectually, their actual, physical union is precluded from the beginning of their acquaintance. The relationship Shelley desires with Teresa/Emily depends upon a break in the law—Teresa's liberation from a convent that is, in a very real sense, her prison. Trapped in a structure that institutionalizes her father's unchecked power—a reminder of Beatrice Cenci's entrapment beneath the grid of patriarchal tyranny—Teresa can never unite with Shelley without violating the patriarchal dictum of law and order, and Shelley realizes that their union can not and will not take place within the confines of the Symbolic Order. Consequently, he looks to an Imaginary space outside of regulation and law—a "far Eden of the purple East"—to which he displaces the fantasy of their erotic union (*Epipsychidion* 417). In the end, Shelley locates his ideal other—even after he has identified a "real" person as the embodiment of that fantasy—outside of, beyond the real world in the inaccessible reaches of the Imaginary. Displacing a physical other into the realm of pure fantasy, Shelley constructs Emily in such a way that confines her "existence" to the Imaginary: he wants her, but he cannot obtain her, so he creates an idyllic life for them in his own mind.[45] Shelley's metaphorization of Teresa as "Emily" functions in terms of what Lacan refers to as "phallic sexuality": she is assigned to a position of mere fantasy, and, in the process, she loses any basis in reality.[46] Teresa Viviani is, for lack of a more eloquent description, flesh and bones, but Emily is nothing more than a highly idealized representation of a vision, an image at least twice-removed—doubly distanced—from reality.

Lifted—or reduced—to the level of pure fantasy, Emily is forced into the act of mime, which Irigaray recognizes as the function men require of women in order to recuperate them in phallocentric discourse and to define them in terms of what they are not (men), even as they act in such a manner that fulfills the expectation of what they are imagined to be; in other words, women are left to masquerade as the objects of desire their paramours have invented (Irigaray, "The Power of Discourse and the Subordination of the Feminine" 76).[47] Throughout *Epipsychidion*, Emily never speaks, and Shelley's complete recuperation of her in his phallocentric discourse reduces her to a mere figment of his imagination. The real person upon whom Shelley's fantasy is based, Teresa Viviani, is silenced as Shelley's monument to his love for the ideal eclipses Teresa's ability to respond in kind, so that all of her actions and intentions become the sole inventions of her male creator.[48] *Epipsychidion* begins not with Shelley's words but with Teresa Viviani's, which Reiman translates as follows: "The loving soul launches beyond creation, and creates for itself in the infinite a world all its own, from this dark and terrifying gulf" (373 n 1).[49] Clearly, *Epipsychidion* recuperates Teresa's idea within Shelley's elaborate fantasy of a displaced erotic union. Thus, from the moment he elaborates upon her words as his own, Shelley robs Teresa/Emily of the ability to think, to speak, and to act as an autonomous subject, independent from her lover. In this way, Shelley reduces even Teresa Viviani to the mere figment of his imagination that Emily more transparently represents.[50]

Shelley exposes his reduction of Teresa/Emily to the level of pure fantasy every time he addresses his beloved as a half-human, half-divine ideal. From the beginning of *Epipsychidion,* he portrays Emily as an angelic sort of fantasy figure, calling her "Sweet Spirit!" "High, spirit-winged Heart!" "Seraph of Heaven!" and "Sweet Lamp!" (1, 13, 21, 53). Indeed, Shelley constructs Emily as "too gentle to be human," and even when he does stoop to describe her human characteristics, he offsets those too-earthly aspects by underscoring her goddess-like nature: not merely a woman, Emily is "one serene Omnipresence" (21, 95). Her effect on him is so ethereal and her very presence so tenuous that Shelley declares her "Scarce visible from extreme loveliness," and he describes the synæsthetic effects of his proximity to her, such as his ability to feel the "odour" of her presence (104, 109). Ironically, Shelley's high praise effaces Emily's material nature and underscores her function as a figure of mere fantasy. Even when he addresses her as the rather mortal "Lady mine," Shelley undermines Emily's reality—as well as the reality of the conditions in which she is being held—by assimilating her into his ultimately narcissistic fantasy:

> Scorn not these flowers of thought, the fading birth
> Which from its heart of hearts the plant puts forth
> Whose fruit, made perfect by thy sunny eyes,
> Will be as of the trees of Paradise.
>
> (384-387)

In an ultimate act of effacement, Shelley turns a blind eye to the more immediate condition of Teresa's unpleasure—her captivity—by projecting her into the space of erotic utopia while doing absolutely nothing to alter her real-life oppression.

Just as Shelley's elevation of Teresa to Emily-the-ideal denies the woman he claims to love any semblance of autonomy, his remarks on the treacherous aspects of her otherwise glorious nature cast Emily as an antagonistic force who threatens to obliterate her would-be paramour: she is a "Vision like incarnate April, warning, / With smiles and tears" (121-122). In this way, Emily replicates the disappointment, deceit, and danger into which Shelley has been lured by other women, all of whom he summarily rejects as false embodiments of his ideal, and all of whom he suggests have proven physically or psychologically threatening: of one early lover, for example, Shelley admits that he "would have followed [her], though the grave between / Yawned like a gulph whose spectres are unseen" (230-231), and of another he recalls that she caused him to

> . . . [turn] upon my thoughts, and [stand] at bay,
> Wounded and weak and panting; the cold day
> [Trembling], for pity of my strife and pain.
>
> (273-275)

Throughout his erotic history, Shelley seems to have remained painfully aware that his true ideal (*objet a*)—regardless of the particular embodiment in whom he has tried to locate her (objet)—has posed considerable risk to his well-being: "Thy wisdom speaks in me, and bids me dare / Beacon the rocks on which high hearts are wreckt" (147-148). At one point in his pursuit, a disembodied voice cautions Shelley that "' . . . O thou of hearts the weakest / The *phantom* is beside thee whom thou seekest'" (233, emphasis added). Throughout his quest, Shelley is haunted by the very vision he seems to desire, an ideal other whose treacherous nature lures him toward death, a *femme fatale* whose beauty blinds him to the evil she represents. At once the hunter and the prey, Shelley slips across the masculine/feminine binary to grapple with the sublime ideal; unmanned—castrated—by his own fantasy, Shelley is reduced to the feminine status of no-thing.[51]

In fact, throughout *Epipsychidion* Shelley ultimately denounces the sublime nature of all women. When he speaks of "Death and Life," "[m]asked like twin babes, a sister and a brother," the grammatical structure of his description genders Death as female-, Life as male-identified (301, 303). Yet the indeterminacy in gender roles I have discussed re-emerges as Shelley recounts falling in love with Emily, from whose masculinized being "life was radiated / Through the grey earth and branches bare and dead" (325-326). The earth and branches represent Shelley's body and soul, weakened by earlier lovers whom Shelley mistook for "[y]outh's vision . . . made perfect" (42). Of course, the reader recognizes at once that Emily, too, will prove false, for the "light" she seems to radiate masks an optical illusion, concealing from his perception and view the beacon of the scopic trap from whose center the beloved beckons, itself the product of the poet's willful denial of the true nature of this new beloved (42). Just as previous false embodiments of his ideal weakened the poet almost to the point of death, so too does Emily radiate a light that will return Shelley to the dark orbit of danger, treachery, and destruction. Nevertheless, he remains undeterred by the education in treachery and danger he has been proffered by so many false embodiments of his fantasy, and he continues to search for his ideal other, first in one embodiment, and then in another, and so on. Ironically, these local failures contribute to the success of Shelley's larger agenda of free love, for if any of these were to emerge as the *objet a* of his fantasy, the rationale behind Shelley's argument for free love would fold. The failures of Emily and the other lovers he describes throughout *Epipsychidion* and elsewhere guarantee the success of the poet's broader sexual creed, which derides any "code of modern morals" that privileges the monogamous couple as love's highest symbol and marriage as its highest expression.

Finally, Shelley's narcissistic production of the ideal—his description of Emily as a "soul out of my soul"—reminds us of the selfish tendency of his entire pursuit and underscores the disappointment to which each embodiment of his fantasy inevitably tends. The first time Shelley attempts to locate his ideal in a mortal woman, he ends up discovering only himself:

> . . . I measure
> The world of fancies, seeking one like thee [the vision],
> And find—alas! mine own infirmity.
>
> (69-71)

Shelley sets the narcissistic terms of the pursuit in his initial exhalation to Emily, which describes her as a "mirror" (30) and thus makes quite clear her function as the narcissistic double he described in "On Love," she who serves as nothing more than "a mirror whose surface reflects only the forms of purity and brightness: a soul within our soul" (*SPP* 474). In adoring Emily, Shelley revisits the narcissistic delusion that leads ultimately and unfailingly to alienation, so that once again he is unable to find sympathy in an other and thus remains trapped in solitude, reeling from erotic disappointment.

Androgyny

P. M. S. Dawson argues that in *Epipsychidion,* Shelley remains "consciously in retreat from the public world."[52] Certainly, the poem gestures toward narcissistic desire, as I have demonstrated. But the erotic tendency that marks Shelley's pursuit is, in fact, not completely esoteric. Quite to the contrary, throughout *Epipsychidion* Shelley remains dedicated—perhaps even desperately so—to outwardly directed erotic engagements, and so he searches the world around him for a physical embodiment of his ideal. His initial dream-like encounter with one manifestation of that ideal suggests the poet's psychological confusion (manifested in the reversal) of internal and external, self and other, fantasy and reality, but even upon awaking, he continues his search undaunted: "I would have followed, though the grave between / Yawned like a gulph whose spectres are unseen" (230-231). Almost overtaken by the beckoning vision, Shelley at last turns

> . . . upon [his] thoughts, and [stands] at bay,
> Wounded and weak and panting; the cold day
> [Trembling], for pity of [his] strife and pain.
>
> (273-275)

Shelley's narcissistic projection of his internal condition upon the world about him reminds the reader of the immediacy of the threat accompanying his pursuit of the ideal: in the poet's view, the suffering and trembling of "the cold day" mirror his own "strife and pain" (274, 275). Such a narcissistic projection of the self onto the natural world reminds us of another of Shelley's tragic heroes, the Poet of *Alastor*, who imagines his melancholic existence to be mirrored in the natural world, and who exclaims,

" . . . O stream!
. . . .
Thou imagest my life . . . ."[53]

Much like Shelley in *Epipsychidion*, the Poet of *Alastor* struggles with the confusion of inside and outside, fantasy and reality, self and (not really) other. In *Epipsychidion*, Shelley corrects the *Alastor* Poet's tragic solipsism by fleeing his "pain and strife" while continuing undaunted in his search for an other. While misery over his inability to locate the beloved weakens and, in the end, overcomes *Alastor*'s Poet, in *Epipsychidion* Shelley refuses to cede ground to frustration and disappointment, so that he moves ever farther away from the vortex of solipsism by turning constantly outward to engage the world about him. The two lines that follow Shelley's brief, narcissistic reflection underscore his efforts to externalize his vision and to code his failure as success—or, at the very least, as progress: "like a noon-day dawn, there shone again / Deliverance" (276-277). Likewise, when Shelley describes a false embodiment of the ideal who left him "nor alive nor dead," he refuses to be defeated by that deceitful lover, and as if to bolster—and, certainly, to insist upon—his own subjectivity and mastery, he urges the reader to "Weep not for me!" (320). Shelley's quest, fruitless thus far, promises not to be blighted by the untimely tragedy of the completely inwardly turned desire that drowns the Poet of *Alastor*. In correcting the solipsism of *Alastor* with a resolute turn to outward engagements, *Epipsychidion* displaces the earlier poem's model of monogamy with a vision of free love, at once triumphing over convention and curing the nihilism of the completely internalized quest that doomed *Alastor*'s Poet to an untimely grave.

Throughout *Epipsychidion*, androgyny plays a primary role in Shelley's descriptions of the lovers' union, as the idealized male and female coalesce—melt—into the one mind. This mixing of gendered identities, this collapsing of the pair of lovers into a single embodiment, foregrounds the central role of androgyny, that psychological combination of masculine and feminine elements, which underwrites the psychological valences that structure Shelleyan love. *Epipsychidion* abounds with images in which diverse elements mix and melt into each other. Early in the poem, Shelley proclaims that "love makes all things equal," so that all lovers may exist in "difference without discord" (126, 144). What appears at first to be a radical democratization—the toppling of difference, the flattening out of the systems of stratification that create oppositions by casting elements in self-other relationships—gives way to a psychological melting of lovers and beloveds in a seamless psycho-erotic community where all members are absorbed into the one mind Shelley so earnestly poses as the universal ideal—and as much more than a mere abstraction.[54]

But androgyny does not come without cost, and as Shelley describes his complete union with the ideal (*objet a*), he points to his repeated emasculation at the hands of the many false embodiments of the ideal (objet) who have pushed him to the brink of spiritual death (285-320).[55] While Shelley trumpets androgyny as the central structure of his erotic model, he also mourns his devolution to a feminine position of passivity, expressing his overt displeasure for what he seems to perceive as a fall into helplessness, over which "[he] wept, and though it be a dream, [he] weep[s]" (307). Shelley exposes androgyny, the only avenue to the ideal, as a process that comes not without cost, a psychological negotiation that engenders anxiety, alienation, and pain. The burden of androgyny is only heightened by that rigid realm under whose law Shelley lies trapped—the Symbolic Order with its inflexible "code of modern morals," which excoriates and punishes any configuration of gendered positionality that deviates from the normative, masculine/feminine opposition. Predicated upon the triumph of androgynous union, Shelley's vision of ideal love is finally unmasked as completely antithetical to the Symbolic Order, so that in *Epipsychidion* the poet is left to search for a way out of that realm, to describe and to activate a means of transport back to the Imaginary.

Even as *Epipsychidion* traces the painful development of the androgynous psyche, Shelley privileges such a feminization of the male subject as the crux upon which the realization of his ideal depends. Shelley's union with Emily is enabled solely by the reversal of gender roles, as Emily assumes the masculine (or active) position while Shelley, asleep and dreaming, assumes the feminine:

> this glorious One [Emily]
> Floated into the cavern where I lay,
> And called my Spirit, and the dreaming clay
> Was lifted . . .
> . . . .
> I knew it was the Vision veiled from me
> So many years—that it was Emily.
>
> (336-344)

Emily, the active, masculine element in this exchange, breathes life into the passive/feminine Shelley; God-like, she animates the poet, who, in a complete psychological reversal, becomes the creature—the Adam (or, more precisely, the Eve) animated by the God-like breath of his own creation. Thus, Shelley cedes creative power to Emily, who in her role as

Shelley's narcissistic projection returns that power back to him in his dream of their erotic union. Here we see the Freudian negotiation of the phallus played out between lover and beloved: Shelley cedes phallic privilege to Emily, who unmans her lover only to guarantee his (never actually threatened) mastery over the entire scene he has constructed.

Androgyny, that odd slip between the parameters of masculinity and femininity, sustains Shelley in his quest for the beloved: mother-like, Emily gives birth to Shelley even as she overtakes him in pleasure and (figuratively) ejaculates life into his passive, receptive body. The phallic mother *par excellence*, Emily returns the dreaming Shelley to a pre-Œdipal stage in which the parameters of gender have yet to be constructed by a social order, and in which endless, polymorphous play guarantees the fulfillment and pleasure of all who participate in the erotic exchange. In lines 345-361, Shelley expresses his desire to erase all structures of differentiation and to participate in the "bothness" of the pairs of objects the poet describes: the couplings of "wind and tide," "cloud and cave," and "grave and cradle" combine seemingly opposite elements to generate single, unified wholes, much in the same way that Shelley hopes to mix and melt with Emily. In a pre-Œdipal oblivion to hierarchy and division, Shelley delights in all things "equal, yet unlike" which lead toward "one sweet end," that state of seamless combination he so desires, itself the manifestation of the androgynous psyche at the site of the erotic body (359). Clearly unacceptable to the Symbolic Order, the seamlessness of androgyny dictates Shelley's opposition to that realm so long as he continues to pursue his vision; in *Epipsychidion*, the poet effects his escape from the Symbolic Order through the unique experience of *jouissance*, which returns him—however briefly—to the pre-Œdipal realm of the Lacanian Imaginary.

Shelley encodes *jouissance* in *Epipsychidion* throughout the second half of line 407. At the instant he speaks—ejaculates—the name of his beloved, "Emily," Shelley envisions a space in which the pair will realize the idyllic love he has described. Prior to this moment, Shelley could but conceptualize the basic model of their relationship as a seamless union, but following his slip into androgyny—his emasculation or death and re-animation at the hands of his beloved[56]—Shelley becomes able to imagine an area in which the pair may express their love apart from the limitations placed upon them by the "code of modern morals" that regulates all erotic negotiations in the Symbolic Order. This is the only time in *Epipsychidion* that Shelley refers to the beloved simply by her name unadorned, unencumbered, by a string of epithets or hyperbolic modifiers. For the first time, it seems, Shelley is able to recognize the beloved in her most pure form, stripped of the many descriptions with which his words have masked her, so that now she appears simply as "Emily," the mere essence of the divine other for whom Shelley has so long searched. But the grammar of Shelley's passage reminds us that his dream has already ended and that the poet is describing a place he has already lost, for although Shelley speaks of their journey to an island

and of the erotic union that takes place there in the present tense, by the time he addresses Emily directly at the end of line 407, Shelley has clearly glimpsed—and lost—the place he is about to describe. In other words, by the end of line 407 Shelley has experienced *jouissance*, an overleaping of the bounds of the Symbolic Order that enables him to peek beyond its vanishing points to access the Imaginary. *Jouissance* always results in one of two ends: a fall back into the Symbolic Order or, in the failure to return to that Order, the death of the subject.[57] As he attempts to describe the place he has seen, Shelley's fall (back) into language underscores his return to the Symbolic Order, and the words that close his description of the island-ideal encode his fall explicitly, as we shall see.

Julia Kristeva posits that in a patriarchal society, women symbolize the edge of the Symbolic Order, the jumping-off place that leads to freedom from patriarchal rule and the lawlessness of chaos. In Kristeva's model, women represent the break between civilization and disorder, a rupture that shatters the integrity of the Symbolic Order by tearing open a closed system and activating the flight of the oppressed toward the liberating space of the Imaginary.[58] But the cost of such a flight is high: in *Epipsychidion*, Shelley bemoans its heavy toll by admitting that he and Emily will obtain complete unity only after their deaths, for only in their "decay" (537) shall they

> become the over-hanging day,
> The living soul of this Elysian isle,
> Conscious, inseparable, one.
>
> (538-540)

Shelley's flight into the Imaginary recalls his initial vision of Emily in which she lured him toward death, for since he and his ideal will realize complete union only after they escape the bounds of modern morals, their idyllic union—their melting into oneness—must surely follow their mortality: in his *envoi* to *Epipsychidion*, Shelley observes,

> "Love's very pain is sweet,
> But its reward is in the world divine
> Which, if not here, it builds beyond the grave."
>
> (596-598)

Shelley consistently constructs his ideal, whether she is embodied in Emily or in earlier, false forms, as a threatening force whose seduction culminates in annihilation. Certainly, Shelley describes Emily as a phallic female, that mother/father-woman who threatens the masculinity, privilege, and power—and even the life—of the man who adores her.

Shelley describes his journey out of the Symbolic Order as a glorious escape. As he and Emily—the creator and the created, the visionary and the vision—sail calmly away from the Order that conspires against their love, various elements of the natural world replicate the lovers' limitless union, so that night and day, storm and calm, disappear into each other to repeat the oneness of the lovers themselves:

> Our bark is an albatross, whose nest
> Is a far Eden of the purple East;
> And we between her wings will sit, while Night
> And Day, and Storm, and Calm, pursue their flight,
> Our ministers, along the boundless Sea,
> Treading each other's heels, unheededly.
>
> (416-421)

This "far Eden of the purple East"—to which, as we shall see, the lovers will never really sail—activates the androgynous union Shelley so desires. He hints at the island's replication of the lovers' blurring of gender roles in his description of the "lone dwelling" on the island, a tower in which "some wise and tender Ocean-King" practiced free love with his sister and his lover (484, 488).[59] Shelley's description of the island's clearly phallic central structure disempowers—de-phallicizes—that tower in the same way that his vision of the ideal other activates his own self-emasculation: like the dreaming poet, the island's aged structure "'Tis not a tower of strength," " . . . scarce [seeming] now a wreck of human art" (486, 493),

> For all the antique and learned imagery
> Has been erased, and in the place of it
> The ivy and the wild-vine interknit
> The volumes of their many twining stems;
> Parasite flowers illume with dewy gems
> The lampless halls . . . .
>
> (498-503)

Overcome and weakened, the tower falters in its usually phallic associations, for the supposed-to-be phallic tower has been feminized in its erasure-by-nature, suggesting to the reader that the island offers a space in which the mixing of binary oppositions—the seamlessness of androgynous union—may be realized. The crawling of the vines up the sides of the tower points to the post-historical place of this world, since an architectural form—a particular artifact of human civilization—is overtaken by the natural world. Just as the Symbolic Order privileges masculinity over femininity, so too does it privilege civilization over nature; but here, in the space of erotic utopia, nature and civilization mingle as one to generate a post-historical ecological wonderland in which natural and architectural forms mix and melt into each other, mirroring the lovers' experience of idyllic union.[60]

The remainder of *Epipsychidion* abounds with descriptions of combination and overlap, images of embracing, combining, and joining that clearly exemplify Shelley's model of erotic union in which one "imagine[s] . . . that the airy children of our brain were born anew within another's," feels "another's nerves . . . vibrate to our own" and sees "the beams of [the beloved's] eyes . . . kindle at once and mix and melt into our own" ("On Love," in *SPP* 473). At the edge of the island, "the Earth and Ocean seem / To sleep in one another's arms," and above them "the blue heavens bend / With lightest winds, to touch their paramour [the island]" (509-510, 544-545). Likewise, the community of lovers Shelley describes replicates the utopic absorption of the landscape itself:

> Possessing and possest by all that is
> Within that calm circumference of bliss,
> And by each other, till to love and live
> Be one: . . . .
>
> (549-552)

As Wasserman notes, Shelley's island is symbolic of the circle, that archetypal symbol of wholeness and eternity (441), and "the lovers, interassimilated by mutual giving and receiving, are also to be absorbed into the circle of their island of bliss, and the island is to be absorbed within their circumference" (449). On this score, lover, beloved, and utopia all mesh in erotic union, achieving the ideal of absolute "interpenetration"—the complete commingling that Shelley celebrates throughout his writing. More narrowly, Shelley and his beloved "shall become the same, we shall be one / Spirit within two frames, oh! wherefore two?" and shall join into

> One hope between two wills, one will beneath
> Two overshadowing minds, one life, one death,
> One Heaven, One Hell, one immortality,
> And one annihilation.
>
> (584-587)

But Shelley codes his entire discussion of combination and fusion in the future tense, which underscores his admission that not only has such a union so far failed to occur, but that the complete absorption of the lovers never will occur—not even on this island—until both of them have died.[61] The gift of seamlessness is deferred, so that the present (tense) is exposed as a mere illusion, a dream, a trick of language, for the island has never existed and, as Shelley knows, it is never going to appear, at least not outside of his language—the very agent and evidence of the poet's entrapment within the Symbolic Order.[62]

Rejection of the Imaginary

I situate the idealized existence Shelley describes throughout *Epipsychidion* in an oppositional relationship to the Symbolic Order for two reasons: first, because it destroys the heteropatriarchal imperative by activating a radical democratization of erotic relationships; second, because it depends upon the collapses—those disintegrations into the ooziness of ambiguity (or "bothness")—that mark the psychological configuration of androgyny.

Consequently, Shelley's model must be located outside the realm of regulation and law in the alternative space I have described in terms of the Lacanian Imaginary. Shelley self-consciously acknowledges the otherworldly location of his ideal in the language of the poem, which gestures toward the improbability of fixing that space in the physical world:

> For in the fields of immortality
> My spirit should at first have worshipped thine,
> A divine presence *in a place divine*.
> (133-135, emphasis added)

Immune to war, famine, pestilence, and all the treacherous aspects of nature that threaten man's security, such as savage wild animals and stormy seas (461-469), Shelley's utopic island emerges as an erotic no-space, a highly refined version of the natural world in which the manifestations of weakness, strife, and turmoil—in particular, disease, brutality, and natural disasters—vanish from our purview.

Shelley first envisioned his erotic utopia as he communed with nature in caves, amid "enchanted mountains," and on imaginary shores (194-197). Each of these formations gestures toward the magic space of the island, for each marks an irregularity in the earth's surface that anticipates the rupture in the Symbolic Order through which one is allowed access to the Imaginary. Shelley's intention for the lovers to retreat to "an isle" (a term whose Italian etymology connotes both "refuge" and "escape," as Wasserman believes Shelley would have known [441]) situates that utopia in an oozy location, surrounded by water and distanced—disconnected, even—from all other land masses (422). Shelley's description of the space reminds us of his usual imbrications of landscapes and bodies, since

> . . . the isle's beauty, like a naked bride
> Glowing at once with love and loveliness,
> Blushes and trembles at its own excess.
> (474-476)

Detached from the rest of the world, Shelley's island-bride hovers between one world and another, " . . . 'twixt Heaven, Air, Earth, and Sea, / Cradled, and hung in clear tranquility" (457-458). Shelley's use of the term "[c]radled" invokes maternal imagery, counterpoising the Symbolic Order (the realm of the Father) to a vision of an "other" society nurtured in the arms of the Mother. "Cradled" in this half-spousal, half-maternal other-space (a combination that extends Shelley's incestuous erotic model to the physical landscape), the island provides access to pre-Œdipal, polymorphous pleasure within a realm of ooziness, moisture, and endless productivity. In returning to the cradle of the island, Shelley sneaks back inside the womb, that warm, moist place in which one is nourished and loved, that enveloping space in which one sleeps, oblivious to the rigid structures that impose so many limitations and constraints on life in the

Revolutionary Landscapes and the Politics of Love 209

Symbolic Order. Shelley encourages us to regard the island as a kind of womb when he remarks on the music of the place, which sounds "in unison," "[l]ike echoes of an antenatal dream" (454, 456). "Echoing"—coming after, repeating—"an antenatal dream," the island must surely activate a return to the womb, a retreat from the Father and a flight to the Mother (454-456).[63] Moist, oozy, life-giving, and productive, Shelley's island hovers, disconnected from the world of language and law and lifted out of the code of modern morals; indeed, Shelley's "far Eden of the purple East" gestures toward the space of the Imaginary.

Throughout *Epipsychidion,* Shelley articulates his outright rejection of the heteropatriarchal imperative, but the fantastic nature of the poem's erotic utopia suggests Shelley's recognition of the improbability of realizing such a model within the limits of his own time and within the confines of his own society. At the most local level, Shelley's would-be lover remains separated from him by a patriarchal dictate that is manifested in a religious system, as Teresa Viviani remains held in the prison-like Convent of St. Anna until she consents to the marriage her father has arranged. Complicating that most immediate of circumstances, Shelley's idealization of the poem's island adds to the incongruity of his vision and the reality of the Symbolic Order. Although he can describe the place he has glimpsed during a moment of *jouissance,* Shelley knows he can never really arrive at that space until he escapes the limits of the Symbolic completely, a dilemma he admits at the poem's conclusion, where he laments that

> "Love's very pain is sweet,
> But its reward is in the world divine
> Which, if not here, it builds beyond the grave."
>
> (596-598)

While it may at first appear that the notoriously atheistic Shelley is buying into a belief in an afterlife as a compensatory fantasy of a deferred union with Teresa, his notion of the afterlife postulates no Christian Heaven but, instead, a world freed from the restrictions and moral codes of the Symbolic Order, an isle "twixt Heaven and earth" where all beings melt into one, an erotic utopia which might be conceived in a moment of *jouissance* but which will only be secured by way of a complete escape from the Symbolic Order—perhaps, as Shelley suggests, through death.[64] Some canceled lines from *Julian and Maddalo* gesture toward the connection between the island's utopic, purple space and the death of the subject:

> "WHAT think you the dead are?" "Why, dust and clay,
> What should they be?" "'Tis the last hour of day.
> Look on the west, how beautiful it is
> Vaulted with burning radiant vapours! the deep bliss
> Of that unutterable light has made
> The edges of cloud   fade
> Into a hue, like some harmonious thought,

>   Purple which is like sweet
>   Wasting itself on that which it had wrought,
>   Till it dies [lingeringly]   and between
>   The light hues of the tender, far, serene,
>   And infinite tranquillity of heaven.
>   Ay, beautiful . . . ."
>
> (WPS 3:196-197).

Telescoping the "far Eden of the purple East" into a post-historical space, Shelley brings full-circle the model of the Imaginary I have described, so that the Symbolic Order, that would-be realm of indisputable power, is shown to be surrounded by the Imaginary, which begins before the Symbolic (in the pre-Œdipal space of the womb) and circles around beyond the ends of it (in the cradling arms of Death, to whom Beatrice referred, we should recall, as an "all-embracing Mother" near the end of *The Cenci* [65]). Shelley's pre-Œdipal/post-mortem conception of erotic utopia marks that space's triumph over history and time, its victory over the Symbolic Order, so that the all-embracing Mother of Death envelops the Symbolic on all sides, (s)mothering it in her grasp.[66]

" . . . *honeyed words betray*"

Throughout *Epipsychidion,* Shelley articulates three specific desires: for an idyllic union with Teresa/Emily, for free love liberated from modern morals, and for transport to an area in which the first two desires might be realized. But all of Shelley's hopes are quashed by the crushing weight of signification, for it is in the very language through which he attempts to articulate his ideal that his entire dream collapses as each utterance falls into the insurmountable trap of signification. A. C. Goodson recognizes language as one of the enemies of Romantic poetry, because "[t]he progress of language serves reason and understanding, which are in the ascendant[, and t]hese are the enemies of poetry."[67] "Where the poetic function fails, . . . there is a general loss of vitality, not just a loss of poetry" (17), Goodson writes, but Kaja Silverman offers a hopeful corrective to Goodson's pessimism—one generally shared by Shelley scholars—in arguing that "[t]o abdicate enunciatory control . . . is, however, not to lose, but rather to find one's language of desire."[68] Indeed, the plotting of utopia involves a stepping-off into the unknown, a charting of somewhat unfamiliar space, both physical and ideological. Deborah Elise White rescues Shelley from charges of what Goodson might characterize as a loss of vitality by remarking that the dedication of Shelley's poetry to an unknowable future requires a language of non-referentiality (103), for if poetry inscribes prophecy, it must be cast in figurative language (105). Poetry, White claims, can never really refer to anything but itself: "[p]oetry points *there* even as, in the gesture of pointing, it says *never*" (125), but yet "[p]oetry points ahead and away from itself, and yet the promise of its truth in each and every case leads one back (or *re-fers* one) 'there' to the supplemental truth that one may, after all, have been *mis*led—that promises are, quite literally, meant to be broken" (128). Kipperman agrees that "utopian language, in its explicit ahistoricality, risks an unself-conscious escapism, denying its grounding in the history it demands to transform" ("Macropolitics of Utopia" 87); yet he finds Shelley's poetry ultimately non-escapist, for it "argues that the very shape and realization of human ideals like peace and equality depend on the progress of history; that struggles for liberation are founded in permanent ideals but expressed and defined only within historical contingency; and that these ideals exist as permanent possibilities of social and spiritual progress, so that even as negatives (utopia is not yet) they persist to negate the negations of imperialism [or, to use a term more specifically suited to the context of my study, *tyranny*] with its delusions of permanent power" (92). And so Shelley pivots back and forth from optimism to despair, his oscillations turning on the failures of language, the snares of signification.

Conscious of the trap of language, Shelley makes clear from the beginning of *Epipsychidion* the false nature of language and its propensity to alter—and, thus, to misrepresent—the ideas it purports to signify: writing of his principal object of desire in pseudonym, Shelley admits her unreality as well as his understanding that even if he were able to retreat to his island of free-love with "Emily," he would remain barred from the lover he truly desires, Teresa Viviani. Ironically, it is Shelley's distinct and explicit articulation of the ideal that prevents him from realizing his desires, for the ultimate object of desire, the Lacanian *objet a*, lies beyond signification and may merely be approximated by the endless succession of embodiments Shelley nominates in his attempts to approach the ideal. Throughout *Epipsychidion,* Shelley's language acknowledges this futility of desire: twice, he exclaims, "woe is me!" (123, 587), a miserable utterance that reminds the reader of exactly the Lacanian argument—that the *objet a* the poem tries to re-present gets lost somewhere in the poet's articulation of that desire.[69] Of Teresa's/Emily's unfortunate situation, Shelley admits that he "weep[s] vain tears" (19), and gradually the whole of *Epipsychidion* emerges as the poet's ineffective lament, his vain weeping of tears, for its drive to articulate an idyllic existence dooms Shelley's fantasy to failure.[70]

Shelley self-consciously addresses the inherent failure of signification throughout *Epipsychidion*. At line 270 he complains that "honeyed words betray" and, about three hundred lines later, he admits that language sounds the death-knell for meaning:

> And we will talk, until thought's melody
> Becomes *too sweet for utterance*, and it die
> In words, to live again in looks, which dart
> With thrilling tone into the voiceless heart,
> Harmonizing silence without a sound.
>
> (560-564, emphasis added)

In short, the act of language murders the very idea(l)s any speaker attempts to express. Only in the move to extra-linguistic communication—only in the escape from language, or the Symbolic Order—can the lovers be resurrected to defeat the trap of signification and, ultimately, to overcome the limits of mortality. While he acknowledges an "other eloquence than words," the paradox of *Epipsychidion* is that Shelley tries to approach that other eloquence on the wings of poesy (567). After he cries "woe is me!" a second time, Shelley is forced to admit the collapse of his vision:

> The winged words on which my soul would pierce
> Into the height of love's rare Universe,
> Are chains of lead around its light of fire.—
> I pant, I sink, I tremble, I expire!

> Weak Verses, go, kneel at your Sovereign's feet,
> And say:—"We are the masters of thy slave . . . ".
>
> (587-593)

With these lines, Shelley leaves us with an ironic commentary on the problem of signification that dooms *Epipsychidion* to its apparent failures. As Ulmer notes, this passage brings the poem full-circle by " . . . [reverting] to its beginning, for the *envoi* develops the self-consciousness about audience that motivated the elaborate machinery of Shelley's prefatory Advertisement" (153); I would add that the *envoi* shifts the register of the poem's concern from the object—Emily—to the act of writing, which the Advertisement addresses directly in its fictional account of the poem's composition.[71] As a poet, Shelley would seem to have language at his command, but ultimately he admits that words are the masters of the writer and, in turn, that they are mastered by the ideal other, whom they are forced to serve. Trapped by the limitations of signification, the "honeyed words" of *Epipsychidion* prove, by their very nature, bound to betray the desire Shelley articulates.[72] Barthes describes the annihilation of love in the traps of signification in a particularly eloquent manner: "To try to write love is to confront the *muck* of language: that region of hysteria where language is both *too much* and *too little*, excessive (by the limitless expansion of the *ego*, by emotive submersion) and impoverished (by the codes on which love diminishes and levels it)."[73] Indeed, the wild swings from excess to impoverishment, from pleasure to pain, contribute to the precariousness under which both the poet and his vision finally collapse.

Reconfiguration

From its very beginning, *Epipsychidion* is overwhelmed by Shelley's attempts to reconcile—to unite—imagination and reality, the internal and the external, the lover and the beloved. Impossible to achieve in the Symbolic Order, such reconciliations lead Shelley out of the physical world and into the Imaginary, for the poem's subject (Shelley) experiences a psychological alteration—a collapse into androgyny—the Symbolic Order deems unacceptable since it manifests the ambiguity and chaos so absolutely inconsonant with its rigid strictures of language and law.

Epipsychidion may, upon a quick reading, seem to offer a positive, tangible vision of idyllic love, but even though the poem is addressed to a real person, the vision of free love and high sexuality Shelley describes remains merely that—a vision. His desire to escape to the "far Eden of the purple East," his attempt to force the external to correspond to the internal by imposing his unique vision upon the actual world around him and then retreating into the solipsistic recesses of his imagination, imprisons Shelley in the realms of fantasy and metaphor, in the wasteland of signification and desire, along with the frustrations endemic to each. At *Epipsychidion*'s conclusion, Shelley acknowledges the poem's failure to deliver him to the place he has described: "Woe is me!" he complains, for he recognizes that even though he has glimpsed an erotic utopia, he must finally fall back into the confines of the Symbolic Order and the disappointments—the traps—of the imperfect world he so abhors (587). But even this moment of agony and defeat may be recuperated into the poem's greater success, for, as Wasserman notes, the poem's linguistic collapse retains the trace of the subject's passivity, which is the primary condition for ascendance to the utopic ideal (427, 439).[74]

Critics who consider Shelley's optimistic vision of a world liberated by love—among them William Hazlitt, Matthew Arnold, T. S. Eliot, and F. R. Leavis—tend to regard the poet as an idealist and escapist who can conceive utopias but who forgets that such fantasies are unrealizable on earth.[75] My argument throughout this chapter—that the act of articulation dooms any ideal to failure—saves Shelley from those charges. The very nature of writing, the inherent failure of signification, limits and weakens any attempt to inscribe an idyllic vision and unveils all utopic scenarios as impossibilities, so that in the end every fantasy will be stripped away, unmasked as disappointment. The "unhealthy" narcissism, the problematic androgyny, and the temporal experience of *jouissance* Shelley describes throughout *Epipsychidion* all get lost in the poet's articulation, so that the poem seems only to offer a pessimistic vision of Shelley's erotic fantasy and, thus, a betrayal of his ideal.

But does the pessimism that pervades the imagined utopia of *Epipsychidion* truly lead to failure? Lucy Newlyn thinks not, for she asserts that "the inability of the imagination to catch up with reason brings with it an awareness of reason's infinite potential; so the subject need not feel humiliated by its apparent 'incapacity'."[76] And if, as Newlyn argues, "[t]he unpleasurable frustration of desire . . . makes possible the triumph of the imagination" (224), then we see how Shelley's vision proceeds from the failure of his language, how the poem unfolds from the very medium through which Shelley attempts to find a mode for self-expression. Newlyn encourages us to see that "writing *recuperates itself* precisely by *allowing itself to be overwhelmed*" (225), finally "to construct a pattern of gain-in-loss . . . by making temporal indeterminacy the register of the subject's power" (227).

What if Shelley were able to locate an embodiment of the *objet a* he so desires? What, then, would become of the philosophy of free love that underwrites all of his erotic poetry? Cixous considers such a problem in her novel, *Angst*: of the inherent "failure" of signification, that elusiveness of "truth" in writing, she admits that, "Every time I have wanted to tell the truth I have lied. It couldn't come out. I chose to use analogies which I vaguely felt would save the truth. . . . If I did succeed it would mean I had failed. I would have brought it down to my level."[77] Were Shelley suddenly able to realize the *objet a*, to locate and to define the ultimate object of desire he merely metaphorizes in "Emily," his philosophy of free love would falter, because its premise would be absolutely compromised. Ironically, it is the apparent "failure" of every individual object of desire to correspond to Shelley's ideal that guarantees the success of his broader model of liberty-through-love.[78] In the end, the shortcomings that appear to problematize Shelley's vision of free love in *Epipsychidion* contribute to a greater success by way of which the poet wages war against the code of modern morals and its elevation of the heteropatriarchal imperative to the erotic ideal. The collapses of Shelley's great love poem thus expose the always already insufficient nature of every human object of desire, so that in the end *Epipsychidion* succeeds in justifying—commanding, even—love's break from the confines imposed upon it by the Symbolic Order and its inflexible "code of modern morals." Shelley's visionary love poem celebrates an/other order in which erotic relationships, unimpeded by social convention, anticipate the physical, psychological, and political landscapes of a liberated world, where rigidity vanishes into permeability as oppression succumbs to ecstatic union.

Notes

1. A number of critics discuss the place of love in the evolution of revolutionary strategies; see, for example, Herbert E. Marcuse, *Eros and Civilization: A Philosophical Inquiry into Freud* (Boston: Beacon Press, 1955), Marilyn Gaull, *English Romanticism: The Human Context* (New York: W. W. Norton, 1988) and Ronald Paulson, *Representations of Revolution (1789-1820)* (New Haven: Yale University Press, 1983), especially 268-269 and 279-280.
2. David Abram, *The Spell of the Sensuous: Perception and Language in a More-Than-Human World* (New York: Pantheon Books, 1996), 80.
3. Ann Bermingham, "System, Order, and Abstraction: The Politics of English Landscape Drawing Around 1795," in *Landscape and Power*, ed. Mitchell, 77.

4. Stephen Daniels, "The Politics of Landscape in European Art," in *The Bulfinch Guide to Art History*, gen. ed. Shearer West (Boston: Bulfinch Press, 1996), 100.
5. W. J. T. Mitchell, Introduction to *Landscape and Power*, ed. Mitchell, 4, 1.
6. William Wordsworth, Preface to *Lyrical Ballads*, in *William Wordsworth*, ed. Stephen Gill. The Oxford Authors (1984; Reprint, New York: Oxford University Press, 1988), 611.
7. Clark notes that Shelley's perspective in *Epipsychidion* is, at times, congruent to the Maniac's: he writes, "The [M]aniac of *Julian and Maddalo* is the victim of a genuine disappointment in love, as is also the case in parts of *Epipsychidion*" (5). Simon Haines considers *Epipsychidion* in the context of *Julian and Maddalo*, primarily to establish *Epipsychidion*'s "direct line of descent" from *Alastor* and *Julian and Maddalo* and to assert its status as "primarily a love poem, then, or at least what love poetry becomes when Shelley writes it," although Haines observes that, just like its predecessors, *Epipsychidion* fails to offer a way out of Shelleyan erotic disappointment; see Haines, *Shelley's Poetry: The Divided Self* (New York: St. Martin's, 1997), 194-195, 203.
8. Greg Kucich notes that Shelley's notion of history reconfigures traditional linear models within a system of cyclicality, for "[s]imply to champion linear progress over decline would be to remain locked within the conflicting and ultimately repressive paradigm of linear structure. Instead, Shelley seeks to refashion the linear conflicts of history's master narratives into a wavelike or cyclical pattern of contrariety that offers a more inspiring vision of cultural and political process"; see Kucich, "Eternity and the Ruins of Time: Shelley and the Construction of Cultural History," in *Shelley: Poet and Legislator of the World*, ed. Bennett and Curran, 25. Ulmer acknowledges the post-historical markers of *Epipsychidion*'s island, the books and music that contain the traces—the history—of civilization, and he argues that "the poem's historical sense refashions Shelley's erotic idealism as a revolutionary agenda aimed at extending human freedom" (146, 147).
9. For accounts of the Shelleys' friendship with Teresa Viviani, see Cameron (275-277), Holmes (624-640), and King-Hele (270-284).
10. Diane Long Hoeveler, *Romantic Androgyny: The Women Within* (University Park: Pennsylvania State University Press, 1990), 147.
11. The term "heteropatriarchal imperative" describes a culture that privileges—demands, empowers, and rewards—the monogamous heterosexual union (the highest expression of which is marriage), the production of the family unit, and all males in general.
12. As before, my use of the phrase "self-involving coils" self-consciously recalls the conditions of complete entrapment in which Beatrice and her family find themselves locked, a condition from which there seems no escape but death.
13. William Godwin, *Enquiry Concerning Political Justice and Its Influence on Morals and Happiness*, ed. F. E. L. Priestley, 2 vols. (1793; reprint, Toronto: University of Toronto Press, 1946), 1:5.
14. Terence Allan Hoagwood, *Skepticism and Ideology: Shelley's Political Prose and Its Philosophical Context from Bacon to Marx* (Iowa City: University of Iowa Press, 1988), 153.

15. Peter Gay, *The Bourgeois Experience: Victoria to Freud,* 3 vols. (New York: Oxford University Press, 1984), 1:8.

16. In his appreciation of Blake, Algernon Charles Swinburne observes that "[h]is republican passion was like Shelley's"; see Swinburne's 1868 study, *William Blake: A Critical Essay,* ed. Hugh J. Luke (Lincoln: University of Nebraska Press, 1970), 17.

17. On the influence of the Joseph Johnson circle on the evolution of Blake's thought and work, see Alexander Gilchrist, "Bookseller Johnson's," in his 1863 critical biography entitled *The Life of William Blake,* ed. Ruthven Todd (London: Everyman's Library, 1982), 78-84. While traditional accounts of Blake's life point to the heavy influence of the Johnson circle, a dissenting voice may be found in Peter Ackroyd's *Blake: A Biography* (New York: Alfred A. Knopf, 1996), in which the author argues that "[Blake's] presumed friendship with these Unitarian dissenters and radicals is a matter of pure speculation" for it might indeed have been "a much more informal and passing arrangement, established upon the duties and coincidences of the day" (88); according to Ackroyd, while "[i]t has often been suggested that Blake was an intimate member of this radical circle, . . . the evidence suggests that Blake only ever attended one of [the group's] dinners" (88).

18. Eugene Victor Wolfenstein, *Psychoanalytic-Marxism: Groundwork* (New York: The Guilford Press, 1993), 1.

19. Ernesto Laclau, introduction to *The Sublime Object of Ideology,* by Slavoj Zizek, trans. Jon Barnes (New York: Verso, 1989), xi.

20. Zizek also gestures toward a revisionary Hegelian model in his observations about political structures and their effects on the individual in order to posit "a kind of 'return to Hegel'—[a reactualization of] Hegelian dialectics by giving it a new reading on the basis of Lacanian psychoanalysis. The current image of Hegel as an 'idealist-monist' is totally misleading: what we find in Hegel is the strongest affirmation yet of difference and contingency— 'absolute knowledge' itself is nothing but a name for the acknowledgment of a certain radical loss" (7). Like Marxism, Hegelian dialecticism might offer another avenue into the concerns of *Epipsychidion* and the failure of the subject (Shelley) to reconcile with the ideal even in a dialectical effort, but such an analysis exceeds my interests in this book. Of course, one could return to Hegel's notion of the "Master-Slave" relationship (see his *Phenomenology of the Spirit* [1807]) for a fruitful discussion of Shelley's relationship to his ideal and to Emily throughout *Epipsychidion,* but such a return is beyond the scope of the present study.

21. Here, Cameron paraphrases an argument made by Robert N. Essick in "'A shadow of some golden dream': Shelley's Language in *Epipsychidion,*" *Papers on Language and Literature* 22 (1986): 165-175.

22. Wasserman argues that for Shelley, fantasy and political reality are always related (431), "that the poet's inner cosmos of loving thoughts may emerge and organize the outward disorder" (433); on a more local level, he notes that "Emily's physical confinement to the convent is . . . a model of all the limitations the poem seeks to overcome" (445). Scrivener notes that *Epipsychidion* situates free love as an agent of liberation, not a consequence that follows from the breakdown of

oppressive structures (268), and Ulmer argues that the island in *Epipsychidion* is transparently political: "The island idyll concluding Shelley's poem resituates its figural politics in polemical contexts that clarify their republican import. Since this politics develops from the earlier visionary passages, Shelley's main political images—the ruined tower and the 'age of gold' (428)—are subject to the familiar rhetorical transformations" (142-143). Jerome McGann acknowledges that Shelley has suffered much at the hands of "critics who deplore, or pity, his social commitments and hopes. Shelley is a cureless idealist—a meliorist, a futurist, an escapist with a vaprous style to match his airy thoughts and dreams"; and like Byron's sensationalism and Keats' aesthetic poetry, Shelley's idealism functions as a "displaced yet fundamental [vehicle] of cultural analysis and critique: a poetry of extremity and escapism which is the reflex of the circumstances" in which he lived and worked; see McGann, *The Romantic Ideology: A Critical Investigation* (Chicago: University of Chicago Press, 1983), 116-117. Finally, McGann points to Shelley's (apparent) flight from politics and into the realm of the erotic as a pointedly socially engaged strategy, for "[e]roticism, Shelley argues, is the imagination's last line of human resistance against what he elsewhere called 'Anarchy': political despotism and moral righteousness on the one hand, and on the other selfishness, calculation, and social indifference" (118).

23. Shelley, *Epipsychidion: Verses Addresses to the Noble and Unfortunate Lady, Emilia V———, Now Imprisoned in the Convent of ———*, in *SPP* 373-388, lines 592-593.

24. Such a failure recalls the collapse of the French Revolution, when the newly empowered dominated their oppressors through exactly the same tactics by which they themselves had been oppressed, a phenomenon mirrored in the Lacanian repetitions that structure *The Cenci* and the contest for power Beatrice wages against her father.

25. Jacques Lacan, "The Mirror Stage as Formative of the Function of the I," in *Écrits: A Selection*, trans. Alan Sheridan (New York: W. W. Norton, 1977), 5.

26. Lacan, "The Subject and the Other: Alienation," in *The Four Fundamental Concepts of Psycho-Analysis*, ed. Jacques-Alain Miller and trans. Alan Sheridan (New York: W. W. Norton, 1981), 203.

27. Both Freudian and Lacanian psychoanalysis exhibit a notorious masculinism. Because I have chosen to implement these models, I follow their biases without comment; however, I believe that my discussion of the various problems that plague *Epipsychidion* (among them Shelley's narcissism and his construction of woman-as-object) demonstrate not only the problems inherent to these models but, more importantly, possible solutions to them. In short, my reading of *Epipsychidion* gestures toward a corrective to masculinism, and my readings of *Laon and Cythna* and *Prometheus Unbound* investigate that corrective as one of the bases for Shelley's liberated worlds.

28. Shelley, "A Discourse on the Manners of the Ancient Greeks Relative to the Subject of Love," in *Shelley's Prose or The Trumpet of a Prophecy*, ed. David Lee Clark (New York: New Amsterdam Books, 1988), 220.

29. Freud, "On Narcissism: An Introduction," in *The Complete Psychological Works of Sigmund Freud,* 14:90.
30. See Freud, "Female Sexuality," in *The Complete Psychological Works of Sigmund Freud* 21:225-243. See also Irigaray's argument that "*It is for that which she is not*—that is, the phallus—*that she [woman] asks to be desired and simultaneously to be loved*" in "Psychoanalytic Theory: Another Look," in *This Sex Which Is Not One,* 62.
31. Lacan, "The Meaning of the Phallus," in *Feminine Sexuality: Jacques Lacan and the école freudienne,* 80-81. Grosz sorts out Lacan's understanding of "demand" and "desire" quite succinctly in her book *Jacques Lacan: A Feminist Introduction* (New York, Routledge, 1990), 59-67. In short, Lacan follows Hegel's formulation of desire in *The Phenomenology of the Spirit* "where Hegel posits desire as a lack and absence. Desire is a fundamental lack, a hole in being that can be satisfied only by one 'thing'—another('s) desire. . . . . Lacan assumes a concept of desire as the *difference* or gap . . . [that] re-establishes the specificity and concreteness of *need*; while it participates in demand's orientation to the other" (64). According to Lacan, desire remains unarticulated and is thereby repressed by the subject, yet its very insatiability leads to a psychic conundrum, a split between fantasy and reality in which the subject is psychically pulled apart, or undone: " . . . as far as Lacan is concerned, the relation between desire and language constitute[s] the twin axes of psychoanalytic interpretation. Together they serve to locate the subject as *split* and divided, a being who fades in the unfolding of discourse" (67).
32. Shelley, "On Life," in *SPP,* 475, 477.
33. Ulmer notes that all of the lovers Shelley memorializes in *Epipsychidion* embody the same ideal. Ulmer's reading of the poet's erotic catalogue thus proves consistent with my understanding of the poem in terms of a Lacanian *objet a* model: " . . . the women encountered along the way—the lady of 'electric poison,' the fair, wise, and true, the Moon, Planet, and Tempest—are Emilys in disguise . . . " (150).
34. Zizek's formulation of the *objet a* as "the object-cause of desire" (163) situates the *objet a* just beyond the subject's grasp, just beyond the circumference of desire. Such a model anticipates the place in which I will finally locate Shelleyan utopia in Chapter V: circling around history and time, existing both before and after the general "fall" of humankind into the Symbolic Order, the exile of Shelleyan utopia is, like the *objet a* itself, circular, enveloping, and it marks the limit—the end—of the Symbolic Order, the triumph of love over domination and peace over tyranny.
35. Lacan, "The Split Between the Eye and the Gaze," in *The Four Fundamental Concepts of Psycho-Analysis,* 76-77.
36. Critics who read *Epipsychidion* as autobiography include Cameron, Holmes, Newman Ivey White, and Nora Crook and Derek Guiton. Crook and Guiton indirectly relate *Epipsychidion* to Shelley's early sexual experiences, stating that in the poem, "life is presented as a prostitute who transmits venereal disease"; see Crook and Guiton, *Shelley's Venomed Melody* (Cambridge: Cambridge University Press, 1986), 152. Cameron's discussion extends beyond biographical concerns and reads the "benignant power" celebrated in the poem

which "stimulates the mind" as a force associated with "elements of love, imagination, mind, good, and happiness" (279). Newman Ivey White describes this power rather vaguely, referring to it simply as intellectual beauty (*Shelley* 2:261). But Cameron does recognize the vision of perfect love *Epipsychidion* offers as pessimistic since it requires a transformed world, a "far Eden of the purple East," for its success; such a requisite transformation implies that this perfect love cannot be realized on earth (279-280; *Epipsychidion* 417). Indirectly, Cameron's observation suggests that *Epipsychidion* articulates a vision of love that must be located outside of the Symbolic Order, an assessment with which my argument will concur.

37. For thorough discussions of slippage and the problems of signification, see Jacques Derrida, *Of Grammatology*, trans. Gayatri Chakravorty Spivak (Baltimore: The John Hopkins University Press, 1976), 1-157, *passim*.

38. Zizek argues that the positive function of the (always insufficient, never the *objet a*) other is that the figure mediates the lack of the subject (his inability to locate the *objet a* in embodied form) in terms of the lack of the Symbolic Order, so that language, and not the subject himself, emerges as the real problem, the real site of failure (122).

39. I use the French to point out the trick of language through which the object of affection (the *objet d'amour*) may be unmasked as such a close—but ultimately false—representation of the ideal other, the *objet a*, which the object of affection only failingly represents.

40. Cameron discusses the real-life corespondents for Shelley's symbols at some length. See his essay, "The Planet-Tempest Passage in *Epipsychidion*," in *SPP*, 640.

41. The language of Shelley's poem suggests this sudden rupture of linearity: penetrative terms such as "burst" (405), "Pierce" (441 and 588), and "Piercing" (400) describe the "invisible violence" (399) of the lovers' ascent to the erotic utopia of the island.

42. Although clearly informed by a model predicting the homosocial triangulation Eve Kosofsky Sedgwick describes in *Between Men: English Literature and Male Homosocial Desire* (New York: Columbia University Press, 1985), the triangle in *Epipsychidion* operates in the interest of democracy, whereas in Sedgwick's model the triangle governs the mediations of power between two men, with a third element—the female—(dis)placed as a mere shield for the linear homoeroticism each man's heterosexual attachment attempts to deflect and thus to deny.

43. See Cameron, "The Planet-Tempest Passage in *Epipsychidion*," 640.

44. For a feminist deconstruction of the place of woman in Freudian psychoanalytic theory, see Irigaray, "The Power of Discourse and the Subordination of the Feminine," in *This Sex Which Is Not One*, 69.

45. Interestingly, Shelley's displacement of Teresa-as-Emily to the Imaginary island duplicates the patriarchal privilege her father has already claimed over her, for just as Teresa's father situates her in a place that guarantees the uninterruption of his fantasy (of marriage) about her, so, too, does Shelley's idealization and displacement of Teresa project her into the space of his desire, into the fantasy of his own creation.

46. Lacan, "God and the *Jouissance* of The Woman," in *Feminine Sexuality*, 137.
47. For more on mimicry and masquerade, see Julia Kristeva, "Revolution in Poetic Language," in *The Kristeva Reader*, trans. Margaret Waller and ed. Toril Moi (New York: Columbia University Press, 1986), 89-136.
48. My model of the idealized other as a figure who gets recuperated within phallocentric discourse as the mere creation of a speaking (male) subject could easily be applied to Mary Shelley's novel *Frankenstein*, which I discuss in these terms in Chapter VI.
49. King-Hele introduces another of Shelley's borrowings from Teresa: in a letter that anticipates the poet's idealization of the "divine presence" of *Epipsychidion*'s Emily, Teresa writes of Shelley that "'he has a human exterior, but the interior is all divine'" (qtd. in King-Hele 271).
50. King-Hele observes that "[b]ecause of *Epipsychidion* Shelley is notorious for idealizing the women he admired" (280); dismissing the "amatory politics of *Epipsychidion*" as neither "revolutionary" nor "feminist," Ulmer states quite pointedly that " . . . there is really no woman in Shelley's poem, where Emily mirrors the poet's narcissism and serves as the object of a rhapsodic lyricism leaving her the mere reflex of his rhetorical virtuosity" (147).
51. Certainly, my coding of the feminine as a reduction of the masculine is meant to ventriloquize, rather than to endorse, the heteropatriarchal assumptions against which feminist theory operates. For a good discussion of the "nothingness" of femininity—by which I mean the reduction of the feminine to the category of lack under the phallocentrism of Freudian theory—see Irigaray, "This Sex Which Is Not One" and "Psychoanalytic Theory: Another Look," in *This Sex Which Is Not One*, 23-33 and 34-67. In "This Sex Which Is Not One," Irigaray considers the plurality of the female sexual organs to argue that because they are "not *one* organ, [they are] counted as *none*. [They are the] negative, the underside, the reverse of the only visible and morphologically designatable organ . . . : the penis" (26); in "Psychoanalytic Theory: Another Look," she observes that the young girl " . . . *recognizes, or ought to recognize,* that compared to the boy she has no sex, or at least that *what she thought was a valuable sex organ is only a truncated penis*" (39). See also Irigaray's attack on Freud's reduction of woman to the status of no-thing in *Speculum of the Other Woman* (25-34, 46-55, 81-98, and 112-129). Jane Gallop also provides a useful discussion of how Lacanian psychoanalytic theory inherits the notion of the nothingness of woman from Freud and thereby elevates man to the status of "whole" while reducing woman to the identity of "hole" or nothing; see Gallop, *The Daughter's Seduction: Feminism and Psychoanalysis* (New York: Cornell University Press, 1982), 22.
52. P. M. S. Dawson, *The Unacknowledged Legislator: Shelley and Politics* (New York: Clarendon Press, 1980), 102.
53. Shelley, *Alastor; or, The Spirit of Solitude,* in *SPP*, 69-87, lines 502 and 505.
54. For more on Shelley's take on the "one mind" and the inherent failure of signification, see "On Life," in *SPP*, 474-478.
55. Zizek describes the effects of the disjunction between the Imaginary and the Symbolic Order as follows: "The main thing here is the opposition between

the imaginary level of the experience of meaning and the meaningless signifier/signifying mechanism producing it. The imaginary level is governed by the pleasure principle, it is striving for a homeostatic balance, and the symbolic order in its blind automatism is always troubling its homeostasis . . . . When the human being is caught in the signifier's network, this network has a mortifying effect on him; he becomes part of a strange automatic order disturbing his homeostatic balance (through compulsive repetition, for example)" (132). Shelley's fruitless pursuit of the *objet a*—his engagement of a variety of "failed" lovers—offers one example of the repetition Zizek describes, one manifestation of the effects of the Imaginary/Symbolic split amidst which Shelley lies trapped.

56. I code emasculation according to the traditional psychoanalytic equation of castration with death. The two might also be aligned in terms of the Renaissance notion of orgasm as "the little death," since it is after what I consider to be Shelley's ejaculation—that single, signal moment in the poem when he calls out the name of his beloved—that Shelley is able to access his vision of "that far Eden of the purple East" (417). In any case, Shelley's vision follows his "death," whether we read that death as emasculation (pain/ castration/ mortality) or ejaculation (pleasure/ orgasm/ transcendence). Felled by death—or falling into voluptuousness—Shelley assumes the position of ecstatic recline as his vision looms over him, so that the passive dreamer is transported out of the Symbolic by the ascendance of the very vision he has created.

57. See Hoeveler on the causal relationship between an escape from Symbolic Order and death (51).

58. Kristeva discusses the function of woman as an agent for the rupture of the Symbolic in her essay "Revolution in Poetic Language," *passim*.

59. Shelley's second invocation of tower-imagery in *Epipsychidion* participates in the poem's thoroughgoing dedication to the recuperation of defeat, or collapse, into victory. Describing his disappointing erotic history, Shelley recalls that at one point

> I questioned every tongueless wind that flew
> Over my tower of mourning, if it knew
> Whither 'twas was fled, this soul out of my soul.

(236-238)

Shelley's recapitulation of his "tower of mourning" in terms of the tower on an island that is consecrated to erotic and political liberation re-casts the figure of disappointment within the space pleasure, rendering defeat as success and disappointment as joy. Ulmer notes that "[i]n its contemporary contexts, the ruined tower of *Epipsychidion* would inevitably suggest a lost democratic past that revolutionary struggle might reclaim" (145). Shelley's language invokes the classical moment to which the island returns:

> The land would have remained a solitude
> But for some pastoral people native there,
> Who from the Elysian, clear, and golden air
> Draw the last spirit of the age of gold,
> Simple and spirited; innocent and bold.

(425-429)

The idyllic island that Shelley places at the center of *Epipsychidion* recalls the great potential and hope that marked the democratic spirit of the classical age and thereby articulates Shelley's politicized vision of an "other" space that fosters freedom, a direct contrast to a "real" world given over to oppression and constraint.

60. In *Political Landscape: The Art History of Nature* (Cambridge: Harvard University Press, 1995), Martin Warnke notes that from the beginning of the eighteenth century, "town fortifications were being dismantled and the ramparts grassed over," a phenomenon he points to as "another development in the political landscape that perhaps did more to promote a sense of freedom than the slow greening of individual free spaces" that accompanied the growing popularity of landscape gardens (82). Warnke observes that the processes of defortification, manifested in nature's overgrowing of the ramparts, "might indeed seem like the return of the Golden Age" (83).

61. Just as *Epipsychidion* begins in the space of death—in the poem itself, Shelley writes that "In my heart's temple I suspend to thee / These votive wreaths of withered memory" (3-4), and in a canceled Advertisement, he reports the drowning of the supposed author of *Epipsychidion*—the poem recuperates such an apparent end (of life, of narrative) within a beginning in at least two ways: first, Shelley points to Venus as " . . . the star of Death / And birth . . . ", his language indicating the synchronicity of life's beginning and end; second, his opening gesture in lines 3-4 invokes not only a funereal ritual, but also the celebration of the marriage-vow (Reiman and Powers note that "votive" describes an act or object that is "[c]onsecrated or dedicated, in fulfillment of a vow" [SPP 374 n 5].) Shelley's recuperation of death and death-ritual into birth and marriage underscores the cyclical model of history he develops throughout *Epipsychidion* as an alternative to rigidly linear epistemologies of space, time, and experience.

62. I draw my metaphors of "gift" and "present" from French feminist revisions of Freudian psychoanalysis, and in particular from Cixous' meditation on a feminine alternative to the Symbolic Order. Cixous poses the Realm of the Gift, the chief marker of which is generosity, as a feminine counter (or antidote) to the masculine, phallocentric Realm of the Proper (the Symbolic Order), where the rigidity of language and law enforce discord and division. See Cixous, "Castration or Decapitation?" 41-45.

63. Wasserman's description of the island reinforces my conception of the pre-Œdipal conditions of that space: "[l]ike the Saturnian condition of belief that Shelley described in *The Witch of Atlas,* [the island] represents a state before the distinction between truth and error became relevant. Even the island's odors, colors, and sounds seem like 'echoes of an antenatal dream' (456), a pre-worldly state in which imagined existence is real" (444). Kristeva's discussion of the function of poetic language describes the way in which such discourse interrupts the domination of the Symbolic Order by puncturing that realm with an other vision: "Language as symbolic function constitutes itself at the cost of repressing instinctual drive and continuous relation to the mother. On the contrary, the unsettled and questionable subject of poetic language . . . maintains itself at the cost of reactivating this repressed instinctual, maternal element. If it is true that the prohibition of

incest constitutes, at the same time, language as communicative code and women as exchange objects in order for a society to be established, *poetic language would be* for its questionable subject-in-process the *equivalent of incest* . . . . [T]his relationship . . . is probably one of the most important factors producing interplay within the structure of meaning as well as a questioning process of subject and history;" see Kristeva, "Desire in Language," in *The Portable Kristeva,* by Julia Kristeva, ed. and trans. Kelly Oliver (New York: Columbia University Press, 1997), 104-105.

64. Nancy Moore Goslee notes that Shelley's original (and rejected) Advertisement to *Epipsychidion* aligns death and the passage to the ideal in its description of the supposed author's drowning in the Sporades. See her essay, "Dispersoning Emily: Drafting as Plot in *Epipsychidion,*" in *The Keats-Shelley Journal* 42 (1993): 104-119.

65. Near the end of *The Cenci,* Beatrice cries,

> . . . Come, obscure Death,
> And wind me in thine all-embracing arms!,
> Like a fond mother hide me in thy bosom,
> And rock me to the sleep from which none wake.

(5.4.115-118)

66. As I have remarked in previous chapters, Shelley's notion of an afterlife replaces the Christian concept of Heaven with his model of love and erotic union.

67. A. C. Goodson, "Romantic Theory and the Critique of Language," in *Questioning Romanticism,* ed. Beer, 17.

68. Kaja Silverman, *World Spectators,* Cultural Memory in the Present, ed. Mieke Bal and Hent de Vries (Stanford: Stanford University Press, 2000), 145.

69. Goslee argues that "the primary meaning of the final 'woe is me' collapse seems to be the inadequacy of words to represent an *achieved* and meaningful sexual union" (118, emphasis added). I depart from Goslee in that my reading of *Epipsychidion* assumes that such a union between Shelley and Emily/Teresa never occurred, that Shelley's "woe is me" gives vent to a cry of frustration motivated by the failure of language to activate the ideal he has envisioned.

70. Agnes Péter provides three motivations or causes for the poem's apparent collapses: first, she points to "Shelley's awareness of the conflict between the creative and the sympathetic aspects of the imagination"; second, she argues that "the lines can be read as Shelley's realization of the inadequacy of language, the error of identifying *logos* with *ratio* in the Western (as opposed to the Oriental) tradition"; third, she cites "Shelley's fear that not only the traditional language is sadly limited by actuality, but that the Platonic dream that behind the actuality there is a realm of permanence is an illusory fixation of the human mind, that behind Plotinus's screen, behind the 'painted veil' of actuality, behind the 'dome of many-colored glass,' or the subtle veil woven by the Witch of Atlas, the wizard lady of the creative imagination, there is only a vacuum, the void"; see Péter, "A Hermeneutical Reading of *Epipsychidion,*" *The Keats-Shelley Journal* 42 (1993): 124-125.

71. Ulmer notes that these final lines signal another type of collapse as the poem "... falls in two in ending, with the speaker's address to Emily finishing at line 590, but with his language continuing until line 604. The two conclusions are linked by their concern with language, of course, and are by no means contradictory. They remain skewed, however, like the edges of a Cezanne table, and confess Shelley's inability to resolve the energies of his poem at a single point of coincidence" (151). I would argue that Ulmer's assessment contributes to the poem's larger success, for just as *Epipsychidion* remains resolutely dedicated to the project of decentering all structures of order, so, too, does the "[fall] in two in ending" play out Shelley's attempts to celebrate the polyvalence of language, power, and desire.

72. Robinson provides evidence for Shelley's belief in man's potential to realize the agenda he explores in *Epipsychidion*: Robinson notes that in a canceled Preface for the poem, Shelley "... concluded that a second Eden for man was only an illusion ... [and] expressed his hope that imaginative knowledge and fulfillment in life were compatible and that man could transcend the physical limitations occasioned by the loss of the first Eden" (9).

73. Roland Barthes, *A Lover's Discourse: Fragments*, trans. Richard Howard (New York: Hill and Wang, 1978), 99.

74. Shelley hints at his intention to recuperate failure, or collapse, into success in the short poem that closes his Advertisement to *Epipsychidion*. Acknowledging that skeptics will reject his description of an erotic utopia, Shelley addresses the poem itself (as he will do again in the *envoi*, thereby creating a self-conscious, writerly frame for the erotic narrative), by saying "My last delight! tell them [skeptical readers] that they are dull, / And bid them own that thou art beautiful" (*SPP* 374).

75. For a thorough review and discussion of nineteenth- and twentieth-century critics who dismiss Shelley as an escapist or an idealist, see Simon Haines, *Shelley's Poetry: The Divided Self* (New York: St. Martin's Press, 1997), 1-31.

76. Lucy Newlyn, "'Questionable Shape': The Aesthetics of Indeterminacy," in *Questioning Romanticism*, ed. Beer, 223.

77. Cixous, *Angst*, trans. Jo Levy (New York: Riverrun Press, 1985), 115-116.

78. Goslee's discussion of the ironic success of *Epipsychidion*'s local failures reinforces the argument I have made: she suggests that "[w]e might well say that [Shelley's] is a Keatsian failure, in which the admission of temporality and mortality frees us from the 'cold pastoral' of a transformative, idealizing rhetoric into a 'burning forehead, and a parching tongue.' Thus words fail in order to succeed, and the allegorization of Teresa as Emily sets up the possibilities of this failure and this success—through the artifice of conventions, of courtly love and the colors of rhetoric that veil the body; through the linguistic artifices of metaphor and of personification that make this veil so nearly opaque that we must see it as well as her; and through the setting of this final encounter in a prophesied future" (118).

CHAPTER V

Mapping the Ideal:
Pleasure and Displacement in *Laon and Cythna* and *Prometheus Unbound*

> ... [T]hose who now live have survived an age of despair. ....
> But mankind appear to me to be emerging from their trance. I
> am aware, methinks, of a slow, gradual, silent change.
> —Percy Bysshe Shelley, Preface to *Laon and Cythna;
> Or, The Revolution of the Golden City*

> The *exilic* intellectual does not respond to the logic of the conventional but to the audacity of daring, and to representing change, to moving on, not standing still.
> —Edward W. Said, *Representations of the Intellectual:
> The 1993 Reith Lectures*

A full four years before he penned *Epipsychidion*, Shelley raged against the code of modern morals in his longest and, perhaps, most controversial poem, *Laon and Cythna; Or, The Revolution of the Golden City, A Vision of the Nineteenth Century in the Stanza of Spenser*. Shelley's publisher, Charles Ollier, withdrew the poem on 11 December 1817, his concerns over *Laon and Cythna*'s content beginning with complaints from the volume's printer and escalating following one customer's exit from his shop "in disgust" over Shelley's latest production (Holmes 390). Ollier's response to his customer's reaction reminds us of the power of the erotic narrative to provoke a reader's response and thus to affect change in the real world, for his customer's reaction to the intimate, or private, relationship between the poem's heroes motivated Ollier's very public act: Ollier suppressed the poem because he perceived that its heroes' erotic excesses posed a threat to his own financial well-being; thus, his act of suppression demonstrates the potential for an erotic narrative to affect the balance of power—in this case, Ollier's reputation and his potential for profit—in the real world. Despite Ollier's efforts, several copies of Shelley's poem remained in circulation among members of his literary circle as well as at the notoriously conservative *Quarterly Review* (389). A twelve-canto attack on monarchy and religion—two forces Shelley constructs throughout the poem as a double-headed embodiment of tyranny—*Laon and Cythna* poses the erotic couple as both emblem and agent for a new revolution. And the title characters are no ordinary couple: in its originally published form, the poem's eponymous lovers/heroes are twins. Shelley thus deploys the incestuous pair as the agents of liberty to demonstrate the potential for subversive eroticism to unsettle the very structures of power and order that would excoriate such a transgressive erotic engagement.

Laon and Cythna describes the parallel adventures of the eponymous twin brother and sister. Nurtured by their mother, the siblings fall in love but separate to pursue the project of liberty. While apart, they experience simultaneous episodes of confinement and torture that underscore their status as a divided self, or halves of a whole being, and eventually they reunite and consummate their relationship in a two-day lovemaking session. Re-invigorated by their erotic union, Laon and Cythna help to overthrow the dictatorship of King Othman of Turkey, who raped Cythna when she was in his custody, siring the child who bears Cythna's physical likeness.[1] Along with the rebels, Laon and Cythna envision a republic, but as Shelley demonstrates in *Swellfoot the Tyrant,* those who unseat power are subject to the temptations of power itself, and before long, the new society Laon and Cythna hope to establish is crushed by the re-emergence of tyranny. Laon is sentenced to execution by burning, and just before his death, Cythna jumps into the pyre as her daughter falls dead, at which point all three figures are magically transported to an island "suspended between two heavens," wrapped in golden mists and bounded on four sides by waterfalls.[2]

Reiman and Powers point to the political significance of Laon and Cythna's relationship in their note to Shelley's Dedication: "Uniting Shelley's philosophical, social, and personal concerns, [*Laon and Cythna*] tells the story of two lovers . . . who inspire and lead a bloodless revolution against the sultan of Turkey—an idealized portrayal of the French Revolution" (*SPP* 96 n 1).[3] Kelly, too, recognizes the real-world political investments of *Laon and Cythna*, which, along with *Frankenstein*, he characterizes as "particular expressions of a major theme of the revolutionary aftermath—the creation of social and national unity infused with the new domesticity and founded on the Romantic feminist version of woman" (78). David Duff considers the relationship between the poem's private and public worlds at some length, arguing that the events in Shelley's poem mirror his contemporary readers' experience of "political faith [having] been first raised and then shattered by the events of the French Revolution" (166). Duff suggests that in *Laon and Cythna* "a 'story of human passion' is . . . superimposed upon the revolutionary narrative" (166) so that "the disillusioned enthusiast of 1817 is supposed to be able to overcome the trauma of the French Revolution by confronting the catastrophe of the Revolution of the Golden City while identifying primarily with the fortunes and feelings of Laon and Cythna" (167). Duff concludes that Laon and Cythna's relationship assumes political importance not only because it is "born of a shared commitment to revolutionary ideals," but, equally if not more importantly, because its subversive nature enables Shelley to launch "an implicit attack on the ideological foundations of the English establishment" (189). Brown, too, recognizes the power of the lovers' incestuous union, noting that Shelley "makes clear the utilitarian foundations of his thinking: incest is a violation of the laws of society and thus 'incorrect,' not a violation of the laws of human nature and hence unnatural" (213). Polhemus reminds us that representations of incest may hold positive social value—they "may hint at a superhuman freedom and intimacy beyond the lot of men and women" (15); such a transcendent, other-worldly meaning of incest informs Shelley's use of that taboo throughout *Laon and Cythna*.

Like Brown, I recognize Shelley's shifting treatment of incest and his understanding of the context-dependent nature of its meaning: while such an act prefigures political liberation in *Laon and Cythna*, in *The Cenci* the same kind of act synecdochizes the structures of patriarchal power. Of course, the relationship between Laon and Cythna is fundamentally different from the relationship between Count Cenci and Beatrice, for the twins' intimacy is based on equality and reciprocity, on mutual pleasure and love, whereas Count Cenci's attack on Beatrice manifests a relationship already stamped with the inequities of patriarchal rule that privilege the father—*any* father—in the matrices of gender, economic status, age, and political affiliation. In *Laon and Cythna,* incest liberates because it originates in the equality characterizing the relationship of lovers devoted to the liberation of the world about them; in *The Cenci,* incest oppresses because it emerges from selfishness and reinforces systems of radical (because omnipotent) inequality. Laon and Cythna's union is, as Brown notes, " . . . the perfect mating of man and womankind, wholly equal, wholly loving, and wholly deserving of one another's love. The epitome of Shelleyan intercourse, all sympathies harmoniously blended, their love stands as the perfected type of all sexual relationship[s]" (185). In short, *Laon and Cythna* articulates Shelley's erotic and political ideal.

Initially, Shelley exploded when learning of Ollier's decision to suppress *Laon and Cythna*. In a lengthy letter dated 11 December 1817, Shelley accuses his publisher of hypocrisy and demands he reverse his decision: "You foresaw, you foreknew, all that these people would say. . . . If I had never consulted your advantage, my book would have had a fair hearing. But now, it is first published, and then the publisher, as if the author had deceived him as to the contents of the work, and as if the inevitable consequence of its publication would be ignominy and punishment, and as if none should dare touch it or look at it, retracts, at a period when nothing but the most extraordinary and unforeseen circumstances can justify his reaction. I beseech you to reconsider the matter, for your sake no less than for my own. Assume the high and secure ground of courage" (*Letters* 1:579). Shelley casts his battle with Ollier in terms of a larger political war, and in so doing he reproduces the poem's elevation of an individual relationship to the status of political model: "I don't believe that if the book was quietly and regularly published the Government would touch anything of a character so refined and so remote from the conceptions of the vulgar. They would hesitate before they invaded a member of the higher circles of the republic of letters. But if they see us tremble, they will make no distinctions; they will feel their strength. You might bring the arm of the law down on us both by flinching now. Directly these scoundrels see that people are afraid of them, they seize upon them and hold them up to mankind as criminals already convicted by their own fears. You lay yourself prostrate and they trample on you" (1:579). Shelley's rather transparent rhetorical strategies throughout the letter are easily charted: he begins by appealing to Ollier as a "refined" man and honorable merchant, and then he casts Ollier as a hero-in-waiting, a figurehead for the trembling masses who nevertheless understand that acknowledging their oppressors will invite further exploitation rather than alliance. Like Laon and Cythna, Shelley and Ollier stand poised to lead the way toward liberation by upsetting the forces that conspire to contain them; in so doing, Shelley elevates a real-life personal relationship to a model for political action, and thus he underscores the immediacy of the personal relationship to the evolution of the social sphere.[4]

However, Shelley's passionate attack on Ollier proved short-lived, for two days later he wrote far more charitably that "[t]he contents of your letter this morning certainly alters the question. No one is to be blamed, however heavy and unexpected is my disappointment [over the suppression of *Laon and Cythna*]" (1:581). On 16 December, Shelley described his intended alterations to the poem to Thomas Moore, and he explained rather dispassionately that "[t]he present edition of 'Laon & Cythna' is to be suppressed, & it will be republished in about a fortnight under the title of 'The Revolt of Islam,' with some alterations which consist in little else than the substitution of the words *friend* or *lover* for that of *brother & sister*" (1:582). Shelley justifies his acquiescence to contemporary moral prudery by privileging *Laon and Cythna*'s broad vision of liberation over the specific nature of the lovers' relationship; in the same letter, Shelley writes that "[a]s soon as I discovered that this effect [revolts & shocks] was produced by the circumstance alluded to, I hastened to cancel it—not from any personal feeling of terror, or repentance, but from the sincere desire of doing all the good & conferring all the pleasure which might flow from so obscure a person as myself" (1:582). In the end, Shelley calculates the loss of erotic specificity against the gain of his "Vision of the Nineteenth Century" and gambles on the effectiveness of the sanitized *Revolt of Islam*; thus modified, the poem re-appeared on 10 January 1818.[5]

Shelley's re-naming of *Laon and Cythna* as *The Revolt of Islam* underscores what I find one of the most significant losses incumbent upon its revision: the transfer of emphasis from a private relationship to a public spectacle, from an explicitly erotic engagement to a more generally political one, for while the original title foregrounds the erotic pair as the central fixture of the poem, Shelley's new title, *The Revolt of Islam*, de-emphasizes the significance of the couple, vanishing them into a larger political effort, reducing them to the status of mere components of an effort for which they once stood as emblems. In short, Shelley's new title diffuses the centrality of the siblings' union, so that the titular status he originally conferred on the incestuous lovers—their "starring role," so to speak—is transferred to a political event: Shelley's revisionary evacuation of the poem's original "sin" of incest reduces the couple to players in the larger production of the Revolution of the Golden City. In the original work, the pair's subversive eroticism elevated the twins to emblematic status, first by differentiating them from their culture at large (and thereby situating them in the figural space of the outlaw, or other) and then by recuperating them as renegade leaders whose shared psychic wholeness embraces the political landscape, (s)mothering it with a love whose seamlessness and self-sacrifice anticipate the model of the feminine community Beatrice envisions at the conclusion of *The Cenci*.

Although *Laon and Cythna* antedates *The Cenci*, it is useful for us to keep Shelley's tragedy in mind as we assess the revolutionary model his "Vision of the Nineteenth Century" describes, particularly since both works situate the domestic sphere as the microcosm of social order, the place that both generates and duplicates political realities.[6] In *The Cenci*, we saw the home as one of so many manifestations of patriarchal tyranny, one of its many vanishing points. In *Laon and Cythna*—which in an 1819 letter to Hunt Shelley describes as a vision " . . . of the beautiful and the just" (*Letters* 2:96)—the poet constructs the domestic sphere more optimistically as the cradle of liberty in which Laon and Cythna are nurtured, suggesting that the siblings' political ideals derive from their formative experiences. But Shelley's vision of a private-public overlap proceeds from no naive sentimentalism; quite to the contrary, Shelley charts liberty as well as oppression according to the contours of domestic harmony and disharmony, respectively. For example, Shelley dramatically underscores the correlation between domestic and political disharmony in Laon's horrific experience with the old woman by the lake. Having left Cythna after two days of love-making to go in search of food, Laon stops to take a drink from the lake and is confronted by

" . . . one woman,
Whom I found wandering in the streets, and she
Was withered from a likeness of aught human
Into a fiend, by some strange misery;
So soon as she heard my steps she leaped on me,
And glued her burning lips to mine, and laughed
With a loud, long, and frantic laugh of glee,
And cried, 'Now, Mortal, thou hast deeply quaffed

> The Plague's blue kisses—soon millions shall pledge the draught!
> My name is Pestilence—this bosom dry
> Once fed two babies—a sister and a brother.
> When I came home, one in the blood did lie
> Of three death-wounds—the flames had ate the other!
> Since then I have no longer been a mother,
> But I am Pestilence;—hither and thither
> I flit about, that I may slay and smother:—
> All lips which I have kissed must surely wither,
> But Death's—if thou are he, we'll go to work together!'"
>
> (2759-2775)

According to the old woman's narrative, the destruction of the domestic milieu results directly in the destruction of the larger world. In Laon's nightmarish vision, the distraught mother no longer functions as a (re-)productive body but is reduced to a morass of death, a dried-up, anti-productive embodiment of the tyranny of lack and its corporeal etiology of starvation, disease, and death. In a later scene that underscores the antithetical relationship between maternity and tyranny, Cythna, in captivity, has a horrifying vision in which her captor orders that her nursing daughter, who resembles Laon, be ripped from her breast. Robbed of the maternal function, Cythna plunges into despair:

> "It seemed that in the dreary night, the diver
> Who brought me thither, came again, and bore
> My child away. I saw the waters quiver,
> When he so swiftly sunk, as once before:
> Then morning came—it shone even as of yore,
> But I was changed—the very life was gone
> Out of my heart—I wasted more and more,
> Day after day, and sitting there alone,
> Vexed the inconstant waves with my perpetual moan."
>
> (3028-3036)

Cythna's vision ultimately proves a false prophecy, for in the end, her child—a literal embodiment of the forces that oppress her, as I shall demonstrate—functions as Cythna's rescuer, her instrument of flight away from tyranny. While in *The Cenci* Beatrice and Lucretia ascend to an abstract other-life in which Beatrice imagines they will be liberated from the orders that attack them, so, too, will Laon, Cythna, and the child who bears Cythna's likeness ultimately ascend to a utopic other-space that will resurrect the harmonious domestic model in which the twins were reared. In both *Laon and Cythna* and *The Cenci*, Shelley correlates domestic disharmony with social turbulence, and he poses idealized domestic models as alternatives to tyrannical political regimes.

Laon and Cythna contributes significantly to the argument I have been making throughout my study, for not only does it demonstrate Shelley's belief in the power of erotic engagements to alter political realities, but it also underscores the permeability of the categories of "the erotic" and "the political" that we have seen throughout the works I have examined. In the discussion that follows, I consider Shelley's development of three concepts throughout *Laon and Cythna*; together, these demonstrate the ways in which the poem occupies a central role in the broader agenda I have described as Shelley's ongoing project of liberty-through-love.[7] To this end, I shall discuss: how *Laon and Cythna* operates pedagogically; how *Laon and Cythna* situates the erotic couple as both the agent and the emblem of liberation, as well as how the lovers' relationship implies Shelley's commitment to feminism; and how *Laon and Cythna* employs landscape metaphors to describe political realities and erotic experiences, and how the poem's utopic landscape celebrates liminality—ooziness—as a political and erotic model through which those ideals may be activated.[8] Throughout my reading of *Laon and Cythna*, I consider the ways in which Shelley goes about "plotting utopia," a concept central to the title of this book: not only do I consider utopia as a narrative, or "plot," but I also consider the particular locations in which Shelley maps, or "plots," his ideal; thus, I investigate the utopian "plot" not only in terms of narrative but also in terms of space, so that "plotting utopia" participates in my mapping of Shelley's agenda of liberty-through-love.

Pedagogy

Shelley's title announces his poem's participation in contemporary political discourse. Proclaiming the work as his "Vision of the Nineteenth Century," Shelley's lengthy Preface sets out three central ideas: the problem with violent revolution, the need for a more gradual program of reform, and the place of erotic engagements within such metamorphoses.[9] Describing *Laon and Cythna* as his "first serious appeal to the public" (104), Shelley acknowledges the slow dissipation of the condition of a "panic which, like an epidemic transport, seized upon all classes of men during those excesses consequent upon the French Revolution," and he appeals to the emerging "sanity" of "those who . . . have survived an age of despair" (101). Shelley argues that the failure of the French Revolution— "the revulsion occasioned by the atrocities of the demagogues and the re-establishment of successive tyrannies in France" (101)—arose from the alarming rapidity of that political reversal: he asks, "Can he who the day before was a trampled slave suddenly become liberal-minded, forbearing, and independent?" (101); indeed, ". . . a nation of men who had been dupes and slaves for centuries were incapable of conducting themselves with the wisdom and tranquillity of freemen so soon as some of their fetters were partially loosened" (101). Shelley argues that the usurpation of tyrannical power leaves the radical discrepancies between the empowered and the disempowered in place and merely reverses the relative positions of those groups with regard to power, an idea to which he returns, as I have shown, in *The Cenci.* In Shelley's view, a more gradual program of political reform—"universal tolerance and benevolence and . . . philanthropy" coupled with "the bloodless dethronement of . . . oppressors and the unveiling of the religious frauds by which [men] had been duped into submission" (100)—will allow the oppressed to "[emerge] from their trance" (102). "In that belief," Shelley writes, "I have composed the following Poem" (102). Thus, Shelley introduces his vision of the nineteenth century by situating *Laon and Cythna* in an explicitly political context, and as Deborah Elise White has argued, "[t]hroughout, the text thematizes the encounter of text and reader so that, from its inception, what is taught includes the apparatus and the act of teaching and what is allegorized includes the possibility of allegory itself" (133). The bastard offspring of a hasty, bloody revolution, *Laon and Cythna* gestures toward the hope Shelley imagines finally to be re-animating even those most thoroughly "[s]eized" by the "epidemic" of "panic" still emanating from the series of political shocks that toppled France (101).[10]

Shelley calls attention to his strategies of textual seduction in the first paragraph of his Preface when he announces that he has brought together a range of devices designed to attract and to please even the most resistant of readers: "I have sought to enlist the harmony of metrical language, the ethereal combinations of the fancy, the rapid and subtle transitions of human passion, all those elements which essentially compose a poem, in the cause of a liberal and comprehensive morality" (99-100). In this way, *Laon and Cythna* marks Shelley's dedicated effort to "[appeal], in contempt of all artificial opinions or institutions, to the common sympathies of every human breast" (100). Anticipating the model of lover and beloved he would develop in his essay "On Love," Shelley evaluates his accomplishments or failures as a poet in terms of his success in impregnating the minds of his readers with his own ideals, so that, like the beloved, his readers offer up a purified mirror of Shelleyan idealism: " . . . if the lofty passions with which it has been my scope to distinguish this story shall not excite in the reader a generous impulse, an ardent thirst for excellence, an interest profound and strong such as belongs to no meaner desires, let not the failure be imputed to a natural unfitness for human sympathy in these sublime and animating themes," Shelley writes, for "[i]t is the business of the Poet to communicate to others the pleasure and the enthusiasm arising out of those images and feelings in the vivid presence of which within his own mind consists his inspiration and his reward" (100-101). Three paragraphs later, Shelley's discussion of the project of poetry anticipates— like the echoes of some antenatal dream, to borrow an image from *Epipsychidion*—the same language he will use in describing the relationship between lover and beloved in "On Love": "How far I shall be found to possess that more essential attribute of poetry, *the power of awakening in others sensations like those which animate my own bosom,* is that which, to speak sincerely, *I know not*; and which, with an acquiescent and contented spirit, I expect to be taught by the effect which I shall produce upon *those whom I now address*" (103, emphasis added).[11] A careful reading of *Laon and Cythna* demonstrates the connection between the act of reading and the scene of seduction in both its erotic and political manifestations, for in digesting the poem, the reader is not only aroused by Shelley's account of the relationship between the incestuous heroes but, by their example, but he or she is educated in the ways of gradual, nonviolent social reform. Tactically, Shelley sets out to seduce the reader with his descriptions of Laon and Cythna's unconventional relationship so that he may sway that reader in favor of the virtues his heroes embody—tolerance and love; in the liberated world Shelley's poem describes, "There is no quarter given to Revenge, or Envy, or Prejudice. Love is celebrated everywhere as the sole law which should govern the moral world" (106). Seduced, Shelley's reader imports the poem's vision back into the world, for in Shelley's model of textual seduction, the pivotal first step in social change derives from the erotic engagement—the seduction—of reading.

Shelley structures *Laon and Cythna* around the device of the mediated narrative, a pedagogical trope to which he returns most famously in "Ozymandias," a sonnet which, as it turns out, appeared in *The Examiner* the day after the publication of *The Revolt of Islam* (SPP 103 n 5). The mediated narrative, as we see so famously in the series of stories-within-stories recorded by Walton for his sister Margaret throughout Mary Shelley's *Frankenstein*, operates pedagogically by reproducing its original exchange of information—from an experienced or knowledgeable figure to an inexperienced one—as a (re-) mediation between text and reader. In its representation of an objective distance between the framing narrative voice and the events it (re-) tells, and in its multiplication of sources—voices, or perspectives, each of which contributes to the credibility of the tale—the mediated narrative lays claim to the status of authority—and, sometimes, to truth.

Laon and Cythna begins with a first-person account of a solitary wanderer who, after " . . . the last hope of trampled France had failed / Like a brief dream of unremaining glory" (127-128), rises "from visions of despair" (129) to glimpse the turbulence in the skies above him and to witness " . . . a monstrous sight" (191): "An Eagle and a Serpent wreathed in fight" (193). The ring, or wreath, of aggression in which these figures are locked metonymizes the eternal struggle between good end evil. Shelley's reversal of the traditional valences of these symbols—the Eagle is unmasked as the figure of evil and the Serpent as a figure of good—reminds the reader of Shelley's investment throughout *Laon and Cythna* in overturning conventional thinking.

The poem's first-person narrator (to whom I shall refer as Shelley, given the exact correspondence of their perspectives, not to mention the poem's first-person perspective) comes upon a beautiful woman who sits gazing into the waters, crying (262-270). A latter-day Eve, the woman offers Shelley infinite knowledge if he will join her as she and the serpent, now fallen from the sky, sail away in a strange boat (311-315). As the three drift to sea, the woman describes the Earth's creation to Shelley, but she reverses the figures of good and evil to lionize the Morning Star, a traditional symbol for Lucifer, whom we soon discover to be the woman's lover. In turn, Shelley speaks of his beliefs about the forces of evil in the universe, which he names as fear, hatred, faith, and tyranny (334-387). The woman recalls her participation in the French Revolution, but she adds that she abandoned the cause when its revolutionary ideals were quashed by the resurgence of tyranny (484-522). In sum, the conversation between Shelley and the mystical woman sets out the poem's political (dis-) allegiances, for in sailing away from the earth, the couple dismiss all conventional structures of power, all systems of belief.

The magical woman delivers Shelley to a dock in the air set in front of a beautiful temple beneath multiple moons in a night sky.[12] The odd celestial circumstances that serve as a backdrop for the scene remind us of the other-worldliness of this place and, I would argue, of its status as a utopic no-space that anticipates *Epipsychidion*'s island of free-love (576-603). Calling out the name of the spirit of the temple, the woman disappears into a vapor and re-assimilates as a planet from which the spirit of the temple emerges (613-639). The spirit brings forth two beautiful figures, Laon and Cythna, both twins and lovers. Looking into the eyes of his sister/lover, an inspired Laon relates the couple's history in the eleven cantos that follow (640-666). Like the speech Shelley shared with the magical woman during their flight away from the familiar world, Laon's narrative clearly lifts biography to history, personal story to universal narrative, so that the education of the siblings/lovers provides the basic model for Shelley's "Vision of the Nineteenth Century."

I offer such a lengthy description of the first canto of *Laon and Cythna* in an attempt to demonstrate the ways in which Shelley makes clear the importance of narration to the project of social change; that is, Shelley suggests that revolutionary ideals and revolutionary hope may be reinvigorated through the telling and re-telling of the histories of individuals and of social movements. We see in Shelley's mystical transport to the magical temple the potential for narration to entrance, to seduce, and thereby to engage the listener (or reader) in the stories to be revealed.[13]

Cantos IV and V, which describe Laon's recuperation from crucifixion and his seven-year tutelage under the care of an odd figure called "the Hermit," re-introduce the poem's pedagogical theme. Removed from the worries and strife of the world that rejected him—just as in the beginning of the poem Shelley himself wandered in self-exile from a post-Revolutionary world of fallen ideals—Laon is re-invigorated by the Hermit's investment in the seductive power of narration, the potential of language to alter political realities:

> "Perchance blood need not flow, if thou at length
>   Wouldst rise; perchance the very slaves would spare
> Their brethren and themselves; great is the strength
>   Of words—...."
>
> (1567-1570)

The Hermit condemns bloody revolutions for the same reason Shelley does—because they mark the transfer of power from one oppressive regime to another—and he urges Laon to sway the masses through his speech, which has the power to charm, rather than through acts of violence and bloodshed:

> "If blood be shed, 'tis but a change and choice
>   Of bonds,—from slavery to cowardice:
> A wretched fall!—Uplift thy charmèd voice!
>   Pour on those evil men the love that lies
>   Hovering within those spirit-soothing eyes—
> Arise, my friend, farewell!" ....
>
> (1657-1662)

Heeding his savior's advice, Laon returns to the Golden City and calms the troops with his words, again underscoring the power of language to seduce, to sway.[14] Shelley's dramatization of the seductive power of language reminds us of the pedagogical devices according to which all of Shelley's works proceed: repeatedly, Shelley relies on poetic, musical language as a mode of instruction, at turns teaching and teasing—conversing with and seducing—his readers, who are swayed not only by the particular arguments he advances but also by the beauty of Shelley's language, itself a seductive device, an instrument of pleasure *and* coercion.[15]

Eroticism

The project of *Laon and Cythna* succeeds because the title characters' deep dedication to each other is matched by their equally deep commitment to the project of liberty. In *Laon and Cythna,* Shelley offers a corrective to the solitary heroes of earlier poems, such as the Poet of *Alastor* who pursues— and is pursued by—his own narcissistic fantasy; in sharp contrast, the heroes of *Laon and Cythna* balance their commitment to each other with an equally indomitable commitment to the liberation of the world. As we will see again in *Prometheus Unbound,* in *Laon and Cythna* Shelley demonstrates the necessity of self-sacrifice to the project of liberty, so that the poem mediates the nihilistic martyrdoms of solitary wanderers (again, *Alastor*'s Poet) through the device of the erotic relationship.[16] In love with each other and dedicated to the absolute freedom—the pleasure, in fact—of the beloved, Laon and Cythna exemplify a model for the re-building of a fractured world, for as they come together in complete erotic union, they self-consciously project the rewards of that union onto the world about them, which they refuse to abandon even in the midst of ecstasy: Laon and Cythna work to liberate the world from its various systems of oppression, and they draw upon the model of their seamless, joyous union as a paradigm for social change. Unable to realize that vision before their expulsion from the world, Laon and Cythna engage in another form of intercourse, the verbal exchange, to impregnate a new visionary—the poet Shelley, who hears their tale—through the seductive device of language, so that in describing their vision of liberation to a voice of another generation, the lovers' seemingly defeated plan—their aborted model—is resurrected, or re-conceived, and engendered in the seductive narrative Shelley re-produces. From Cythna through Laon through Shelley, the reader is seduced by the language of the poem, realizing perhaps, as Baudrillard has suggested, that "seduction is destiny. It is what remains of a magical, fateful world, a risky, vertiginous and predestined world; it is what is quietly effective in a visibly efficient and stolid world" (180); through the seductions of *Laon and Cythna*, the reader is transported to the other world of liberty and love, a world that, importantly, begins with the vision of a woman—Cythna.

The significance of Cythna in Laon's narrative must not be overlooked, for it is Cythna who inspires Laon to speak, and in fact it is she who generates the words he articulates. After arriving at the temple, Shelley meets the lovers and receives their tale:

> Beneath the darkness of [Laon's] outspread hair
> He stood thus beautiful; but there was One
> Who sate beside him like his shadow there,
> And held his hand—far lovelier; she was known
> To be thus fair, by the few lines alone
> Which through her floating locks and gathered cloak,
> Glances of soul-dissolving glory, shone:—
> None else beheld her eyes—in him they woke
> Memories which found a tongue as thus he silence broke.
>
> (658–666)

Interestingly, during their intercourse with Shelley, Laon and Cythna exchange gendered positionalities: Cythna assumes the masculine position of the impregnator (here, through the instrument of her gaze), and Laon assumes the feminine position of the mother who delivers the narrative, who figuratively gives birth to the textual body that is the story of the sibling-lovers' shared experience. The metaphor may be extended and the gendered positionalities even further complicated, for it is Shelley who is ultimately impregnated by Laon's speech—his overflow or ejaculation—

and it is Shelley who will re-produce, or give birth to, the textual embodiment of the lovers' history.[17] These perpetual mediations in gendered positionalities cohere around the act of intercourse—the erotic exchange of language—for it is through language that pleasure proliferates in the emergence of the lovers' revolutionary agenda. Mother-Father of the lovers' extraordinary exchange, Cythna stands as the primary source, the first voice, that underwrites Laon's articulation (and, by extension, Shelley's as well), and her role throughout the poem as the origin of the seductive narrative—indeed, as the incarnator of the liberated world—cannot be overestimated.

Cythna corresponds to the image of the beloved Shelley describes in "On Love": she stands as Laon's complement, his other, in part because she is his sister (and therefore shares the same formative experiences as he) and in part because she embodies his own psychic projections.[18] Laon describes how Cythna awakes from sleeping entwined in his arms to sing the very hymns to freedom and justice his sleeping soul just composed. The siblings' nocturnal embrace activates the convergence of their individual minds into one, so that each manifests the ideals of the other. Of his sister/beloved, Laon observes that

> ... she did seem
> Beside me, gathering beauty as she grew
> Like the bright shade of some immortal dream
> Which walks, when tempest sleeps, the wave of life's dark stream.
> (870-873)

Cythna functions as Laon's mirror—"As mine own shadow was this child to me, / A second self, far dearer and more fair" (874-875)—and thus as his perfect complement.

The first recollection Laon provides of the lovers' activities underscores the seamlessness of their union:

> —so she was made
> My sole associate, and her willing feet
> Wandered with mine where earth and ocean meet,
> Beyond the aëreal mountains whose vast cells
> The unreposing billows ever beat,
> Through forests wide and old, and lawny dells
> Where boughs of incense droop over the emerald walls.
> (885-891)

The particular locations Laon describes remark the pair's affinity with the natural world and remind the reader that the revolutionary lovers exemplify the natural condition of liberty. More to the point, though, the first place in which the lovers commune also marks the space "where earth and ocean meet"—the beach, a liminal space across which the borders between apparently separate entities (earth and ocean) dissolve. So, too, do the borders between the (apparently separate) bodies of brother and sister dissolve into liminality, so that as Cythna wakes from dreaming to sing the hymns Laon has composed, her voice energizes the "boundless universe" (929), and the entire natural world resounds with the lovers' song (928-945).

Shelley devotes the whole of canto 7 to the story of Cythna's separation from Laon. We learn that, following epic tradition, Cythna was captured, led underwater, and held prisoner in a cave. Chained, she was tortured by cannibalistic dreams of her sibling, just as Laon dreamt of Cythna during his crucifixion (2911-2694), a reciprocal experience that underscores the complete psychic union, or oneness, of the siblings/lovers. Like Laon, Cythna learns the utility of language and masters the non-verbal language of the gaze: her affect and her language so move King Othman that he temporarily renounces his notoriously tyrannical ways (2857-2874), and her powerful stare mesmerizes an Eagle, who is dissuaded from attacking a soldier merely by the power of Cythna's extra-linguistic command (2974-3000). Like her brother's experience in exile, Cythna's education under tyranny teaches her the virtues of nonviolent revolution; and reading the narrative of her experience, the reader is meant to be educated in kind. Together, the educations of Laon and Cythna stress language over force and tolerance over hatred—exactly the program of reform Shelley hopes his readers will adopt.[19]

The erotic relationship enjoyed by the poem's heroes serves more than a merely provocative function, however, for we find that through their reciprocal understanding, each lover is cleansed and purified by the best qualities of the other in exactly the way Shelley described in "On Love." In short, Laon, tutored by Cythna, becomes wise, and Cythna, who learns from her brother/lover/student, is cleansed of fear and evil (946-951). This fluctuation in positionality—now one lover assumes a dominant role, now the other—underscores the place of ambiguity and seamlessness in Shelley's erotic model, for it is only through these re-mediations of power (or positionality) that true equality emerges in the lovers' relationship: were one lover always the teacher and the other always the pupil, the seemingly fixed hierarchies of power and order in the world about them would remain uncontested and, at the most local level, would inform their relationship. Rather than dismantling the teacher/pupil structure and proposing another model in its place, Shelley leaves that structure intact to demonstrate that while one cannot destroy the forces that regulate relationships in the world, one can alter the relativity of their positions by decentering them, or removing them from a fixed, hierarchical relationship—and thus replacing power with equality, tyranny with communication. Instead, Shelley invokes a sense of play—and, relatedly, of *pleasure*—by perpetually shifting the positions the lovers occupy, so that the back-and-forth motion of reciprocity anticipates the radical liberation of the world about them, even as it duplicates the movements of intercourse, both sexual and verbal.

Laon and Cythna introduces the twin problems that plague *The Cenci*: sex and text. In *The Cenci*, Shelley demonstrates how both sex and text may take oppressive forms—specifically, in the Count's rape of Beatrice and in what I have described as her "perpetual violation" in the narratives-to-be-written about her family, narratives Beatrice fears will exculpate her father by casting the members of his family as merciless, bloodthirsty parricides. But in *Laon and Cythna,* Shelley situates incest as the highest expression of love between equal partners whose ultimate (and, importantly, absolutely unselfish) goal is the liberation of the world. Shelley thus demonstrates the double-valenced potential of incest: in *Laon and Cythna* incest tends toward freedom, where in *The Cenci* it reinforces larger systems of oppression. In both works, Shelley reminds us of the inextricability of pleasure and power, or eroticism and politics, by privileging the erotic relationship as a locus for social structures. Thus, while Beatrice despairs over the perpetual rape to be waged upon her reputation in the histories that will be written about the Cenci family, Cythna understands the ultimate good to which her political martyrdom will lead:

> "The good and mighty of departed ages
>   And in their graves, the innocent and free,
> Heroes, and Poets, and prevailing Sages,
>   Who leave the vesture of their majesty
>   To adorn and clothe this naked world—and we
> Are like to them—such perish, but they leave
>   All hope, or love, or truth, or liberty,
> Whose forms their mighty spirits could conceive,
> To be a rule and law to ages that survive."
>   (3712-3720)

As Hogle notes, ". . . for sympathetic onlookers and readers," Laon and Cythna's self-sacrifice transforms the pair "into a 'memory, ever burning' beyond their execution, which allows all hopeful inhabitants of this present 'dark night of things' to look ahead toward 'an eternal morning' due to reappear some day in an existence newly perceived" (102). The death of the lovers *is* the resurrection of the other—the marginalized individual(s)—that Beatrice calls for in *The Cenci* when she instructs Bernardo to set down the true narrative of her family's plight: in *Laon and Cythna,* the immolation of the lovers/heroes marks the symbolic triumph of liberty, and their self-sacrifice unfurls as an unassailable example for the generations to follow.

The incestuous nature of the twins' union allows Shelley to stress his ardent belief that women can be free only when they are afforded the same life-experiences as men: reared in the same household with a shared set of formative moments, the siblings/lovers manifest Shelley's feminist sympathies and demonstrate how social change derives from a domestic model. Laon, acutely aware of the evil that has overtaken the earth, admits that:

> This misery was but coldly felt, till she
>   Became my only friend, who had endued
> My purpose with a wider sympathy;
>   Thus, Cythna mourned with me the servitude
>   In which the half of humankind were mewed
> Victims of lust and hate, the slaves of slaves:
> . . . .
>   Never will peace and human nature meet
>   Till free and equal man and woman greet
> Domestic peace; and ere this power can make
>   In human hearts its calm and holy seat,
> This slavery must be broken . . . .
>
> (982-998)

In fact, it is Cythna who first utters the prophecy of the liberation of the Golden City (1000-1006), and it is she who rescues Laon from certain attack by a band of soldiers (2497-2523). Shelley situates Cythna as the inspiration for Laon's revolutionary narrative, both in that she serves as his muse and in that she functions as a savior/teacher who heals his psychic wounds and articulates the agenda of liberty her brother/lover endorses. The apparent hero of Shelley's poem, as I have suggested, is Cythna, whom Cameron designates as "the first intellectual, radical heroine in English literature, anticipating the 'new woman' heroines of Shaw and others later in the century" (322).[20] But that it is Laon, not Cythna, who narrates the lovers' history reminds us of Shelley's focus on the erotic couple (as opposed to the individual hero or heroine) in the revolutionary paradigm: speaking for the poem's real hero—its primary narrator, as I have argued—Laon launches the parallel voices, the harmonic conversation, which Shelley calls for in "On Love" and which, throughout *Laon and Cythna*, activates the incarnation of a liberated world.

Shelley claims he composed *Laon and Cythna* without concern for what he knew would be the critics' reaction to his heroes' relationship, and he contextualizes his writerly defiance in terms of the giants of literary history: "I have sought therefore to write, as I believe that Homer, Shakespeare, and Milton wrote, with an utter disregard of anonymous censure" (104). Before broaching the topic of incest directly, Shelley distances himself from possible misreadings of *Laon and Cythna* as an argument for atheism: "The erroneous and degrading idea which men have conceived of a Supreme Being . . . is spoken against, but not the Supreme Being itself" (105). In a similar way, Shelley removes himself from the erotic "crime" of the poem's heroes, acknowledging that "[i]n the personal conduct of my hero and heroine, there is one circumstance which was intended to startle the reader from the trance of everyday life" (106). Underscoring the power of subversive eroticism "to startle the reader" to attention—if not to action—Shelley suggests that at least part of the power of the incest-motif lies in its ability to provoke and thus to demand a reaction from readers who might otherwise be unmoved by a narrative of political revolution. Here we find Shelley's explicit articulation of the coercive power that lies embedded in the erotic narrative as the poet lauds the sexy text's potential to tease a reader into action and thus to generate a truly reciprocal intercourse—a conversation—between the reader and the text. Insisting that "[t]he circumstance of which I speak [incest] was introduced . . . merely to accustom men to that charity and toleration which the exhibition of a practice widely differing from their own has a tendency to promote," (106), Shelley adds in a note that "[t]he sentiments connected with and characteristic of this circumstance have no personal reference to the writer" (106 n 1).[21] Although he distances himself from the subversive erotic practices of his heroes, Shelley concludes the final paragraph of his original Preface by gesturing toward his tacit acceptance of such a practice: "[n]othing indeed can be more mischievous than many actions innocent in themselves, which might bring down upon individuals the bigoted contempt and rage of the multitude" (106). Shelley acknowledges the sheer weight of the subject of incest by deliberately and carefully calling the reader's attention to his delicate denial of such an activity even as he points to that subversive erotic engagement as a vehicle for reform, an instrument that, once deployed, develops and motivates the reader's capacity for tolerance and understanding.

As we have seen, Shelley's Preface announces *Laon and Cythna*'s political engagements and situates these in tandem with subversive eroticism. His fourteen-stanza Dedication "To Mary" reiterates the correspondence between political and erotic engagements, between social and private concerns:

> The toil which stole from thee so many an hour,
>   Is ended,—and the fruit is at thy feet!
> No longer where the woods to frame a bower
>   With interlacèd branches mix and sweet,
>   Or where with sound like many voices sweet,
> Waterfalls leap among wild islands green,
>   Which framed for my lone boat a lone retreat
> Of moss-grown trees and weeds, shall I be seen:
> But beside thee, where still my heart has ever been.
>
>   (10-18)

His poetic task complete, Shelley returns his attention from work to love, from his public vocation to his domestic relationship, and he lays the product of his labor at the feet of his lover. In this way, Shelley returns a public task—the composition of political poetry which, importantly, occurs *in nature*—to the space of the erotic by apostrophizing his "Vision of the Nineteenth Century" as a love-offering to his wife. Shelley acknowledges Mary's role as paramount in the development of his thought, as stanza 11 makes clear:

> And what art thou? I know, but dare not speak:
>   Time may interpret to his silent years.
> Yet in the paleness of thy thoughtful cheek,
>   And in the light thine ample forehead wears,
>   And in thy sweetest smiles, and in thy tears,
> And in thy gentle speech, a prophecy
>   Is whispered, to subdue my fondest fears:
> And through thine eyes, even in thy soul I see
> A lamp of vestal fire burning internally.
>   (91-99)

Ruminating on the possible failure of *Laon and Cythna,* Shelley poses Mary—his inspiration, his life-mate, a Cythna to his Laon—as a savior into whose embrace he may retreat from a public that fails to understand him:

> If men must rise and stamp with fury blind
>   On his pure name who loves them,—thou and I,
>   Sweet friend! can look from our tranquillity
> Like lamps into the world's tempestuous night,—
>   Two tranquil stars, while clouds are passing by
> Which wrap them from the foundering seaman's sight,
> That burn from year to year with unextinguished light.
>   (120-126)

Reinscribing the relationship enjoyed by his heroes, Shelley constructs himself and Mary as twin outlaws—"two . . . stars"—who find "tranquillity" in each other's orbit and security in the atemporal, boundless nature of their love for each other; and, like the heroes of *Laon and Cythna,* the misunderstood poet and his muse ascend together to the heavens.[22] Shelley thus insists that his political poem derives from his own domestic harmony: writing of his love for Mary and their children, he concludes that " . . . these delights, and thou, have been to me / The parents of the Song I consecrate to thee" (80-81). As we have seen, Shelley privileges erotic relationships—conceived here in the broad sense of the family—as the primary models, the antecedents, even, for political engagements. Having completed his political engagement in the form of *Laon and Cythna,* Shelley now returns his full attention to the domestic sphere, turning away from the public word of politics and publication to the private world of love, demonstrating, as his Dedication and the whole of the poem show, how those two spheres become so completely interwoven that finally they melt into one.

Landscape and Liminality

My readings of the topographies Shelley explores throughout the works I have discussed bears out Kathleen M. Kirby's claim that "[s]pace can be a site to bring together and understand the connections between the psychic and the social, the personal and the political."[23] Schama points to landscape—in my study, representations of literal and symbolic space, at once natural and psychological—as a vista whose "scenery" derives as much from human memory and hope as from the natural world (14, 7). Schama argues that "inherited landscape myths and memories share two common characteristics: their surprising endurance through the centuries and their power to shape institutions that we still live with" (15). In his Preface to *Laon and Cythna*, Shelley includes the natural landscape among the various texts that inform his vision of a liberated world: "I have considered Poetry in its most comprehensive sense; and have read the Poets and the Historians and the Metaphysicians whose writings have been accessible to me, and have looked upon the beautiful and majestic scenery of the earth, as common sources of those elements which it is the province of the Poet to embody and combine" (103). In plotting utopia, Shelley turns to the natural landscape for the raw material that underwrites his vision of a liberated world, and landscape offers throughout his works a canvas upon which the poet paints his vision.[24]

Twice in the poem, Shelley transforms the landscape into a sort of tablet onto which the narrative of freedom may be inscribed. Upon his arrival at the lovers' temple, Shelley finds their story depicted in paintings that adorn the cavern walls:

> And on the jasper walls around, there lay
> Paintings, the poesy of mightiest thought,
> Which did the Spirit's history display;
> A tale of passionate change, divinely taught,
> Which, in their wingèd dance, unconscious Genii wrought.
> (599-603)

This shift in media from poetry to painting, from the verbal to the visual arts, reminds us of the cave-narrative's proximity to truth, for we tend to regard painting as a less mediated form of narrative than writing. S(h)ifted into a purely visual medium, the refined narrative anticipates the history Shelley is about to receive in language, so that his memory of the paintings will function as a visual mnemonic for the important lessons he is about to learn. In canto 7, Shelley effects a similar representational turn to landscape as Cythna inscribes the characteristics of the "One Mind" into the "cave" of her own consciousness:

> "My mind became the book through which I grew
> Wise in all human wisdom, and its cave,
> Which like a mine I rifled through and through,
> To me the keeping of its secrets gave—
> One mind, the type of all, the moveless wave
> Whose calm reflects all moving things that are:
> Necessity, and love, and life, the grave
> And sympathy (fountains of hope and fear),
> Justice, and truth, and time, and the world's natural sphere.

> "And on the sand would I make signs to range
>   These woofs, as they were woven, of my thought;
> Clear, elemental shapes, whose smallest change
>   A subtler language within language wrought:
>   The key of truths which once were dimly taught
> In old Crotona;—and sweet melodies
>   Of love, in that lorn solitude I caught
> From mine own voice in dream, when thy dear eyes
> Shone through my sleep, and did that utterance harmonize."
> (3100-3117)

Cythna's speech poses the physical body as the nexus between landscape and text, for it is in "the cave" of her own mind that she inscribes the "signs" of the "secrets" she has come to understand. "Clear, elemental shapes," these signs take extra-linguistic form—they are images rather than letters—so that in drawing them upon the sand of the cave, Cythna symbolically inscribes knowledge upon the landscape—the "cave"—of her consciousness. Cythna's body registers as the site of poetry, which Shelley encourages his reader to regard as the transmission of truth into consciousness. Reverberating with the harmony of her extraordinary experiences, the psychic space of Cythna's mind anticipates—and is finally manifested in—the physical space to which the lovers ascend at the play's end. Cythna's speech thus attests to the power of the liberated mind to incarnate its ideal, to turn psychic into physical space, to unite the types of landscapes I have described in the plot—both the narrative and the place—of utopia.

Throughout *Laon and Cythna,* Shelley draws on the pastoral tradition of the bower of bliss to describe the heroes' ascent to the space of complete freedom, a space whose tangibility, importantly, is remarked by its grounding in elements of the natural world. Duff points to Shelley's appropriation of the Spenserian landscape trope of the bower of bliss as the device that enables him to overlap the political and the erotic throughout *Laon and Cythna.* As we have seen, it is Cythna who articulates the promise of hope, and her images are coded specifically in terms of the natural cycles of landscape:

> "This is the winter of the world;—and here
>   We die, even as the winds of Autumn fade,
> Expiring in the frore and foggy air.—
>   Behold! Spring comes, though we must pass, who made
>   The promise of its birth,—even as the shade
> Which from our death, as from a mountain, flings
>   The future, a broad sunrise; thus arrayed
> As with the plumes of overshadowing wings,
> From its dark gulph of chains, Earth like an eagle springs.

> "O dearest love! we shall be dead and cold
>   Before this morn may on the world arise;
> Wouldst thou the glory of its dawn behold?
>   Alas! gaze not on me, but turn thine eyes
>   On thine own heart—it is a paradise
> Which everlasting Spring has made its own,
>   And while drear Winter fills the naked skies,
> Sweet streams of sunny thought, and flowers fresh-blown,
> Are there, and weave their sounds and odours into one."
> (3685-3702)

Cythna figuratively maps landscape along the contours of the human body, so that just as the natural world progresses through successive seasons of life and death, so, too, is the human body re-invigorated by the "everlasting Spring" in its bosom. Deriving from nature's seasonal cycles, this re-animation of the human body anticipates the cyclical nature of history: just when we despair over the world's fall into tyranny, the cyclical model promises the re-animation of despair as *hope* in the eventual return of liberty. Cythna, as Duff notes, "[forecasts] . . . a political spring that will eventually succeed the encroaching winter" (208-209), thus echoing Shelley's investment in the cyclicality of political progress that we see, for example, in "Ode to the West Wind."[25] Duff argues that "whereas the political prophecy turns on the image of the cycle of seasons, the personal revelation is expressed by [Cythna's] metaphor of an '*everlasting* spring'— this being, of course, a traditional attribute of the earthly paradise, or the Bower of Bliss. By extending the image of spring, Shelley thus manages to create a perfect link between his public and private themes, between the prophecy of revolution and the doctrine of individual transcendence" (209). As we have seen in *Epipsychidion* and in *The Cenci*, the landscape metaphor functions as a pivotal device in linking the putatively separate categories of public and private, the political and the erotic.

Three pivotal moments in *Laon and Cythna* underscore the importance of landscape metaphors to Shelley's model. The poem's opening stanzas demonstrate the effects of political unrest on the natural landscape: "When the last hope of trampled France had failed," Shelley writes, " . . . the firm earth was shaken, / As if by the last wreck its frame were overtaken" (127, 134-135). Shortly after, as "Darkness more dread than night was poured upon the ground" (144), Shelley observes a catalogue of atmospheric disturbances and is struck by the sudden quiet that follows:

> Hark! 'tis the rushing of a wind that sweeps
>   Earth and the ocean. See! the lightnings yawn
> Deluging Heaven with fire, and the lashed deeps
>   Glitter and boil beneath: it rages on,
>   One mighty stream, whirlwind and waves upthrown,

> Lightning, and hail, and darkness eddying by.
> There is a pause—the sea-birds, that were gone
> Into their caves to shriek, come forth, to spy
> What calm has fall'n on earth, what light is in the sky.
>
> (145-153)

These frightening transformations of land and sky echo the reverberations of political unrest, but just as the world seems to be lurching toward complete chaos, the heavens open to reveal an expanse of blue sky, green ocean, and calm (154-162). Even as it duplicates the spasms of political turmoil, landscape thus offers the promise of hope, for its opening onto a scene of calm foretells the inevitable toppling of tyranny. The poem's opening scene situates landscape as the mirror *and* the lamp of the human condition: at first a reflection of the chaos all around him, landscape finally offers Shelley a glimpse of the more desirable world yet to emerge.[26] The culmination of Shelley's odd journey to the lovers' temple also emphasizes the importance of landscape to the poem's vision: suspended between the sea and the sky in a liminal space that remarks the fluidity, or ooziness, of its unusual location, the temple straddles the borders between particular landscape elements to reconcile topographical difference. The space of oozy reconciliation, the lovers' temple stands as the repository of pleasure, both in the narrow sense of the lovers' union and in the broader sense of Shelley's vision of a world liberated by love.

Landscape metaphors also emerge in Shelley's location of Laon's recovery from crucifixion in what we might call a vegetized landscape; that is, Laon's recuperation and tutelage take place in a green world whose peace and tranquillity stand in stark contrast to the strife-ridden society from which the Hermit has delivered the hero. At the beginning of canto 4, the Hermit takes Laon across the water to a ruined island at " . . . the margin of a lake" (1442). Shelley describes the Hermit's home as a tower so overgrown with vines that the couch on which he places the hero is literally made ". . . of grass and oak-leaves interlaced" (1431). Anticipating both the ruined tower on *Epipsychidion*'s island and the madhouse in *Julian and Maddalo*, the Hermit's home signals the blurring of fixed categories of order: this " . . . small chamber, which with mosses rare / Were tapestried . . . " repairs the chasm between the worlds of nature and culture (1429-1430). Like the towers we have seen before, the Hermit's abode is yet another liminal space in which elements of nature and civilization mix and melt together. A place—or plot—of respite for the poem's embattled hero, the Hermit's odd home offers Laon a space in which he may be nourished and (re-) educated, a womb-like space from which Laon will finally emerge, better equipped for the struggle against tyranny.

Shelley's second important use of landscape metaphors occurs in cantos 8 and 9, where Cythna warns the sailors who have captured her about the dangers incumbent upon "'the dark idolatry of self'" (3390).[27] Seduced by

Mapping the Ideal

her locution, the sailors vow allegiance to Cythna's feminist political ideals and liberate their female captives (3469-3480). Overnight, the vegetation of the land near which the ship has docked completely overtakes the vessel, symbolizing the redemption of the sailors that results from their rejection of the pursuits of power, prestige, and reward, three manifestations of selfishness and tyranny (3481-3486). A similarly vegetal landscape marks the scene of Laon and Cythna's reunion in canto 6:

> But I to a stone seat that Maiden led,
>   And kissing her eyes, said, "Thou hast need
> Of rest," and I heaped up the courser's bed
> In a green mossy nook, with mountain-flowers dispread.
>
> Within that ruin where a shattered portal
>   Looks to the eastern stars (abandoned now
> By man, to be the home of things immortal,
>   Memories, like awful ghosts which come and go,
>   And must inherit all he builds below
> When he is gone), a hall stood, o'er whose roof
>   Fair clinging weeds with ivy pale did grow,
> Clasping its gray rents with a verdurous woof,
> A hanging dome of leaves, a canopy moon-proof.
>   (2565-2577)

But the world around the lovers continues to be plagued by tyranny, and the shocks of political upheavals are felt even in this seemingly paradisiacal space:

> And then I saw and felt. The moon was high,
>   And clouds, as of a coming storm, were spread
> Under its orb,—loud winds were gathering overhead.
>
> . . . .
>   And we sate calmly, though that rocky hill,
>   The waves contending in its caverns strook,
> For they foreknew the storm, and the gray ruin shook.
>   (2665-2667; 2674-2676)

The experience of complete commingling metaphorized in Laon and Cythna's consummation proves incommensurate with a world hostile to the siblings'-lovers' transgression, so that, much like the ruin in which the couple lie sheltered, their security is threatened by the political storms that conspire against their agenda of ceaseless reciprocity, the platform of liberty-through-love. Further, the reverberations of the landscape demonstrate the continuing hold of tyranny on the world about the lovers: through his depiction of the landscape's response as particularly anxious, Shelley turns once again to the natural world as a register for the unnatural condition of tyranny.

Finally, Shelley returns to landscape metaphors in the last stanzas of *Laon and Cythna* as he describes the arrival of the heroes (accompanied by Cythna's daughter) at the utopic other-space that is to be their eternal home. Too weak to ascend the pyre upon which Laon is to be executed, Cythna once again draws on the seductive power of language to woo the onlookers, who help bind her near her lover so that the two may perish together (4567-4577). As the fire soars upward, Cythna's daughter falls dead next to Othman's throne, but when the flames begin to encircle the lovers, everything suddenly disappears before them. After passing for three days through " . . . winding watery ways" (4745), the three suddenly stop, suspended, on the fourth day of their journey:[28]

> The torrent of that wide and raging river
>   Is passed, and our äereal speed suspended.
> We look behind; a golden mist did quiver
>   Where its wild surges with the lake were blended,—
>   Our bark hung there, as on a line suspended
> Between two heavens,—that windless waveless lake
>   Which four great cataracts from four vales, attended
> By mists, aye feed; from rocks and clouds they break,
> And of that azure sea a silent refuge make.
>
>   (4801-4809)

Cameron compares these metaphors to those of *Queen Mab* to conclude that the cataracts at the borders of this paradise represent "space, matter, time, and mind" (340). The waterfalls might also be contextualized in terms of the four components of language the Hermit describes to Laon—the Serpent, the Dove, Wisdom, and Innocence (1584). Following Schama's reading of Bernini's Fountain of the Four Rivers, one could also argue that the four cataracts suggest " . . . the four continents of the world (as well as, perhaps, the four elements)" (302); from this perspective, Shelley's heroes are transported not outside of the world at all but to its very center, to the space from which the world's vital forces may be re-generated.[29] Certainly, Laon, Cythna, and Cythna's daughter have arrived at something like *Epipsychidion*'s "far Eden of the purple East," a natural wonderland that reinscribes the oozy borders so central to the cartographies of Shelley's liberated worlds, among them the homeland from which Shelley's Rosalind and Helen feel exiled, the one of which they are reminded when they hear its echoes, importantly, in the trickling of the brook, a watery reminder of the oozy landscape of utopia the women mourn. In *Laon and Cythna*, the watery borders of the utopic other-space—its very limits—symbolize the breakdown of binary systems of order: the cataracts emanate from both rocks and clouds, ground and sky in an atemporal space where neither wind nor wave belies the progress of time through the revolutionary scene. Having arrived at utopia, it seems, time has stopped.

Mapping the Ideal

But the ascent to the paradisiacal realm comes at no small cost. Like so many other Shelleyan heroes, Laon and Cythna are granted release from the constraints imposed upon them by the Symbolic Order only after they sacrifice their lives to the project of freedom.[30] Burned at the stake in punishment for his transgressive politics, Laon never resorts to hatred or revenge; indeed,

> There are no sneers upon his lip which speak
> That scorn or hate has made him bold; his cheek
> Resolve has not turned pale,—his eyes are mild
> And clam, and, like the morn about to break,
> Smile on mankind . . . .
>
> (4471-4475)

Just as he is about to be executed, Laon is joined by Cythna who—reprising her role as her brother's savior in canto 6—arrives on a horse to join him on the pyre (4558-4566). The lovers' kiss activates the only weapon they deploy against the forces that condemn them—their erotic relationship, through which the lovers are ennobled.[31] Paradise, Shelley argues, *is* the erotic connection, in both its sexual and familial components.

At the poem's end, Laon and Cythna find themselves in an idyllic setting on a shore beside a stream that recalls the scene with which Shelley's poem began (4585-4602). The circularity of Shelley's narrative re-invokes the poem's opening image of the serpent and the eagle wreathed in fight, which reminds the reader of the constant struggle between good and evil (freedom and oppression) that marks the human condition, as well as of the circularity—the fluidity—of infinity.[32] And just as in the poem's opening Shelley boards a boat to be delivered to a beautiful temple, here, at the poem's end, a boat sails softly toward Laon and Cythna, steered by a silver-winged cherub—that same child who perished at the sight of the lovers' martyrdom (4603-4629). The child announces that she is the daughter of Laon and Cythna, thus transferring her paternal heritage from tyrant (Othman) to redeemer and correcting the teleology of incest-as-oppression that Shelley exposes throughout *The Cenci* (4657-4665). As the revolutionary "family" prepare to sail away, the child tells Laon that despair functions to activate wisdom (4699-4701), and thus she encourages the reader of Shelley's poem—he or she who is "emerging from [the] trance" induced by the "shocks" of the French Revolution (Preface to *Laon and Cythna* 102)—to look beyond disappointment to enlightenment. The child's message of peace, of course, derives from Cythna's conception of the coming spring, which I have considered at length. Thus, the political optimism that closes *Laon and Cythna* may be traced backward through a pattern of (narrative) intercourse, from the poem's speaker (Shelley), to the child, to Laon, and finally to the first voice—the incarnator—of the poem, Cythna.[33]

∞ ∞ ∞ ∞ ∞

Laon and Cythna stands at the intersection of the objectives Shelley hopes to realize through the project of liberty-through-love. Specifically, the poem poses tolerance and love as the conditions that prefigure the transformation of the world, and it embraces an incestuous relationship as an occasion for invoking and testing the development of those conditions in Shelley's readers. Throughout the poem, Shelley demonstrates how what we might classify as "private" engagements—the familial, erotic relationship of the poem's heroes—facilitate "public" or political work in the remaking of the world or, as the title describes it, in "the Revolution of the Golden City." In particular, *Laon and Cythna* underscores Shelley's argument that global change begins in that most local of spheres, the home. Demonstrating that political movements replicate domestic relationships, *Laon and Cythna* investigates the overlaps between individual and social bodies, between private and public spaces, and between the categories I have designated as "the erotic" and "the political."

A similar set of concerns informs *Prometheus Unbound: A Lyrical Drama in Four Acts* (1820), which many scholars regard as Shelley's finest achievement. Certainly, the play articulates the poet's belief in the power of love to conquer tyranny, and it emphasizes the place of language within the project of revolution, but a thorough examination of Shelley's development of those concepts is far beyond the scope of the present project.[34] Rather than engage in a close reading of *Prometheus Unbound*, I want instead to point to the ways in which the play reiterates the agenda I examined throughout my reading of *Laon and Cythna*. Specifically, I summarize the place and function of three concepts in *Prometheus Unbound*: the construction of Prometheus as redeemer; the liberating power of love and the relationship between language and liberty; and the model of utopia and the place of landscape—the physical world—within Shelley's imaginative revolution. As in my reading of *Laon and Cythna*, I turn to both narrative and space as I examine the strategies through which Shelley's play participates in the plotting of utopia.

The similarities between *Prometheus Unbound* and *Laon and Cythna* are staggering, both in number and in kind, as countless critics have noted.[35] Both poems describe the extraordinary struggle of a pair of lovers against the forces of oppression; both position the bastard-issue of rape (in *Prometheus Unbound*, Demogorgon) as a re-mediator of power and an ironic foil to tyranny; and both conclude with the displacement of the heroic couple to a utopic other-space situated in a green world, a vegetized wonderland. Both works investigate the movement of time and the progression of political power as cyclical phenomena, and both interrogate the complicity of language and power, as I discuss below. Like *Laon and Cythna*, *Prometheus Unbound* insinuates the erotic couple—Prometheus and Asia—as the agents of liberation, and just as in the former poem Laon is educated and inspired by his sister's speech, so, too, is Prometheus inspired by the agenda for intellectual revolution Asia describes early in the play.[36] While the erotic union between Laon and Cythna prefigures the (temporary) liberation of the world, the love between Prometheus and Asia similarly functions to bring about universal freedom.[37] Finally, in what seems to be a re-writing of the conclusion of *Laon and Cythna,* the fourth act of *Prometheus Unbound* describes the lovers'/heroes' ascent to a utopic other-space from which liberty and, in this poem, culture and the arts are re-generated, themselves figuring as forces for the perpetual renewal of liberty.

Near the conclusion of *Laon and Cythna,* the silver-winged cherub explains to Laon that despair proffers an ultimately positive function, for it teaches men wisdom;[38] similarly, Prometheus, who at the play's beginning has been chained to a rock for 3000 years, his entrails scavenged daily by a ravenous eagle in punishment for his curse on Jupiter, finally realizes the pedagogical reward of his centuries-old torture:

> . . . I speak in grief,
> Not exultation, for I hate no more,
> As then, ere misery made me wise. . . .
>
> (1.56-58)

Prometheus's speech reminds us the power of language to affect and even to alter social realities. In *The Cenci,* language takes its most affective form in the legal sentence, a discursive pronouncement publicized by its utterance and manifested in direct action on the body of the (so-called) criminal; in *Prometheus Unbound,* Shelley postulates the potential for language, in its "unsaying," to un-do social realities, so that *contra-diction*—speaking against (itself)—emerges as one rhetorical strategy through which oppression may be undone. And just as *Laon and Cythna* points to the heroine as the first interlocutor of freedom, so, too, does *Prometheus Unbound* place the initial call for an intellectual revolution not in the mouth of Prometheus, but in the mouth of Asia:

> . . . in Heaven-defying minds
> As thought by thought is piled, . . . some great truth
> Is loosened, and the nations echo round
> Shaken to their roots: as do the mountains now.
>
> (2.3.39-42)

Like *Laon and Cythna, Prometheus Unbound* situates the heroine as a figure pivotal to the articulation of the revolutionary agenda, a feminist character without whom the play's putative hero would be so overcome by the forces leagued against him that he would certainly plunge into despair, never to realize the healing potential of hope. In short, *Prometheus Unbound* follows *Laon and Cythna* by pointing to the heroine as the ultimate figure from whom freedom is generated and by privileging the erotic couple, rather than the individual redeemer, as the true agents of social change.

As in *Laon and Cythna,* in *Prometheus Unbound* Shelley locates the no-space of utopia outside of time and place in an imaginary world in which time stands still.[39] For while the utopic space of *Prometheus Unbound* is surely an earthly one, as I discuss below, the play's heroes ascend to it only at the onset of eternity, as Time is carried to his grave. "A Train of dark Forms and Shadows" passes the scene and sings:

> Here, oh here!
> We bear the bier
> Of the Father of many a cancelled year!
> Spectres we
> Of the dead hours be,
> We bear Time to his tomb in eternity.
>
> (4.9-14)

Divorced from Time, the utopia of *Prometheus Unbound,* like that of *Laon and Cythna,* plots a space marked by liminality and transgression, by reciprocity and overlap, a condition manifested most clearly in the visible union of Heaven and Earth, which Panthea describes:

> ... Heaven and Earth united now,
> Vast beams like spokes of some invisible wheel
> Which whirl as the Orb whirls, swifter than thought,
> Filling the abyss with sunlike lightenings,
> And perpendicular now, and now transverse.
>
> (4.273-277)

Re-writing the interlocking grid of patriarchal power that dominated the world of *The Cenci,* the liberating potential of Shelley's redeemed universe shines its life-affirming light throughout the entire world; no longer trapped in the darkness of despair, the redeemed world is illuminated by the natural processes of freedom. Even the markers of human progress and ownership—which now seem "monstrous works and uncouth skeletons" (4.299)—are overgrown with vegetation and bizarre life forms, symbolizing the triumph of nature over culture in the subsumption of man's artifacts to his own achievement beneath the mighty power of the natural world. Even much more assuredly than he does in *Laon and Cythna,* in *Prometheus Unbound* Shelley points to a terminus in the cyclical struggle between good and evil, utopia at and as the death of time, when the world turns away from tyranny and civilization and embraces instead nature, love, and generation.

O'Neill's observation that in writing *Prometheus Unbound* "Shelley has his eye firmly on the climate of opinion in the second decade of the nineteenth century, on the way in which, in his view, it was frustrating—temporarily, as he hoped—the progress of reform" (87) reminds us of how closely and specifically *Prometheus Unbound* articulates Shelley's reformist agenda. Shelley's work on the poem was interrupted by an important political event, the government's massacre of a number of peaceful protesters on 16 August 1819—"Peterloo," as the bloody spectacle came to be known. Scrivener argues that "[s]omething like Peterloo could have frightened the aristocratic Shelley out of his more radical tendencies, but it did not. Rather, it emboldened him to go as far as he ever went in a radical direction" (140). *Prometheus Unbound* thus emerges from a political climate in which the effects of governmental power have been demonstrated upon the bodies of revolutionaries in the most dramatic of ways, an era in which power is registered on the bodies of the oppressed as complete powerlessness, evacuation, vanishing—somatic inscriptions echoing those we have seen in all the works I have examined thus far.

Almost one year to the day after the Peterloo massacre, Shelley published *Prometheus Unbound: A Lyrical Drama in Four Acts; With Other Poems,* and Scrivener emphasizes the importance of the entire volume to the reading of Shelley's play (234). Of the nine works that follow *Prometheus Unbound,* six address elements of the natural world, and three focus on specific political concerns, such as the fight for freedom in Spain. While a review of the entire *Prometheus Unbound* volume is certainly beyond my intention in the present study, two of its poems are particularly relevant to my reading of the play.[40] "Ode to the West Wind," the fifth poem following the *Prometheus Unbound,* turns to the seasonal cycles of the natural world to locate proof of the cyclical pattern of history, finally anticipating the onset of liberty in the winds of Spring. "Ode to Liberty," the final poem in the volume, traces the movement of (the personified) Liberty throughout history to counterpoise freedom to religion and tyranny.[41] Both poems call for the re-emergence of freedom, and both underscore the place of the natural world in that resurrection. Throughout, the *Prometheus Unbound* volume remains committed to an investigation of the confluence of politics and the natural world, and all of the poems in the volume herald liberty as a natural state, the absolute antithesis of the unnatural, man-made systems of oppression beneath which the world lies locked.

Prometheus as Redeemer

The eponymous hero of *Prometheus Unbound* functions as one of the play's symbols for the new age of love, and Shelley provides a number of images that underscore the links between Prometheus and Christ. In his Preface to the poem, Shelley compares his hero to quite another Biblical figure, but the correspondence between Prometheus and Christ nevertheless emerges in the subtext of the following passage:

> The only imaginary being resembling in any degree Prometheus, is Satan; and Prometheus is, in my judgement, a more poetical character than Satan because, in addition to courage and majesty and firm and patient opposition to omnipotent force, he is susceptible of being described as exempt from the taints of ambition, envy, revenge, and a desire for personal

> aggrandisement, which in the Hero of *Paradise Lost*, interfere with the interest. The character of Satan engenders in the mind a pernicious casuistry which leads us to weigh his faults with his wrongs and to excuse the former because the latter exceeded all measure. In the minds of those who consider that magnificent fiction with a religious feeling, it engenders something worse. But Prometheus is, as it were, the type of the highest perfection of moral and intellectual nature, impelled by the purest and truest motives to the best and noblest ends. (133)

In describing Prometheus in the image of Milton's Satan, Shelley constructs his hero in the tradition of a figure punished for his refusal to bow to the might of his creator. But in rejecting the aspects of Satan's character that tend toward self-interestedness, Shelley suggests Prometheus's correspondence to another Biblical figure, Jesus Christ. Though not traditionally represented in an oppositional relationship with his creator, Christ, like Satan, is a figure who complicates God's law by offering an alternative to the inflexibility of his Father's tyrannical rule. Shelley's description of Prometheus as "of the highest perfection of moral and intellectual nature," as "impelled by the purest and the truest motives to the best and noblest ends," sounds remarkably like his description of Christ in the "Essay on Christianity," in which Shelley argues that "Jesus Christ opposed with earnest eloquence the panic fears and hateful superstitions which have enslaved mankind for ages."[42] While Shelley faulted Christ for the highly derivative nature of his doctrines as well as for his belief (misguided, Shelley argued) in his direct descent from the tyrannical Father, Shelley nevertheless admired Christ even as he deplored Christianity, which he excoriated as the appropriation of a well-intentioned philosophy by an oppressive, politically self-interested regime.

Prometheus Unbound opens with the image of Prometheus chained to a rock and tortured as two female figures attend him, a scene that recalls the crucifixion of Christ and the ministrations of his mother and Mary Magdalene.[43] Halfway through the first act, Panthea experiences a vision of the crucified Christ as she overhears an exchange between Prometheus and the Furies, again reminding the reader of the correspondence between Shelley's hero and the figure of Jesus (1.585). Twice, the Spirits point to Prometheus as both the beginning and the end of their prophecy of wisdom, justice, love, and peace (1.796-800). Both creator and redeemer, God and Christ, Prometheus is, as God Himself claims to be in the book of Revelation, the Alpha and the Omega, the first and the last, the beginning and the end.[44] As the play continues, the correspondence between the functions of Prometheus and Christ comes into focus even more clearly: Prometheus will resuscitate and complete the mission of Christ which the world has forgotten—the establishment of an order based on peace and love. In some sense, Prometheus might be regarded as Christ's redeemer, or resurrector, because he will re-claim Christ's message from its tyrannical re-locutions and because his name will avoid the taint of its association

Mapping the Ideal

with oppression in the way that the name of the Christian savior has been forever besmirched.[45]

When Prometheus begins to fulfill his mission as the bringer of peace, Ione and Panthea recognize that even though the dawn of the new age will destroy the old system of language—including the codes of law, custom, and belief—language ultimately must be reborn as a new means of expression, enabling love to reverse sadness and oppression and to transform them into freedom and joy (1.752-779). As the play's first act concludes, Prometheus accepts his mission as peace-bringer, as the New Christ:

> ... I would fain
> Be what it is my destiny to be,
> The saviour and strength of suffering man,
> Or sink into the original gulph of things. . . .
>   There is no agony or solace left;
> Earth can console, Heaven can torment no more.
> . . . .
> I said all hope was vain but love— . . . .
>
> (1.815-820, 824)

Perhaps the most significant pairing of the figures of Prometheus and Christ occurs even before Shelley's hero accepts his mission, suggesting (as does line 816 in the extract above) that like Christ, Prometheus is fated to stand for the causes of freedom and love, that his acceptance of his "mission" merely marks his tacit acknowledgment of the heroic role already carved out for him. When in act 1 the Furies recognize the power of speech, language, and knowledge to strengthen Prometheus's resolve against Jupiter, they respond by tearing the veil (1.525-539), and just as the Veil of the Temple was suddenly and violently rent at the crucifixion of Jesus Christ[46]—the moment at which Jesus gave his life for the sins of man and saved the world through his own suffering and death—so, too, is this veil torn exactly at the moment the Furies articulate the key to Prometheus's victory—the power of language to oppose tyranny, the revolutionary force of contra-diction. In the most vivid reference to Christ, Shelley describes Prometheus in imagery clearly invoking Christ's crown of thorns, that symbolic marker placed upon Christ's head before his trial for blasphemy:[47] the Chorus sings,

> Past ages crowd on thee, but each one remembers,
> And the future is dark, and the present is spread
> Like a pillow of thorns for thy slumberless head.
>
> (1.561-563)

Eternal ("slumberless") even after his crucifixion, Prometheus, like Christ, stands as the fulfillment of a prophecy, as the figure of hope and redemption for the generations to follow. Like Christ, Prometheus is, without a doubt, the savior of the human race, and the only weapons he deploys against tyranny are language and love.

Gerald McNiece reads *Prometheus Unbound* as Shelley's argument that "[a]ll the static and dogmatic forms of worship, all that customarily passes for theology or ultimate and absolute truths of divinity must be eliminated. Jupiter is the one name for the older names and forms of worship."[48] More narrowly, if we read Prometheus as Christ, then Jupiter, the hero's tormentor under whose self-interested command Prometheus lies enchained—crucified—must, of course, be God. Richardson reads Prometheus and Jupiter in terms of each other, so that, at the play's beginning, each is the complement of the other: "Prometheus bound emblematizes Jupiter's power, while the god's 'unenvied' throne provides the standard against which Prometheus measures his psychic empire" (126); in short, "Fiend and Tyrant, God and Titan, begin to blur together as complementary terms in a struggle that paradoxically sustains twin antagonists, each committed to the other's downfall yet invested in the other's recognition" (129). As the play opens, the stagnant battle between Prometheus and Jupiter lies locked in a struggle for power, and the progress of the play explores how Prometheus's turn away from the tyrannical nature of his curse on Jupiter releases him entirely from the struggle for power, thus modeling contra-diction as a strategy for freeing Prometheus from torment and, by extension, liberating the world.

While Prometheus and Jupiter function as complements in the play's opening scene, as soon as Prometheus revokes his curse on Jupiter, Shelley develops the hero's complementary relationship with his lover, Asia, as the play's central paradigm. Curran reads Prometheus as the figure of logic and Asia as the figure of intuition (100), and he suggests that it is only in the melding of these two very different types of psychologies that liberation may occur. He extends his reading of the lovers by considering the first two acts, which he argues reveal the quite different natures of each lover's psychology: acts 1 and 3, which center on Prometheus and his struggles against Jupiter, demonstrate the obstinance of the oppressed which, ironically, empowers the oppressor; but acts 2 and 4, which center on Asia and Demogorgon, "[suggest] that the wisdom of the heart, once impassioned, subsumes intellectual analysis within a harmonious and progressive vision" (102-103). King-Hele's understanding of the place of Asia in Shelley's drama echoes Curran's: she is the figure without whom Prometheus would remain powerless to affect change in the world (197). In their union, the lovers combine knowledge and wisdom, coded throughout the play as, respectively, masculine and feminine embodiments of potential, but each lover lies powerless, impotently (because solitarily) awaiting the activation of the other. It would thus be a mistake to read Prometheus, as has Hoeveler, as the embodiment of the androgynous ideal (148, 150), for even if he were such a figure, he would be unable to bring about the liberation of the world, since in Shelley's system, the individual hero, no matter how noble his intentions, will be vanquished by tyranny and despair, as are the primary figures in *Alastor* and *Epipsychidion*. Only when the hero locates his ideal in the figure of an other does he begin to envision a viable alternative to a world that inevitably inveighs and ceaselessly conspires against the lovers; in short, liberation proceeds from the erotic union, and without Asia, Prometheus would remain crucified, both literally and figuratively.[49]

Language, Love, and Revolution

In his Preface to *Prometheus Unbound,* Shelley foregrounds love among the psychological conditions that set the stage for the return of liberty: " . . . until the mind can love, and admire, and trust, and hope, and endure, reasoned principles of moral conduct are seeds cast upon the highway of life which the unconscious passenger tramples unto dust, although they would bear the harvest of his happiness" (135). From the play's beginning, Shelley encourages his reader to appreciate the powers of language and love to undo the shackles of tyranny. Love is the mission and the message that emerge from the struggle between Prometheus and Jupiter; after all, although Prometheus was enchained for cursing the God of the universe, his release was brought about not by an act of hate (selfishness), but by an act of love (selflessness)—Prometheus' utterance of pity for his tormentor. Similarly, the love-relationship between Prometheus and Asia functions in the interest of liberty, as did the union of Laon and Cythna. Finally, the play's celebration of the erotic relationship between Asia and Lucifer (the latter Shelley's symbol for true goodness in the universe, as we saw at the beginning of *Laon and Cythna*), emphasizes the subversive eroticism that links all three figures in an abstract ménage-à-trois reminiscent of both the high sexuality of *Epipsychidion* and the incest of *Laon and Cythna*:

> Before Jove reigned
> [The Morning-Star, Lucifer] loved our sister Asia, and it came
> Each leisure hour to drink the liquid light
> Out of her eyes, for which it said it thirsted
> As one bit by a dipsas; and with her
> It made its childish confidence, and told her
> All it had known or seen, for it saw much,
> Yet idly reasoned what it saw; and called her—
> For whence it sprung it knew not nor do I—
> "Mother, dear Mother."
>
> (3.4.15-24)

Positioned as the mother of the figure of universal love, Asia re-places the Christian icons of God and Christ as an atemporal deity, a role her lover/double Prometheus also assumes, as I have discussed. We see in this pivotal description the convergence of three significant components that underwrite Asia's role in Shelley's play: the construction of Asia as one of the new deities in the age of peace and love; the doubling of Asia and Prometheus in their assumptions of the corrective roles to the Christian God and Christ; and the place of incest—or at least incestuous desire—in Lucifer's clearly sexual attraction to his own "'Mother, dear Mother,'" whose love provides him comfort and joy, and whose vision—"the liquid light / Out of her eyes"—serves as Lucifer's physical and psychical nourishment. In act 2, we discover that Asia becomes love itself and, as love (in the forms of selfless and reciprocal engagements) she remarks on her transformative power to undo systems of oppression (2.5.32-47).

Shelley's initial gestures toward the transformative power of love occur in the play's first act, in which he suggests that love may serve as the agent for a universal revolution, a sea-change from tyranny to liberation (1.763-779). The Chorus urges Prometheus to follow an agenda of love, even though its initial costs are high:

> Though Ruin now Love's shadow be,
> Following him destroyingly
>   On Death's white and winged steed,
> Which the fleetest cannot flee—
>   Trampling down both flower and weed,
> Man and beast and foul and fair,
> Like a tempest through the air;
> Thou shalt quell this Horseman [i.e., Ruin] grim,
> Woundless though in heart or limb.—
>
> (1.780-788)

Armored by the power of love, Prometheus gains immunity from injury and death, even though his struggles on love's behalf will bring him in direct confrontation with the enemies of love and eternity.

Cameron notes that the logistics of Prometheus and Asia's relationship duplicates the condition of Laon and Cythna's: both lovers have been separated by some tyrannical force and must defeat that force to achieve an erotic union, the effects of which will ultimately extend to all of humanity (510). Scrivener notes that, as in *Laon and Cythna*, "[i]n *Prometheus Unbound* sexual pleasure is celebrated as a triumph of liberated humanity, and pleasure itself, not ascetic purity, is the ruling idea of the poem" (154). But drawing on an argument first advanced by Stuart Sperry, Ulmer assesses the place of the erotic in Shelley's poem a bit more cautiously: "Shelleyan eros underlies the liberating promise of Promethean myth, but also its 'dark underside' and 'potential for either hope or despair'" (79). Asia's dream in act 2 clarifies the sexual component of the relationship between the poem's heroes. Gazing into Panthea's eyes, Asia envisions Panthea's sexually ecstatic dream of Prometheus and remembers the experience as her own, and in the dream, Prometheus utters Asia's name as he achieves orgasm (2.1.71-92). Panthea recalls that

Mapping the Ideal

> ... in the deep night
> My being was condensed, and as the rays
> Of thought were slowly gathered, I could hear
> His voice, whose accents lingered ere they died
> Like footsteps of far melody. Thy name,
> Among the many sounds alone I heard
> Of what might be articulated though still
> I listened through the night when sound was none.
>
> (2.1.85-92)

Asia interprets Panthea's vision as a prophecy of her union with Prometheus in an ecstatic world—that utopic space we will see at the play's end, where pleasure, love, and reciprocity replace the systems of tyrannical domination that keep individuals separated from one another by the false constructs of politics, prejudice, belief, and creed:

> I see a shade—a shape—'tis He, arrayed
> In the soft light of his own smiles which spread
> Like radiance from the cloud-smothered moon.
> Prometheus, it is thou—depart not yet!
> Say not those smiles that we shall meet again
> Within that bright pavilion which their beams
> Shall build o'er the waste world? The dream is told.
>
> (2.1.120-126)

Casting Prometheus as a radiant vision, Asia speaks in a voice that will find its echo in *Epipsychidion,* and in so doing she complicates the dynamics of gender that mark this exchange. Like so many of Shelley's male heroes— the speaker of *Epipsychidion* and the Poet of *Alastor* among them—Asia calls up a vision of her beloved and predicts that the mere force of that vision will transport the lovers to utopia. While this strategy fails in *Alastor* (because of the Poet's complete self-involvement) and in *Epipsychidion* (because Shelley cannot work his way out of the limits of signification), in *Prometheus Unbound,* Asia's vision succeeds in transporting the lovers to utopia, as we shall see, because it follows from an erotic union that is neither produced by mere fantasy (as in *Alastor*) nor barred by real-life structures of law and convention (as in *Epipsychidion*).

One reason the erotic union of *Prometheus Unbound* succeeds in manifesting utopia is that the lovers, like Laon and Cythna, engage in a relationship of complete reciprocity, equality, and selflessness. Neither is (de-) limited by the fantasy of the other, and each is dedicated not only to the couple's liberation but also to the freedom of humankind. In every way, Prometheus and Asia function as each other's perfect complement,[50] and their relationship stands in sharp contrast to the play's other pairings of Jupiter and Prometheus and of Jupiter and Thetis. Where Prometheus's opening speech reveals his refusal to give into selfishness and hatred,

Jupiter's opening lines emphasize his self-centeredness and bespeak his swaggering braggadocio:

> Ye congregated Powers of Heaven who share
> The glory and the strength of him ye serve,
> Rejoice! henceforth I am omnipotent.
> All else has been subdued to me—alone
> The soul of man, like unextinguished fire,
> Yet burns towards Heaven with fierce reproach and doubt
> And lamentation and reluctant prayer,
> Hurling up insurrection, which might make
> Our antique empire insecure, though built
> On eldest faith, and Hell's coeval, fear.
>
> (3.1.1-10)

Smug and proud, Jupiter exposes himself as the vain ruler of the universe, the tyrant whose self-satisfaction—like Count Cenci's—derives from the degree to which he dominates all others.

Just as Jupiter stands in opposition to Prometheus, so, too, does Jupiter's relationship with Thetis counter Prometheus' love for Asia. Prometheus and Asia engage in a relationship of equality and reciprocity, but Jupiter's relationship with Thetis is marked by inequities of power; Jupiter's rape of Thetis spawns the bastard—Demogorgon, the embodiment of oppression—whom the tyrant poses as pivotal to his selfish schemes:

> Even now I have begotten a strange wonder,
> That fatal Child, the terror of the Earth,
> Who waits but till the destined Hour arrive,
> Bearing from Demogorgon's vacant throne
> The dreadful might of ever living limbs
> Which clothed that awful spirit unbeheld—
> To redescend and trample out the spark . . .
> . . . .
> Two mighty spirits [Jupiter and Thetis], mingling, made a third [Demogorgon],
> Mightier than either—which unbodied now
> Between us, floats, felt although unbeheld,
> Waiting the incarnation, which ascends—
> Hear ye the thunder of the fiery wheels
> Griding the winds?—from Demogorgon's throne.—
> Victory! victory! Feels't thou not, O World,
> The Earthquake of his chariot thundering up
> Olympus?
>
> (3.1.18-24, 3.1.43-51)

The ruler of the universe, Jupiter presumes to announce the fate—the mission, even—of his son, whom he envisions as a henchman from whom all the world will cower in fear.

In his celebration of the bastard as the figure who will perpetuate his unchecked tyranny, Jupiter recalls Count Cenci, but, as is the case in *Laon and Cythna,* in *Prometheus Unbound* the bastard figure repudiates the tyrannical father to activate the transcendence of the lovers, and thus to hasten the liberation of the world. As King-Hele observes, "[Jupiter] believes Demogorgon will, like a dutiful child, stamp out the only troublesome 'spark' in the world, the soul of Man. After that, Jupiter expects to reign omnipotent" (183). But Demogorgon, the "fatal child" of his father's selfish schemes, lies dormant until the moment Curran describes as "the visionary marriage of Prometheus and Asia at the end of act 2 [which] fulfills the dream union of the act's beginning" and from which "Demogorgon comes to life, not as the child confidently expected by Jupiter and Thetis, but as the issue of Prometheus and Asia: a potential now informed and empowered" (101). In short, Demogorgon transfers his filial loyalty from one erotic couple to another, from oppressors to liberators, and in so doing he reverses the role his father had imposed upon him. Like a resentful Christ, Demogorgon turns his back on his father's wishes, and he chooses instead to assist Asia in her quest to re-unite with her lost lover. As Hoeveler notes, "Jupiter falls, not through Prometheus's efforts, but because of his own arrogant and misguided maleness," his blind assumption of patriarchal privilege (152). McNiece points to Demogorgon as the central figure in Shelley's model for the defeat of tyranny: in refusing his father's command, Demogorgon unmasks the tyrant's impotence, ripping from him the power to which he falsely and selfishly lays claim, for "[i]n Shelley's view, the tyrant, a creature of solitude and self-contempt, is destroyed when recognized as a corrupt mask" (230). Like Cythna's child, the bastard-offspring of rape transforms oppression into liberation simply by interrupting the oppressor's power: through his mere denunciation of the tyrant, the bastard of rape becomes the child of hope; in short, Demogorgon, conceived in the service of oppression, transforms himself—translates himself, even—through an act of sheer will and through the mechanism of language into the voice and vehicle of liberty.

Throughout *Prometheus Unbound,* Shelley explores the potential of language to work in concert with power, just as he has throughout the other works I have discussed. In act 2, Shelley points to the notion of a God of the universe as nothing more than a merely linguistic construction and, anticipating the object/*objet a* model of *Epipsychidion,* he concludes that "God" is a mere name that may be appropriated by any individual who declares supremacy over the universe (act 2, *passim*). Asia, too, intuits the purely linguistic nature of the concept of God, and she implores Demogorgon to "Utter his name—a world pining in pain / Asks but his name; curses shall drag him down" (2.4.29-30). The ambiguous response Demogorgon offers no less than three times—"He reigns" (2.4.28 and 2.4.31 [twice])—suggests that names are unimportant in the matrices of power, for whenever inequality is systematized, the resulting hierarchies will privilege some—or one—at the expense of others so that *some* figure will "reign" as long as the general condition of inequality persists. Jupiter also understands the linguistic nature of his apparent omnipotence, as we see at the beginning of act 3 when Jupiter, flanked by minor gods, celebrates his might in a speech that acknowledges the power of language to change the world:

> Ye congregated Powers of Heaven who share
> The glory and the strength of him ye serve,
> Rejoice! henceforth I am omnipotent.
> . . . .
> . . . [M]y curses through the pendulous air
> Like snow on herbless peaks, fall flake by flake
> And cling to it— . . . .
>
> (3.1.1-3, 3.1.11-13)

Jupiter's omnipotence begins with his declaration in line 3, the absence of which would have left his unchecked power unremarked and, by extension, unfelt. Jupiter's claim to omnipotence thus underscores the place of language in the accession of power as well as in power's maintenance, for if power is a force that, tending toward oppression, is coded into law, it proceeds from the utterance of self-proclaimed lawgivers—the self-appointed gods of the universe. Appropriately, the eventual proof of Jupiter's disempowerment will emerge as a crisis in incarnation, as the failure of his words to bring about the events they describe:

>   Ai! Ai!
> The elements obey me not . . . I sink . . .
> Dizzily down—ever, forever down—
> And, like a cloud, mine enemy above
> Darkens my fall with victory!—Ai! Ai!
>
> (3.1.79-83)

Following the heroes' ascent to the poem's utopia, Panthea reminds Prometheus and Asia of the power of language and its potential to be directed either in the service of oppression or in the service of liberation (4.316-318). In the new world, the Earth proclaims, the potential of language will be unlimited, and man will be free to direct language toward the project of peace and love:

> Language is a perpetual Orphic song,
>   Which rules with Dædal harmony a throng
> Of thoughts and forms, which else senseless and shapeless were.

> The Lightning is his slave; Heaven's utmost deep
> Gives up her stars, and like a flock of sheep
> They pass before his eye, are numbered, and roll on!
> The Tempest is his steed,—he strides the air;
> And the abyss shouts from her depth laid bare,
> "Heaven, hast thou secrets? Man unveils me, I have none."
> (4.415-423)

Prometheus Unbound concludes with Demogorgon's announcement that despotism has been defeated—at least for the present—and that love " . . . folds over the world its healing wings" (4.561). To mark the onset of the new age, Demogorgon names the four qualities that will sustain the reign of love and guarantee its perpetual victory over despotism, if ever despotism threatens to return:

> Gentleness, Virtue, Wisdom, and Endurance,—
> These are the seals of that most firm assurance
> Which bars the pit over Destruction's strength.
> (4.562-564)

Demogorgon closes the play by listing the Promethean abilities that characterize the age of love, and, in recognizing that " . . . Hope creates / From its own wreck the thing it contemplates," he returns the reader to the idea of the power of language to manifest ideals, the potential of words to serve the project of peace through the phenomenon of incarnation (4.573-574). Shelley's play thus concludes by acknowledging man's potential to align the power of language with the project of peace and love: God-like, redeemed man may appropriate language to breathe the age of freedom into existence, to incarnate liberty just as, according to legend, Prometheus stole from the gods the power to breathe life into clay figures, to incarnate life (liberty) from lifelessness (stillness, inanimation, oppression).

Landscape and Utopia

Shelley's Preface foregrounds the importance of the natural landscape to *Prometheus Unbound*: "This Poem was chiefly written upon the mountainous ruins of the Baths of Caracalla, among the flowery glades, and thickets of odoriferous blossoming trees which are extended in ever winding labyrinths upon its immense platforms and dizzy arches suspended in the air. The bright blue sky of Rome, and the effect of the vigorous awakening of spring in that divinest climate, and the new life with which it drenches the spirits even to intoxication, were the inspiration of this drama" (133). Shelley's composition of *Prometheus Unbound* was thus inspired to no minor degree by the vigor and promise of the natural world as it burst into spring, a demonstration of Abram's claim that "[h]uman languages, then, are informed not only by the structures of the human body and the human community, but by the evocative shapes and patterns of the more-than-human terrain. Experientially considered, language is no more the special property of the human organism than it is an expression of the animate earth that enfolds us" (90). Another poem in the *Prometheus Unbound* volume, "Ode to the West Wind," celebrates the political implications of the cycle of the seasons in order to attest to the potential of the "animate earth" to speak, as I have discussed. Cameron argues that, for Shelley, the egalitarian world will prove completely "in tune with nature, as depicted in [a]cts 3 and 4 of *Prometheus Unbound*" (167); and in the final act of the drama, Shelley articulates such a congruence explicitly as Earth rejoices in humankind's liberation from Jupiter:

> The Lightning is [Man's] slave; Heaven's utmost deep
> Gives up her stars, and like a flock of sheep
> They pass before his eye, are numbered, and roll on!
> The Tempest is his steed,—he strides the air;
> And the abyss shouts forth from her depth laid bare,
> "Heaven, hast thou secrets? Man unveils me, I have none."
> (4.418-423)

Just prior to these lines, Earth rebukes Jupiter for his tyrannical ways in an attack thoroughly couched in the language of the natural landscape (4.332-355). But in the passage above, Earth celebrates the transfer of power from Jupiter to Man, for he understands that in the utopic age of freedom, when man has been released from all forms of oppression, Man's benevolence—his selflessness—will elevate him above the selfish rule of Jupiter, and Man will emerge as the selfless god of the natural world, the benevolent ruler of a liberated universe.

Near the end of his Preface, Shelley considers the effect of the natural world on the mind of the poet: "A Poet, is the combined product of such internal powers as modify the nature of others, and of such external influences as excite and sustain these powers; he is not one, but both. Every man's mind is in this respect modified by all the objects of nature and art . . . . [The mind of the Poet] is the mirror upon which all forms are reflected, and in which they compose one form" (135). Shelley extends his initial image of the Roman landscape to metaphor, arguing that the effects of the poet's mind find form in the physical landscape: "The great writers of our own age are, we have reason to suppose, the companions and forerunners of some unimagined change in our social condition or the opinions which cement it. The cloud of mind is discharging its collected lightning, and the equilibrium between institutions and opinions is now restoring, or is about to be restored" (134). This transposition of nature from the physical landscape to the poet's psychology repeats the conflations of natural and psychological landscapes I have discussed in previous chapters, and it anticipates the pairing of nature and psychology we see throughout *Prometheus Unbound*.

The imagery of *Prometheus Unbound* is dominated by these links between political structures, psychological phenomena, and the landscape of the natural world. As the play opens, Prometheus' enslavement to Jupiter's tyrannical, anti-productive rule is manifested in the scene's setting: "*Scene: A Ravine of Icy Rocks in the Indian Caucasus. Prometheus is discovered bound to the Precipice. Panthea and* Ione *are seated at his feet*" (136). Curran argues that, aside from Miltonic Christianity, geography is the most important allegory Shelley develops throughout *Prometheus Unbound* (60). He points to the play's opening scene to demonstrate how landscape functions prophetically, for the "legendary" Indian Caucasus was "a focus of history and myth. . . . a landscape of fertile suggestiveness . . . " (61).[51] Shelley's placement of the crucified hero in an ironic setting underscores the rejuvenative powers of landscape and anticipates the inevitable transfiguration of the now-vanquished hero. In his initial speech, Prometheus bemoans his entrapment to a tyrannical ruler, and the landscape around him echoes his sense of isolation and hopelessness: for 1000 years, the ravine has been "Black, wintry, dead . . . without herb, / Insect, or beast, or shape or sound of life" (1.21-22). But as Holmes notes, this desolation "is also the winter of political hope, the frozen misery of the sick and hungry and the ignorant" (498).[52] Locked under the ice-floes of an apparently perpetual winter, the world awaits the eventual return of the spring that Prometheus' release will activate.

The play's opening thus sets the stage for the confluence of landscape, politics, and psychology upon which the utopic agenda of *Prometheus Unbound* depends. Three passages in act 2 extend this construction. First, in her dream of erotic union with Prometheus, Panthea takes the form of a dewdrop and is absorbed into Prometheus by the strength of his sun-like rays:

> . . . in the deep night
> My being was condensed, and as the rays
> Of thought were slowly gathered, I could hear
> [Prometheus's] voice, whose accents lingered ere they died
> Like footsteps of far melody. . . .
>
> (2.1.85-89)

Panthea's dream of sexual ecstasy metaphorizes an orgasmic encounter as an exchange between elements of the natural world, and the pleasures of lovemaking are translated as the approach of the sun over the cold, neverending night of winter:

> I lifted [my eyes]—the overpowering light
> Of that immortal shape was shadowed o'er
> By love; which, from his soft and flowing limbs
> And passion-parted lips, and keen faint eyes
> Stream'd forth like vaprous fire; and atmosphere
> Which wrapt me in its all-dissolving power
> As the warm ether of the morning sun
> Wraps ere it drinks some cloud of wandering dew.
>
> (2.1.71-78)

Significantly, Panthea's dream codes the female body as the site of potential, the corporeal register that functions in the same way as the natural landscape in the play's opening—as the site from which liberation will be born.

Later in act 2, Asia pays homage to the natural beauty of the world (2.3.11-16) and prophesies the coming of an intellectual revolution so powerful that it will radically alter the whole of the earth. Near the end of her speech, she assures Panthea that she can hear this inevitability in the landscape around them, once again emphasizing the female body's particular proximity to the project of revolution:

> —Hark! the rushing snow!
> The sun-awakened avalanche! whose mass,
> Thrice sifted by the storm, had gathered there
> Flake after flake, in Heaven-defying minds
> As thought by thought is piled, till some great truth
> Is loosened, and the nations echo round
> Shaken to their roots: as do the mountains now.
>
> (2.3.36-42)

Asia's metaphor is an important one, for not only does it suggest the correspondence between the landscapes of nature, politics, and individual psychologies, but it also demonstrates the ironic potential of inclement weather: like snows "sifted" by successive storms, the human mind under the "winter" of oppression sifts with each cataclysmic event, gradually refining into a superior form that will slip through the openings in the interlocking grid of oppression and break free from tyranny's stranglehold—an ironic effect of the swollenness of tyranny somatically inscribed upon the emaciated bodies of the oppressed, as we have seen in *Swellfoot the Tyrant*. We see in Asia's metaphor how the effects of political realities register at the level of landscape, both natural and psychological. In the turn from (a political) winter to spring, refined thoughts break free from winter's hold in an avalanche of freedom, and liberty bursts through the prison-bars of oppression.

One scene later, Asia confronts Demogorgon and demands to know

> ... who made terror, madness, crime, remorse,
> Which from the links of the great chain of things
> To every thought within the mind of man
> Sway and drag heavily—and each one reels
> Under the load towards the pit of death.
>
> (2.4.19-23)

Demogorgon answers her only obliquely, prefacing his non-answer by saying " ... —If the Abysm / Could vomit forth its secrets ... " (2.4.114-115). Quelling Demogorgon's fears about speaking against the tyrannical god of the universe, Asia poses Prometheus as the redeemer who will protect

Demogorgon from his master's wrath, and she, too, invokes the imagery of the natural landscape in describing Prometheus's triumphant ascent: "... —Prometheus shall arise / Henceforth the Sun of this rejoicing world" (2.4.126-127). At the conclusion of this exchange, Demogorgon releases blazing chariots into the sky and, as Holmes observes, "[t]he volcanic fire of history begins to erupt" (502). Time and again, a variety of narratives—some explicitly erotic (Panthea's dream) and others more clearly political (the exchange between Asia and Demogorgon)—draw the vocabulary of revolution from the imagery of the natural world, so that landscape metaphors function as the leitmotifs of freedom in the erotic cartography that plots utopia.

The utopia to which Prometheus and Asia ascend is, as I have suggested, a space marked by liminality and ooziness, or the melting of binary divisions, a phenomenon manifested most dramatically in the erasure of the border between the Earth and the Heavens.[53] Such a model is predicated in act 2 during Asia's epic descent to the underworld, where she realizes that the key to liberation lies in the complete dissolution of binary divisions (2.3.79-80).[54] In act 3, Hercules releases Prometheus from the chains of his enslavement and praises the hero as a symbol of strength. Liberated, Prometheus declares—decrees, one might say—that he and Asia shall never part from each other or from the assemblage of lovers who join them, and he calls for the entire community of lovers to retire to a cave, this poem's equivalent to *Laon and Cythna*'s shimmering island between the heavens (3.3.4-10). The imagery of the cave participates in traditional utopic landscape constructions; Bloch writes that in utopia, "an objective, a highly objective hollow space ... is opened," and in such openings, such caves, "the *aesthetic utopian meanings* of the beautiful, even of the sublime, reveal their conditions" (150). Prometheus' description of the cave is replete with images of the natural world, a condition key to Shelley's utopic landscapes, his vegetized wonderlands:

> There is a Cave
> All overgrown with trailing odorous plants
> Which curtain out the day with leaves and flowers
> And paved with veined emerald, and a fountain
> Leaps in the midst with an awakening sound;
> From its curved roof the mountain's frozen tears
> Like snow or silver or long diamond spires
> Hang downward, raining forth a doubtful light;
> And there is heard the ever-moving air
> Whispering without from tree to tree, and birds,
> And bees; and all around are mossy seats
> And the rough walls are clothed with long soft grass;
> A simple dwelling, which shall be our own.
>
> (3.3.10-23)

The cave combines elements of the utopic spaces we have seen in both *Laon and Cythna* and *Epipsychidion,* yet it corrects the pessimism of those poems by locating utopia upon the Earth, rather than in an imaginary space between the heavens or in the reaches of an elaborate erotic fantasy. A vegetized wonderland, the design, structure, and decoration of the cave all follow from natural forms, and the movement of the wind outside of the cave functions as an oracle that heralds the dawn of the new age of peace and love. Even gems are stripped of their associations with oppression—in the civilized world, they are regarded as markers of personal wealth and power, but here they are re-naturalized as part of the cave's decor, now sparkling testaments to the beauty of the unadorned, unencumbered world. In this utopia, which Richardson describes as "the ultimate classless society of interrelated minds" (142), landscape functions as a language, so that the beauty and productivity of natural forms articulate the promise of the new age of freedom.

Like the utopic space to which Laon and Cythna retire, the cave Prometheus describes serves as the sepulchre of time: " . . . we will sit and talk of time and change / As the world ebbs and flows, ourselves unchanged—" (3.3.23-24). Hoeveler interprets this death of time in terms of the evolution of the lovers' relationship, which, having progressed to a state of perfection, finally achieves immortality: " . . . love for an ideal beloved is not merely a transition from the mortal to the immortal, but instead produces a complete union of the two states" (121). Eternal and yet still quite human, Prometheus and Asia step out of the chasm between life and death to enter into the realm of eternity.[55] The cave also serves as the birthplace—or re-birthplace—of artistic production, a cradle for a new age of art now divorced from the tyrannical agendas it had been made to serve in the fallen world. At long last liberated, art, too, may be re-born:

> . . . the mind . . .
> . . . .
> Shall visit us, the progeny immortal
> Of Painting, Sculpture, and rapt Poesy
> And arts, though unimagined, yet to be.
>
> (3.3.50-56)

Prometheus's cave is the womb that engenders the entire potentiality of the new world, the re-birthplace of existing arts and the fertile ground from which all new artistic forms shall emanate, a claim and condition that mirrors Shelley's insistence in his "Essay on Christianity" that the proliferation of knowledge will lead to justice and equality, that utopia follows from enlightenment. In the womb-like utopia of *Prometheus Unbound,* in this magic space of peace, love, and knowledge, " . . . veil by veil evil and error fall . . . / Such virtue has the cave and place around" (3.3.62-63).[56] Clearly a feminine space, the cave corrects the rigid inflexibility of the patriarchal system over which it has triumphed, and it assumes the feminine function

Mapping the Ideal

of fecundity as the space from which new artistic forms and political hope are born—a marked contrast to the sterility of the systematic grid of patriarchal order beneath which all things lie paralyzed, trapped. At last, the cave marks the triumph of love over time, peace over history, and creativity over oppression.

Bloch insists that "[t]*he concrete utopia stands at the horizon of every reality*" (155); and while Shelley displaces the utopias of *Laon and Cythna* and *Epipsychidion* to purely imaginative spaces, he situates Prometheus's cave in a decidedly real-world location. *Prometheus Unbound* thus corrects the pessimism of the earlier works by arguing that liberty may be found in life rather than after death; as Curran has noted, "to depend on blandishments of a heavenly pantheon spun from wish fulfillment is to delude oneself into contentment with worldly justice, to play into Jupiter's hands" (111). By locating the space of liberty in the real world, *Prometheus Unbound* offers an alternative to the problematic utopias we have seen in *Epipsychidion* and *Laon and Cythna,* and the poem suggests that any reader may access this space through a mere shift in perspective, a new way of thinking about the world. The play's opening act anticipates this ideology, as Richardson notes, for it is "Prometheus's turn from introspective anguish to self-distancing sympathy [that] disarms the Furies' temptation of its crippling force"; indeed, "Prometheus seeks now to end his three millennia of isolation by renewing a sympathetic relation that would replace and counteract the enclosing struggle for power with Jupiter," so that "[s]elf-liberation becomes the foundation for a new social order" (132, 133, 145).[57] In act 4, Shelley suggests that the spirits released over the peaceful world emanate from within the human mind, thus implying that peaceful revolution proceeds from Man's imaginative potential:

> We come from the mind
> Of human kind
> Which was late so dusk and obscene and blind;
> Now 'tis an Ocean
> Of clear emotion,
> A Heaven of serene and mighty motion.
>
> (4.93-98)

In the age of intellectual revolution, a simple shift in perspective rips the many veils of custom, law, and belief from humans' eyes so that we may see the world anew, no longer blinded by the inequities of class, tribe, and nation that marked the age of tyranny (3.4.190-204).

The play's final act reiterates Shelley's investment in the confluence of landscape, politics, and psychology by depicting the liberation of the human mind in terms of the transformation of the natural landscape. Continuing their speech, the Chorus of Spirits sings,

> From that deep Abyss
> Of wonder and bliss

> Whose caverns are chrystal palaces;
> From those skiey towers
> Where Thought's crowned Powers
> Sit watching your dance, ye happy Hours!
>
> (4.99-104)

First projecting the effects of the liberated mind onto the landscape, which bursts from "dusk" onto "an Ocean / Of clear emotion," Shelley then describes the effects of liberation in terms of what seems to be the orgasm of the natural universe. The shock of liberation proves so great that its force registers even on the surface of the Moon, whose topographical alterations suggest the spasms of sexual pleasure, as well as the phenomenon of mixing and melting—commingling—so key to Shelley's model of love:

> The snow upon my lifeless mountains
> Is loosened into living fountains,
> My solid Oceans flow and sing and shine
> A spirit from my heart bursts forth,
> It clothes with unexpected birth
> My cold bare bosom: Oh! it must be thine
> On mine, on mine!
>
> Gazing on thee I feel, I know,
> Green stalks burst forth, and bright flowers grow
> And living shapes upon my bosom move:
> Music is in the sea and air,
> Winged clouds soar here and there,
> Dark with the rain new buds are dreaming of:
> 'Tis Love, all Love!
>
> (4.356-369)

In response to his lover's exaltation, the Earth, too, describes the orgasmic intensity it experiences in the toppling of tyranny by love:

> [A spirit] interpenetrates my granite mass,
> Through tangled roots and trodden clay doth pass
> Into the utmost leaves and delicatest flowers;
> Upon the winds, among the clouds 'tis spread,
> It wakes a life in the forgotten dead,
> They breathe a spirit up from their obscurest bowers
>
> And like a storm, bursting its cloudy prison
> With thunder and with whirlwind, has arisen
> Out of the lampless caves of unimagined being,
> With earthquake shock and swiftness making shiver
> Thought's stagnant chaos, unremoved forever,
> Till Hate and Fear and Pain, light-vanquished shadows, fleeing,

> Leave Man, who was a many-sided mirror
> Which could distort to many a shape of error
> This true fair world of things— . . .
> . . . .
> Man, one harmonious Soul of many a soul
> Whose nature is its own divine controul
> Where all things flow to all, as rivers to the sea.
>
> (4.400-402)

Echoing the language of "On Love," Shelley argues that in the pleasure of intellectual revolution, man is freed from what Blake described as "the mind-forg'd manacles" that enchain him (Pl. 46), and his freedom, his ascension to peace and love, is felt not only by the earth, but by the entire universe, whose "shiver[s]" of pleasure drive out the forces of tyranny (4.379). As Brown observes, "[t]he joys of sexual intercourse are raised to a cosmic level in *Prometheus Unbound,* which in its conclusion is a paean of universal eroticism. Earth's volcanic rebirth of love is repeatedly figured in terms of orgasmic release, with nature, at last resuscitated from its winter of sensual death in Christian repression, asceticism, and self-contempt, spending itself in love's delight" (61). Earth observes that, now united in liberty,

> Man, [is] one harmonious Soul of many a soul
> Whose nature is its own divine controul
> Where all things flow to all, as rivers to the sea.
>
> (4.400-402)

Earth's imagery tropes human liberation in terms of topographic commingling, so that the breakdown of all barriers of difference—the undoing of the vanishing points of tyranny—unites all humans as one, just as all rivers collect and become inseparable from one another in the vast sea. In short, the orgasmic cataclysm of man's protracted release from tyranny registers in this world and beyond to re-construct the entire universe in the image of Shelley's agenda of peace and love, and the erotic cartography of the redeemed world of *Prometheus Unbound* echoes the oozy pleasures of the lovers' ceaseless reciprocity. In plotting utopia, Shelley co-aligns erotic and political engagement, whose effects interpenetrate the natural world to manifest the utopia which in *Epipsychidion* disappears into that "far Eden of the purple East," but which in *Prometheus Unbound* appears first in the lovers' embrace and then, through the power of their erotic energy, across the diverse landscapes—physical and psychological, natural and man-made—of the redeemed world.

∞ ∞ ∞ ∞ ∞

In his study of what he calls the "art history of nature," Warnke notes that "after the French Revolution the air was perhaps so full of political watchwords that the slogans of Liberty could actually be read into the lava spewed forth by Mount Vesuvius," and he reproduces an image by

Desperet entitled "The Third Eruption of the Volcano of 1789" in which the word "LIBERTÉ" appears in volcanic matter as it spews straight up into the air (95, 110).⁵⁸ According to Warnke, "the upheaval in human affairs seemed to be accompanied by an equally violent upheaval in nature. Freaks of nature that seemed to defy natural laws were interpreted as confirming the revolutionary impulse" (95). Warnke's observation points to a transhistorical regard for nature as a space outside of order, where one discombobulated by the turmoil of society returns to seek solace and reprieve: "There was a time when we liked to think of landscape as something that compensated us for a loss. In it we sought what was no longer ours by right. It was a refuge for the civilized, in which they could experience what was missing, suppressed or forgotten in the economic, social or private world they inhabited. Landscape could be deliberately sought as an ideal destination only when human life was no longer led in natural landscape conditions" (145). Warnke argues that landscape, idealized and thus constructed as the other of society, figures as the place to which those who have been marginalized by society wish to return. He suggests that we regard this crossing of an imaginary self/other, subject/object line, this return to the place of liberty (nature) by way of a rejection of the space of oppression (society), as an empowering move, since a marginalized figure—society's other—turns away from the order that has rejected him to establish a new place in a prelapsarian realm where nature exists in an apparently pristine—an uncorrupted, we might say—condition.

This movement of a disenfranchised being from the social to the natural realm is far more complicated, however, than Warnke suggests. For even as one so moving asserts his subjectivity to claim his own place in the world, and even as he returns to what seems to be an earlier—even a "primary"— condition, that individual in fact remains an exile, a being who has been jettisoned from the sphere of privilege, law and order, pushed away from the world into which he was born and "out" into a sort of frontier space.⁵⁹ Like the frontier, the natural world thus conceived is located at both the beginning and the end of history: a blank slate upon which an individual's narrative has yet to be plotted—utopia is the beginning of history—but it is also the space, the plot, at which one arrives after having been expelled from society—and thus it is the end of history. The exile, moving from society "back"—or forward—to nature, finds himself at the end of one life and the beginning of another, in the void of a space that is both before and after, at the beginning and the end of a historical record. It is in this void, this no-space of a post-historic Eden, that Shelley finally situates the heroes of *Epipsychidion, Laon and Cythna,* and *Prometheus Unbound*.⁶⁰ Far from sinking beneath the weight of nostalgia, Shelley's revolutionary no-space is displaced into the future, underscoring the poet's hope for its perpetual manifestation rather than his mourning of the vision as an artifact of an irrecoverable world. To put it simply, Shelley's lovers do not retreat to spaces that have already been lost, that have already disappeared; quite to the contrary, they move forward to landscapes—natural, psychological, and political—that have yet to evolve. In this way, Shelley's visionary poems anticipate the birth of liberty rather than looking mournfully—or nostalgically—back at the death of a Golden Age that has already been forfeited.

Notes

1. The symbolic physicality of Cythna's child anticipates one of the means through which oppression gets inscribed in *The Cenci*, as I have discussed: in *Laon and Cythna*, the echo of Cythna's aspect in the face of the child suggests the potential for that child to follow her in its ideological sympathies and, thus, to work as an agent for liberty-through-love, a fate that will in fact be proven by the whole of the poem; on the other hand, the (predicted, desired) echo of Count Cenci's aspect in face of the offspring of his rape of Beatrice will, he believes, mark that child as an embodiment of his power over her, a tangible reminder of his repeated "rape" of Beatrice, first literally and forever after symbolically in the physiognomic echo of the legacy born of that union.
2. Shelley, *Laon and Cythna; Or, The Revolution of the Golden City, A Vision of the Nineteenth Century in the Stanza of Spenser*, in *The Complete Poetical Works of Percy Bysshe Shelley*, ed. Thomas Hutchinson (New York: Oxford University Press, 1934; New York: Oxford University Press, 1956), 12.40.
3. A number of critics cite *Laon and Cythna* as Shelley's retelling of the French Revolution; in terms of my reading, the most useful of these are Duff and Scrivener. David Duff argues that "the Revolution of the Golden City bears an unmistakable resemblance to the French Revolution," and he discusses the Revolution-era political theory that informs Shelley's composition of the poem; see Duff, *Romance and Revolution: Shelley and The Politics of a Genre* (New York: Cambridge University Press, 1994), 158. Scrivener, too, recognizes the importance of the events of 1789 to Shelley's thought, and he concludes that "[t]he French Revolution is a point of reference because revolution [seemed] imminent in England" at the time Shelley composed *Laon and Cythna* (129). In Scrivener's reading, "the French Revolution parallels and allusions [in *Laon and Cythna*] are ways of trying to comprehend the present and shape the future" (128). Scrivener states bluntly that "Shelley wanted *Laon and Cythna* viewed as a political action. One should not despair at the French Revolution's failure . . . . [for] [t]emporary defeats are simply a part of the process," and he concludes that the poem should be contextualized not only in terms of that pivotal event, but also in terms of "the English situation of 1816-1817" (123, 128). Scrivener examines *Laon and Cythna* to demonstrate how the structure of the poem affirms Shelley's belief in gradual progression, or reform, so that every defeat is mitigated by some other victory (127), and he concludes that "however remote the

poem appears from the realities of 1817 politics, it is actually an attempt to arouse the leisure-class liberals to lead a radical social transformation" (125).

4. Shelley underscores the importance of personal relationships to models of political action in a letter purportedly written to Longman and Company, the publishers of Thomas Moore's *Lalla Rookh*: "I have attempted in the progress of my work to speak to the common & elementary emotions of the human heart, so that, tho it is the story of violence & revolution, it is relieved by milder pictures of friendship & love & natural affections" (*Letters* 1:563 and n).

5. For discussions about the extent of Shelley's revisions to *Laon and Cythna,* see Cameron (312), King-Hele (86), and Michael O'Neill, *Percy Bysshe Shelley: A Literary Life* (New York: St. Martin's Press, 1990), 49.

6. As I have suggested throughout this book, in Shelley's model, the domestic sphere of home and family functions as a microcosmic model for the world at large, for even as the domestic order reflects social values and political structures, it is from the domestic order (for example, the family relationship that Beatrice shares with her survivors, or the fellow-feeling that Julian and Maddalo share with the Maniac) that alternative social models emerge.

7. Although a number of scholars have written insightful critiques of *Laon and Cythna,* the most useful in terms of my own argument are those by Brown, Cameron, Duff, Hogle, Kelly, Scrivener, and Ulmer. Brown considers the function of erotic union in the poem and discusses the poem's evidence of Shelley's feminist political vision (59, 181). Cameron treats the place of *Laon and Cythna* in Shelley's canon as well as the place of the poem's heroine in the history of feminist literature in English, and he argues that the poem demonstrates Shelley's understanding of the importance of the intellectual in a post-revolutionary world (311, 322, 324). Duff, whose chapter on *Laon and Cythna* offers perhaps the most thorough and original of the readings I cite here, considers the poem in terms of Shelley's meta-textual concerns as well as the poet's development of those interests in *Prometheus Unbound,* and he demonstrates the political use of the erotic as it is manifested here and in other works by both Percy and Mary Shelley (154-216, *passim*). Hogle examines what he describes as the "primary narcissism" that informs the relationship between the poem's heroes (97, 101) and argues that *Laon and Cythna* demonstrates "the movement of desire" to be the force behind both freedom and oppression (96-97)—something my comparison of *Laon and Cythna* to *The Cenci* will suggest. Kelly argues that *Laon and Cythna* proves Shelley's dedication to a feminist agenda, and he reads that text alongside Mary Shelley's *Frankenstein* to demonstrate how both works engage in a "revolutionary social critique" (74). Scrivener, who describes *Laon and Cythna* as Shelley's "uncompromising vision of the ideal" (107), discusses the poem's model of love-as-victory (125), argues that the French Revolution and contemporary literary responses to it helped shape Shelley's poem (128-129), and suggests that feminism marks *Laon and Cythna*'s "most atypical aspect" (132). Finally, Ulmer considers the poem's investigation of the leaguing of language and oppression (122)—a phenomenon we have seen throughout the works I have examined thus far—but points to Laon as a figure who

learns to appropriate the coercive power of language and to recuperate that power in the interest of freedom (70).

8. My definition of landscape remains rather broad, as my readings in Chapters III and IV have demonstrated. To wit, I include both physical and psychological formations in that category as well as an array of spaces in the natural world—the earth, the sea, the heavens—and, finally, the markers of human civilization that dot the natural landscape, such as the Maniac's tower in *Julian and Maddalo*. In short, my notion of "landscape" derives from the kind of picture, or perspective, a subject experiences upon gazing at the world about him: in taking in the objects that make up the view, the subject forms an image of the landscape itself, and in examining those elements, in contemplating the "picture" he has taken, the subject gains perspective—an altered way of thinking about—the world of which he is a part, or, in the case of the exile, the world from which he is *apart*.

9. As Scrivener notes, Shelley's "philosophical anarchism establishes a political ideal, a utopia, toward which society is moving in stages; it rejects a millenarian logic whereby utopia could be achieved immediately; it accepts politics as a process of gradual reforms and compromise, as well as ethical idealism" (xii).

10. I refer to Shelley's poem as "the bastard offspring of the French Revolution" for a variety of reasons. The poem issues from a failed union—a political ideal that turned into the very tyranny it sought to overcome. Unplanned, unwanted, unaffordable, the effects of the French Revolution remained, like the (stereotypical) figure of the bastard, an emblem of poor judgement and regret, a constant reminder of the breaking of an ideal, the recall of a promise. Conceived in selfish passion without regard for the well-being of its future, the bastard, like the Revolution, is the product of carelessness and haste, rather than of love, compassion, and a real dedication to an agenda of liberty. Finally, my description of Shelley's poem as a "bastard offspring" of the French Revolution demonstrates the way in which the poem functions like a particularly sexualized and "othered" body to disrupt hegemonic assumptions, and the epithet anticipates my discussion of the bastard in the poem—Cythna's child by Othman, who, as I discuss below, re-writes the teleology of rape by posing the so-called "illegitimate" as a self-conscious symbol for the triumph of liberty over oppression, thus reinscribing "bastardry" as liberation by translating selfishness into love.

11. In particular, I am thinking of the following language from "On Love": "Love ... is that powerful attraction towards all that we conceive or fear or hope beyond ourselves when we find within our own thoughts the chasm of an insufficient void and seek to awaken in all things that are, a community with what we experience within ourselves. If we reason, we would that the airy children of our brain were born anew within another's; if we feel, we would that another's nerves should vibrate to our own, that the beams of their eyes should kindle at once and mix and melt into our own, that lips of motionless ice should not reply to lips quivering and burning with the heart's best blood. This is Love" (*SPP* 473); and, even more directly, "I know not the internal constitution of other men, or even of thine whom I now address" (473).

12. In his discussion of fluvial myths, Simon Schama remarks on the ship as a traditional metaphor for the Church; see Schama, *Landscape and Memory* (New York: Alfred A. Knopf, 1995), 290. Throughout my discussions of *Laon and Cythna* and *Prometheus Unbound*, I consider the place of religion in Shelley's vision, and while I remain cognizant of Shelley's desire to dismantle the tenets of religion that perpetuate tyranny (i.e., blind obedience), I also find useful the correspondence between Shelley's vision of a world liberated by the selfless acts of lovers and the Christian plan of salvation. However, Shelley's model of liberty-through-love replaces the single male hero-figure with the erotic couple, whose sexual relationship sketches the contours for a map of liberation, as I have suggested. But Shelley's location of that couple in a beautiful temple, a kind of heaven Shelley approaches by way of a boat, draws so heavily on traditional religious metaphors that I think that correspondence cannot and should not be overlooked. In rescuing the hallmarks of Christianity (selflessness and salvation) from the shackles of patriarchal tyranny under which they have labored (a belief in a jealous God and the glorification of the individual hero), Shelley builds a new mythology out of the old, appropriating Christian signs and symbols and re-animating—re-incarnating—them with erotic energy.

13. Scrivener agrees that Shelley's purpose in writing *Laon and Cythna* is to encourage "revolutionary principles and ideals" (120). He describes the poem's political agenda in terms of "Godwinian anarchy, nonviolence, the 'bloodless dethronement' of the oppressors, 'universal toleration and benevolence of true philanthropy'" (the original language is Shelley's), and he locates vegetarianism, feminism, egalitarianism, and freedom of thought among the poem's ideals (124, 133). Duff comments on what we might refer to as the "percolating potential" implicit throughout *Laon and Cythna*—Shelley's hope that the poem will speak to later generations of political radicals to construct their own agendas and inform their actions (214).

14. As Laon delivers his message of peace, a soldier pierces his hand with a spear, and the stigmata somatically inscribes the peace-bringer as a revisionary Christ-figure (1774-1800). In both his message of tolerance and love and his status as a revisionary Christ-figure, Laon anticipates the figure of Prometheus, whom Shelley takes up as a revolutionary symbol about one year later in *Prometheus Unbound*, a poem to which I devote the second part of this chapter.

15. Here, I am thinking of lines from the Preface I have already quoted: "I have sought to enlist the harmony of metrical language, the ethereal combinations of the fancy, the rapid and subtle transitions of human passion, all those elements which essentially compose a poem, in the cause of a liberal and comprehensive morality" (99-100).

16. One could argue that Shelley's solitary wanderers remain equally invested in erotic relationships (for example, the *Alastor* Poet's obsession with the veiled maiden of whom he has dreamed), but in the case of the solitary wanderer who pursues his own fantasy, the "erotic" relationship is completely inwardly turned, completely solipsistic. My understanding of the erotic—as a category that describes relationships between and among individuals and groups—precludes such self-

absorbed models. In *Laon and Cythna*—as well as in, for example, *Prometheus Unbound, Epipsychidion, Julian and Maddalo,* and *The Cenci*—Shelley rejects solipsism and celebrates outwardly directed erotic engagement, and he demonstrates how the building of personal relationships dedicated to mutuality and reciprocity pave the way for the re-building of the larger world.

17. The cross-gendered exchanges that mark the story's overarching narrative duplicate a scene in canto 7 where Cythna, in captivity, imagines herself first as pregnant and then as nourishing and playing with a daughter who bears a strong resemblance to Laon (2974-2991). The place of maternity as a counter to oppression underwrites the scene, which also anticipates the redemptive function of the so-called "illegitimate" child, the bastard who, at the poem's end, delivers Laon and Cythna from the world that excoriates them.

18. Cythna is not to be confused with the Shelleyan *femme fatale,* for although she embodies Laon's psychic projections—just as the veiled maiden embodies the Poet's thoughts in *Alastor*—Cythna is a real person, Laon's actual sister. In uniting with her, Laon engages in outwardly directed love, not in the solipsism that traps the Poet of *Alastor* within his own fantasy and ultimately starves him of human companionship to such a degree that, in the end, he dies of disappointment and fatigue.

19. I juxtapose "language" and "force" to emphasize the incongruity between what Shelley regards as real progress toward liberty as mediated through language and the mere *illusion* of progress toward freedom that results from forceful physical confrontation (specifically, violent revolution). However, as my discussion throughout has suggested, I do unveil Shelley's deployment of language as a form of seduction—flirting, teasing, and sometimes even tricking the reader (for example, by veiling "public" matters beneath sexy narratives). Thus, I understand the potency of Shelley's language in terms of its very real, physiological effects on his readers; by extension, I also understand the ability of Shelley's language to motivate readers to some sort of action, but I see that action as the result of communication, of rational discussion, and therefore, I believe, such action stands in sharp contrast to acts of force motivated by ignorance and hatred and manifested in physical and psychological domination.

20. King-Hele also identifies Cythna as "the first 'new woman' in English poetry" (85), and Duff notes that it is Cythna, not Laon, who realizes the way out of disappointment and oppression (170, 205). Hoeveler, on the other hand, offers an alternative reading of Shelley's construction of Cythna, which she dismisses as antifeminist (98).

21. Ulmer considers Shelley's reasons for distancing himself and Mary from the incest-motif at some length (53).

22. The excoriation Shelley anticipates casts the poet and his wife as intellectual exiles in the sense that Edward W. Said describes: "Exile for the intellectual in this metaphysical sense is restlessness, movement, constantly being unsettled, and unsettling others"; see Said, *Representations of the Intellectual: The 1993 Reith Lectures* (New York: Pantheon Books, 1994), 53. I depart from Said's view of the trajectory of exile, however, for Said describes the exile as participating in a dialectical engagement with the past he has lost and with the present in which he suffers that loss

(60); Shelley's sense of exile is decidedly not dialectical, however, for the poet's exiles contemplate the world from a remove in a conversation not between two elements, but at least three—the past, the present, and *the future,* to which Shelley's exiles look for the hope of change. Said's notion of the exile is far less optimistic than Shelley's, not to mention far more time-bound: Shelley's exiles never mourn the loss of a past that may never be recovered, but they draw instead on the lessons of the past and on the wisdom of their present situation in order to envision—and to activate—a future in which liberty reigns, a future Deborah Elise White characterizes as "the promise of dawn and the artifice of poiesis—a bright and mourning star" (163), a characterization that reminds us of utopia's overlappings of pleasure and pain, or optimism and disappointment: utopia is the place for which we believe ourselves destined, but the place that remains tantalizingly out of reach, and so just from outside of it we float in exile. I discuss the "place" of the Shelleyan exile at much greater length in the conclusion to this chapter. (In writing above that "Shelley's exiles never mourn," I deliberately echo lines from Oscar Wilde's *The Ballad of Reading Gaol*, which were chosen as the writer's epitaph: "For his mourners will be outcast men / And outcasts always mourn.")

23. Kathleen M. Kirby, *Indifferent Boundaries: Spatial Concepts of Human Subjectivity* (New York: The Guilford Press, 1996), ix.

24. Timothy Morton discusses the subject of Shelley and ecology at some length; see Morton, "Shelley's Green Desert," *Studies in Romanticism* 35 (Summer 1996): 409-430; and Morton, *Shelley and the Revolution in Taste: The Body and the Natural World* (Cambridge: Cambridge University Press, 1994).

25. "Ode to the West Wind" extols the perpetual power of nature in moving the world through cycles of oppression to those of liberation, coded in the poem as decay and death (oppression) and as the spring of new life (liberation):

> Wild spirit, which art moving everywhere;
> Destroyer and Preserver; hear, O hear!
> . . . .
> The trumpet of a prophecy! O wind,
> If Winter comes, can Spring be far behind?

(SPP 14-15, 69-70)

26. My image deliberately gestures toward a seminal work of twentieth-century Romantic criticism, M. H. Abrams' *The Mirror and the Lamp: Romantic Theory and the Critical Tradition* (New York: Oxford University Press, 1953).

27. Shelley's phrase "the dark idolatry of self" reminds us of "self-anatomizing," the dysfunction Shelley marks as the curse of the Cenci family, the tendency toward narcissism and an investment in the self at the expense of all others which, at its most extreme, is manifested in and as sadism.

28. Obviously, the length of this journey proves significant because it corresponds to the three days between the crucifixion and resurrection of Jesus Christ, that figure who informs Shelley's construction of Laon throughout this poem, and of other selflessly invested hero-liberators throughout his *œuvre*.

29. Negotiations of marginality and centrality prove particularly difficult to disentangle, especially in narratives dedicated to the complicating of such oppositions. As much feminist theory has argued, the marginal (i.e., woman) truly occupies a central role in traditional (patriarchal) culture, for at least two reasons: first, because it defines the edges, the borders, of the central/the empowered, the marginal/disempowered also functions as its limit, as a boundary and, thus, a restriction to the central/empowered, so that marginality/disempowerment contains, polices, and controls centrality/empowerment; second, the central/empowered remain so focused on the marginal/disempowered as a threat that the marginal assumes a place of great cultural weight—a preoccupation for the central, a site of cathexis—because the marginal, ironically, occupies a position at and in the very middle of the space of centrality/empowerment. In both formulations, the places of the central and the marginal remain as ambiguous, as shifting—indeed, as oozy—as the functions of each category, and any complete disconnection of one from the other proves impossible, suggesting finally the radical contingency the marginal and the central share and, thus, their potential for commingling, for a giving in to liberating embrace.

30. Bonca offers one explanation for the apparent necessity of death as a doorway to Shelley's utopia: "Shelley's deep distrust of human sexuality usually compels him to escort his fictive lovers through 'the dark gate of death' before he allows them the consummate (Shelleyan) form of mingled being: transcendental intercourse (*Alastor*, 1.211)" (175). I depart from Bonca in such thinking, since I believe Shelley situates sexuality as a key means for achieving "transcendental" union, completion; and, as I have discussed, the cartographies of his utopias follow from the forms of the lovers' intercourse, itself the most extreme version of *verbal* intercourse, of mere communication, the balm so central to much Romantic writing, Charles Robert Maturin's *Melmoth the Wanderer*, Mary Shelley's *Frankenstein* and Samuel Taylor Coleridge's *The Rime of the Ancient Mariner* three among many such works.

31. I borrow the term "ennobled" from Shelley's language, which I quote in the epigraph to Chapter III. In his letter to Thomas Jefferson Hogg, Shelley discusses the effect of his relationship with Mary Godwin as ennobling, as having made him "a more true & constant friend, a more useful lover of mankind, a more ardent asserter of truth & virtue—above all more consistent, more intelligible[,] more true" (*Letters* 1:402).

32. In his discussion of fluvial myths—a conceptual category in which I would lump *Epipsychidion, Laon and Cythna,* and *Prometheus Unbound,* since each concludes with an erotic couple crossing some sort of body of water to arrive at utopia—Schama notes that such narratives foreground the circulation and, thus, the infinite cyclicality of water (258). Schama's description of bodies of water as "temporal and topographical loops" (261) meshes exactly with the place of water in the works I have named: water operates as a permeable boundary that both encloses and releases space and time, so that, in many ways, Shelley reminds us of water's function as the nexus to infinity.

33. By situating Cythna as the incarnator of *Laon and Cythna*, I replace the patriarchal notion of a (male-identified) God in Heaven (who functions as the incarnator, or "first voice" of the universe) with an alternative model similar to the one Beatrice invokes at the end of *The Cenci* when she speaks so lovingly of death, the eternal peace, as an "all-embracing Mother." My description of Cythna as the poem's "first voice" avoids the trap of simply replacing a male-identified deity with a female-identified one, however, for it re-distributes the "role" of God away from the individual patriarch to the erotic couple, who remain dedicated to the freedom of all people: even though Cythna's is the poem's "first voice," that voice exists only as it is mediated to the poet by her lover, Laon, and, through the poet, to the reader. The voice, or narrative, of liberty depends on and in fact proceeds from conversation, communication, and exchange, all of which Shelley opposes to silence, domination, and oppression.

34. The rich critical history of *Prometheus Unbound* is far too lengthy to review here. In addition to the those I note throughout my discussion, the following arguments inform my reading of the play. Cameron argues that *Prometheus Unbound* is grounded in Shelley's idea of historical evolution, the notion that tyranny will eventually give way to a more progressive government (475-564, especially 558-564). Hogle considers the place of myth and anti-myth in *Prometheus Unbound* and situates the drama in the context of Shelley's writing from 1818-1820 to argue that Shelley's use of mythographs "acquires a distinct moral mission with a series of tasks leading to its accomplishment, tasks that his poems from *Prometheus Unbound* to 'The Witch [of Atlas]' must try to fulfill or at least to begin" (220, 167-221); Ulmer (78-108) and Wasserman (255-305) also consider the place of myth in Shelley's project. Curran argues for a reading of *Prometheus Unbound* as psychodrama, suggesting that one should understand the revolutionary narrative as the projection of an internalized fantasy of utopic progression (*Shelley's Annus Mirabilis* 96-103). O'Neill summarizes the crux of *Prometheus Unbound* in terms of the place of necessity and love in bringing about the revolution of the world (81-92). Apostrophizing *Prometheus Unbound* as the most complete expression of the Shelleyan ideal, Wasserman points to the play as one among many of Shelley's works that locate revolution in the destruction of binaries and the concomitant reunion of the world into a condition of oneness (271). Wasserman also considers the function of the natural world in the drama (326-358) and the place of history in the past and future of the imaginative revolution at the play's end (374-413). Linda Brigham places *Prometheus Unbound* in the context of late twentieth-century debates about "postmodern connections of politics, aesthetics, and economics" in order to consider "postmodernism's problem . . . [of *preventing*] history's erasure rather than . . . [accomplishing] it. The question," Brigham argues, "is how can we *save* history, if we should, rather than how we can *erase* history, if we should"; see Brigham, "*Prometheus Unbound* and the Postmodern Political Dilemma," in *Shelley: Poet and Legislator of the World,* ed. Bennett and Curran, 253.

35. Two of these discussions are particularly relevant to my own. Hogle argues that "when [Shelley] composes . . . *Prometheus Unbound: A Lyrical Drama in Four Acts* (written between September 1818 and the very end of 1819), he emphasizes

Mapping the Ideal

the figural, verbalized nature of 'upthrown' god-kings, thereby reworking the reflective position of *Laon and Cythna* . . . " (103). Alan Richardson notes that "*Prometheus Unbound* can be read as Shelley's critical response to the failure of the French Revolution, which he had analyzed in the preface to *Laon and Cythna*"; see Richardson, *A Mental Theater: Poetic Drama and Consciousness in the Romantic Age* (University Park: Pennsylvania State University Press, 1988), 131.

36. Shelley, *Prometheus Unbound,* in *SPP* 132-210, lines 2.3.39-42. Brown notes the correspondence between the feminist agendas of *Prometheus Unbound* and *Laon and Cythna* and discusses the identical functions of Cythna and Asia (180-181).

37. As Brown argues, "*Prometheus Unbound* represents the high watermark in Shelley's celebration of sex" (63).

38. In its recuperation of despair as wisdom, the cherub's explanation recalls the project of *Epipsychidion*: the recuperation of failure as success, the reversal of defeat into victory.

39. Scrivener has observed of *Prometheus Unbound* that "[t]he poem describes the process of breaking out of history and into utopia" (152).

40. Scrivener examines the entire volume in a chapter entitled "*Prometheus Unbound* in Context" (140-246).

41. One of the cancelled stanzas of the "Ode to Liberty" re-invokes the image of *Prometheus Unbound*'s utopic cave; thus, in Shelley's early drafts, the *Prometheus Unbound* volume concluded by returning to the space of liberation that his four-act drama anticipated:

> Within a cavern of man's trackless spirit
>   Is throned an Image, so intensely fair
> That the adventurous thoughts that wander near it
>   Worship, and as they kneel, tremble and wear
> The splendour of its presence, and the light
>   Penetrates their dreamlike frame
> Till they become charged with the strength of a flame.
>   (*WPS* 2:315)

42. Shelley, "Essay on Christianity," in *Shelley's Prose,* 205.

43. Matt. 27:55-56. Bryan Shelley provides a lengthy reading of the place of Christ and the Christian belief in *Prometheus Unbound*; see "Providence and Prometheus" in his book *Shelley and Scripture: The Interpreting Angel* (New York: Clarendon Press, 1994), 96-116. Among the many references to Christ he traces in the play's first act are the crown of thorns (1.290, 1.563-565, 1.598-599), the robe of mockery (1.289), the nails of crucifixion (1.20), the piercing spear (1.31-32), and the succession of mockers (1.36-38) (106).

44. Rev. 22:13. That another character—Demogorgon—is consistently coded throughout Shelley's play as the "last" reminds us of his correspondence to Prometheus, as well. Demogorgon is one of several characters without whom the utopia at the play's end would never have been activated, for it is largely through his efforts that Prometheus and Asia are reunited. Shelley's decision to distribute the

traditionally singular (individual) status of the hero across several "couples"—Prometheus and Asia on the one hand, and Prometheus and Demogorgon on the other—reminds us of the importance of external engagement to the success of Shelley's agenda of liberty-through-love: idealists, such as *Alastor*'s Poet or like the poet of *Epipsychidion*, whose real-life circumstance separates him from his beloved, fail miserably when they are alone, in solitude; but when joined in the struggle for freedom with like-minded thinkers, Shelleyan idealists work through communal efforts to manifest utopia in the real world.

45. Other scholars who provide readings of Prometheus as Christ include Richardson (131), Cameron (542), King-Hele (199), Curran (*Shelley's Annus Mirabilis* 54-65, especially 55 and 58), and Carl Grabo in *Prometheus Unbound: An Interpretation* (New York: Gordian Press, 1968), 10.

46. Matt. 27:51-53.

47. Matt. 27:29.

48. See Gerald McNiece, *Shelley and the Revolutionary Idea* (Cambridge: Harvard University Press, 1969), 226-227.

49. Ulmer's reading of the function of androgyny in the play strikes me as far more accurate than Hoeveler's: rather than pointing to a single individual as the embodiment of the androgynous ideal, Ulmer, following Ross Woodman, points to the erotic union of Prometheus and Asia as the epitome of androgyny, or oneness (84). Like Ulmer, I find that Shelley emphasizes the couple (or, elsewhere, the community of lovers) rather than the individual, as the forerunners of freedom; in short, Ulmer's reading of *Prometheus Unbound* is similar to mine, except that he codes erotic union as androgyny, and in so doing I believe he effaces an important component of the Shelleyan model—the outward turn to the beloved, the power of an intimate connection with an other or, in the case of the free-love community, with others, rather than the collapsing of (gendered) difference within the singular self, as "androgyny" suggests.

50. Richardson notes that Prometheus must call upon Asia before he can break free from isolation (136), and Ulmer reads what he describes as the "androgynous union" of Prometheus and Asia as the ultimate image of Shelleyan oneness and, by extension, of revolution (84). McNiece reads Asia as a corrective to the French Revolution, "the energy and beauty of love which would have prevented the excesses of fanatical rationalism" (233). Hogle also considers Asia's feminist significance (109) and compares her role to Cythna's (110-111), yet he argues that Asia must be understood not as Prometheus's complement, but as All (182, 184) so that Asia serves as the true—and only—liberator in the poem (185-186), an argument clearly counter to mine, given its privileging of the lone figure (rather than the erotic couple or community) as a hero.

51. For Curran's full account of the legendary status of the Indian Caucasus, see *Shelley's Annus Mirabilis*, 60-63.

52. Such a bleak setting reappears in Shelley's last major effort, *The Triumph of Life*, as the speaker observes the approach of the chariot (lines 62-95). In their introduction to the poem, Reiman and Powers note that *The Triumph of Life* warns against "[running] to the extremes of optimism and . . . [giving] way to despair

when idealized expectations fail," both in "the political sphere and in love" (*SPP* 455). Thus, *The Triumph of Life* underscores the bastard's message at the conclusion of *Prometheus Unbound*—that despair will cede to wisdom as time passes; and *The Triumph of Life* also recalls the bleak setting of the opening of *Prometheus Unbound*, again underscoring the incongruity between that poem's utopic vision and the apparent barrenness of its initial scene, which eventually bursts forth into vegetation when the world is liberated by love.

53. McNiece also remarks on the psychopolitics of this utopia, albeit in language slightly different from my own. While I describe utopia in terms of the collapsing of binary oppositions, McNiece considers utopia with regard to the unmasking of false systems of belief: "When the foul shapes and loathsome masks which have been interposed between man and man [sic] and reality have fallen away, men and women self-governed by love, hope, and a freely ranging imagination are left" (243).

54. Richardson catalogues the binaries resolved in this utopia as follows: "Heaven and Earth are one of a number of paired contraries that meet here to dissolve. Masculine and feminine, matter and spirit, actual and potential, sense and imagination, nature and consciousness reveal themselves as arbitrary oppositions rendered obsolete by a force that eradicates conventional boundaries" (150).

55. Ulmer offers a reading of the place of utopia far less optimistic than either Hoeveler's or mine. Arguing that Shelley's utopia "wanders between two worlds as a reflex of the transitional struggles of nineteenth-century politics," Ulmer concludes that the negations of power we see in this place underscore the ironic presence of power that subverts the utopia (100); according to Ulmer, this utopia is no space of perfection but "a prison with tragedy at its center," not a figural womb from which the world may be reborn but the excluded, oppressed space of the Other that labors under tyranny's domination and rule, the no-man's land into which the dissenting figures of Prometheus and Asia are expelled.

56. Shelley's line reminds us again of the power of language to undo, to contradict, itself, here by way of the anagrams "veil" and "evil," words whose letter-content is identical, but whose arrangement—which shapes the perspective through which we perceive that letter-content—shifts the meaning of each entirely, individuating the one from the other, when in fact both contain, both inscribe, the same material.

57. Other scholars write less effusively about the liberatory potential of a mere shift in perception. Holmes dismisses Prometheus's change in attitude as " . . . a rejection of the world rather than universal social revolution. In this sense Shelley's poetry remains more honest than his ideology, for the actions of Prometheus . . . are those of a leader who has escaped defeat and gone into a jaded exile, rather than those of a genuine victor" (507). Dawson, too, complicates the utopic nature of the poem's final location by suggesting that the supposed places to which all of the poem's major figures retire—Prometheus and Asia, Jupiter and Demogorgon—is in fact the same cavernous abyss. Thus, Dawson argues, "[i]f we follow the mplications through we shall conclude that Prometheus, Asia, and Jupiter are all aspects of the human mind, who disappear as separate entities when the mind heals its own divisions," and so "[t]he natural conclusion would seem to be that Jupiter,

Prometheus, and Asia have all been reabsorbed into this realm, the ultimate source of all potentiality. This is death, as far as death is possible for immortals" (127, 126).

58. Interestingly, Desperet's image anticipates the ooziness that marks the revolutionary landscapes Shelley will describe: in Desperet's depiction of the eruption of Liberty, physical states mix into each other as the solid earth spews forth a molten liquid that gets transformed into a vaporous cloud over the landscape. Desperet's image, dated 1789—the year of the French Revolution—depicts the eruption of Liberty as a moment in which material difference is suspended as solid, liquid, and gas commingle in a hybrid state of freedom. Paulson, too, notes the overcoding of landscape with revolutionary imagery in nineteenth-century art: Paulson remarks that depictions of "revolutionary 'people' . . . distinguished the crowds that appear (like flowing masses of lava) as part of the sublime landscapes of John Martin and J. M. W. Turner" (*Representations of Revolution* 21). Elizabeth Helsinger also notes the explicit connections J. M. W. Turner made between landscape painting and contemporary debates over politics and representation; see Helsinger, "Turner and the Representation of England," in Mitchell, ed., 103.

59. Robert D. Newman considers the processes of narrative engagement in terms of a model of exile and return, and his argument about the place of exile in the activity of reading is instructive to my argument about Shelley's utopic no-spaces. According to Newman, "[t]he narrative recreation of the exile reveals the fluidity of a genre between biography and history as symptomatic of a more profound unsettling of fixed binaryism. Exiles continually define themselves in relation to what is absent, their homeland, which they simultaneously embrace and deny. Their recreation of that homeland . . . demonstrates memory as a revisionary act and history as an exercise in narrative memory. Exiles' memories of homeland are not constants, but are constantly changing due to their experience as exiles. Their mental returns are guided by necessity of making that home, which was once an extension of Self, Other, in part so as to preserve the home that now is. This necessitates alienation from oneself, the Self that was and that still is present as an influence upon and aspect of the present Self"; in short, "[t]he exile . . . creates a mirror for the reader's experience while infiltrating and modifying that experience"; see Newman, *Transgressions of Reading: Narrative Engagement as Exile and Return* (Durham: Duke University Press, 1993), 1-2.

60. Hogle's reading of the "place" of *Prometheus Unbound*'s utopia anticipates what I suggest here: he notes that it is at once before and after the present moment, and he concludes that "[a] partial regression to the figural revolution behind all perceived changes . . . is radical forward progress at the same time" (192).

CHAPTER VI

Conclusion
Re-Tracing Seduction:
The Influence of Shelley on Nineteenth-Century British Culture

> In the infancy of society, every author is necessarily a poet, because language itself is poetry; and to be a poet is to apprehend the true and the beautiful, in a word the good which exists in the relation, subsisting, first between existence and perception, and secondly between perception and expression.... For [the poet] not only beholds intensely the present as it is, and discovers those laws according to which present things ought to be ordered, but he beholds the future in the present, and his thoughts are the germs of the flower and the fruit of latest time.
> —Percy Bysshe Shelley, *A Defence of Poetry*

> Literature always anticipates life. It does not copy it, but moulds it to its purpose.
> —Oscar Wilde, *The Decay of Lying: An Observation*

In *A Defence of Poetry,* Shelley underscores his belief in the social role of the poet and in the empowering potential of poetry, and he describes the function of the poet-as-seer in the terminology of the natural landscape: the poet's vision draws from and reproduces "the germs of the flower and the fruit of . . . time" (*SPP* 482). In what has become the most famous passage from the *Defence,* Shelley concludes his valorization of the poet by heralding that figure's central role in activating social change: "[p]oets are the hierophants of an unapprehended inspiration, the mirrors of the gigantic shadows which futurity casts upon the present, the words which express what they understand not; the trumpets which sing to battle, and feel not what they inspire: the influence which is moved not, but moves. Poets are the unacknowledged legislators of the world" (508). The importance of the poet is indeed social, and his "place" is transhistorical, for even as he writes with an eye both to history and to his own day, the poet, as seer, accesses a vision of the future, and his works transmit that knowledge to any reader who studies them: " . . . the office and character of a poet participates in the divine nature as regards providence, no less than as regards creation" (492). Looking backward and forward, the poet functions as a pantemporal mediator of knowledge, a historian of man's accomplishments and shortcomings, a visionary for the future of humankind.

Cameron notes that Shelley recognizes reading as the first important step in social change (213), and O'Neill turns to the Preface to *Prometheus*

Unbound for proof of Shelley's "growing sense of the importance of the imagination and the part played by the audience" in the realization of that poem's political ideal (84). Klancher argues that Shelley regards the function of reading not as redemptive, as do Wordsworth and Coleridge (135, 171), but as empowering: "[f]or Shelley, reading and writing *as acts* do not offer escape from or transcendence of an early-nineteenth-century class-structured, commodified, and technologized social order. Language can only clarify the intellectual, social, and political frames that constitute the cultural order while being formed by it"; in the end, then, "Shelley's political poems explore and clarify the conditions under which the subjects of power might become fully human in acts of mind and will that lie beyond the scope of any poem" (171). "Literature," Jeanette Winterson writes, "is not a lecture delivered to a special interest group, it is a force that unites its audience. The sub-groups [of audience members] are broken down," and it is through the processes of reading, "through the acceptance of breakdown; breakdown of fellowship, of trust, of community, of communication, of language, of love, that we begin to break down ourselves, a fragmented society afraid of feeling."[1] The effects of literary engagement Winterson describes all operate toward unification—of the reader with the writer though the hinge of the text; of the reader/text/writer with the larger world—and thus reading makes porous the boundaries that seem to separate us in the real world, allows us to ooze slowly toward the erotic embrace, the intellectual commingling, that Shelley situates as the platform of liberty-through-love. Shelley regards reading as the process that precedes—precipitates, even—social change; the problem he must confront, then, is the drawing in of an audience—the seduction of the reader.

Barthes might well have been speaking of Shelley's work when he observed that "[t]he text is a fetish object, and *this fetish desires me*" (*The Pleasure of the Text* 27). For Barthes, the very essence of the erotic is language—discourse, or the linguistic exchange (*Sade, Fourier, Loyola* 27). At once the desiring subject and the object of desire, the text, no less than the reader, operates as an agent of consumption: text and reader—fetish and fetishizer—oscillate in a seductive game of looking and being looked at, acting and being acted upon, until the distinctions between them vanish in the ooziness of narrative engagement. In the end, the text seduces and impregnates the reader, who reproduces the text's ideal in the world about him (or her). Textual seduction thus depends upon the power of the text to lure the reader into an erotic engagement from which the textual ideal will re-emerge in the reader's (no less erotic) engagements of the world at large. And what textual seduction produces, what gestates through its deployment, is something like what Baudrillard describes as "the triumph of a soft seduction, a white, diffuse feminization and eroticization of all relations in an enervated social universe" (2) as "[s]eduction rises like the phoenix from the ashes" (121) and transforms everything in its wake,

Conclusion

re-making the world in the image of itself, by and through the powerful-pleasurable lure of the erotic.

But what is this lure by which a text arouses the reader's interest, and how does that lure operate in terms of the model I have been exploring? Newman argues that the act of reading begins in the space of exile and that readers look to texts as links—psychic bridges, perhaps—to homelands they want desperately to recover. For Newman, this homeland is, to borrow a phrase from *Epipsychidion*, the "antenatal dream"—that space before the subject's fall into the organizational grids of the Symbolic Order and its panoply of proscriptive languages, laws, and regulations: " . . . the loss engendered by the invasion of the Imaginary by the Symbolic Order in the individual's psychic life motivates the reading process in an attempt to recover the ideal Imaginary state while narrative memory inevitably recapitulates this loss" (1). Newman casts the reader as the exile returning home, but the distance between reader and homeland (or ideal), ironically, becomes magnified—rather than reduced—by the act of reading: "We might view memory as a narrative of homecoming just as we see narrative as an act of memory. In either case, readers function as wanderers, perpetually exiled by their desire for the order of metanarration which both obstructs and enters into their engagement with the narrative. Just as they wander the text in search of the illusion of unity, smoothing its folds to meet the contours of their present desires, the margins of the text invade and alter the path they wander. Their return home can never be completed because their image of home changes" (3). Newman's model charts narratives as figural maps of lands long lost, lands to which we imagine we can return in the act of reading. But such returns hinge on the solipsistic act of textual engagement—the selfish act of textual ingestion in which the reader devours the text in an effort to triumph over exile. Such a journey strikes me as very much like the "edge-pursuit" that characterizes much of Cixous' work, which Catherine A. F. MacGillivray describes as "a pursuit of the edge, practiced on the edge; an edgy pushing at edges in an effort to feel and fall over them," a process through which "Cixous's poetic practice critiques and performatively deconstructs . . . [rigid] categories and therefore must be understood as an attempt 'to cause contradictions to vibrate,' as exactly the extent to which it cannot be pinned down but remains as movement, as escape."[2] Shelley's insistence on the importance of outwardly directed engagement precludes the success of such a solipsistic model of reading, as I have argued, and heralds instead commingling, the interpenetration of reader and writer that duplicates the ecstatic union of lover and beloved, whose interplay Shelley characterizes in "On Love" in language that anticipates MacGillivray's: "If we reason, we would be understood; if we imagine, we would that the airy children of our brain were born anew within another's; if we feel, we would that another's nerves should vibrate to our own, that the beams of their eyes should kindle at once and mix and melt into our own, that lips of motionless ice should not reply to lips quivering and burning with the heart's best blood. This is love" (*SPP* 473). Throughout his work, Shelley plots utopic spaces as sites for the realization of his vision of human liberation, a vision that begins in textual engagement and depends finally upon the reader's (re-) engagement of the world-at-large through various sorts of erotic relationships—sometimes sexual, sometimes familial, sometimes relationships of fellow-feeling—all of which derive from the models explored in the works I have discussed. Phyllis Rose describes love as "the momentary or prolonged refusal to think of another person in terms of power";[3] certainly, the mode of the erotic destabilizes relations of power by re-mediating power as pleasure, leading to the mixing and melting (again to return to the language of "On Love") of the lovers' embrace. Grimshaw writes that, " . . . the erotic seems to me frequently to involve some sense of 'loss' of the boundaries of self; the temporary erosion of the bodily boundaries between one person and another, and the temporary obliteration of one's normal or everyday sense of oneself" (182). And not only does the erotic erode borders of subjectivity, senses of self, but it activates a leap outside of time, since "[s]exual intercourse"—for me but one manifestation of erotic engagement, yet one that speaks volumes about the others it metonymizes—"is commonly marked by a forgetting and a shutting out of everything else, a collapsing of *before* and *after* into *now*," "[obliterating] chronology and the alienation of normal consciousness. [Sexual ecstasy] becomes a real but alternative world, where self and the object of desire fuse in a spot of timelessness" (188). Sexualized and textualized, Shelley's narratives beckon readers into negotiations from which social re-engagements are sure to follow.

Through close readings of six works, I have begun to tease out the political engagements embedded in Shelley's erotic narratives, and I have considered the public implications of private relationships, the social consequences of the erotic in its various manifestations. While *Swellfoot the Tyrant* demonstrated Shelley's understanding of the intrinsic links between political and sexual machinations as well as the potential for the exile's return to complicate power and privilege, *Epipsychidion* provided a rich analysis of the model of love that informs all of Shelley's works as well as a vivid description of the utopia from which the poem's lover and beloved remain forever barred, that extra-linguistic space of memory, fantasy, and psychic projection that lies just beyond the reach of poetry. And while *The Cenci* exemplified the links between political and domestic oppression and gestured toward the family as the locus from which an alternative political model might develop, *Julian and Maddalo* turned to friendship and fellow-feeling as antidotes to the private experience of erotic disappointment and its very public manifestation in the exile and containment of the Maniac. Finally, *Laon and Cythna* and *Prometheus Unbound* resurrected the fallen utopia of *Epipsychidion* to offer returns to natural wonderlands not only as correctives to the orders that beset each poem's heroes, but also as viable alternatives—tangible utopias—to the never-never land of *Epipsychidion*'s far Eden of the purple East. In each case, Shelley blurs the line between public and private life, so that lovers, families, and friends look beyond the vanishing points of tyranny as they envision alternate social models, as they trace and re-trace the seductive cartographies of worlds liberated by love, all in their efforts to plot utopia.

While these texts represent only a fraction of Shelley's *œuvre*, I find them integral to the processes of plotting utopia I have described. However, one could turn to a variety of Shelley's works for analogues to the readings I have provided. For example, the narcissism and selfishness that perpetuate tyranny's grip on the human race, which I have explored in *Swellfoot the Tyrant* and *Epipsychidion*, is duplicated in *Alastor; Or, the Spirit of Solitude*, in which a well-meaning Poet impedes the progress of liberty by way of his self-interestedness, his narcissistic disregard for the people and circumstances around him. The turn to fellow-feeling and to the family as sites for the evolution of alternate social orders, seen most clearly in the present study in *Julian and Maddalo* and in the final portions of *The Cenci*, appears again in *Rosalind and Helen: A Modern Eclogue* and in *The Witch of Atlas* (1820), all of which exhibit extensive investments in the belief that "[l]ove is the counteraction to lack and exclusion" (Polhemus 171). And while the soaring utopias of *Prometheus Unbound* and *Laon and Cythna* remain, in my opinion, unmatched in Shelley's other works, their shared paradigm of liberty-through-love underwrites the majority of Shelly's *œuvre*, including the shorter and longer poems, the dramas, and the essays. In mapping the political in Shelley's erotic narratives, I have traced the erotic cartographies according to which virtually all of the poet's works may be charted, the various modes of textual seduction through which Shelley plots utopia.

But the model of textual seduction is not particular to the works of Shelley; that model may in fact inform readings of a variety of texts throughout the nineteenth century—not only literary texts, but paintings, home decoration, and architecture, as well. Such broad applications demonstrate the richness of Shelley's model of textual seduction and gesture toward its importance beyond the poet's narrow historical moment; nevertheless, I have limited the present study because I find the model of textual seduction most fully developed throughout the works of Shelley: because Shelley investigates the power of the erotic not only to liberate but also to oppress, his investigations mine an entire continuum between freedom and constraint to mark—to map, or plot—a whole range of nooks and crannies in the apparent gulphs between private and public life, between oppression and liberation, ultimately to locate spaces for negotiation—"room for maneuver," to borrow Chambers' phrase.

Certainly, my discussion could be broadened to include the works of Shelley's contemporaries as well as his inheritors, and in concluding my study, I want to trace some outlines for a larger project by offering general observations about the place of Shelley's model of textual seduction throughout nineteenth-century British literature and culture. In general, I focus on Shelley's contemporaries and on two schools one might point to as Shelley's inheritors, the Pre-Raphaelites and the Aesthetes; specifically, I touch on works by William Wordsworth, Samuel Taylor Coleridge, William Blake, Mary Wollstonecraft, Mary Wollstonecraft Godwin Shelley, John Keats, and Lord Byron; by Christina Rossetti, Dante Gabriel Rossetti, and Algernon Charles Swinburne; and by Oscar Wilde, John Gray, and Aubrey Beardsley. Throughout, the Shelleyan model forms the locus of a counter-tradition that situates the erotic as a trope for political discourse, seducing readers with a wide variety of sexual milieux in which pleasure and love are posed as symbols for liberation from oppressive regimes and selfishly invested individuals: time and again, Shelley and his inheritors stage the erotic as a device for renegotiating power and privilege, so that every context in which the erotic figures must be understood as a resolutely political one.

∞ ∞ ∞ ∞ ∞

Shelley's Contemporaries

In my Introduction, I traced the genesis of Shelley's model of textual seduction to French Revolution-era representations of erotic revolution, in which erotic images (of bare-breasted women, for example) collapsed the distinction between private pleasures and public acts, offering up texts that clearly operated as political pornography. Such a collapse does not disappear in the first decade of the nineteenth century, however; one could point to William Wordsworth's idealization of rural scenes and family life as another moment in which the private pleasures of home and the retreat to nature assume social significance, for Wordsworth clearly models his idyllic vision of life in the nineteenth century on the individual or family who remains willfully distanced from the pressures of city life, self-exiled from "society." Samuel Taylor Coleridge, too, understood the public ramifications of private engagements, and his spiritual meditations—themselves acts of study and introspection—likewise emerged as forces for the betterment of the world at large. While Wordsworth's Preface to *Lyrical Ballads* (1801) glorifies the simple, country life as both a cure from the ills of the city and a model for the re-making of a fallen world, Coleridge's odd Gothic poem "Christabel" (1816) investigates the consequences of the violation of the public/private division as well as the problems intrinsic to sexual excess: from the moment Christabel carries Geraldine over the threshold into Sir Leoline's castle, the political and erotic relationships throughout that household alter dramatically and irreversibly.

Two other significant predecessors to the Shelleyan model may be located in the works of William Blake and Mary Wollstonecraft. Blake's *Songs of Innocence and of Experience, Shewing the Two Contrary States of the Human Soul* (1794) describes a world constantly under threat from the innovations of modern English life, and both books point to the family and to the education of the child as sites for reform. Blake's insistence on the power of education (which includes but is not limited to reading) to induce the "mind-forg'd manacles" (Pl. 46) of custom and law demonstrates his understanding of the effects of internal states and private relationships upon the world at large. But perhaps the most direct influence on Shelley's model is Mary Wollstonecraft, the mother of the poet's wife, Mary Wollstonecraft Godwin Shelley. The Shelleys knew Wollstonecraft's works well, and a number of scholars have located in Wollstonecraft's polemical texts, such as *A Vindication of the Rights of Man* (1790) and *A Vindication of the Rights of Woman* (1792), source documents for the feminist passages in Shelley's works. While the influence of Wollstonecraft's polemical work cannot be overestimated, I also find an important influence in the novel she left unfinished at the time of her death from complications following the birth of Mary Godwin: *The Wrongs of Woman; Or, Maria* (1789) exerted a particularly potent influence on Shelley's work, for the alternative social order Wollstonecraft explores throughout that novel underwrites the conclusion of *Julian and Maddalo* and, even more clearly, the vision of the maternal social model—the feminine community—that Beatrice describes at the end of *The Cenci*. Like Wollstonecraft's novel, both works by Shelley predicate the undoing of oppression and exclusion upon the emergence of a matriarchal order in which comfort and care soothe the wounds inflicted by the tyranny of patriarchal privilege or, as Wollstonecraft so eloquently describes them, "the misery and oppression, peculiar to women, that arise out of the partial laws and customs of society."[4] Wollstonecraft's valorization of a matriarchal order also informs Mary Shelley's *Frankenstein; or, The Modern Prometheus* (1818), in which the machinations of science (coded throughout the novel as analogous to patriarchy and its masculinist assumptions) threaten the sanctity of nature as well as the security of the home and family (coded throughout as feminine). In *Frankenstein*, Mary Shelley revisits her mother's concerns about the "place" of woman in society to demonstrate how the conditions of tyranny and oppression arise from masculinist obsessions with power, glory, might, and exclusion.

Another of Shelley's contemporaries, John Keats, deploys the erotic as a device for mediating power between and among individuals to chart politicized relationships according to the contours of erotic engagements, all in a manner completely consistent with Shelley's carefully plotted erotic cartographies. The final lines of *Lamia* (1820) evince Keats' belief in the power of erotic engagement to determine the sense of subjectivity, to set the registers of pleasure or pain. As his bride disappears, finally exposed as an embodiment of evil, a broken Lycius mourns: "And Lycius' arms were empty of delight, / As were his limbs of life, from that same night. / On the high couch he lay!—his friends came round / Supported him—no pulse, or breath they found, / And, in its marriage robe, the heavy body wound."[5] For Keats, the failure of the erotic—its rupture, its fracture—holds the most dire of consequences, visited on the body as the extreme of unpleasure and oppression, as literal, physical death.

In *The Eve of St. Agnes* (1820) Keats points to the power of illicit relationships to unsettle social structures, but he explores that theme more thoroughly and to much more interesting ends in *Isabella; or, The Pot of Basil* (1820), a poem that describes the struggle for power between the title character and her brothers. While *Isabella* concludes with a shocking finale that undercuts our expectations of the triumph of the hero(ine), Keats' poem nonetheless comments upon the potential for erotic engagements to upset relationships of power. Lorenzo's murder—and, in the end, Isabella's death—result from the lovers' violations of class hierarchies: in crossing the lines of privilege, their erotic engagement threatens to unsettle all other structures of order and power in the world of the poem. Threatened by an erotic relationship whose very nature compromises their claims to power and prestige, Isabella's brothers murder Lorenzo to protect their selfish financial interests. In short, *Isabella; or, The Pot of Basil* stages an ideological war mediated through—or deflected into—a clash over an erotic object: ultimately, Lorenzo's murder symbolizes the myriad anxieties the poem explores with regard to public life (specifically, politics and economy); and while Keats's poem ends in chaos—the murder of the lover, the flight of the brothers, and the insanity and subsequent death of the heroine—it nevertheless gestures toward the productive potential of love in the basil plant, which, as William Holman Hunt's 1867 painting inspired by the poem suggests, symbolizes the power of love to triumph over the destructive forces of hatred, jealousy, and deceit, the potential for an erotic engagement to triumph over time, to outlive even death. Hunt's painting spectacularizes the implicit message of Keats's poem—that from love proceeds the birth of a new world; in short, Isabella's pot of basil stands as a Shelleyan utopian landscape-in-miniature, as symbol of a liberated world in which love grows despite the efforts of those who would impede it, and in which erotic relationships triumph even over death.

Shelley's good friend, George Gordon, Lord Byron, the most famous writer of the day, must certainly be acknowledged as an influence on Shelley's thought and work, as Shelley's thinly veiled representation of Byron as Maddalo suggests, and Shelley exerted an equally strong influence on Byron as well, for we find in Byron occasional experiments with the model of textual seduction to which all of Shelley's works contribute. In *Heaven and Earth: A Mystery* (1821), Byron's portrayal of the lovemaking

Conclusion

between angels and mortal women, which is interrupted by the chaos an angry God imposes upon the Earth, conflates erotic transgression and the effects of power on the physical world to remind us that the violation of boundaries (here, the heavenly and the earthly) ushers forth tangible, chaotic change, and the play recalls Shelley's portrayal in *Prometheus Unbound* of the volcanic eruption that precipitates the ascension of Prometheus and Asia to a redeemed world liberated from the forces of oppression. By depicting the effects of power and pleasure as they are registered in the landscape of the real world, Byron demonstrates his understanding of the fecundity of the landscape metaphor, the power of erotic cartography.

In *Sardanapalus* (1821), Byron considers how the transvestite-King's violations of gendered behavior motivate political rebellion, and he closes the tragedy by encouraging his reader to make sense of Sardanapalus' self-immolation as a revolutionary act that celebrates the ironic victory of a self-consciously "feminine" regime of pleasure and love over the "masculine" rebellion that has risen in response to what it regards as Sardanapalus's perversions of power. In the far more playful *Beppo, A Venetian Tale* (1818) as well as in the epic that *Beppo* inspired, *Don Juan* (1819-1824), Byron anticipates *Sardanapalus'* investigations of the places of dress, mannerism, and behavior within the mediations of power. In *Beppo,* Byron examines the unique occasion afforded by the tale's liminal setting—Carnival—for exploring the uses of costume and masquerade as devices for altering identity and, consequently, as opportunities for re-mediating power and social position: Beppo may reclaim the object of his erotic desire, his long-estranged wife, only because he hides behind a mask and seduces her unawares across a crowded room. Byron's Venetian tale also spectacularizes the place of clothing in the authentication of identity, as Beppo's wife demands that he drop his masquerade costume and borrow the clothes of her lover—clothes she deems more indicative of Beppo's "true" identity—so that he may be re-baptized and thereby legitimated by a ritual act that conveys social "presence," or "place." In *Beppo,* authenticity and power are accessed through the feminine strategies of dress, affectation, and pretense, all of which are played up in the liminal context of the masquerade. But where such feminine affectations encourage the horrors of a violent revolution in *Sardanapalus,* in *Beppo* the same strategies enable the title character to return to the pleasure and security of patriarchal privilege, so long as he revokes them and dresses in the "proper" clothes that befit a "man" of his public station by the poem's end. And throughout *Don Juan,* Byron's best-known account of seduction and its triumphs, the poet deploys strategies identical to those I have described to investigate behavior and identity as the grounds from which individuals may negotiate power by mediating public presence and reputation: in both Don Juan's idealized romance with Haidée and his sensational tryst with the Duchess Fitz-Fulke, Byron investigates the potential for erotic relationships to affect social standing and individual power, for both relationships unmask the purely illusory nature of any sort of separation between sexual engagements and social presence, or erotic pleasures and political power.

Any discussion of Byron is bound to take into account the significance of his eponymous hero, and certainly the Byronic hero operates as a revolutionary, for in his diverse experiences, this broody, introspective iconoclast invariably affects others around him, whether by way of his self-exile from traditional values, Christianity among them, or by way of his ambiguous erotic reputation, which distributes his name as tainted currency throughout society by way of the seductive mechanism of gossip and which, ironically, enlarges his symbolic presence in public life. In *Manfred: A Dramatic Poem* (1817), the Byronic hero emerges as a foundational source for the cult of personality we see developed throughout the nineteenth century, especially in the Aesthetic period in the works of Oscar Wilde. The misanthropic Byronic hero, wallowing in self-exile from the human race as he contemplates his personal history and its carefully guarded secret (in the case of Manfred, his incestuous relationship with his sister, Astarte), proves a powerful personality whose mediations of identity, whose disinclination to tell, whose highly eroticized nature, and whose self-perception as a body marked as a criminalized figure—a latter-day Cain, we might say—situate Manfred as a force that complicates the borders between the proper and the improper, the inside and the outside, the innocent and the criminal. The Byronic hero functions as a liminal character whose ambiguous nature and unclear history threaten to throw the world around him into chaos, a transgressor whose brooding presence inaugurates a powerful erotic type in Byron's day that remains central to nineteenth- and twentieth-century culture.

The Pre-Raphaelites

Historical geographer David Harvey argues that space operates as a type of code, or shorthand, during periods of political upheaval, and he points to the manipulations of space—in his terminology, aesthetics, or, in my own, plotting—as processes that help to bring about, to deliver, a new age of social and personal relationships.[6] Surely the nineteenth century was among the most fraught ages in recent historical memory, as wealth transferred from landed gentry to industrialists, as women emerged from the home to claim new roles in business and social life, and as power remained in flux, often suspended precariously between and among so many political factions. The nineteenth century lay ripe for the plotting of a better age, and the re-emergence of erotic cartographies in the Victorian and Aesthetic periods may be read as symptomatic of larger anxieties about fragmentation, fears of a breaking into pieces of the literal and figurative maps—plots—that wrote and re-wrote that era's history—values, beliefs, and ideologies, themselves structures according to which upheaval may be charted.

While my discussion of erotic cartographies in the works of Shelley has, in part, considered the chasm between the realms generally described as "public" and "private" as well as the imbrications of these spheres in the project of liberty-through-love, the public/private binary, like British culture itself, becomes increasingly fragmented throughout the nineteenth century. With heightened concerns about propriety, *property*—in particular, the home—came increasingly to function as a theatre for public consumption, where the "value"—and the values—of families and individuals might be "read" through a variety of markers of allegiance, wealth, and taste.[7] Beatriz Colomina describes the house as "the stage for the theater of the family," and Mark Wigley remarks that "[t]he house is itself a way of looking, a surveillance device monitoring the possessions that occupy it. It is really the house, provided by the man, that stands in his place."[8] Anxious to make a good impression—and thus to impress himself or herself into the map of social standing—the nineteenth-century individual turned to modes of self-representation as means for achieving public presence and visibility. Ironically, nowhere was self-representation practiced to a greater effect than in the home, which had heretofore been regarded as a primarily private space.[9]

Decades before Colomina and Wigley, Gaston Bachelard considered the intimate connections between architecture and personal experience as well, and he pointed to the house as the space of intimacy, arguing that "even more than landscape, [it] is a 'psychic state' . . . [that] bespeaks intimacy."[10] According to Bachelard's model, "the house is one of the greatest powers of integration for the thoughts, memories, and dreams of mankind" (6). Following Bachelard, Michelle Perrot observes that the home is the "theatre of private life, scene of the most personal of learning experiences, and focus of childhood memories, . . . the fundamental place of commemoration in which our imaginations dwell forever" (357). Perrot credits Immanuel Kant with recognizing the crucial function of the home in the formation of one's self-identity; for Kant, "'Man's identity is . . . residential'" (342). Perrot adds that the home is a "fortress of privacy, . . . protected by walls, servants, and darkness. . . . a place seething with internal conflict, a microcosm through which [run] the tortuous boundaries between public and private, male and female, master and servant, parent and child, family and individual" (346)—a home that sounds remarkably like the Cencis'. In Perrot's view, "great things were at stake in private space. Here the ambitions of power were realized in material form, personal relations took shape, and people discovered themselves" (356). In its hallways, staircases, and specialized rooms, the home seems a space obsessed with secrecy, and Perrot concludes that "at the center of all this secrecy was sex" (346). In the newly fragmented space of the home, secrecy gets negotiated through, around, and by physical space, so that just like Basil Hallward's portrait of Dorian Gray, which I discuss below, "secret" activities became farther and farther removed from public view into that realm of the home I will describe as a particularly nineteenth-century innovation: the space of the "cloistered-private."

A number of scholars have considered the power of architecture to activate the dynamic function of space, leading Alberto Pérez-Gómez to argue that "[a]rchitecture is a verb rather than a noun."[11] Pérez-Gómez reads the 1499 architectural text *Hypnerotomachia Poliphili* as a document that bespeaks the erotic nature of the discipline; according to Pérez-Gómez, "*Hypnerotomachia* . . . [demonstrates] how architectural meaning is not something intellectual . . . but rather originates in the erotic impulse itself . . . . [and shows that] the effect of architecture is always beyond the purely visual, evoking the memory and expectation of erotic fulfillment" (xv). Pérez-Gómez considers the possible functions of architecture as poiesis, as a "recognition through personal experience of the body as the site of meaning, to which the work of art and architecture speak in the medium of the erotic" (xxvi). He concludes that "erotic knowledge is a paradigm of truth as 'unveiling'" and suggests that it is in the spaces of buildings that we come to know the secrets of the universe (xxvi). Mark C. Taylor regards architecture even more explicitly as moral and spiritual in its effects: he observes that "without the guidance of visionary artists and architects, entry into the Promised Land is believed to be impossible" (12).[12] Clearly, my considerations of the representations of public and private space in erotic narratives are underwritten by the assumption that in manipulating these spaces, nineteenth-century writers and artists are struggling to locate a kind of "promised land," some sort of new world liberated from the oppressive structures particular to each writer's historical moment. Throughout my readings, erotic cartographies proceed from manipulations of space by means of erotic engagements that overlap public and private spheres, so that in the model of erotic cartography, space and behavior speak in tandem about the real worlds from which each narrative only seems to depart.

Unsurprisingly, nineteenth-century architectural innovations reveal the fragmentation of the once-private space of the home into areas newly demarcated private and public.[13] Wigley traces the history of the confluence of architecture and patriarchal authority to conclude that " . . . architecture's complicity in the exercise of patriarchal authority . . . [defines] a particular intersection between a spatial order and a system of surveillance which turns on the question of gender" (332). In this way, the nineteenth-century home becomes a fragmented territorial ground, and individuals' anxieties about their presence in the home—both with regard to how their homes would be evaluated by visitors, as well as how their "secrets" might be revealed when they opened their homes to public scrutiny—reflected the changing place of the home, its evolution into a spectacle for public (re-) view. In short, the "spatial and ideological transformations" of the nineteenth century led to the "formal establishment," Wigley claims, "of privacy" (350). Such recapitulations of public and private space within the home precipitated the innovation of a new type of space, I argue: the "cloistered-private," those areas within the home where individuals could escape the unforgiving scrutiny of the public gaze. Throughout the century, specific rooms, alcoves, and hallways became increasingly marked as off-limits to public view, and within those spaces, the erotic cartographies of the later nineteenth century begin to take shape as transgression moved from the stage of the world into the private reaches of the home; in short, revolution became privatized as it retreated from public acts to private pleasures, at times finally slipping from acts of political revolt to episodes of mere misbehavior.[14]

The gradual evolution of what I call the "cloistered-private" space both reflected and reinforced a variety of cultural and psychological transformations that began around the historical moment of the later Romantic period and continued throughout the nineteenth century.[15] Anxious Victorian campaigns to cleanse the world of the excesses of the generation that preceded their own—an age wallowing in what many Victorians would surely have considered depravity—necessitated a heightened awareness of the connections between the public and private realms, so that one's "private" identity came increasingly to be regarded as signifying the "truth" of one's political sympathies. This invasion or co-optation of the private space in the service of the public forced many Victorians who felt unbearably restrained by the moral temper of the day to innovate a dual conception of domestic space: while the "private" continued to designate a space for the activities in which one could "properly" indulge at home—activities that observed the "proper" Victorian temper—what I have described as the "cloistered-private" space operated as a site for the enjoyment of "improper" pleasures, and it found form in a variety of areas located in the deepest reaches of the private space of the home, such as the bathroom, the closet, and the library.[16] This Victorian double-removal of the erotic—a move not just from the public sphere to the private but even further into the reaches of the cloistered-private—appeared even more definitively to disengage erotic literature from the realm of public activity and, therefore, to reduce its social significance.[17]

The Victorian innovation of the cloistered-private space may have resulted directly from the Romantics' highly self-conscious presentation of erotic narratives as exclusively sexual and resolutely esoteric; that is, the mechanisms that motivated reading practices for Victorian erotica may actually have been improvised in the Romantics' deliberate efforts to separate erotic narratives from the public realm of political engagement by appearing to situate them in the private realm of imaginative literature, in narratives of pure fantasy. Yet, in both the Romantic and Victorian periods, this displacement of the erotic ultimately served to affect change in the public sphere either by subverting hegemonic codes directly (in the Romantic period) or by appearing to uphold those codes through a persistent refusal to confront them publicly (in the Victorian period), through a fear of bringing into public space or even into (non-cloistered) private space the erotic narratives that created, marked, pervaded, and informed the cloistered-private realm of Victorian life. In sum, the erotic continued to operate effectively as a mechanism for re-mapping the social and political worlds of the Romantic and Victorian periods, even as it appeared to slip more deeply into the reaches of the private: in the Romantic period, erotic literature seemed disengaged from political discourse and therefore offered a means for speaking treason in a protected space; in the Victorian period, the consumption of such texts in "cloistered-private" spaces served both as a means of confirming hegemonic codes (through the readerly effect of shame, the awareness of impropriety and, thus, of the need to be hidden) and as a means of rebelling against the increasingly stringent moral climate of the period. The erotic thus continued to figure in public space— and its consumption continued to function as a public act—throughout the Victorian period just as it had in the Romantic era, so that even though the "space" of the erotic appears to remain in flux throughout these periods, its function—its effect or "place"—remains fixed. These negotiations and re-negotiations of the erotic in the Romantic and Victorian periods functioned as public acts and activated directly social effects and consequences; in this way, the broad categories of "public" and "private"—though useful ways for (re-) moving the erotic into "safe" areas of examination—ultimately functioned as false categories, merely other names for social interaction, other masks for political engagement.

The rise of the Pre-Raphaelite Brotherhood in mid-Victorian culture signals yet another collapse in the separation of public and private engagements as artists and their patrons began increasingly to situate subversive works of art amidst the decor of the "respectable" mid-Victorian home. The Pre-Raphaelite period overlaps with the vogue of the house beautiful in England; together, these movements constitute a transitional generation in which we see the "place" of revolutionary art move into the home as an aspect of decor, an artifact of taste, and an occasion for pleasure. Invading the private under the guise of the "house beautiful," the art of the Pre-Raphaelite period transplants the social issues it confronts into the space of the home, imbricating public and private through its representations of the erotic *as display* (of wealth, taste, and cultivation). Just as Byron and Shelley displace social concerns into erotic narratives that traverse space (in *Don Juan*) and time (in *Prometheus Unbound*), three figures associated with the Pre-Raphaelite movement—Christina Rossetti, Dante Gabriel Rossetti, and Algernon Charles Swinburne—return the "space" of eroticism to a more familiar ground firmly situated within the codes of mid-Victorian bourgeois morality and experience. While Dante Rossetti turns to medieval imagery and describes natural landscapes seemingly divorced from any particular historical moment (the countryside, forests, heaven), and while Swinburne retreats to what retrospectively would be regarded as the "decadent" spaces of the transgressively erotic and the pagan, both write from perspectives thoroughly informed by—and derivative of—contemporary bourgeois values, the subject with which all of Christina Rossetti's works remain deeply engaged.

Christina Rossetti's religious devotion and her work with so-called "fallen women" provide some basis for regarding her literary productions as rather hegemonic in their allegiances. However, her oft-anthologized poem *Goblin Market* (1862) articulates a particularly erotic cartography by plotting a world whose bifurcations, principally demarcated by gender, are everywhere linked by highly eroticized exchanges. Rossetti's poem counterpoises the loving, feminine realm of the home to the exploitative masculine realm of the marketplace, and beneath the veil of sisterly affection and familial duty—which have encouraged many to misread the poem as nothing other than a *paean* to filial devotion—lurks a series of intensely erotic exchanges between the sisters and the goblins: with their succulent fruits, the goblins symbolically rape first Lizzie and then Laura, and, in her desire to save her "fallen" sister, Laura offers her juice-covered body to Lizzie in a bizarre improvisation of Christian communion. Whether Rossetti intended for sisterly devotion or lesbian eroticism to emerge as the poem's central political trope has been widely debated, but as we have seen throughout the works of Shelley—and in this chapter, in the works of Mary Wollstonecraft and Mary Shelley—Rossetti privileges the "feminine" space of the domestic as the ground from which a new world may emerge, liberated from the tyranny of patriarchal order.

Like his sister, Dante Gabriel Rossetti both reflects and departs from the traditional values of his day, and his poetry and paintings complicate the neat divisions between private and public engagements in the tradition of the other writers I have mentioned. Rossetti's use of the erotic as a political device clearly derives from Shelley's, as a close study of influence would indicate, but his mediations of hetero- and homo-eroticism extend the heterocentrism of Shelley's texts to anticipate the so-called "decadent" engagements of the Aesthetic period. For example, the "Willowwood" sequence from *The House of Life* (1881) demonstrates the effects to which Rossetti recuperates heterosexual desire in a homoerotic context: rather than gazing at his male companion, the protagonist looks in the water between them at his companion's reflection, which dissolves into the image of his (female) beloved as the protagonist leans over to kiss it; in doing so, the protagonist consequently engages the eroticized space of the masculine image to participate in a homoerotic pleasure carefully mediated through—diffused by—the veil of heterosexual fantasy. More generally, the poems that comprise *The House of Life* demonstrate how Rossetti's connection of a universal order to the individual erotic experience builds on the implications of Shelley's erotic narratives, and the poetic sequence follows the

Shelleyan proposition that if oppression follows from division (selfishness), liberation must proceed from the erotic union of self and other in a seamless combination and ceaseless reciprocity (selflessness).

Like his poetry, Rossetti's paintings also examine the mediations of public and private space as well as the overlaps in erotic and political experiences that inform his attempts at textual seduction, his representations of erotic cartography. Increasingly popular in the mid-nineteenth century, Rossetti's paintings assumed importance as status symbols for an aspiring middle class, but their particular narratives interrupted hegemonic assimilation by insinuating artistic representations of erotic engagements into the space of the home. One could read *Paolo and Francesca* (1862), a painting that situates an erotic engagement around the central figure of an open book, as suggesting that the sensual experience is born from the act of reading; *Girl At a Lattice* (1862) as posing the female body as a force for problematizing the boundaries of inside and outside; *Pandora* (1869) as casting the *femme fatale* as the holder of all knowledge and as the figure who can release evil into the world (much like Lilith in Rossetti's poem "Eden Bower"); *Ecce Ancilla Domini* (1850) as celebrating the ascetic pleasures of Christian conversion; and *Beata Beatrix* (c. 1864-1870) as portraying the ecstatic pleasures of prayer and piety. Part of the power of Rossetti's paintings lies in their spectacularization of the erotic *as* the image, for Rossetti's figural plottings of the intrinsic links between public and private life are meant for display, intended to be offered up for public consumption and scopophilic pleasure. With their characteristically lush colors and arresting images, Rossetti's eye-catching paintings undoubtedly seduce the admirers who gaze at them.

Finally, I point to Algernon Charles Swinburne, an important nexus between the darker strains of Romanticism and the decadent tendencies of the fin-de-siècle Aesthetic movement. Another clear inheritor of Shelley's narrative and ideological strategies, Swinburne conflates religious and erotic engagements in a way that both contributes to my concerns about the imbrications of public and private spheres and anticipates the strategy Wilde will develop in a number of works, *Salome* (1893) and *La Sainte Courtesaine* (1894) chief among them: just as Swinburne noted his intellectual indebtedness to Shelley, so, too, did Wilde acknowledge his tutelage through the works of Swinburne. While Swinburne announces his engagement with politics rather directly in poems such as "Ode on the Proclamation of the French Republic" (1870) and "The Eve of Revolution" (1871), his portrayal of erotic relationships in *Atalanta in Calydon* (1865) underscores the processes through which the domestic sphere encourages struggles for power and presence in the various machinations of private life that are motivated by a host of jealousies and clashings of wills.

Swinburne's notorious *Poems and Ballads* (1866) launched a perverse model for the new age by rejecting the "proper" values of mid-Victorian bourgeois society in favor of a new trinity of paganism, lesbianism, and sadomasochism. Throughout *Poems and Ballads,* paganism and eroticism replace Christianity, and pain replaces pleasure as Swinburne sketches out his vision of a world completely counter to his own. Swinburne describes such a world in "A Cameo," where he overcodes the typical image of the "proper" Victorian lady with a disturbing scene in which Desire, Pain, Pleasure, Satiety, and Death march in a procession that both recalls Keats's "Ode on a Grecian Urn" and anticipates the nihilistic sacrifices we see in so much Aesthetic literature and art. In "Sapphics," Swinburne glamorizes lesbian desire and points to perverse erotic energy as a force for liberating a world struggling beneath the weight of oppression—the very model Shelley sketched out a generation before in his musings on the revolutionary, liberatory power of love.

As we have seen in the works of Dante Gabriel Rossetti, and as we shall observe again in works from the Aesthetic period, throughout the writings of Swinburne, the *femme fatale* appears as an erotic figure whose body generates perverse spirituality even as it incubates a range of destructive powers. *Laus Veneris* (In Praise of Venus) demonstrates that the truest and highest occasion for celebration is the destruction of the soul through turbulent and painful erotic engagements. In short, Swinburne advocates a revolutionary program that pushes one to joy—an ecstatic state Swinburne regards as the complete liberation from all structures of oppression—through the symbolically humiliating acts of ritualistic, masochistic pleasure, which the speaker enjoys under the direction of the *femme fatale.* Finally, Sappho's paean to one of her lovers in *Anactoria* overturns bourgeois conceptions and discourses of love by pushing masochism to a necrophilic extreme. In a passage that culminates with her ecstatic verbal ejaculation, Sappho admits that she becomes aroused by fantasies of watching her lover die, eating her lover's flesh, and, perhaps recalling the finale of Byron's *Sardanapalus,* burning to ash with her lover so that their bodies may melt and mix together in eternal inseparability. In celebrating lesbianism, masochism, cannibalism, and necrophilia, *Anactoria* unleashes a revolutionary vision of a world poised to overturn completely the tenets of mid-Victorian bourgeois morality. As throughout *Poems and Ballads,* in *Anactoria* Swinburne maps a new social vision that depends upon the suspension of social codes and the vanishing of the divisions between the political and the erotic, a complete and joyful giving in to the ooziness of excess.

The Aesthetes

Like its predecessors, the Romantic and the Pre-Raphaelite movements, the short-lived Aesthetic movement of the 1890s staged the erotic as a device for complicating the distinction between public and private engagements. Peter Gay draws on contemporary responses to Oscar Wilde's *The Picture of Dorian Gray* (1890, 1891) to conclude that the prevailing mode of criticism rendered Wilde an outsider, a criminal: "Bluntly[, the reviews suggest that] . . . in the hands of this decadent, literature had corrupted life. The critic had turned into a criminal simply by being the critic he was."[18] Certainly, Wilde's influence was feared by many who recognized its seductive potential, its ability to sway "good" readers toward decadent engagements. Saint-Amand notes that "[the seducer's] knowledge of desire accords him a privileged, yet isolated, position in the community" (10), and I would argue that Wilde occupies such a space, as does Shelley, not only for their shared investments in the seductive valences of reading, but also for their commitments to the revolutionary power of nontraditional erotic experiences. "The language of things is a language of presence. Desire, on the other hand, is virtually synonymous with absence" writes Silverman (144), and certainly her wisdom proves most true when the nature of that desire has no language of its own, no means or modes for expression—a condition central not only to Shelley's plottings of utopia, but to his and to the Aesthetes' efforts to textualize excoriated forms of eroticism. In fact, the homosexuality of many of Aestheticism's principle figures—Wilde, John Gray, Aubrey Beardsley, Charles Ricketts, Charles Shannon, and André Raffalovich, to name a few—necessitated the innovation of strategies for coded discourse whereby erotic "secrets" could proliferate in ways that only those-in-the-know could decode; thus, many of the artifacts of the Aesthetic movement participate in oppositional narrative by veiling anti-hegemonic engagements, transgressions, beneath *bildungsroman*, comedies of manners, mythological and Biblical narratives, and philosophical discourses about art and life.

Just as Shelley, Byron, and the intellectual circles in which they moved were attacked in their day in a discourse of moral judgment through which reactionaries sought to expose their dangerous influence upon British culture, so, too, were Wilde, Beardsley, and the school to which they were said to "belong" chastised in a wide range of late nineteenth-century attacks.[19] Well-known figures at the fin de siècle, Wilde and Beardsley lived and worked in an age of weariness and anxiety, at the end of a century fatigued by tremendous changes in politics, science, and culture. Elaine Showalter characterizes what she calls "the terminal decades of a century" as "the death throes of a diseased society and the winding down of an exhausted culture," an age in which "crises . . . are more intensely experienced, more emotionally fraught, more weighted with symbolic and historical meaning, because we invest them with metaphors of death and rebirth that we project onto the final decades and years of a century."[20] While post-Revolutionary optimism and outrage spurred early nineteenth-century writers and artists to political engagement, the *ennui* that has so often been said to characterize the 1890s has been generally characterized as an indomitable force that reduced writers and artists alike to a state of profound apathy about the world around them. In their inheritance of the French *Symboliste* movement and its doctrine of "*l'art pour l'art* [art-for-art's-sake]," English Aesthetes have traditionally been regarded as resolutely disengaged from political matters and adamantly disinterested in anything outside the purely aesthetic experience.

But in his study of *Fin-de-siècle Vienna,* Carl Schorske argues that art becomes political in its very retreat from politics: "[i]f the Viennese burghers had begun by supporting the temple of art as a surrogate form of assimilation into the aristocracy, they ended by finding in it an escape, a refuge from the unpleasant world of increasingly threatening political reality."[21] In Schorske's view, art that facilitates a turn away from the horrors of the world becomes the medium of that world's salvation—a new religion for a dying time, a panacea for an exhausted population (8-9): "[i]ndeed, as civic action proved increasingly futile, art became almost a religion, the source of meaning and the food of the soul" (9).

The relative congruence of lived experiences at a wide range of fins de siècle has been demonstrated by numerous scholars.[22] Schorske's study of 1890s Vienna, then, proves helpful in making sense of the place of art in the cultural imagination at such highly fraught historical moments. Another important study is Max Nordau's *Degeneration,* first published in Germany in 1892, which so inflamed the public's imagination that it went through seven printings in the six months following its initial English translation in 1895. The general argument of *Degeneration*—that art is a product of neurosis, and that "degenerate" art emerges in times such as the late nineteenth century, when all elements of culture are breaking down, among them tradition, language, behavior, and health—proves apropos of the criticisms of Wilde and Beardsley I discuss below, for it employs exactly the discursive forms implemented throughout the nineteenth century to attack what were perceived to be revolutionary movements in the arts, such as the Cockney and Satanic schools of the Romantic period, the Pre-Raphaelite Brotherhood, and, at the century's end, the Aesthetic movement.

Nordau argues that "all these *fin-de-siècle* cases have . . . a common feature, to wit, a contempt for traditional views of custom and morality"; more particularly, he targets as the principle characteristic of fin de siècle degeneracy the "practical emancipation from traditional discipline."[23] Nordau describes what he calls "the *fin-de-siècle* disposition" as "the confluence of two well-defined conditions of disease . . . viz. degeneration (degeneracy) and hysteria . . . " (15). He then provides his readers with the symptomology of degeneration, and he focuses at length on the degenerate's predilections for what he dismisses as frivolous, affected art. Finally, Nordau concludes that degenerates tend to be "rich educated people, or . . . fanatics" (7). Here, we see something of a turn back to antilibertinism as Nordau highlights economic privilege among those qualities one must possess in order to fall into degeneracy: wallowing in sin and degradation, the degenerate must, of course, enjoy an independent income that guarantees his physical well-being in spite of his resolute disengagement from the "traditional discipline" of the Protestant work ethic (5, 7).[24]

Nordau's drive to catalogue the "symptoms" of degeneracy—an interesting turn on Sade's fetish for cataloguing—participates in the same pathologizing tradition we have seen in French Revolution-era efforts to locate the "problem" of Marie Antoinette at the site of her erotic body, as well as in the *Blackwood's* description of Leigh Hunt's associates as "the Cockney school," a term that connotes not only its members' physical degeneracy (their ill health and poor posture) but also their psychological dysfunction (their manias).

Almost predictably, Nordau returns to revolutionary France as the womb of degeneracy, and he argues that the groundwork for the ideology that would cohere in the *Symboliste* movement was born of and from that particular site of excess (112). He adds that degenerate artists, who introduced to the world "the literary phases called Diabolism and Decadentism," may be "distinguished from *ordinary criminals* merely in that the former [artists] content themselves with dreaming and writing, while the latter [criminals] have the resolution and strength to act" (260-261, emphasis added). Weaker and less respectable even than criminals, those most outcast members of society, the degenerate artist "concoct[s] philosophic systems to justify his depravity or . . . employ[s] an accommodating rhetoric in verse and prose to celebrate it, bedizen it and present it under as *seductive* a form as possible" (261, 260, emphasis added). In Nordau's taxonomy, the degenerate lures society to destruction through a form of textual seduction, by way of works that embed an erotic cachet that "bedizen[s]"—decorates—his poisonous art to infuse it with seductive power. But even more important to Nordau is the fact that these seductive artifacts are the products of "anarchists" and, therefore, that they constantly threaten to erode the structures of rule and order that govern society (302).

In meditating on the "seductive masks" of such decadent "tendencies," Nordau returns to a medicalizing discourse similar to the language that informs the *Blackwood's* attacks on Keats and Hunt, which I reviewed in the Introduction: Nordau argues that "[degenerate] art, without being properly a disease of the human mind, is yet an incipient, slight deviation from perfect health," that "the truth is . . . that degenerates . . . are weirdly senile" (553). In a vocabulary that echoes the *Blackwood's* diatribes, Nordau attacks the stated political goals of these artists as irreligious: "They have the name of liberty on their lips when they proclaim as their god their corrupt self, and call it progress when they extol crime, deny morality, raise altars to instinct, scoff at science, and hold up loafing aestheticism as the sole aim of life. But their invocation of liberty is a shameless blasphemy" (554). Nordau closes his tome by invoking the Bible as a corrective to the tendencies of degeneracy, posing "the Good Book" as an antidote for the collective diseases of the fin de siècle: "In the profoundly penetrating words of Scripture (Matt. v. 17), 'Think not that I am come to destroy the law, or the prophets; I am not come to destroy, but to fulfill'" (560). Nordau thus sanctions *Degeneration* as an evangelical weapon, faithful to the Word of God and delivered to man in an inspired effort to save the world from the irreligious tendencies of an historical moment Murray G. H. Pittock has characterized as symptomatic of "subjectivism, alienation, the apotheosis of the artist, [and] a sense of fragmentation at the heart of Western culture."[25] Unsurprisingly, Nordau's evangelical witch-hunt was easily appropriated by a variety of social critics, often in the interest of national stability, and so the language of *Degeneration* informed many fin-de-siècle attacks on the so-called "decadent" works of Wilde and others in his circle.

Even as it labored under unprecedented scrutiny, the increasingly specialized nature of the Victorian home provided, ironically, an opportunity for Aesthetic decadence to interrogate "improper" erotic engagements by playing up the draw of cloistered-private spaces in which titillating "secrets" were imagined to be engendered. Wilde's extremely popular play *The Importance of Being Earnest* (1895) oozes such an epistemology of space, and its mediations of identities and behaviors as they are parceled out "in the city" and "in the country" prove quite instructive to my argument about the mediations of public and private space through the mechanism of the erotic. As Jack and Algernon go off "Bunburying"— indulging in an array of pleasures purchased by lies, secrets and selfish, duplicitous engagements—we see the notion of the "double life" emerge that would come to haunt Wilde at his trials later that year. In addition to its epistemology of space, *The Importance of Being Earnest* contributes to the tradition of erotic cartography by alluding to geographic sites as registers of political excess: while the place of the French Revolution as a counter to traditional English values is emphasized throughout the play, so, too does Germany register ironically as a nation—a landscape, one could say—dedicated to the pursuits of decadent pleasure, in particular, to homosexual engagements.[26]

Even more overt in its "decadence" than *The Importance of Being Earnest,* Wilde's novel *The Picture of Dorian Gray* (1890-1891) stages the delights of homoeroticism in passages so shocking they were read at Wilde's trials in an effort to "prove" the writer inclined to the "immoral" tendencies encoded in his writing. Throughout the novel, Dorian's traversals through various spaces in the city and his repositioning of his degenerating portrait throughout various rooms of his house (ultimately in the attic schoolroom, to which only Dorian holds the key) remind us of the increasingly specialized nature of domestic space as well as of the oppressive monitorization of the private sphere by the coercive forces of the public, all of which motivate Dorian's panic over the possible revelation of his erotic secrets by anyone who might unveil the tell-tale portrait in the relatively "public" domestic space of the parlor.

In the tradition of Z's attacks against the Cockney School, fin-de-siècle attacks against Wilde and his works appropriated vocabularies variously medical, political, and legal. Such discursive diversity informs the *St. James's Gazette*'s review of *The Picture of Dorian Gray* on 24 June 1890 entitled "A Study in Puppydom." By referring to the principle characters in the novel—Basil Hallward, Henry Wotton, and the eponymous Dorian—as "puppies," *St. James's* casts Wilde's work in terms of the effeminacy of its characters: "puppy," an epithet applied to a person as a term of contempt, usually described "a vain, empty-headed, pertinent young man; a fox, a coxcomb" (*OED*).[27] From its very title, the *St. James's* review of Wilde's novel conjoins effeminacy and shame, one the symptom and the other the product of otherness, to expose *The Picture of Dorian Gray*—and, by extension, its author—as manifestations of effeminacy, and the reviewer castigates the magazine in which the novel first appeared, *Lippincott's*, for not being "ashamed to circulate [*The Picture of Dorian Gray*] in Great Britain."[28] Predictably, the reviewer locates the impetus for such a subversive work in the literary revolution of French *Symbolisme* (all things French, by the end of the nineteenth century, seemed to Britons always to pose a threat to established order [see Introduction, n 23]), complaining that Wilde "airs his cheap research among the garbage of the French *Décadents* like any driveling pedant" (333). Scoffed as decadent "French" garbage, Wilde's novel comes under attack as a locus of the revolutionary excesses against which the "decent" organs of the English press continued to labor, even at the end of the nineteenth century.

The second paragraph of the *St. James's* review closes by alluding to the real problem with *The Picture of Dorian Gray*—its celebration of the homoerotic. But here, the reviewer avoids uttering the unspeakable by contextualizing Wilde's novel among the "classics," a reference many *St. James's* readers would have recognized immediately as a code for representations of aberrant sexual practices. The reviewer presses the allusion farther, mentioning the "infamies believed by many scholars to be accurately portrayed in the lost works of Plutarch, Venus, and Nicodemus, especially Nicodemus. . . . . Why, bless our souls! haven't we read something of this kind somewhere in the classics? Yes, of course we have! But in what author? Ah—yes—no—yes, it *was* Horace! What an advantage it is to have received a classical education!" (334). Here, the reviewer glosses his initial reference to the "classics" by ironically praising the benefits of an education such as Wilde would have received at Oxford, a site which, as Dowling has demonstrated, had by this time become "visible less as a concrete educational entity . . . than as 'Oxford,' a symbolic site upon which are felt to converge a multiplicity of discrete and competing power relations, constantly shifting and entering into new strategic combinations" (117), particularly given the relatively well-known controversy over Oxford's program of Greek studies and the scandals of the intergenerational homosexual relationships enjoyed by two of its professors, Arthur Symons and Walter Pater.[29]

Next, the *St. James's* reviewer launches into a passage loaded with adjectives—"dull," "nasty," "[depraved]," "[wicked]," "[filthy]," and "[vile]" (334-335)—that render Wilde, vis-à-vis his novel, the embodiment of otherness. The reviewer concludes that such tendencies in the novel—which, throughout the review, are carefully attributed to Dorian Gray rather than to Wilde himself, yet clearly in the belief that in writing his beautiful dandy Wilde is writing his own life—do in fact tell us something about the novel's author, "that he derives pleasure from treating a subject merely because it is disgusting" (335). Just as Lockhart attacked Keats for his choice of audience, now Wilde gets similarly upbraided for his choice of subject matter.

On 25 June 1890, *St. James's* editors acknowledged Wilde's angry response to their initial review but perpetuated the ill-feeling by once again inveighing against "his mawkish and nauseous story" and by claiming that "the greater part of our criticism was devoted not so much to the nastiness of 'The Picture of Dorian Gray,' but to its dullness and stupidity" (337). In a similar note published the next day, the editors denounced the still-complaining Wilde for behaving "like any young lady who has published her first novel 'at the request of numerous friends' [only to fall] back on the theory of the critic's 'personal malice'" (339). The note closes on the following phrase: the "dullness and incompetence [of any work of art] are not redeemed because it constantly hints, not obscurely, at disgusting sins and abominable crimes—as 'The Picture of Dorian Gray' does" (340). The *St. James's* review thus concludes with ringing indictments against Wilde carefully coded in legal and religious terminologies: a criminal and a sinner, Wilde gets dismissed as what Nordau would certainly have recognized as a fin-de-siècle degenerate, a threat to social order.[30]

The *Daily Chronicle*'s review of *The Picture of Dorian Gray* proved no less severe in its attacks on Wilde's degeneracy which, the reviewer stated, find form in his "poisonous book" (*The Picture of Dorian Gray* 343). The review begins with the observation that "Dulness and dirt are the chief features of *Lippincott's* this month. The element in it that is unclean, though undeniably amusing, is furnished by Mr Oscar Wilde's story of 'The Picture of Dorian Gray'" (342). The review opens by invoking terms connoting mental deficiency and filth and by lamenting Wilde's spiritual well-being: like his book, the author's soul, the review implies, is "unclean" (342). Along with this religious language, the review draws on the vocabulary of disease, and the reviewer, in a manner we have seen throughout nineteenth-century reactionary responses to "revolutionary" art, indicts Wilde's novel for publicizing and glamorizing "French" excess: "It is a tale spawned from the leprous literature of the French *Décadents*—a poisonous book, the atmosphere of which is heavy with the mephitis odours of moral and spiritual putrefaction—a gloating study of the mental and physical corruption of a fresh, fair and golden youth, which might be horrible and fascinating but for its effeminate frivolity, its studied insincerity, its theatrical mysticism, its flippant philosophizings, and the contaminating trail of garish vulgarity which is over all Mr Wilde's elaborate Wardour Street aestheticism and obtrusively cheap scholarship" (342-343). One could place this passage alongside Lockhart's attack on Keats, for both reviews construct binary models according to which each author's deficiencies—each writer's stigmata—are carefully charted. Like *Blackwood's* attacks on Keats and Hunt, *The Daily Chronicle*'s attack on Wilde focuses its moralizing gaze on the vulgarity and effeminacy of his work.

Just as *St. James's Gazette* avoids the utterance of the unspeakable in its review of *The Picture of Dorian Gray, The Daily Chronicle* gestures towards homosexuality only by way of a highly connotative language: "Dorian's only regret is that unbridled indulgence in every form of secret and unspeakable vice ... will leave traces of premature age and loathsome sensualness on his pretty facy, rosy with the loveliness that endeared youth of his odious type to the paralytic patricians of the Lower Empire" (343). At once effeminizing and diminishing, the description of Dorian's "pretty facy" reminds us of the subversive appeal of the erotic body of the *homme fatal* as it evolves throughout Wilde's novel. *The Daily Chronicle* comes much closer than *St. James's* to invoking homosexuality directly in its attack on Basil Hallward, whom it describes as "an artist, who raves about [Dorian] as young men do about the women they love not wisely but too well" (343).[31] Characterizing the novel's title character as a recklessly selfish individual who wants to "[defile] English society with the moral pestilence which is incarnate in him," the review concludes by warning readers away from *The Picture of Dorian Gray,* "the book which will taint every young mind that comes in contact with it" (344). This last phrase proves particularly important in situating attacks on Wilde in the context of lingering anxieties about the French Revolution: just as Rousseau "warned ominously" that the presence of a woman (Marie Antoinette) in the public sphere would feminize that entire milieu and consequently turn men into women,[32] the conclusion of the *Daily Chronicle*'s review of *The Picture of Dorian Gray* locates in that novel the textual embodiment of a similar problem: the decadent book, the sustained celebration of effeminacy in all of its guises—vulgarity, blasphemy, and aberrant sexuality among them—*The Picture of Dorian Gray* threatens to throw the world into chaos and ruin by seducing impressionable readers into antihegemonic engagements by way of its celebration of resolutely "feminine" pleasures, by way of its seduction of the reader through the lure of its transgressively erotic appeal.

In *Salome* (1893), Wilde's decision to situate a religious drama in an erotic context hints at intrinsic links between Christianity and sex, a model his Victorian audience would have been likely to contest if not to reject outright. Whereas one might argue that in *The Picture of Dorian Gray* the spheres of religion and sex do not necessarily overlap but that Dorian's own "perverse" or "confused" desire leads him to combine them artificially, so that he mixes them up in his thoughts, tastes, words, and actions, in *Salome* we see the Christian doctrine directly linked to erotic engagements. My reading of the play hinges on an alignment of the "proper" with Christian doctrine or the "sacred," for the realm of the "proper" may be unmasked as the space of the Christian promise of the Word-Made-Flesh. The "improper," on the other hand, represents the undoing of that realm, the negation of the Christian covenant.

Throughout *Salome*, the "proper" and the sacred occupy one space, the "improper" and the profane another, but the play demonstrates how the movement from the proper to the improper is mediated by erotic engagements, as well as how that movement parallels the shift from the sacred to the profane. In its conflations of the spiritual and the sexual and its transgressions of the boundary between the proper and the improper, *Salome* slowly unravels, exposing itself as a text that seems constantly to be moving out of control. Of course, the ultimate action of the play, the assassination of Salome, demonstrates Herod's desperate attempt to reassert control over a domestic drama that has effectively castrated him of all power; that is, Herod's call for the death of Salome clearly follows from his fear of the consequences to which his excesses have led. The destruction of Salome, that figure who problematizes gendered access to power through a deliberate commodification of her own sexuality, serves as the vehicle by way of which Herod moves back into an area of fixity in which men no longer need to fear decapitation (symbolic of castration) and loss of power. In an odd way, Herod's move from a revolutionary, erotic space in which sexual and familial roles become blurred to a reactionary one in which such differences are likely to be reasserted suggests that the ultimate gesture of the drama is not simply from the "proper" to the "improper" and back again but, instead, from the "proper" through the mediations of erotic engagement to the "improper" and, finally, to a new realm of configurations in which the "proper" doctrine of the Word-Made-Flesh gets reasserted in Herod's anxious rejection of erotic transgressions in the wake of the (highly "improper") decapitation of the prophet of the Lord. *Salome* thus concludes in the reactionary space of patriarchal certainty: Herod's camp continues to function as an erotic utopia no longer threatened by the wailings of God's mouthpiece from the dungeon, and Herod's call (for Salome's death) engenders a world in which his own word once again guarantees the fleshy response he desires, a secular/sexual world in which Herod alone lays claim to the Word-Made-Flesh power of incarnation. Indeed, the play's final move to contain the figure of excess is repeated in a variety of Wilde's works, among them "The Sphinx," *The Picture of Dorian Gray,* and *The Importance of Being Earnest*: by mapping the space of the transgressive within the ideological parameters of traditional structures of power and pleasure, in each of these works, Wilde sketches a plot for subversive literary engagement, for in their apparent denunciations of excess (now political, now erotic), Wilde's texts nevertheless allow for the representation of subversive activity within the frame—the parameters, the borders—of traditional morality.[33]

The strategies of textual seduction and erotic cartography also lurk in the works of John Gray, the young man widely reported to be the inspiration for Wilde's Dorian. Frequently cited as the highest accomplishment of the Aesthetic movement, Gray's *Silverpoints* (1893) contains poetry printed in tiny italics in the middle of pages given over almost entirely to blank space. Bound in green leather pressed with an intricate gold leaf design, *Silverpoints* quickly gained acclaim as the perfection of the book-as-*objet d'art*, and the fact that thirteen of its twenty-nine poems offered translations of works by Baudelaire and Verlaine certainly aligned Gray's project with the notorious continental movement of *Symbolisme*. Although most critics have emphasized the artifact of Gray's book at the expense of its poetry, Gray's writings serve significantly to advance my model of textual seduction: careful readings of "Les Demoiselles de Sauve," "Heart's Demense," "Song of the Seedling," "Complaint," "The Barber," "Mishka," "On a Picture," "Mon Dieu M'a Dit . . . " "A Une Madone . . . " and "La Voyage à Cythère" reveal Gray's deep investment in the mediation of the homoerotic through the realms of the private (where it leads to pleasure) and the public (where its necessary veiling leads to anxiety). Throughout these mediations, Gray makes clear the transgressive nature of such behavior to suggest what contemporary press accounts of Wilde's trials prove: that at the fin de siècle, homosexuality emerges as a powerful and revolutionary force recognized as a threat not only to the (private, erotic) sanctity of the home but also to the (public, political) stability of the British empire. In its newly publicized status, this decadent "secret," this "aberrant" lifestyle is poised to infect the private (the home) as well as the public (the nation), so that homosexuality looms as an erotic specter that unhinges the public/private split and contributes to fin-de-siècle anxieties about individual degeneration and cultural disintegration—collectively, anxieties about the collapse of the British Empire.

Finally, I turn to Aubrey Beardsley's drawings, which provide perhaps the most spectacular representation of the model of textual seduction I have described. Beardsley's drawings demonstrate the mechanics of ooziness, which I have discussed throughout this book as a trope for transgression and revolution, for pleasure, flux, and change. Positioned as spaces of pleasure and meaning—or pleasure-in-meaning—Beardsley's drawings "open up" in order to reveal passageways between generally bounded, restricted or exclusive spaces, such as inside and outside, private and public, artificial and natural, traditional and progressive, "proper" and "improper." In his drawings for Sir Thomas Malory's *Le Morte D'Arthur*, Wilde's *Salome*, and Aristophanes' *Lysistrata*, Beardsley provides openings in each text that function as lacunae from whose blankness a multiplicity of narratives are generated. Not at all gaps in narrative, not "holes" or voids in meaning, these openings function as narratives in and of themselves, as sites from which meanings may be born; in short, Beardsley's drawings offer spaces of both pleasure and (re)production, slippery passages that give birth to revolutionary worlds throughout which oscillate a multiplicity of narratives. In the beginning there was the Word, our phallogocentric culture claims, but Beardsley re-places the Word—phallic mastery or "Meaning"—with(in) oozy imagery, inside narrative-lacunae of pleasure and (re)production, multiplying-spaces inside of which new worlds are conceived.

In his drawings for *Le Morte D'Arthur,* Beardsley includes a number of empty boxes in the drawings that mark off spaces for description or narration. Beardsley's boxes cover elements of both nature and society, private and public, so that these openings—which function as passages between and among the drawings, the narrative, and the reader—educate the reader about the ways in which narration operates as a device that dismantles the boundaries meant to keep the "spaces" depicted in Beardsley's drawings (private and public, for example) free from the influence—or infection—of the other.[34] In his drawings for *Salome,* Beardsley's deliberate caricatures of Wilde at once engage the reader in an extra-textual narrative—Wilde's reputation—and, perhaps more importantly, they insinuate the image of Wilde within the subversive erotic acts they depict. As a host of monstrously deformed characters gaze directly at *Salome*'s reader while gesturing toward particular aspects of the drawings, these bizarre figures encode a sort of "monstrous" complicity between the reader and the (so-called) "perverse" acts Beardsley's images celebrate—and, indeed, flaunt.

Divorced from their narrative context, Beardsley's drawings for *Lysistrata* might seem simply pornographic, but we can re-construct the specifically political significance of the drawings by reading them back through the text of Aristophanes' play. Such an approach accomplishes two ends: first, it demonstrates how the drawings imply an inextricable link between private and public life; second, it suggests that in choosing *Lysistrata* as a medium for his drawings, Beardsley proves his particular investment in exposing the diverse ways in which private relationships (marital habits) mediate the stability of the public world by exerting a pronounced influence in matters of public policy and political strategy. As in his drawings for *Le Morte D'Arthur,* Beardsley's drawings for *Lysistrata* constantly remind us that the text—the narrative of *Lysistrata*—functions as the means by which passages between public and private may be bridged. Thus, Beardsley teaches us to read the links, the windows, between private and public, between the bedroom and society, as spaces for the re-mediations of pleasure and power, and his drawings spectacularize the function of representations of erotic engagements as maps of political models, plots of both the existing (status quo) and the ideal (utopia).

Milly Heyd remarks that "much of the early criticism [of Beardsley's art] is predominantly concerned with moral evaluation of both the man and his work. Terms such as 'evil' and 'sin' are widely used."[35] Heyd reminds us that Beardsley's art is often excoriated in a religious terminology that claims to uncover countless manifestations of evil in the art itself. In 1894, *The Westminster Gazette* suggested that Beardsley's works posed such a risk to readers that the images should be scrutinized by the highest powers in the country: stating that the artist "'achieves excesses hitherto undreamt of,'" the *Gazette* attacked the subjects of Beardsley's drawings as "'the most morbid of grotesque[s]'" and concluded that "' . . . we do not know that anything would meet the case [that Beardsley's work presents] except a short Act of Parliament to make this kind of thing illegal'" (qtd. in Heyd 1). That same year, an article in *The Studio*—the magazine in which appeared "the first [piece] ever published on Beardsley together with some of his drawings" (5)—acknowledged Beardsley as perhaps the most important illustrator of his day, even as it bemoaned the "'presence of the unhealthy spirit'" in his work (qtd. in Heyd 5). As we saw in *The Daily Chronicle*'s review of *The Picture of Dorian Gray*, this anxious response to Beardsley couches commentary about his art within an assessment of the state of his soul. While *The Daily Chronicle* suggests that Wilde's spirit is "unclean," here Beardsley's is characterized as "unhealthy": in their twin manifestations of evil, Wilde and Beardsley are imagined to embody the perceived decline in English values that fueled anxieties about the turn of the oncoming century, so that in attacking the artists as well as their work, Beardsley's and Wilde's numerous detractors displace an array of anxieties about the dawn of a new era. Critically constructed as embodiments of the excesses feared to be waiting just around the turn of the century, Wilde and Beardsley loom as common sites at which Victorian values and ideals appear to fracture and dissolve as the transgressions of their "French" decadence throw the world into the chaos of another revolution—this time, the very sort of revolution in culture and art that Shelley envisioned, and the very project he plotted through the strategies of textual seduction.

∞ ∞ ∞ ∞ ∞

In his study of "Men, Women, Architecture, and the Construction of Sexuality," Aaron Betsky observes that in the sixteenth century, "[t]he painter, mirror maker, and map maker all performed a similar function within [the] emerging man-made world (the Dutch invented the word 'landscape,' or 'made land'): [t]hey framed, reflected, and fixed that world so that it could be known. There was no other world here than that which was continually remade by man through observation and craft."[36] As I have demonstrated, Shelley and his inheritors drew on the function of these early "land makers," but rather than sketching out the parameters of the known world, rather than mirroring the experience of life around them, these visionaries looked beyond the edges of the canvas or parchment upon which they "painted" their visions, behind the backs of the mirrors in which they reflected upon the world about them, and from those ambiguous voids, those overlaps just beyond the edges of the visible, they generated visions of other worlds, utopic landscapes in which the grids of order and regulation ceded to oozy images of seamlessness and reciprocity. "For the Dutch, the model of a painting was a mirror, not a window," Betsky argues (111); but Shelley and his inheritors broke through the mirrored, self-replicating walls of the Symbolic Order that surrounded them to open vantage points—windows, perspectives—through which they could access the path to freedom.

As Shelley remarks in the passage that serves as the epigraph for this chapter, "[i]n the infancy of society, every author is necessarily a poet, because language itself is poetry; and to be a poet is to apprehend the true and the beautiful, in a word the good which exists in the relation, subsisting, first between existence and perception, and second between perception and expression" (*SPP* 482). Kristeva points to poetic language as "the very place where social code is destroyed and renewed" as writers "sound a dissonance within the . . . paternal function of language" ("Desire in Language" 101). As I have shown, the Shelleyan model of textual seduction appropriates the tool of patriarchal dominance—language—but transforms that tool by directing it toward a utopian, democratic ideal; thus, the processes of textual seduction plot utopia from beneath the vanishing points of tyranny by establishing symbolic links between this world and the better one to come. Evan Eisenberg observes that one of the positive effects of our search for an Eden-like wonderland is "a search for wholeness," for complete re-integration with those parts of ourselves and our natures we imagine we have lost, and we fear we may never find again.[37] But Shelley undoes that sense of loss through the strategies of textual seduction, which allow him to plot the utopia he so believes has yet to emerge: dissolving the chains of oppression with the seductive power of language, Shelley and his inheritors draw their readers into the struggle for freedom, generating a virtual army of lovers whose individual and social engagements trace a course beyond exile and excoriation as they find their way home to liberty through love.

Notes

1. Jeanette Winterson, *Art Objects: Essays on Ecstasy and Effrontery* (New York: Vintage International, 1995), 106, 108-109.
2. Catherine A. F. MacGillivray, Preface to *FirstDays of the Year*, by Hélène Cixous (Minneapolis: University of Minnesota Press, 1998), xxi, xiv.
3. Phyllis Rose, *Parallel Lives: Five Victorian Marriages* (New York: Alfred A. Knopf, 1984), 8.

4. Mary Wollstonecraft, *The Wrongs of Woman, or Maria*, in *"Mary" and "The Wrongs of Woman,"* by Mary Wollstonecraft, ed. Gary Kelly (1798; reprint, New York: Oxford, 1990), 73.
5. John Keats, *Lamia*, in *The Poems of John Keats*, ed. Jack Stillinger (Cambridge: The Belknap Press of Harvard University Press, 1978), 2.307-311.
6. David Harvey, *The Condition of Postmodernity* (Oxford: Basil Blackwell, 1989), 273. I am indebted to Brigham for mentioning this source in her essay "*Prometheus Unbound* and the Postmodern Political Dilemma," which I cite in Chapter V.
7. For thorough discussions of the permutations of style and taste in nineteenth-century interior decoration, see Charlotte Gere, *Nineteenth-Century Decoration: The Art of the Interior* (New York: Harry N. Abrams, 1989) and Peter Thornton, *Authentic Decor: The Domestic Interior 1620-1920* (New York: Viking, 1984), 138-388. Linda Parry's discussion of the influence of William Morris's interiors and Frances Collard's review of Morris's innovations in furniture also speculate about the place of decor in the nineteenth-century British home; see Parry, "Domestic Decoration," in *William Morris,* ed. Parry (New York: Harry N. Abrams, 1996), 148-154 and Collard, "Furniture," in *William Morris,* ed. Parry, 155-179.
8. Beatriz Colomina, "The Split Wall: Domestic Voyeurism," in *Sexuality and Space,* ed. Colomina, 85. Mark Wigley, "Untitled: The Housing of Gender," in *Sexuality and Space,* ed. Colomina, 341.
9. Wigley argues that "discrete representational systems, like those of . . . makeup and clothing, . . . cannot be detached from those of architecture" (386); for Wigley, " . . . identity theory *is* necessarily spatial theory" (388, emphasis added), and "[t]o rethink identity spatially would involve interrogating the multiplicity of decorative surfaces that produce the sense of sexuality installed, along with the institutions of private space, in the nineteenth century" (388).
10. Gaston Bachelard, *The Poetics of Space*, trans. Maria Jolas (New York: Orion Press, 1964; Boston: Beacon Press, 1994), 72.
11. Alberto Pérez-Gómez, *Polyphilo, or, The Dark Forest Revisited: An Erotic Epiphany of Architecture* (Cambridge: Cambridge University Press, 1990), xvi.
12. Mark C. Taylor, *Disfiguring: Art, Architecture, Religion* (Chicago: University of Chicago Press, 1992), 12.
13. In an appendix entitled "The Nineteenth Century," British architect Thomas Dinham Atkinson provides a fascinating discussion of the evolution of architectural styles throughout the century, and his remarks are of particular interest to me given Atkinson's proximity to the nineteenth century itself; see Atkinson, *English Architecture* (New York: E. P. Dutton and Company, 1903), 193-219. A more concise and objective discussion of nineteenth-century architecture can be found in David N. Durant, *The Handbook of British Architectural Styles* (London: Barrie and Jenkins, 1992), 126-191. Perrot, with Roger-Henri Guerrand, discusses the architecture of the nineteenth-century home and the significance of its decor in *A History of Private Life, Vol. IV: From the Fires of Revolution to the Great War*, 339-449. Finally, Christina Crosby's chapter entitled "Reading the Gothic Novel: 'History' and *Hints on Household Taste*" demonstrates the processes through

which Gothic revival architecture emerged as both commodity and fetish; see Crosby in *Rewriting the Victorians: Theory, History, and the Politics of Gender*, ed. Parrish, 101-115.

14. See Perrot and Guerrand, *A History of Private Life*, Vol. IV, 339-449.

15. The later Romantic period, also commonly referred to as the "second-generation Romantic period," begins around 1812.

16. Quite interestingly, most Victorian photographic pornography features nude or partially clad young women in such cloistered-private spaces, usually in the bathroom. By contrast, a great many pornographic representations produced before the advent of photographic technology in the Victorian period—that is, in the engravings that predate even the Romantic period—feature the more "public" private space of the boudoir (a room that until about the middle of the Romantic period was still employed in the public function of receiving guests) as well as spaces that are even more clearly marked as "public," such as streets and parks.

17. Wigley traces the origin of a gradual development of what he calls "secret privacy" in domestic architecture to a fifteenth-century treatise by Leon Battista Alberti entitled *On the Art of Building in Ten Books* (345). Although he locates the evolution of variously secret places within the already-private space of the home at a much earlier historical moment, Wigley's understanding of the function and importance of these spaces of "secret privacy" is quite similar to my argument about the cloistered-private space: Wigley writes, "[t]his new sense of privacy was gradually produced throughout the next centuries by redefining the spaces of the house into a complex order of layered spaces and subdivisions of spaces that map a social order by literally drawing the lines between hierarchies of propriety. . . . A new kind of space emerged in which distance is no longer the link between two visible objects in space but is the product of a mask whose surface is scrutinized for clues about what lies beyond it but can never simply be seen[, an] economy of vision founded on a certain blindness . . . " (345). According to Wigley, "[t]he first truly private space was the man's study, a small locked room off his bedroom which no one else ever enters, an intellectual space beyond that of sexuality. Such rooms emerged in the fourteenth century and gradually became a commonplace in the fifteenth century. They were produced by transforming a piece of furniture in the bedroom—a locked writing desk—into a room, a 'closet' off the bedroom. Indeed, it was the first closet" (347). Wigley's association of the private space of the study with "the first closet" reminds us of the nature of such "closety" spaces in general: at once hidden and exposed, the closet, as Eve Kosofsky Sedgwick has demonstrated, is the defining structure for oppression; see Sedgwick, *Epistemology of the Closet* (Berkeley: University of California Press, 1990).

18. John Gay, *Pleasure Wars*, The Bourgeois Experience: Victoria to Freud. 5 vols. (New York: W. W. Norton, 1998), 5:134.

19. As we have seen in the case of the "Cockney School," "belonging" to one school or another is largely a function of public and critical opinion; thus, Wilde and Beardsley get grouped with a number of other figures, both English and French—among them Charles Ricketts, Charles Shannon, André Raffalovich, John Gray, Joris Karl Huysmans, Stéphane Mallarmé, Arthur Rimbaud, and Paul

Verlaine—as members of the "Aesthetic" or "Decadent" school of art. The connections (and rifts) between the English writers in this list become increasingly well-known during the period 1890-1895, when the major works of the movement were produced. Technically, French writers in the tradition are called "*Symbolistes*," and their "movement" predates English Aestheticism, so that early attacks on Aesthetic projects usually import the specter of France and its (always revolutionary) tendencies into critiques of English literary and artistic productions. English writers who adopt the *Symboliste* tradition are called "Aesthetes" or, more commonly, "Decadents." The pivotal link between the later Romantics and the Aesthetes comes in Robert Buchanan's notorious attack on Dante Gabriel Rossetti and the Pre-Raphaelite Brotherhood, *The Fleshy School of Poetry,* which appeared in 1871. Significantly, the language through which Buchanan attacks Rossetti and his circle sounds remarkably similar to the language of Z's attacks on the Cockney School, which I consider at length in the Introduction, and it participates in an ongoing, reactionary discursive model that we see resurrected in late nineteenth-century attacks against Wilde, Beardsley, and other members of their intellectual milieu. Dowling provides fascinating insights into the failure of Buchanan's essay in terms of its author's naiveté regarding then-current discourses of civic engagement and outdated ideas about masculinity; see 12-15, 24.

20. See Elaine Showalter, *Sexual Anarchy: Gender and Decadence at the Fin de Siècle* (New York: Viking, 1990), 1-2.

21. Carl E. Schorske, *Fin-de-Siècle Vienna: Politics and Culture* (New York: Random House, 1980; New York: Vintage, 1981), 8.

22. See, for example, Showalter; Elaine Scarry, *Fins de siècle: English Poetry in 1590, 1690, 1790, 1890, 1990* (Baltimore: The Johns Hopkins University Press, 1995); Karl Beckson, *London in the 1890s: A Cultural History* (New York: W. W. Norton, 1992); Stjepan G. Mestrovic, *The Coming Fin de Siècle: An Application of Durkheim's Sociology to Modernism and Postmodernism* (New York: Routledge, 1991); and Robert D. Newman, ed., *Centuries' Ends, Narrative Means* (Stanford: Stanford University Press, 1996).

23. Max Nordau, *Degeneration,* trans. George L. Mosse. (1892; reprint, Lincoln: University of Nebraska Press, 1993), 5.

24. In fact, Nordau draws a clear distinction between members of the "rich, educated" class and "the Philistine or Proletarian [who] still finds undiluted satisfaction in the old and oldest forms of art and poetry," the good worker whose aesthetic sensibilities have remained loyal to traditional subjects and forms (7).

25. Murray G. H. Pittock, *Spectrum of Decadence: The Literature of the 1890s* (New York: Routledge, 1993), 181.

26. Though seldom remarked upon in Wilde scholarship, Germany occupies a central ideological position in *The Importance of Being Earnest*. That play's figure of traditional Victorian values, Lady Augusta Bracknell, is coded in terms of what, for lack of a better description, we might regard as quasi-German identity twice in the play, first when Algernon comments upon her ringing of the doorbell as "Wagnerian" and later when Lady Bracknell discusses the selection of music for her final social occasion: "I'm sure the program will be delightful, after a few

expurgations. French songs I cannot possibly allow. People always seem to think they are improper, and either look shocked, which is vulgar, or laugh, which is worse. But German sounds a thoroughly respectable language, and indeed, I believe is so"; see Wilde, *The Importance of Being Earnest*, in *The Norton Anthology of English Literature*, ed. M. H. Abrams, et al., 6th ed., vol. 2 (New York: W. W. Norton, 1993), 1635-1636. While Lady Bracknell appears to eschew revolutionary excess (elsewhere, she says of the French Revolution that "To be born, or at any rate, bred in a handbag, whether it had handles or not, seems to me to display a contempt for the ordinary decencies of family life and reminds one of the worst excesses of the French Revolution. And I presume you know what that unfortunate movement led to" [1639]), she unknowingly endorses erotic excess by lauding the music of Germany: as Wilde certainly knew, the terms "German" and "musical" functioned as codes for the homosexual sensibility emerging in fin-de-siècle London; see Sedgwick, *Tendencies* (Durham: Duke University Press, 1993), 65-67. Thus, the play's figure of traditional morality, Lady Bracknell, lambastes public displays of excess (political revolutions) even as she implicitly endorses the "private" excesses of transgressive erotic engagements.

27. Older meanings for "puppy" included "a woman likened to a doll as a dressed-up inanity" (*OED*, s.v. "puppy").

28. See "A Study in Puppydom," in *The Picture of Dorian Gray*, by Oscar Wilde, ed. Donald L. Lawler (New York: W. W. Norton, 1988), 335.

29. See Dowling, 67-103, *passim*.

30. In fact, Nordau writes at some length about Wilde's degeneracy; see *Degeneration*, 317, 319, 320.

31. This indictment might be read as particularly damning to Wilde, since many interpreted the painter Basil Hallward as a thinly veiled portrait of the author. Yet *The Daily Chronicle* locates Wilde in more than just one of the novel's characters, and in the end, the review describes Dorian as the physical embodiment of Wilde's Decadent agenda: "Dorian [Gray is a] cool, calculating, conscienceless character, evolved logically enough by Mr Wilde's 'New Hedonism'" (344). My use of the term "homosexual" here is more convenient shorthand than historical precision: as Ed Cohen and others have shown, the term "homosexual" entered public vocabulary around the time of Oscar Wilde's trials, before which, many scholars agree, there was no such thing as a homosexual in terms of the way we now conceive that term—as naming a lifestyle, an identity; see Cohen, *Talk on the Wilde Side: Toward a Genealogy of a Discourse on Male Sexualities* (New York: Routledge, 1993), *passim* and especially Chapter 5, "Typing Wilde: Construing the 'Desire to Appear to Be a Person Inclined to the Commission of the Gravest of All Offenses'," 126-172

32. See Hunt, *The Family Romance of the French Revolution*, 90.

33. One could argue that, like Wilde, Nordau contains degenerate behavior only to celebrate it covertly, but such an assumption would prove incorrect, for where Nordau exposes "decadent" behavior in order to flay it, Wilde's containment of the revolutionary (or decadent) impulse within the frame of the reactionary narrative may be exposed as a transparently ironic move, reminding the reader that what Wilde is *really* interested in is neither the containment nor the excoriation but,

indeed, the celebration of transgressive behavior, which Wilde accomplishes from the ironic remove of the voice of "proper" Victorian values.

34. Laura Mulvey notes that the box, like the mask, " . . . [conceals] a secret that is dangerous to man"; see Mulvey, "Pandora: Topographies of the Mask and Curiosity," in *Sexuality and Space,* ed. Colomina, 63.

35. Milly Heyd, *Aubrey Beardsley: Symbol, Mask and Self-Irony* (New York: Peter Lang, 1986), 2.

36. Aaron Betsky, *Building Sex: Men, Women, Architecture, and the Construction of Sexuality* (New York: William Morrow and Company, 1995), 111.

37. Evan Eisenberg, *The Ecology of Eden* (New York: Alfred A. Knopf, 1998), 144.

References

Abram, David. *The Spell of the Sensuous: Perception and Language in a More-Than-Human World.* New York: Pantheon Books, 1996.

Abrams, M. H. *The Mirror and the Lamp: Romantic Theory and the Critical Tradition.* New York: Oxford University Press, 1953.

Ackroyd, Peter. *Blake: A Biography.* New York: Alfred A. Knopf, 1996.

Arac, Jonathan, and Harriet Ritvo. Introduction to *Macropolitics of Nineteenth-Century Literature: Nationalism, Exoticism, Imperialism.* Edited by Jonathan Arac and Harriet Ritvo, 1-11. New Cultural Studies Series, ed. Joan DeJean, Carroll Smith-Rosenberg, and Peter Stallybrass. Philadelphia: University of Pennsylvania Press, 1991.

Arac, Jonathan, and Harriet Ritvo, eds. *Macropolitics of Nineteenth-Century Literature: Nationalism, Exoticism, Imperialism.* New Cultural Studies Series, ed. Joan DeJean, Carroll Smith-Rosenberg, and Peter Stallybrass. Philadelphia: University of Pennsylvania Press, 1991.

Atkinson, Thomas Dinham. *English Architecture.* New York: E. P. Dutton, 1903.

Bachelard, Gaston. *The Poetics of Space.* Translated by Maria Jolas. New York: Orion Press, 1964; Boston: Beacon Press, 1994.

Baker, Carlos. *Shelley's Major Poetry: The Fabric of a Vision.* New York: Russell and Russell, 1961.

Barthes, Roland. *A Lover's Discourse: Fragments.* Translated by Richard Howard. New York: Hill and Wang, 1978.

———. *The Pleasure of The Text.* Translated by Richard Miller. New York: Hill and Wang, 1994.

———. *Sade, Fourier, Loyola*. Translated by Richard Miller. Baltimore: Johns Hopkins University Press, 1997.

Bataille, Georges. *Story of the Eye*. Translated by Joachim Neugroschel. San Francisco: City Lights Books, 1987.

Bate, Walter Jackson. *John Keats*. London: Hogarth, 1979.

Baudrillard, Jean. *Seduction*. Translated by Brian Singer. CultureTexts. New York: St. Martin's Press, 1990.

Beckson, Karl. *London in the 1890s: A Cultural History*. New York: W. W. Norton, 1992.

Beer, John. "Fragmentations and Ironies," in *Questioning Romanticism*. Edited by John Beer, 234-264. Baltimore: The Johns Hopkins University Press, 1995.

Beer John. ed. *Questioning Romanticism*. Baltimore: The Johns Hopkins University Press, 1995.

Benét, Laura. *The Boy Shelley*. New York: Dodd, Mead and Company, 1964.

Benét's Reader's Encyclopedia. Edited by Bruce Murphy. 4th edition. New York: HarperCollins, 1948. Reprint, New York: HarperCollins, 1996.

Bennett, Betty T., and Stuart Curran, eds. *Shelley: Poet and Legislator of the World*. Baltimore: The Johns Hopkins University Press, 1996.

Bermingham, Ann. "System, Order, and Abstraction: The Politics of English Landscape Drawing Around 1795." In *Landscape and Power*. Edited by W. J. T. Mitchell, 77-101. Chicago: University of Chicago Press, 1994.

Bernier, Olivier. "France's Weak and Frivolous Ruling Couple." In *The French Revolution*. Edited by Don Nardo, 48-54. Turning Points in World History, ed. Bonnie Szumski. San Diego: Greenhaven Press, 1999.

Betsky, Aaron. *Building Sex: Men, Women, Architecture, and the Construction of Sexuality*. New York: William Morrow and Company, 1995.

Blake, William. *Songs of Innocence and of Experience Shewing the Two Contrary States of the Human Soul*. 1794. Reprint, New York: Oxford University Press, 1991.

Bloch, Ernst. *The Utopian Function of Art and Literature: Selected Essays*. Translated by Jack Zipes and Frank Mecklenberg. Studies in Contemporary German Social Thought, ed. Thomas McCarthy. Cambridge: The MIT Press, 1993.

Bonca, Tedi Chichester. *Shelley's Mirrors of Love: Narcissism, Sacrifice, and Sorority*. Psychoanalysis and Culture, ed. Henry Sussman. Albany: State University Press of New York, 1999.

Boyer, M. Christine. *The City of Collective Memory: Its Historical Imagery and Architectural Entertainments*. 1994. Reprint, Cambridge: The MIT Press, 1996.

Brigham, Linda. "*Prometheus Unbound* and the Postmodern Political Dilemma." In *Shelley: Poet and Legislator of the World*. Edited by Betty T. Bennett and Stuart Curran, 253-262. Baltimore: The Johns Hopkins University Press, 1996.

Brown, Nathaniel. *Sexuality and Feminism in Shelley*. Cambridge, Mass.: Harvard University Press, 1979.

Burke, Edmund. *Reflections on the Revolution in France*. Edited by J. G. A. Pocock. 1789-1790. Reprint, Indianapolis: Hackett Publishing Company, 1987.

Butler, Judith. *Bodies That Matter: On the Discursive Limits of "Sex."* New York: Routledge, 1993.

Butler, Marilyn. *Romantics, Rebels, and Reactionaries: English Literature and its Background 1760-1830*. New York: Oxford University Press, 1981.

Cameron, Kenneth Neill. "The Planet-Tempest Episode in *Epipsychidion*." In *Shelley's Poetry and Prose*. Edited by Donald H. Reiman and Sharon B. Powers, 637-658. New York: W. W. Norton, 1977.

———. *Shelley: The Golden Years*. Cambridge: Harvard University Press, 1974.

Cameron, Vivian. "Political Exposures: Sexuality and Caricature in the French Revolution." In *Eroticism and the Body Politic*. Edited by Lynn Hunt, 90-107. Parallax: Re-Visions of Culture and Society, ed. Stephen G. Nichols, Gerald Prince, and Wendy Steiner. Baltimore: The Johns Hopkins University Press, 1991.

Chambers, Ross. *Room for Maneuver: Reading (the) Oppositional (in) Narrative*. Chicago: University of Chicago Press, 1991.

Chodorow, Nancy J. "Feminism, Femininity, and Freud." Chap. 8 in *Feminism and Psychoanalytic Theory*. New Haven: Yale University Press, 1989.

Cixous, Hélène. *Angst*. Translated by Jo Levy. New York: Riverrun Press, 1985.

———. "Castration or Decapitation?" Translated by Annette Kuhn. *Signs* 7 (Fall 1981): 41-55.

ld of Percy Bysshe Shelley. Gainesville: University of Florida Press, 1993.

Clark, Anna. "Queen Caroline and the Sexual Politics of Popular Culture in London 1820." *Representations* 31 (Summer 1990): 47-68.

Clark, Timothy. *Embodying Revolution: The Figure of the Poet in Shelley*. New York: Oxford University Press, 1989.

Cohen, Ed. *Talk on the Wilde Side: Toward a Genealogy of a Discourse on Male Sexualities*. New York: Routledge, 1993.

Collard, Frances. "Furniture." In *William Morris*. Edited by Linda Parry, 155-179. New York: Harry N. Abram, 1996.

Colomina, Beatriz. "The Split Wall: Domestic Voyeurism." In *Sexuality and Space*. Edited by Beatriz Colomina, 73-128. Princeton Papers on Architecture. Princeton: Princeton University Press, 1992.

Colomina, Beatriz, ed. *Sexuality and Space*. Princeton Papers on Architecture. Princeton: Princeton University Press, 1992.

Cooperman, Robert. *In the Household of Percy Bysshe Shelley*. Gainesville: University of Florida Press, 1993.

Cox, Jeffrey N. "Shelley's *The Cenci*: The Tragedy of 'Self-Anatomy'." Chap. 6 in *In The Shadows of Romance*. Athens: University of Ohio Press, 1987.

———. "Staging Hope: Genre, Myth, and Ideology in the Dramas of the Hunt Circle." *Texas Studies in Language and Literature* 38 (Fall/Winter 1996): 245-264.

Cox, Jeffrey N., ed. *Seven Gothic Dramas* 1789-1825. Athens: University of Ohio Press, 1992.

Cronin, Richard. *Shelley's Poetic Thoughts*. New York: St. Martin's Press, 1981.

Crook, Nora, and Derek Guiton. *Shelley's Venomed Melody*. Cambridge: Cambridge University Press, 1986.

Crosby, Christina. "Reading the Gothic Novel: 'History' and *Hints on Household Taste*." In *Rewriting the Victorians: Theory, History, and the Politics of Gender*. Edited by Linda M. Shires, 101-115. New York: Routledge, 1992.

Curran, Stuart. *Shelley's Annus Mirabilis: The Maturing of an Epic Vision*. San Marino: The Huntington Library, 1975.

———. *Shelley's "Cenci": Scorpions Ringed With Fire*. Princeton: Princeton University Press, 1970.

Daniels, Steven. "The Politics of Landscape in European Art." In *The Bulfinch Guide to Art History*, 96-108. Ed. Shearer West. Boston: Bulfinch Press, 1996.

Darnton, Robert. *The Forbidden Best-Sellers of Pre-Revolutionary France.* New York: W. W. Norton, 1995.

Dawson, P. M. S. *The Unacknowledged Legislator: Shelley and Politics.* New York: Clarendon Press, 1980.

Derrida, Jacques. *Of Grammatology.* Translated by Gayatri Chakravorty Spivak. Baltimore: The Johns Hopkins University Press, 1976.

Dollimore, Jonathan. *Sexual Dissidence: Augustine to Wilde, Freud to Foucault.* New York: Clarendon Press, 1991.

Douglas, Alfred (Lord). "Two Loves." *The Chameleon* (December 1894): n.p.

Dowling, Linda. *Hellenism and Homosexuality in Victorian Oxford.* Ithaca: Cornell University Press, 1994.

Doyle, William. *The Oxford History of the French Revolution.* Oxford: Clarendon Press, 1989.

Du Plessix Gray, Francine. *At Home with the Marquis de Sade: A Life.* New York: Simon and Schuster, 1998.

Duff, David. *Romance and Revolution: Shelley and the Politics of a Genre.* New York: Cambridge University Press, 1994.

Durant, David N. *The Handbook of British Architectural Style.* London: Barrie and Jenkins, 1992.

Eisenberg, Evan. *The Ecology of Eden.* New York: Alfred A. Knopf, 1998.

Erkenlenz, Michael. "Unacknowledged Legislation: The Genre and Function of Shelley's 'Ode to Naples'." In *Shelley: Poet and Legislator of the World.* Edited by Betty T. Bennett and Stuart Curran, 63-72. Baltimore: The Johns Hopkins University Press, 1996.

Essick, Robert N. "'A shadow of some golden dream': Shelley's Language in *Epipsychidion.*" *Papers on Language and Literature* 22 (1986): 165-175.

Fay, Elizabeth. "Introduction: Passion in a Barren Field." In *Romantic Passions.* Edited by Elizabeth Fay. Romantic Circles Praxis Series, ed. Orrin N. C. Wang and John Morillo. <http://www.umd/edu/praxis/passions/fay/intro.html>.

Ferris, Suzanne. "Reflections in a 'Many-Sided Mirror': Shelley's *The Cenci* through the Post-Revolutionary Prism." *The Wordsworth Circle* 23 (Spring 1992): 134-144.

Frappier-Mazur, Lucienne. "The Social Body: Disorder and Ritual in Sade's *Story of Julliette.*" In *Eroticism and the Body Politic.* Edited by Lynn Hunt, 131-143. Parallax: Re-Visions of Culture and Society, ed. Stephen G. Nichols, Gerald Prince, and Wendy Steiner. Baltimore: The Johns Hopkins University Press, 1991.

———. *Writing the Orgy: Power and Parody in Sade*. Translated by Gillian C. Gill. Philadelphia: University of Pennsylvania Press, 1996.

Fraser, Flora. *The Unruly Queen: The Life of Queen Caroline*. New York: Alfred A. Knopf, 1996.

Freud, Sigmund. *The Complete Psychological Works of Sigmund Freud*. 24 vols. Edited and translated by James Strachey with Alix Strachey and Alan Tyson. London: The Hogarth Press, 1986.

Frosh, Stephen. *The Politics of Psychoanalysis: An Introduction to Freudian and Post-Freudian Theory*. New Haven: Yale University Press, 1987.

Fulford, Roger. *The Trial of Queen Caroline*. New York: Stein and Day, 1968.

Gallop, Jane. "Beyond the Phallus." Chap. 6 in *Thinking Through the Body*. New York: Columbia University Press, 1988.

———. "Writing Erratic Desire." Chap. 7 in *The Daughter's Seduction: Feminism and Psychoanalysis*. Ithaca: Cornell University Press, 1982.

Garside, Peter, ed. *The Black Dwarf*. New York: Columbia University Press, 1993.

Gaull, Marilyn. *English Romanticism: The Human Context*. New York: W. W. Norton, 1988.

Gay, Peter. *Education of the Senses*. Vol. 1 of *The Bourgeois Experience: Victoria to Freud*. New York: W. W. Norton, 1984.

———. *Pleasure Wars*. Vol. 5 of *The Bourgeois Experience: Victoria to Freud*. New York: W. W. Norton, 1998.

Gere, Charlotte. *Nineteenth-Century Decoration: The Art of the Interior*. New York: Harry N. Abrams, 1989.

Gilchrist, Alexander. *The Life of William Blake*. Edited by Ruthven Todd. 1863. Reprint, London: Everyman's Library, 1982.

Godwin, William. *Enquiry Concerning Political Justice and Its Influence on Morals and Happiness*. 2 vols. Edited by F. E. L. Priestley. 1793. Reprint, Toronto: University Press of Toronto, 1946.

Gold, Elise M. "*King Lear* and Aesthetic Tyranny in Shelley's *The Cenci, Swellfoot the Tyrant,* and *The Witch of Atlas*." *English Language Notes* 24 (September 1986): 58-70.

Goodson, A. C. "Romantic Theory and the Critique of Language." In *Questioning Romanticism*. Edited by John Beer, 3-28. Baltimore: The Johns Hopkins University Press, 1995.

Goslee, Nancy Moore. "Dispersoning Emily: Drafting as Plot in *Epipsychidion*." *The Keats-Shelley Journal* 42 (1993): 104-119.

Grabo, Carl. *Prometheus Unbound: An Interpretation*. New York: Gordian Press, 1968.

Grimshaw, Jean. "Ethics, Fantasy and Self-Transformation." In *The Philosophy of Sex: Contemporary Readings*. Edited by Alan Soble, 175-188. Lanham: Rowman and Littlefield Publishers, 1997.

Grose, Francis. *Classical Dictionary of the Foreign Tongue*. London: Routledge and Kegan Paul, 1963.

Grosz, Elizabeth. "Bodies-Cities." In *Sexuality and Space*. Edited by Beatriz Colomina, 241-253. Princeton Papers on Architecture. Princeton: Princeton University Press, 1992.

———. *Jacques Lacan: A Feminist Introduction*. New York: Routledge, 1990.

Gubar, Susan. "'The Blank Page' and the Issue of Female Creativity." In *The New Feminist Criticism: Essays on Women, Literature, and Theory*. Edited by Elaine Showalter, 292-313. New York: Pantheon Books, 1985.

———. "Representing Pornography: Feminism, Criticism, and Depictions of Female Violence." In *For Adult Users Only: The Dilemma of Violent Pornography*. Edited by Susan Gubar and Joan Hoff, 47-67. Bloomington: Indiana University Press, 1989.

Gubar, Susan, and Joan Hoff, eds. *For Adult Users Only: The Dilemma of Violent Pornography*. Bloomington: Indiana University Press, 1989.

Guillaumin, Colette. "Race and Nature: The System of Marks." In *French Feminism Reader*. Edited by Kelly Oliver, 81-99. Lanham: Rowman and Littlefield Publishers, 2000.

Habermas, Jürgen. *The Structural Transformation of the Public Sphere: An Inquiry into a Category of Bourgeois Society*. Translated by Thomas Burger with Frederick Lawrence. Cambridge: MIT Press, 1994.

Haines, Simon. *Shelley's Poetry: The Divided Self*. New York: St. Martin's Press, 1997.

Harrison, Charles. "The Effects of Landscape." In *Landscape and Power*. Edited by W. J. T. Mitchell, 203-249. Chicago: University of Chicago Press, 1994.

Harvey, David. *The Condition of Postmodernity*. Oxford: Basil Blackwell, 1989.

Hawthorne, Melanie C. "'Comment Peut-on Être Homosexuel?': Multinational (In)Corporation and the Frenchness of *Salomé*." In *Perennial Decay: On the Aesthetics and Politics of Decadence*. Edited by Liz Constable, Dennis Denisoff, and Matthew Potolosky, 159-182. New Cultural Studies, ed. Joan DeJean, Carroll Smith-Rosenberg, Peter Stallybrass, and Gary A. Tomlinson. Philadelphia: University of Pennsylvania Press, 1999.

Hegel, G. W. F. *Phenomenology of the Spirit.* Translated by A. V. Miller. 1807. Reprint, New York: Clarendon Press, 1977.

Helsinger, Elizabeth. "Turner and the Representation of England." In *Landscape and Power.* Edited by W. J. T. Mitchell, 103-125.

Heyd, Milly. *Aubrey Beardsley: Symbol, Mask, and Self-Irony.* New York: Peter Lang, 1986.

Hoagwood, Terence Allan. *Skepticism and Ideology: Shelley's Political Prose and Its Philosophical Context from Bacon to Marx.* Iowa City: University of Iowa Press, 1988.

Hoeveler, Diane Long. *Romantic Androgyny: The Women Within.* University Park: Pennsylvania State University Press, 1990.

Hogle, Jerrold E. *Shelley's Process: Radical Transference and the Development of His Major Works.* New York: Oxford University Press, 1988.

Holmes, Richard. *Shelley: The Pursuit.* New York: E. P. Dutton, 1974; New York: Penguin Books, 1987.

Hould, Claudette. *Images of the French Revolution.* Québec: Musée de Québec/Les Publications du Québec, 1989.

Huet, Marie-Hélène. "Thunder and Revolution: Two Hundred Years of Rethinking." In *The French Revolution 1789-1989: Two Hundred Years of Rethinking.* Edited by Sandy Petrey, 13-32. Lubbock: Texas Tech University Press, 1989.

Hunt, Leigh. *The Descent of Liberty: A Mask.* London: James Cawthorn, 1815.

Hunt, Lynn. "The Bad Mother." Chap. 4 in *The Family Romance of the French Revolution.* Berkeley: University of California Press, 1992.

———. *The Family Romance of the French Revolution.* Berkeley: University of California Press, 1992.

———. "How the Revolution's Divorce Laws Affected Private Life." In *The French Revolution.* Edited by Don Nardo, 112-117. Turning Points in World History. San Diego: Greenhaven Press, 1999.

———. "The Many Bodies of Marie Antoinette: Political Pornography and the Problem of the Feminine in the French Revolution." In *Eroticism and the Body Politic.* Edited by Lynn Hunt, 108-130. Parallax: Re-Visions of Culture and Society, ed. Stephen G. Nichols,

Gerald Prince, and Wendy Steiner. Baltimore: The Johns Hopkins University Press, 1991.

———. *Politics, Culture, and Class in the French Revolution.* Berkeley: University of California Press, 1984.

Hunt, Lynn, ed. *Eroticism and the Body Politic.* Parallax: Re-Visions of Culture and Society, ed. Stephen G. Nichols, Gerald Prince, and Wendy Steiner. Baltimore: The Johns Hopkins University Press, 1991.

Ingraham, Catherine. "Initial Properties: Architecture and the Space of the Line." In *Sexuality and Space.* Edited by Beatriz Colomina, 255-271. Princeton Papers on Architecture. Princeton: Princeton University Press, 1992.

Irigaray, Luce. "Commodities Among Themselves." Chap. 9 in *This Sex Which Is Not One.* Translated by Catherine Porter. Ithaca: Cornell University Press, 1985.

———. "The Power of Discourse and the Subordination of the Feminine." Chap. 4 in *This Sex Which Is Not One.* Translated by Catherine Porter. Ithaca, N.Y.: Cornell University Press, 1985.

———. "Psychoanalytic Theory: Another Look." Chap. 3 in *This Sex Which Is Not One.* Translated by Catherine Porter. Ithaca.: Cornell University Press, 1985.

———. *Speculum of the Other Woman.* Translated by Gillian C. Gill. Ithaca: Cornell University Press, 1985.

———. *This Sex Which Is Not One.* Translated by Catherine Porter. Ithaca: Cornell University Press, 1985.

Itzin, Catherine, ed. *Pornography: Women, Violence, and Civil Liberties.* New York: Oxford University Press, 1992.

Jones, Steven E. "Shelley's Satire of Succession and Brecht's Anatomy of Regression: 'The Mask of Anarchy' and *Der anachronistische Zug oder Freiheit und Democracy.*" In *Shelley: Poet and Legislator of the World.* Edited by Betty T. Bennett and Stuart Curran, 193-200. Baltimore: The Johns Hopkins University Press, 1996.

———. *Shelley's Satire: Violence, Exhortation, and Authority.* DeKalb: Northern Illinois University Press, 1994.

Kappeler, Suzanne. "Pornography: The Representation of Power." In *Pornography: Women, Violence, and Civil Liberties.* Edited by Catherine Itzin, 88-101. New York: Oxford University Press, 1993.

Keats, John. *Lamia. The Poems of John Keats.* Edited by Jack Stillinger, 452-474. Cambridge: Belknap Press of Harvard University Press, 1978.

Kelly, Gary. "From Avant-Garde to Vanguardism: The Shelleys' Romantic Feminism in *Laon and Cythna* and *Frankenstein*." In *Shelley: Poet and Legislator of the World*. Edited by Betty T. Bennett and Stuart Curran, 73-87. Baltimore: The Johns Hopkins University Press, 1996.

Kendrick, Walter. *The Secret Museum: Pornography in Modern Culture*. Berkeley: University of California Press, 1987. Reprint, with a new Afterword, Berkeley: University of California Press, 1996.

Kenyon, J. P., ed. *The Wordsworth Dictionary of British History*. Hertfordshire: Wordsworth Editions Limited, 1994.

King, Geoff. *Mapping Reality: An Exploration of Cultural Cartographies*. New York: St. Martin's Press, 1996.

King-Hele, Desmond. *Shelley: His Thought and Work*. Rutherford: Farleigh Dickinson University Press, 1960.

Kipperman, Mark. "Macropolitics of Utopia: Shelley's *Hellas* in Context." In *Macropolitics of Nineteenth-Century Literature: Nationalism, Exoticism, Imperialism*. Edited by Jonathan Arac and Harriet Ritvo. New Cultural Studies, ed. Jean De Jean, Carol Smith-Rosenberg, and Pater Stallybrass. Philadelphia: University of Philadelphia Press, 1991.

———. "Shelley and the Ideology of the Nation: The Authority of the Poet." In *Shelley: Poet and Legislator of the World*. Edited by Betty T. Bennett and Stuart Curran, 49-59. Baltimore: The Johns Hopkins University Press, 1996.

Kirby, Kathleen M. *Indifferent Boundaries: Spatial Concepts of Human Subjectivity*. New York: The Guilford Press, 1996.

Klancher, Jon P. *The Making of English Reading Audiences, 1790-1832*. Madison: University of Wisconsin Press, 1987.

Kristeva, Julia. "Desire in Language." In *The Portable Kristeva*. Edited and translated by Kelly Oliver, 93-115. New York: Columbia University Press, 1997.

———. *The Kristeva Reader*. Edited by Toril Moi. Translated by Margaret Waller. New York: Columbia University Press, 1986.

———. *The Portable Kristeva*. Edited and translated by Kelly Oliver. New York: Columbia University Press, 1997.

———. *Powers of Horror: An Essay in Abjection*. Translated by Leon Roudiez. New York: Columbia University Press, 1982.

Kucich, Greg. "Eternity and the Ruins of Time: Shelley and the Construction of Cultural History." In *Shelley: Poet and Legislator of the World*. Edited by Betty T. Bennett and Stuart Curran, 14-29. Baltimore: The Johns Hopkins University Press, 1996.

Lacan, Jacques. "God and the *Jouissance* of The Woman." Chap. 6 in *Feminine Sexuality: Jacques Lacan and the école freudienne*. Edited and translated by Juliet Mitchell and Jacqueline Rose. New York: W. W. Norton, 1982.

———. "The Meaning of the Phallus." Chap. 2 in *Feminine Sexuality: Jacques Lacan and the école freudienne*. Edited and translated by Juliet Mitchell and Jacqueline Rose. New York: W. W. Norton, 1982.

———. "The Mirror Stage as Formative of the Function of the I." Chap. 1 in *Écrits: A Selection*, translated by Alan Sheridan. New York: W. W. Norton, 1977.

———. "Of the Network of Signifiers." Chap. 4 in *The Four Fundamental Concepts of Psycho-Analysis*. Edited by Jacques-Alain Miller and translated by Alan Sheridan. New York: W. W. Norton, 1981.

———. "The Split Between the Eye and the Gaze." Chap. 6 in *The Four Fundamental Concepts of Psycho-Analysis*. Edited by Jacques-Alain Miller and translated by Alan Sheridan. New York: W. W. Norton, 1981.

———. "The Subject and the Other: Alienation." Chap. 16 in *The Four Fundamental Concepts of Psycho-Analysis*. Edited by Jacques-Alain Miller and translated by Alan Sheridan. New York: W. W. Norton, 1981.

Laclau, Ernesto. Introduction to *The Sublime Object of Ideology*, by Slavoj Zizek. Translated by Jon Barnes. New York: Verso, 1989.

Lajer-Burcharth, Eva. *Necklines: The Art of Jacques-Louis David after the Terror*. New Haven: Yale University Press, 1999.

Laqueur, Thomas. "The Queen Caroline Affair: Politics as Art in the Reign of George IV." *Journal of Modern History* 54 (September 1982): 417-466.

Lever, Evelyne. *Marie Antoinette: The Last Queen of France*. Translated by Catherine Temerson. New York: Farrar, Straus, Giroux, 2000.

Lever, Maurice. *Sade: A Biography*. Translated by Arthur Goldhammer. San Diego: Harvest, 1993.

Levinson, Marjorie. *The Romantic Fragment Poem: A Critique of Form*. Chapel Hill: University of North Carolina Press, 1986.

Lord, M. G. "Pornutopia: How Feminist Scholars Learned to Love Dirty Pictures." *Linguafranca* 7 (April/May 1997): 40-48.

Macdonald, D. L., and Kathleen Scherf, eds. *Frankenstein; or, The Modern Prometheus*, by Mary Shelley. Orchard Park: Broadview Literary Texts, 1994.

MacGillivray, Catherine A. F. Preface to *FirstDays of the Year*, by Hélène Cixous. Translated by Catherine A. F. MacGillivray, vii-xxiii. Minneapolis: University of Minnesota Press, 1998.

Marcuse, Herbert E. *Eros and Civilization: A Philosophical Inquiry into Freud*. Boston: Beacon Press, 1955.

Maurois, André. *Ariel: A Shelley Romance*. London: John Lane, 1924.

Maza, Sara. "The Diamond Necklace Affair Revisited (1785-1786): The Case of the Missing Queen." In *Eroticism and the Body Politic*. Edited by Lynn Hunt, 63-89. Parallax: Re-Visions of Culture and Society, ed. Stephen G. Nichols, Gerald Prince, and Wendy Steiner. Baltimore: The Johns Hopkins University Press, 1991.

McCalman, Iain. *Radical Underworld: Prophets, Revolutionaries, and Pornographers in London, 1795-1840*. New York: Clarendon Press, 1993.

McGann, Jerome. *The Romantic Ideology: A Critical Investigation*. Chicago: University of Chicago Press, 1983.

McNeice, Gerald. *Shelley and the Revolutionary Idea*. Cambridge: Harvard University Press, 1969.

Mellor, Anne K. *Romanticism and Gender*. New York: Routledge, 1993.

Mestrovic, Stjepan. *The Coming Fin de Siècle: An Application of Durkheim's Sociology to Modernism and Postmodernism*. New York: Routledge, 1991.

Miller, Richard B. "Violent Pornography: Mimetic Nihilism and the Eclipse of Difference." In *For Adult Users Only: The Dilemma of Violent Pornography*. Edited by Susan Gubar and Joan Hoff, 147-162. Bloomington: Indiana University Press, 1989.

Mitchell, W. J. T. Introduction to *Landscape and Power*. Edited by W. J. T. Mitchell, 1-4. Chicago: University of Chicago Press, 1994.

Mitchell, W. J. T., ed. *Landscape and Power*. Chicago: University of Chicago Press, 1994.

Moi, Toril. *Sexual/Textual Politics: Feminist Literary Theory*. New York: Routledge, 1985.

Morton, Timothy. *Shelley and the Revolution in Taste: The Body and the Natural World*. Cambridge: Cambridge University Press, 1994.

———. "Shelley's Green Desert." *Studies in Romanticism* 35 (Summer 1996): 409-430.

Mulvey, Laura. "Pandora: Topographies of the Mask and Curiosity." In *Sexuality and Space*. Edited by Beatriz Colomina, 53-71. Princeton Papers on Architecture. Princeton: Princeton University Press, 1992.

Newlyn, Lucy. "'Questionable Shape': The Aesthetics of Indeterminacy." In *Questioning Romanticism*. Edited by John Beer, 209-233. Baltimore: The Johns Hopkins University Press, 1995.

Newman, Robert D. *Transgressions of Reading: Narrative Engagement as Exile and Return*. Durham: Duke University Press, 1993.

Newman, Robert D., ed. *Centuries' Ends, Narrative Means*. Stanford: Stanford University Press, 1996.

Nardo, Don, ed. *The French Revolution*. Turning Points in World History. San Diego: Greenhaven Press, 1999.

Nordau, Max. *Degeneration*. Translated by George L. Mosse. 1895. Reprint, Lincoln: University of Nebraska Press, 1993.

Oliver, Kelly, ed. *French Feminism Reader*. Lanham: Rowman and Littlefield Publishers, 200.

O'Neill, Michael. *Percy Bysshe Shelley: A Literary Life*. New York: St. Martin's Press, 1990.

Parry, Linda. "Domestic Decoration." Chap. 1 in *William Morris*. Edited by Linda Parry. New York: Harry N. Abrams, 1996.

Parry, Linda, ed. *William Morris*. New York: Harry N. Abrams, 1996.

Paulson, Ronald. "Burke's Sublime and the Representation of Revolution." In *Culture and Politics from Puritanism to the Enlightenment*. Edited by Perez Zagorin. Berkeley: University of California Press, 1980. 241-269.

———. *Representations of Revolution (1789-1820)*. New Haven: Yale University Press, 1983.

Paz, Octavio. *An Erotic Beyond: Sade*. Translated by Eliot Weinberger. New York: Harcourt Brace and Company, 1998.

Pérez-Gómez, Alberto. *Polyphilo; or, The Dark Forest Revisited: An Erotic Epiphany of Architecture*. Cambridge: Cambridge University Press, 1990.

Perrot, Michelle. *A History of Private Life, Vol. IV: From the Fires of the Revolution to the Great War*. 4 vols. Edited by Philippe Ariès and Georges Duby. Translated by Arthur Goldhammer. Cambridge: The Belknap Press of Harvard University Press, 1990.

Péter, Agnes. "A Hermeneutical Reading of *Epipsychidion*." *The Keats-Shelley Journal* 42 (1993): 120-127.

Pinch, Adela, "Thinking about the Other in Romantic Love." In *Romantic Passions*. Edited by Elizabeth Fay. Romantic Circles Praxis Series, ed. Orrin N. C. Wang and John Morillo. <http://www.umd.edu/praxis/pas sions/pinch/pinch.html>.

Pittock, Murray G. H. *Spectrum of Decadence: The Literature of the 1890s.* New York: Routledge, 1993.

Polhemus, Robert M. *Erotic Faith: Being in Love from Jane Austen to D. H. Lawrence.* Chicago: University of Chicago Press, 1990.

Reading Shelley's Interventionist Poetry, 1819-1820. Edited by Michael Henry Scrivener. Romantic Circles Praxis Series, ed. Orrin N. C. Wang and John Morillo. <http://www.umd.edu/praxis/intervention ist/>.

Reiman, Donald H. "Shelley and the Human Condition." In *Shelley: Poet and Legislator of the World.* Edited by Betty T. Bennett and Stuart Curran, 3-13. Baltimore: The Johns Hopkins University Press, 1996.

Richardson, Alan. *A Mental Theater: Poetic Drama and Consciousness in the Romantic Age.* University Park: Pennsylvania State University Press, 1988.

Robinson, Charles E. *Shelley and Byron: The Snake and Eagle Wreathed in Fight.* Baltimore: The Johns Hopkins University Press, 1976.

Robinson, Jeffrey C., "Passion and Romantic Poets." In *Romantic Passions.* Edited by Elizabeth Fay. Romantic Circles Praxis Series, ed. Orrin N. C. Wang and John Morillo. <http://www.umd.edu/praxis/passions/robinson/rbsn.html>.

Roe, Nicholas. Untitled seminar discussion delivered to the Interdisciplinary Group for Historical Literary Study, Texas A&M University, College Station, Tex., April 1996.

Romantic Passions. Edited by Elizabeth Fay. Romantic Circles Praxis Series, ed. Orrin N. C. Wang and John Morillo. <http://www.umd/edu/praxis/passions/fay/intro.html>.

Rosario, Vernon A. *The Erotic Imagination: French Histories of Perversity.* New York: Oxford University Press, 1997.

Rose, Phyllis. *Parallel Lives: Five Victorian Marriages.* New York: Alfred A. Knopf, 1984.

Rzepka, Charles J. "Re-collecting Spontaneous Overflows: Romantic Passions, the Sublime, and Mesmerism." In *Romantic Passions.* Edited by Elizabeth Fay. Romantic Circles Praxis Series, ed. Orrin N. C. Wang and John Morillo. <http://www.umd.edu/ praxis/passions/rzepka/rzp.html>.

Sade, Donatien Alphonse (Marquis de). *The 120 Days of Sodom and Other Writings.* Compiled and translated by Austryn Wainhouse and Richard Seaver. New York: Grove Weidenfeld, 1966.

Said, Edward W. *Representations of the Intellectual: The 1993 Reith Lectures.* New York: Pantheon Books, 1994.

Saint-Amand, Pierre. *The Libertine's Progress: Seduction in the Eighteen-Century French Novel*. Translated by Jennifer Curtiss Gage. Hanover: Brown University Press, 1994.

Scarry, Elaine. *Fins de siècle: English Poetry in 1590, 1690, 1790, 1890, 1990*. Baltimore: The Johns Hopkins University Press, 1995.

Schama, Simon. *Citizens: A Chronicle of the French Revolution*. New York: Alfred A. Knopf, 1989.

———. *Landscape and Memory*. New York: Alfred A. Knopf, 1995.

Schorske, Carl. *Fin-de-siècle Vienna: Politics and Culture*. New York: Random House, 1961. Reprint, New York: Vintage, 1981.

Scrivener, Michael Henry. *Radical Shelley: The Philosophical Anarchism and Utopian Thought of Percy Bysshe Shelley*. Princeton: Princeton University Press, 1982.

Sedgwick, Eve Kosofsky. *Between Men: English Literature and Male Homosocial Desire*. Gender and Culture, ed. Carolyn G. Heilbrun and Nancy K. Miller. New York: Columbia University Press, 1985.

———. *Epistemology of the Closet*. Berkeley: University of California Press, 1990.

———. *Tendencies*. Durham: Duke University Press, 1993.

Shattuck, Roger. *Forbidden Knowledge: From Prometheus to Pornography*. New York: St. Martin's Press, 1996.

Shelley, Bryan. *Shelley and Scripture: The Interpreting Angel*. New York: Clarendon Press, 1994.

Shelley, Mary. *Frankenstein; or, The Modern Prometheus*. 3 vols. London: Lackington, Hughes, Harding, Mavor, and Jones, 1818.

———. "Note to Œdipus Tyrannus; or, Swellfoot the Tyrant." In *The Complete Works of Percy Bysshe Shelley*. 10 vols. Edited by Roger Ingpen and Walter E. Peck, 2:360. New York: Charles Scribner's Sons, 1928.

Shelley, Percy Bysshe. *Alastor; or, The Spirit of Solitude*. In *Shelley's Poetry and Prose*. Edited by Donald H. Reiman and Sharon B. Powers, 70-87. New York: W. W. Norton, 1977.

———. *The Complete Works of Percy Bysshe Shelley*. Edited by Roger Ingpen and Walter E. Peck. 10 vols. New York: Charles Scribner's Sons, 1928.

———. *The Cenci: A Tragedy, in Five Acts*. In *Shelley's Poetry and Prose*. Edited by Donald H. Reiman and Sharon B. Powers, 237-301. New York: W. W. Norton, 1977.

———. *A Defence of Poetry.* In *Shelley's Poetry and Prose.* Edited by Donald H. Reiman and Sharon B. Powers, 478-508. New York: W. W. Norton, 1977.

———. "A Discourse on the Manners of the Ancient Greeks Relative to the Subject of Love." In *Shelley's Prose or The Trumpet of a Prophecy.* Edited by David Lee Clark, 216-223. New York: New Amsterdam Books, 1988.

———. *Epipsychidion: Verses Addressed to the Noble and Unfortunate Lady, Emilia V———, Now Imprisoned in the Convent of ———.* In *Shelley's Poetry and Prose.* Edited by Donald H. Reiman and Sharon B. Powers, 373-388. New York: W. W. Norton, 1977.

———. "Essay on Christianity." In *Shelley's Prose or The Trumpet of a Prophecy.* Edited by David Lee Clark, 196-214. New York: New Amsterdam Books, 1988.

———. *Julian and Maddalo; A Conversation.* In *Shelley's Poetry and Prose.* Edited by Donald H. Reiman and Sharon B. Powers, 112-127. New York: W. W. Norton, 1977.

———. *Laon and Cythna; or, The Revolution of the Golden City. A Vision of the Nineteenth Century in the Stanza of Spenser.* In *The Complete Works of Percy Bysshe Shelley.* Edited by Thomas Hutchinson. New York: Oxford University Press, 1934; New York: Oxford University Press, 1956.

———. *The Letters of Percy Bysshe Shelley.* Edited by Frederick L. Jones. 2 vols. Oxford, England: Clarendon Press, 1964.

———. "Lines Written Among the Euganean Hills." In *Shelley's Poetry and Prose.* Edited by Donald H. Reiman and Sharon B. Powers, 103-112. New York: W. W. Norton, 1977.

———. "Ode to Naples." In *The Complete Works of Percy Bysshe Shelley.* Edited by Roger Ingpen and Walter E. Peck, 10 vols. 4:51-56. New York: Charles Scribner's Sons, 1928.

———. *Œdipus Tyrannus, or Swellfoot the Tyrant.* In *The Complete Works of Percy Bysshe Shelley.* Edited by Roger Ingpen and Walter E. Peck, 10 vols. 2:317-350. New York: Charles Scribner's Sons, 1928.

———. "On Life." In *Shelley's Poetry and Prose.* Edited by Donald H. Reiman and Sharon B. Powers, 474-478. New York: W. W. Norton, 1977.

———. "On Love." In *Shelley's Poetry and Prose.* Edited by Donald H. Reiman and Sharon B. Powers, 473-474. New York: W. W. Norton, 1977.

———. "Ozymandias." In *Shelley's Poetry and Prose*. Edited by Donald H. Reiman and Sharon B. Powers, 103. New York: W. W. Norton, 1977.

———. *Prometheus Unbound: A Lyrical Drama in Four Acts.* In *Shelley's Poetry and Prose*. Edited by Donald H. Reiman and Sharon B. Powers, 132-210. New York: W. W. Norton, 1977.

———. *Rosalind and Helen: A Modern Eclogue. Percy Bysshe Shelley: Complete Poems*, 136-151. New York: Book-of-the-Month Club, 1993.

———. *Shelley's Poetry and Prose.* Edited by Donald H. Reiman and Sharon B. Powers. New York: W. W. Norton, 1977.

———. *Shelley's Prose or The Trumpet of a Prophecy.* Edited by David Lee Clark. New York: New Amsterdam Books, 1988.

———. *The Triumph of Life.* In *Shelley's Poetry and Prose*. Edited by Donald H. Reiman and Sharon B. Powers, 453-470. New York: W. W. Norton, 1977.

Shires, Linda M. "Of Maenads, Mothers, and Feminized Males: Victorian Readings of the French Revolution." In *Rewriting the Victorians: Theory, History, and the Politics of Gender*. Edited by Linda M. Shires, 147-165. New York: Routledge, 1992.

Shires, Linda M., ed. *Rewriting the Victorians: Theory, History, and the Politics of Gender.* New York: Routledge, 1992.

Showalter, Elaine. *Sexual Anarchy: Gender and Decadence at the Fin de Siècle.* New York: Viking, 1990.

Silverman, Kaja. *World Spectators.* Cultural Memory in the Present, ed. Mieke Bal and Hent de Vried. Stanford: Stanford University Press, 2000.

Siskin, Clifford. *The Historicity of Romantic Discourse.* New York: Oxford University Press, 1987.

Smith, Bruce. "Premodern Sexualities." *PMLA* 115.3 (May 2000): 318-329.

Smith, E. A. *A Queen on Trial: The Affair of Queen Caroline.* Dover: Alan Sutton, 1993.

Soble, Alan, ed. *The Philosophy of Sex: Contemporary Readings.* 3rd edition. Lanham: Rowman and Littlefield Publishers, 1997.

Stahmer, Charles. "A Language That Both Is and Is Not Their Own: Another Look at the Efficacy of Language in Shelley's *The Cenci*." Paper presented at the "Re-Reading Romanticism" conference at Duke University, Durham, N.C., November 1993.

Stevenson, John. *London in the Age of Reform.* New York: Oxford University Press, 1977.

Straub, Kristina. *Sexual Subjects: Eighteenth-Century Players and Sexual Ideology.* Princeton: Princeton University Press, 1992.

Swinburne, Algernon Charles. *William Blake: A Critical Essay.* Edited by Hugh J. Luke. 1868. Reprint, Lincoln: University of Nebraska Press, 1970.

Taylor, Mark C. *Disfiguring: Art, Architecture, Religion.* Chicago: University of Chicago Press, 1992.

Thornton, Peter. *Authentic Decor: The Domestic Interior 1620-1920.* New York: Viking, 1984.

Tripp, Edward. *The Meridian Handbook of Classical Mythology.* New York: New American Library, 1970.

Turner, James. "Pepys and the Private Parts of Monarchy." In *Culture and Society in the Stuart Restoration.* Edited by Gerald Maclean, 95-110. Chicago: University of Chicago Press, 1995.

Ulmer, William. *Shelleyan Eros: The Rhetoric of Love.* Princeton: Princeton University Press, 1990.

von Kuehnelt-Leddihn, Eric. "The Age of the Guillotine (Sade, Robespierre, and the Consequences)." In *Reflections on the French Revolution: A Hillsdale Symposium.* Edited by Stephen J. Tonsor, 71-81. Washington, D.C.: Rignery Gateway, 1990.

Walkowitz, Judith R. *City of Dreadful Delight: Narratives of Sexual Danger in Late-Victorian London.* London: Virago Press, 1992.

Warnke, Martin. *Political Landscape: The Art History of Nature.* Cambridge: Harvard University Press, 1995.

Wassermann, Earl. *Shelley: A Critical Reading.* Baltimore: The Johns Hopkins University Press, 1971.

Watkins, Daniel P. *Sexual Power in British Romantic Poetry.* Gainesville: University Press of Florida, 1996.

White, Deborah Elise. *Romantic Returns: Superstition, Imagination, History.* Stanford: Stanford University Press, 2000.

White, Newman Ivey. *Shelley.* 2 vols. New York: Alfred A. Knopf, 1940.

———. "Shelley's Swell-Foot the Tyrant in Relation to Contemporary Political Satires." *PMLA* 36 (1921): 332-346.

Wigley, Mark. "Untitled: The Housing of Gender." In *Sexuality and Space.* Edited by Beatriz Colomina, 327-389. Princeton Papers on Architecture. Princeton: Princeton University Press, 1992.

Wilde, Oscar. *The Decay of Lying*. In *Complete Works of Oscar Wilde*, 1071-1092. 1948; Reprint, Glasgow: HarperCollins Publishers, 1994.

———. *The Importance of Being Earnest*. In *The Norton Anthology of English Literature, Vol. 2. 6th ed.* Edited by M. H. Abrams, et. al., 1628-1667. New York: W. W. Norton, 1993.

———. *The Picture of Dorian Gray.* Edited by Donald L. Lawler. A Norton Critical Edition. New York: W. W. Norton, 1988.

Williams, Linda. "Fetishism and Hard Core: Marx, Freud, and the 'Money Shot'." In *For Adult Users Only: The Dilemma of Violent Pornography*. Edited by Susan Gubar and Joan Hoff, 198-217. Bloomington: Indiana University Press, 1989.

Williams, Raymond. *Culture and Society 1780-1950*. New York: Harper Torchbooks, 1958.

Winterson, Jeanette. "Ecstasy and Energy: The Semiotics of Sex." In *Art Objects: Essays on Ecstasy and Effrontery*, 103-118. New York: Vintage, 1995.

Wolfenstein, Eugene Victor. *Psychoanalytic-Marxism: Groundwork*. New York: The Guilford Press, 1993.

Wollstonecraft, Mary. *The Wrongs of Woman; or, Maria*. 1798. In *"Mary" and "The Wrongs of Woman."* Reprint, edited by Gary Kelly, 69-204. New York: Oxford, 1991.

Wordsworth, William. Preface to *Lyrical Ballads*. In *William Wordsworth*. Edited by Stephen Gill. The Oxford Authors, ed. Frank Kermode. New York: Oxford University Press, 1988.

Worton, Michael. "Speech and Silence in *The Cenci*." In *Essays on Shelley*. Edited by Miriam Allot, 78-94. Liverpool: Liverpool University Press, 1982.

Zizek, Slavoj. *The Sublime Object of Ideology.* Translated by Jon Barnes. New York: Verso, 1989.

Index

A

Abram, David, 175
  The Spell of the Sensuous, 173
Ackroyd, Peter, 216 n 17
Aesthetes, 290, 294, 299, 300, 301–12, 316 n 19
Alberti, Leon Battista, *On the Art of Building in Ten Books,* 315 n 17
Alphonse, Donatien. *See* Sade, Marquis de
androgyny, 182, 201–07, 213, 282 n 49
architecture, 152–54, 164 n 26, 183, 295–98, 312, 314 n 9, 314 n 13, 315 n 17
Aristophanes, 61
  Lysistrata, 310–11
Arnold, Matthew, 41 n 35, 109 n 1, 213
Atkinson, Thomas Dinham, 314 n 13

B

Bachelard, Gaston, 295
Baker, Carlos, 55
Bakhtin, Mikhail, 113 n 29

Barthes, Roland, 5, 6, 15, 42 n 42, 212
  Le Plaisir du Texte [The Pleasure of the Text], 14, 286
  Sade, Fourier, Loyola, 286
Bataille, Georges, *Histoire de l'oeil [Story of the Eye],* 114 n 35
Bate, Walter Jackson, 44 n 66
Baudrillard, Jean, 8, 12, 128, 179, 236, 286
Beardsley, Aubrey, 36, 290, 302, 303, 310–12, 316 n 19
Beer, John, 8, 177
Benét, Laura, 109
Bermingham, Ann, 176
Bernier, Oliver, 44 n 62
Betsky, Aaron, 312
Bible, 70, 115 n 41, 116 n 52, 253–55, 302, 304
  Tower of Babel, 183
Blake, William, 36, 41 n 35, 216 n 16, 216 n 17, 271, 290
  Songs of Innocence and of Experience, 181, 291
Bloch, Ernst, 40–41 n 31, 269
Bonca, Tedi Chichester, 4, 38 n 11, 44 n 65, 279 n 30

339

Boyer, M. Christine, 162 n 16
Brigham, Linda, 280 n 34
Brougham, Henry, 55
Brown, Nathaniel, 227, 271, 274 n 7, 281 n 36, 281 n 37
Buchanan, Robert, 316 n 19
Burke, Edmund, 44 n 65, 60, 61
   Reflections on the Revolution in France, 21, 23, 111 n 14
Butler, Marilyn, 17–18
Byron, Lord, George Gordon, 17, 29, 33, 39 n 23, 147, 217 n 22, 290, 292–94, 302
   Beppo, 293
   Cain, 33
   Childe Harold's Pilgrimage, 67
   "Darkness," 68
   Don Juan, 33, 293, 298
   The Giaour, 117 n 58
   Heaven and Earth: A Mystery, 292–93
   Manfred, 294
   Sardanapalus, 293, 301

C

Cameron, Kenneth Neill, 57, 60–61, 66, 110 n 8, 116 n 50, 118 n 69, 119 n 72, 178, 183, 215 n 9, 216 n 212, 218–19 n 36, 219 n 40, 240, 248, 258, 274 n 5, 274 n 7, 280 n 34, 282 n 45, 285
Cameron, Vivian, 40–41 n 31
Carlile, Richard, 113 n 28
Caroline of Brunswick (queen of England), 7, 19, 43 n 58, 52–64, 74, 75, 78, 99, 102, 110 n 7, 110 n 10, 111 n 14, 112 n 20, 112 n 21, 113 n 31, 118 n 69.
   See also Queen Caroline Affair

cartography, 248
   erotic, 175, 176, 182, 190, 267, 271, 289, 293, 294–97, 299, 300, 305
castration, 15, 59, 65, 75–76, 103, 114 n 35, 116 n 50, 118 n 68, 157, 199, 309
centrality, 248, 279 n 29
Chambers, Ross, 9, 153, 168–69 n 59
Charles II (king of England), 7, 40 n 24, 40 n 25
Chodorow, Nancy J., 117 n 54
Christ, Jesus, 10, 23, 31, 50–51, 70, 184, 253–55, 257–58, 276 n 14, 281 n 43, 282 n 45
Christianity, 6, 33, 38 n 11, 50–51, 69–70, 184, 209, 223 n 66, 254–55, 257–58, 276 n 12, 281 n 43, 294, 299, 301, 308–09
Cixous, Hélène, 287
   Angst, 214
   "Castration or Decapitation," 222 n 62
Clairmont, Claire, 196
Clark, Anna, 55, 62–63, 118 n 64
Clark, Timothy, 147, 167 n 48, 167 n 49, 215 n 7
class, 5, 6, 7, 20, 25, 29, 31, 44 n 68
Clément, A., 23, 31, 62
cloistered-private, 296–98, 305, 315 n 16
Cobbett, William, 53
cockney: definitions of, 26
Cockney School, 25–33, 113 n 32, 303, 304, 305, 315–16 n 19
Cohen, Ed, 317 n 31
Coleridge, Samuel Taylor, 36, 286, 290
   "Christabel," 290
   The Rime of the Ancient Mariner, 279 n 30

Colomina, Beatriz, 295
community, feminine. *See* feminine community
Confédération de la nature, ou L'Art de se reproduire, avec figures, La [The Confederation of Nature, or The Reproductive Art, with Pictures], 20
Cooperman, Robert, *In the Household of Percy Bysshe Shelley*, 109 n 1
Cox, Jeffrey N., 113–14 n 32, 118 n 58, 165 n 29, 166 n 33, 166 n 36
Cronin, Richard, 94, 168 n 53
Crook, Nora, 218 n 36
Crosby, Christina, 314 n 13
Cruikshank, George, 59
Curran, Stuart, 78–79, 162 n 13, 162 n 15, 256, 267, 280 n 34, 282 n 45

D

Daniels, Stephen, 176
Darnton, Robert, 3, 5, 12–13, 42 n 40
Dawson, P. M. S., 201, 283–84 n 57
decadence, 299, 300, 302, 304, 305, 308, 310, 317 n 33
Decadents, 304, 306, 307, 316 n 19
Deleuze, Gilles, 152, 163 n 22
Derrida, Jacques, 195
  Of Grammatology, 219 n 37
Desperet, 272, 284 n 58
didacticism. *See* pedagogy
Douglas, Lord, Alfred, "Two Loves," 109 n 2
Dowling, Linda, 24, 45 n 70, 316 n 19
Duff, David, 226, 273 n 3, 274 n 7, 276 n 13, 277 n 20
Durant, David N., 314 n 13

E

Eisenberg, Evan, 313
Eliot, T. S., 213
Erkelenz, Michael, 66
Essick, Robert N., 182–83, 216 n 21

F

family, 51, 55, 64–65, 116 n 51, 130, 133–42, 161 n 10, 196, 242, 291, 295
father, 15, 64–65, 124, 130, 133–42, 162 n 16, 174, 208, 237, 254
feminine community, 20, 128, 129, 143–46, 166 n 40, 167 n 45, 229, 291
femininity, 8, 24, 27–28, 44 n 68, 52, 55, 85, 110 n 7, 112 n 18, 161 n 10, 165 n 27, 182, 197–201, 236, 283 n 54, 291, 293, 299, 300.
  See also feminine community; feminism; feminization
feminism, 27, 116 n 54, 226, 231, 247, 279 n 29, 281 n 36
  feminist theory, 220 n 51
  French, 161 n 10, 185, 219 n 44, 222 n 62.
  See also psychoanalysis: feminist; *jouissance*
feminization, 15, 22, 23, 26, 28, 31, 79, 206, 308
Ferris, Suzanne, 162 n 12
Frappier-Mazur, Lucienne, 2, 4–5, 10, 38 n 4, 134
Fraser, Flora, 40 n 26, 58, 59
free love, 11, 35, 161 n 10, 183, 190–93, 197, 201, 210, 211, 213, 214
French Revolution, 1–2, 7, 17–20, 23, 25, 34, 62, 128, 130, 217 n 23, 231, 234, 271, 275 n 10,

282 n 50, 284 n 58, 290, 304, 305, 308, 317 n 26
Freud, Sigmund, 45 n 71, 116–17 n 54, 124–25, 186, 187, 220 n 51
   "Beyond the Pleasure Principle," 136, 140
   "Civilization and Its Discontents," 124.
   See also psychoanalysis: Freudian
Frosh, Stephen, 18, 180
Fulford, Roger, 111 n 12

G

Gallop, Jane, 117 n 54, 220 n 51
Gaull, Marilyn, 214 n 1
Gay, Peter, 180, 301–02
gender, 5, 107
George IV (king of England), 7, 54, 56–59, 75, 78, 111 n 12
Gere, Charlotte, 314 n 7
Gilchrist, Alexander, 216 n 17
Gillray, James, 60
God, 124–25, 131, 135, 162 n 16, 163 n 19, 165 n 28, 175, 178, 183–84, 192, 240, 254, 256, 257, 276 n 12, 280 n 33, 309.
   See also Romantic pantheism
Godwin, Mary Wollstonecraft, 118 n 67, 121, 126–27, 161 n 8, 279 n 31.
   See also Shelley, Mary
Godwin, William, 180, 181
Gold, Elise M., 94, 113 n 29, 118 n 66
Goodson, A. C., 210
Goslee, Nancy Moore, 223 n 64, 223 n 69, 224 n 78
Grabo, Carl, 282 n 45
Gray, John, 36, 290, 302, 310, 315 n 19
   "The Barber," 310
   "Complaint," 310
   "Les Demoiselles de Sauve," 310
   "Heart's Demense," 310
   "Mishka," 310
   "Mon Dieu M'a Dit," 310
   "On a Picture," 310
   Silverpoints, 310
   "Song of the Seedling," 310
   "A Une Madone," 310
   "La Voyage à Cythère," 310
Grimshaw, Jean, 3, 178
Grose, Francis, 119 n 74
Grosz, Elizabeth, 42 n 38, 218 n 31
Guattari, Félix, 152, 163 n 22
Gubar, Susan, 117 n 54, 169 n 64
Guillaumin, Colette, 162 n 16, 163 n 22
Guiton, Derek, 218 n 36

H

Habermas, Jürgen, 16–17
Haines, Simon, 215 n 7
Hallward, Basil, 296, 308, 317 n 31
Harrison, Charles, 45–46 n 79, 176
Harvey, David, 294
Hawthorne, Melanie C., 39 n 23, 112 n 20
Hazlitt, William, 53, 213
Hegel, Georg Wilhelm Friedrich, The Phenomenology of the Spirit, 216 n 20, 218 n 31
Helsinger, Elizabeth, 284 n 58
Hénaff, Marcel, 162 n 13
heteroeroticism, 299
heteropatriarchy, 15, 179, 183, 191, 193, 196, 207, 209, 220 n 51
   heteropatriarchal imperative, definition of, 215 n 11
heterosexuality, 299
Heyd, Milly, 311–12
history, 49, 130, 196, 245, 294, 296–97

Hoagwood, Terence Allan, 180
Hoeveler, Diane Long, 178, 179, 188, 195, 221 n 57, 282 n 49, 283 n 55
Hogg, Thomas Jefferson, 121, 127, 279 n 31
Hogle, Jerrold E., 162 n 15, 166 n 33, 166 n 36, 168 n 54, 169 n 63, 239, 274 n 7, 280 n 34, 280 n 35, 284 n 60
Holmes, Richard, 45 n 77, 115–16 n 49, 167 n 47, 167 n 48, 215 n 9, 218–19 n 36, 283 n 57
Homer, 240
homoeroticism, 219 n 42, 299, 305, 306, 310
homosexuality, 109 n 2, 305, 306, 308, 310, 317 n 26, 317 n 31
Hone, William, 113 n 28
  A New Catechism, 60
Hould, Claudette, 60, 163 n 19
Huet, Marie-Hélène, 40 n 27
Hunt, Leigh, 25, 26–33, 44 n 66, 45 n 70, 60–61, 63, 229, 304
  The Descent of Liberty, 53, 63–64, 70, 113 n 32
  Foliage, 44 n 69, 113 n 31,
  The Story of Rimini, 28–31, 44–45 n 69, 113–14 n 31, 304
Hunt, Lynn, 6, 19–21, 39 n 21, 39 n 22, 53, 130, 163 n 17
Hunt, William Holman, 291
Huysmans, Joris Karl, 315 n 19

I

incest, 20, 23, 33, 36, 125, 129–32, 133–42, 160 n 6, 174, 208, 226, 227, 239–41, 249–50, 258, 277 n 21, 294
Ingraham, Catherine, 152
Irigaray, Luce, 45 n 71, 105, 117 n 54, 161 n 10, 189, 218 n 30, 219 n 44, 220 n 51
  "The Power of Discourse and the Subordination of the Feminine," 198

J

Jesus Christ. *See* Christ, Jesus
Johnson, Joseph: Johnson circle, 181, 216 n 17
Jones, Steven E., 110 n 4, 110 n 10, 118 n 62, 119 n 70, 119 n 72, 119 n 73
jouissance, 185, 187, 189, 193, 204–05, 209, 213

K

Kant, Immanuel, 295
Kappeler, Susanne, 169 n 64
Keats, John, 25, 29–33, 36, 44 n 66, 45 n 70, 217 n 22, 290, 291, 304, 307, 308
  Endymion, 29
  The Eve of St. Agnes, 292
  Isabella; or, The Pot of Basil, 292
  Lamia, 291–92
  "Ode on a Grecian Urn," 301
Kelly, Gary, 12, 39–40 n 23, 44 n 68, 226, 274 n 7
Kendrick, Walter, 39 n 23
Kenyon, J. P., 40 n 24
King, Geoff, 10, 152, 176
King-Hele, Desmond, 167 n 47, 182–83, 215 n 9, 220 n 49, 220 n 50, 256, 261, 274 n 5, 277 n 20, 282 n 45
Kipperman, Mark, 35, 144, 211
Kirby, Kathleen M., 242
Klancher, Jon P., 18, 286
Kristeva, Julia, 41–42 n 37, 189, 205, 221 n 58, 222 n 63, 313
Kucich, Greg, 215 n 8

L

Lacan, Jacques, 35, 117 n 54, 140, 185, 187, 188–89, 198, 218 n 31. *See also* psychoanalysis: Lacanian

Lajer-Burcharth, Eva, 6, 151

landscape, 149–51, 154, 159, 163 n 21, 168 n 53, 168 n 56, 168 n 58, 174, 175, 179, 207, 208, 229, 231, 243–48, 250, 263–71, 272, 273, 284 n 58, 293, 295, 313

    definitions of, 176, 275 n 8. *See also* cartography

Laqueur, Thomas W., 53, 58–59

Lawrence, James Henry, 126

Leavis, F. R., 213

Lely, Sir Peter, 40 n 24

lesbianism, 299, 300, 301

Lever, Evelyne, 22, 43 n 60

Lever, Maurice, 2, 6, 37 n 1, 37 n 4, 43 n 60

Levinson, Marjorie, 154, 168 n 51, 168 n 56

liberation, 2, 7–8, 36, 128, 160 n 6, 161 n 10, 175, 178, 183, 190, 193–94, 227, 231, 237, 240, 243–44, 256–57, 259, 261, 291, 300. *See also* liberty; liberty-through-love

libertinism, 7, 21, 39 n 22, 131, 166 n 33

liberty, 49, 66–73, 92–94, 107, 118 n 60, 237, 240, 250, 257, 266, 273, 275 n 10, 284 n 58, 289. *See also* liberation

liberty-through-love, 51, 73, 75, 87, 108, 127, 214, 247, 250, 276 n 12, 286, 289, 295, 313

Lockhart, John Gibson, 25, 27–33, 45 n 70, 45 n 77, 307, 308

love, 11, 49–52, 73, 121–28, 150–51, 177, 179, 182–86, 190–94, 250, 256, 257, 270, 275 n 10, 287–89, 292, 301, 313. *See also* free love, liberty-through-love

Lucifer, 71, 234, 257–58. *See also* Satan

M

Macdonald, D. L., 39 n 23

MacGillivray, Catherine A. F., 287

Mallarmé, Stephan, 315 n 19

Malory, Sir Thomas, *Le Morte D'Arthur,* 310–11

Man Ray, 38 n 4

map(ping). *See* cartography

Marcuse, Herbert E., *Eros and Civilization,* 180, 214 n 1

marginality, 279 n 29

Marie Antoinette (queen of France), 21–24, 27, 34, 39 n 21, 43 n 57, 43 n 58, 43 n 60, 44 n 62, 45 n 74, 54, 62, 74, 111 n 14, 304, 308

marriage, 7, 49, 52–53, 55, 118 n 67, 126–27, 160–61 n 7, 161 n 8, 167 n 40, 178, 191–92, 196, 222 n 61

Martin, John, 284 n 58

Marx, Karl, *Economic and Philosophical Manuscripts,* 118 n 61. *See also* psychoanalysis: psychoanalytic-Marxist theory

masculinism, 217 n 27, 291, 299

masculinity, 23, 27–28, 84–85, 112 n 18, 165 n 27, 200, 236, 283 n 54

masturbation, 154–55, 159

maternity. *See* mother

Index

Maturin, Charles Robert, *Melmoth the Wanderer*, 279 n 30
Maurois, André, 109 n 1
Maza, Sara, 55
McCalman, Iain, 19, 40 n 26
McGann, Jerome, 217 n 22
McNiece, Gerald, 256, 261, 282 n 50, 283 n 53
Medwin, Thomas, 56, 114 n 37
Mellor, Anne K., 17–18
Mercier, Louis-Sébastien, 42 n 40
   De la Littérature et des littéraries, 12
Merrick, Jeffrey, 19
Miller, Richard B., 169 n 64
Milton, John, 240
   Paradise Lost, 254
Mitchell, W. J. T., 176
Moi, Toril, 161 n 10, 186, 188
monarchy, 11, 12-13, 69-70, 105.
   See also Caroline of Brunswick; Charles II; George IV; Marie Antoinette; Queen Caroline Affair
monogamy, 192–93, 201.
   See also marriage
Moore, Thomas, 228, 274 n 4
Morris, William, 314 n 7
Morton, Timothy, 278 n 24
mother, 23–24, 30, 44 n 62, 52, 64–65, 86, 140, 143–44, 167 n 40, 186, 208, 210, 230, 236–37, 258, 277 n 17, 280 n 33, 291

N

natural world, 176, 208, 244, 253, 263, 264–66, 267–68, 269–70, 285, 288, 298
nature, 208, 245, 252, 272, 283 n 54, 283 n 55, 290, 291, 311

Newlyn, Lucy, 213–14
Newman, Robert D., 284 n 59, 287
Nordau, Max, 303–04, 316 n 24, 317 n 30, 317–18 n 33
   Degeneration, 303
North, Francis, *The Kentish Barons*, 117–18 n 58

O

Ollier, Charles, 225, 227–28
O'Neill, Michael, 274 n 5, 285–86
ooziness, 3, 8, 11, 50, 128, 143, 146, 151, 159
   definition of, 41 n 37, 177, 179, 207, 208–09, 231, 246, 267, 271, 310
oppositionality, 8, 9, 56–57, 71, 75, 79, 80, 83, 102–03, 112 n 18, 134, 161 n 10, 165 n 27, 169 n 59, 203, 207–08, 260
oppression, 2, 22, 49–50, 71, 86–87, 94, 145–47, 190, 214, 239, 249, 254, 260, 261, 266, 313
Orwell, George, *Animal Farm*, 113 n 27

P

paganism, 299, 300–01
Paine, Thomas, 45 n 75
Parry, Linda, 314 n 7
Pater, Walter, 306
Paterman, Carole, 6
patriarchy, 11, 15, 52–53, 55, 74, 112 n 18, 128, 130–132, 133–42, 144–47, 157–58, 161 n 10, 165 n 27, 178, 187, 190, 209, 227, 261, 276 n 12, 291, 293, 296, 299, 309.
   See also father; heteropatriarchy; psychoanalysis

Paulson, Ronald, 2, 8, 21, 60, 181, 214 n 1, 284 n 58
Paz, Octavio, 129, 131, 166 n 33
Peacock, Thomas Love, 56, 113 n 31
pedagogy, 12, 51, 148, 231–35, 251
penis, 78, 157, 187, 220 n 51.
    See also phallus
Penley, Constance, 3
Pérez-Goméz, Alberto, 296
Perrot, Michelle, 55, 295, 314 n 13
Péter, Agnes, 223 n 70
Peterloo Massacre, 62, 66, 253
phallicism. *See* phallus
phallus, 59, 74–77, 83–85, 94, 103–05, 108, 114 n 35, 164 n 24, 165 n 27, 187, 198, 204, 206, 311
    phallic female, 205
Pittock, Murray G. H., 305
Pocock, J. G. A., 111 n 14
Polhemus, Robert M., 42 n 45, 129, 151, 227
polygamy, 193
pornography, 1, 3, 5, 12, 19–22, 45 n 74, 56, 290, 315 n 16
Powers, Sharon B., 67, 226, 282 n 52
Pre-Raphaelites, 290, 294–301, 303, 316 n 19
private, 1, 16, 22, 34, 36, 43 n 60, 44 n 62, 49, 62, 64–65, 114 n 37, 228, 290, 295–98, 299, 300, 305, 310–11.
    See also cloistered-private
prostitution, 20, 160–61 n 7
psychoanalysis, 180–82
    feminist, 116–17 n 54, 219 n 44, 222 n 62
    Freudian, 116–17 n 54, 204, 217 n 27, 219 n 44, 222 n 62
    Lacanian, 116–17 n 54, 141, 174, 180, 182, 184–85, 187–89, 193, 204, 208, 211, 216, 217 n 27, 220 n 51
    patriarchal agenda of, 84, 114 n 35, 217 n 27
    psychoanalytic-Marxist theory, 181–82.
    See also jouissance
public, 1, 16, 22, 34, 36, 43 n 60, 44 n 62, 49, 62, 64–65, 103, 114 n 37, 228, 290, 292, 295–98, 299, 300, 305, 308, 310–11

Q

Queen Caroline Affair, 7, 19, 40 n 26, 43 n 57, 43 n 58, 52–63, 65, 73, 75, 108, 113 n 29, 119 n 72

R

Raffalovich, André, 302, 315 n 19
rape, 2, 116 n 52, 129–32, 133–42, 164 n 23, 226, 239, 250, 260, 261, 275 n 10, 299
Reich, Wilhelm, 18
    The Function of the Orgasm, 180
    The Mass Psychology of Fascism, 180
Reiman, Donald H., 67, 147, 199, 226, 282 n 52
religion, 28, 49, 67, 69, 71, 81, 89, 107, 116 n 50, 116 n 51, 116 n 52, 124, 131, 132–33, 135, 163n19, 174, 178, 192, 209, 225, 256, 276 n 12, 312
revolution(ary), 2, 34, 49, 52, 55, 62, 72, 79, 92, 99, 101, 105, 108, 112 n 18, 128, 135, 142, 144, 237, 240–41, 250, 266, 269, 271, 290, 301, 310, 311.
    See also French Revolution; Spanish Revolution

Index

Richardson, Alan, 256, 267, 282 n 45, 282 n 50, 283 n 54
Ricketts, Charles, 302, 315 n 19
Rimbaud, Arthur, 315 n 19
Robinson, Charles E., 167 n 47, 224 n 72
Robinson, Jeffrey C., 26
Robinson, John, 25
Roe, Nicholas, 28, 31, 45 n 75
Romanticism, 2, 7, 8, 10, 17–19, 27, 163–64 n 22, 177, 226, 297–98, 300, 301, 303, 316 n 19
    Romantic pantheism, 125
Rosario, Vernon A., 13, 39 n 23
Rossetti, Christina, 36, 290, 298
    Goblin Market, 299
Rossetti, Dante Gabriel, 36, 290, 298, 301, 316 n 19
    Beata Beatrix, 300
    Ecce Ancilla Domini, 300
    "Eden Bower," 300
    Girl at a Lattice, 300
    The House of Life, 299–300
    Pandora, 300
    Paolo and Francesca, 300
Rousseau, Jean-Jacques, 13, 22, 167 n 49, 176
Rzepka, Charles J., 163–64 n 22

S

Sade, Marquis de (Donatien Alphonse), 1–7, 10, 20–21, 33, 36–37 n 1, 39 n 23, 40 n 27, 129, 131–32, 134, 151, 162 n 13, 166 n 33, 304
    Cent Vingt Journées de Sodome [The 120 Days of Sodom], 2, 37 n 4
    La Philosophie dans le Boudoir [Philosophy in the Bedroom], 2, 6, 39 n 21
Said, Edward W., *Representations of the Intellectual*, 225, 277–78 n 22
Saint-Amand, Pierre, 1–2, 4, 7–8, 162 n 13, 302
Satan, 71, 90, 91, 92, 254. *See also* Lucifer.
Satanic School, 33, 303
Schama, Simon, 23, 36 n 1, 242–43, 248, 276 n 12, 279 n 32
Scherf, Kathleen, 39 n 23
Schorske, Carl, 303
Scrivener, Michael Henry, 61, 66, 114 n 37, 116 n 50, 119 n 72, 162 n 15, 216–17 n 22, 253, 258, 273–74 n 3, 274 n 7, 275 n 9, 276 n 13, 281 n 39, 281 n 40
Sedgwick, Eve Kosofsky, 219 n 42, 315 n 17
seduction, 126, 293
    textual, 7–8, 9, 10, 14, 15, 18, 34, 44 n 68, 127, 146, 148, 232, 235, 277 n 19, 284 n 60, 286–87, 289, 290, 292, 300, 304, 308, 310, 312, 313
Shakespeare, William, 240
    King Lear, 118 n 66
Shannon, Charles, 302, 315 n 19
Shaw, George Bernard, 240
Shelley, Brian, 281 n 43
Shelley, Harriet Westbrook, 127. *See also* Westbrook, Harriet
Shelley, Mary (née Wollstonecraft Godwin), 36, 54, 56, 57, 61, 78, 164 n 24, 274 n 7, 290, 291, 299
    Frankenstein, 136, 160 n 1, 195, 220 n 48, 226, 233, 241–42, 279 n 30, 291. *See also* Godwin, Mary Wollstonecraft

Shelley, Percy Bysshe: letters:
  to the Gisbornes, 112 n 19
  to Thomas Jefferson Hogg, 121, 127, 279 n 31
  to Leigh Hunt, 229
  to James Henry Lawrence, 126
  to Longman and Company, 274 n 4
  to Thomas Medwin, 56
  to Charles Ollier, 227–28
  to Thomas Love Peacock, 56
works:
Adonais (poetry), 45 n 69
Alastor (poetry), 122, 135, 160 n 1, 160 n 2, 168 n 55, 201, 215 n 7, 235, 257, 259, 276 n 16, 277 n 18, 279 n 30, 282 n 44, 289
The Cenci (drama), 5, 15, 16, 35, 44 n 69, 49, 50, 52, 73, 114 n 39, 117 n 56, 117 n 58, 118 n 60, 118 n 66, 118 n 68, 127, 128, 129–47, 149, 157–58, 159, 162 n 12, 163 n 19, 163 n 20, 166 n 40, 167 n 45, 168 n 51, 174, 176, 177–78, 179, 198, 210, 217 n 24, 222, 229, 230, 232, 239, 249, 251, 252, 261, 273 n 1, 274 n 6, 277 n 16, 280 n 33, 288, 289, 291
A Defence of Poetry (prose), 12, 13–14, 15, 64, 173, 185, 285
"A Discourse on the Manners of the Ancients" (prose), 185
Epipsychidion (poetry), 9, 35, 49, 52, 73, 115 n 41, 118 n 60, 122, 128, 143, 155–56, 160, 173, 174, 175, 176, 177, 178–214, 215 n 7, 217 n 27, 222 n 61, 223 n 64, 223 n 69, 224 n 71, 224 n 72, 224 n 74, 224 n 78, 225, 232, 257, 259, 269, 271, 272, 277 n 16, 279 n 32, 281 n 38, 282 n 44, 287, 288–89
"Essay on Christianity" (prose), 9, 254, 268
Julian and Maddalo (poetry), 15, 16, 35, 49–50, 52, 73, 122, 127, 128, 129, 147–59, 167 n 48, 168 n 51, 168 n 56, 174, 177–78, 179, 209, 215 n 7, 274 n 6, 275 n 8, 277 n 16, 288, 289, 291
Laon and Cythna (poetry), 9, 35–36, 49, 50, 52, 68, 73, 115 n 41, 128, 143, 160, 160 n 6, 173, 174, 175, 176, 177, 217 n 27, 225–250, 251–52, 258, 259, 261, 269, 272, 273 n 1, 273 n 3, 276 n 13, 277 n 16, 277 n 18, 279 n 32, 280 n 33, 281 n 35, 281 n 36, 288, 289
"Lines Written Among the Euganean Hills" (poetry), 169 n 60
"Lines Written During the Castlereagh Administration" (poetry), 66
The Mask of Anarchy (poetry), 66, 110 n 4
"Ode to Liberty" (poetry), 53, 61, 65–73, 114–15 n 40, 118 n 62, 253
"Ode to Naples" (poetry), 66, 169 n 60
"Ode to the West Wind" (poetry), 253, 264, 278 n 25
Œdipus Tyrannus; or, Swellfoot the Tyrant (drama), 34–35, 49, 51–54, 57–58, 60–62, 64–65, 73, 74–109, 110 n 4,

110 n 8, 110 n 10, 112 n 19, 117 n 58, 118 n 60, 118 n 66, 173, 174, 177, 226, 266, 288, 289
"On Love" (prose), 14, 122–25, 127, 149, 160 n 1, 174, 179, 185–86, 190, 198, 232, 240, 271, 275 n 11, 287
"Ozymandias" (poetry), 233
A Philosophical View of Reform (prose), 66
Prometheus Unbound (drama), 9, 50, 52, 73, 115 n 41, 118 n 60, 128, 143, 160, 173, 174, 175, 176, 177, 217 n 27, 235, 250–71, 272, 276 n 14, 277 n 16, 280 n 34, 281 n 36, 281 n 37, 281 n 39, 283 n 52, 284 n 60, 285–86, 288, 293, 298
Prometheus Unbound (volume), 66, 279 n 32, 281 n 40, 281 n 41, 289
Queen Mab (poetry), 121, 248
The Revolt of Islam (poetry), 45 n 77, 228–29, 233
Rosalind and Helen (poetry), 4, 151, 167 n 45, 289
"Similes for Two Political Characters" (poetry), 66
"Song to the Men of England" (poetry), 66
"Sonnet: England 1819" (poetry), 66
Tasso (fragment), 167 n 48
The Triumph of Life (poetry), 4, 110 n 4, 176, 282 n 52
The Witch of Atlas (poetry) 118 n 66, 188, 195, 222 n 63, 223 n 70, 280 n 34, 289
Shires, Linda M., 25
Showalter, Elaine, 302

Silesius, Angelus, 14
Silverman, Kaja, 302
Siskin, Clifford, 18
Smith, Bruce, 13
Smith, E. A., 54
Sophocles, *Œdipus Rex*, 53, 64–65, 73
Southey, Robert, *The Vision of Judgment*, 33
Spanish Revolution, 66–67, 253
Speech from the Throne, A, 63
Sperry, Stuart, 258
Stahmer, Charles, 162 n 12
Straub, Kristina, 128–29
Swinburne, Algernon Charles, 36, 216 n 16, 290, 298, 300–01
Anactoria, 301
Atalanta in Calydon, 300
"A Cameo," 301
"The Eve of Revolution," 300
Laus Veneris [In Praise of Venus], 301
"Ode on the Proclamation of the French Republic," 300
Poems and Ballads, 300–01
Symbolisme, 302, 306, 310, 316 n 19
Symons, Arthur, 306

T

Tasso, 147
Taylor, Mark C., 296
Tennyson, Lord, Alfred, 41 n 35
Textual seduction, *see* seduction: texual
Thérèse Philosophe, 5
Thornton, Peter, 314 n 7
transgression, 16, 19–20, 73, 83, 93, 104, 129, 297, 310, 312
 definitions of, 3–4
 erotic/sexual, 2–4, 7, 24, 33, 52–53, 57, 65, 73, 102–08, 125, 293, 299, 308, 318 n 33
transgressive texts/narratives, 163 n 20

Turner, J. M. W., 284 n 58
Turner, James, 40 n 24
tyranny, 1, 14–15, 49, 60, 67, 69, 74, 76, 79–91, 108, 116 n 52, 144, 146–47, 148, 174, 190, 225, 231, 234, 246, 257, 271, 276 n 12, 280 n 34, 289, 291

U

Ulmer, William, 164 n 23, 165–66 n 32, 166 n 33, 166 n 36, 179, 182–83, 212, 215 n 8, 217 n 22, 218 n 33, 220 n 50, 224 n 71, 258, 274–75 n 7, 277 n 21, 280 n 34, 282 n 49, 282 n 50, 283 n 55
utopia, 9, 10, 35, 63, 73, 92, 143, 163 n 20, 178, 179, 197, 208–09, 231, 243–44, 248, 250, 252, 259, 263–71, 272, 283 n 53, 283 n 54, 283 n 55, 288, 289, 311, 313

V

vagina, 114 n 35
Verlaine, Paul, 315–16 n 19
Victorians, 294, 297–98, 301, 315 n 16, 318 n 33
Viviani, Teresa, 178, 189, 197–99, 201, 209, 215 n 9, 220 n 49, 223 n 69, 224 n 78
von Kuehnelt-Leddihn, Erik, 36 n 1

W

Walkowitz, Judith R., 18–19
Warnke, Martin, 222 n 60, 271
Wasserman, Earl, 164 n 23, 168 n 51, 168 n 53, 207, 208, 213, 216 n 22, 222 n 63, 280 n 34
Watkins, Daniel P., 1–2, 39 n 23
Westbrook, Harriet, 118 n 67, 126, 161 n 8.
    See also Shelley, Harriet
White, Deborah Elise, 5, 210, 232, 278 n 22
White, Newman Ivey, 54, 56, 57, 58, 63, 78, 112 n 24, 113 n 31, 115 n 46, 118 n 65, 167 n 47, 218–19 n 36
whore, 23, 24, 30, 52
Wigley, Mark, 295, 314 n 9, 315 n 17
Wilde, Oscar, 36, 290, 294, 302, 300, 305–12, 316 n 19, 317 n 30, 317–18 n 33
    The Ballad of Reading Gaol, 278 n 22
    The Decay of Lying, 285
    The Importance of Being Earnest, 305, 309, 316 n 26
    The Picture of Dorian Gray, 190, 301–02, 305–08, 309
    La Sainte Courtesaine, 300
    Salome, 300, 308–09, 310–11
    The Sphinx, 309
Williams, Linda, 169 n 64
Williams, Raymond, 17–18
Wilson, John, 25, 45 n 70
Winterson, Jeanette, 286
Wolfenstein, Eugene, 181–82.
    See also psychoanalysis: psychoanalytic-Marxist theory
Wollstonecraft, Mary, 36, 40 n 27, 45 n 75, 181, 290, 299
    A Vindication of the Rights of Man, 291
    A Vindication of the Rights of Woman, 291
    The Wrongs of Woman: Or, Maria, 166–67 n 40, 291
woman. *See* femininity
Woodman, Ross, 282 n 49
Wooler, Thomas Jonathan, 113 n 28
Wordsworth, William, 10–11, 36, 41 n 35, 176, 286, 290

Lyrical Ballads, 290
Worton, Michael 162 n 12
Wycherly, William, 40 n 24

Z

Zizek, Slavoj, 182, 188, 216 n 20, 218 n 34, 219 n 38, 220 n 55

For Product Safety Concerns and Information please contact our EU representative GPSR@taylorandfrancis.com
Taylor & Francis Verlag GmbH, Kaufingerstraße 24, 80331 München, Germany

www.ingramcontent.com/pod-product-compliance
Lightning Source LLC
Chambersburg PA
CBHW050429240426

43661CB00055B/2317